dBASE IV

The Master Reference

Robin Stark
Mason Sharp

For John Watson,
and for the Brothers of
Delta Tau Delta,
Theta Beta at U.C.S.D.

— Mason Sharp

FIRST EDITION
SECOND PRINTING

Published by Windcrest Books, an imprint of TAB Books.
TAB Books is a division of McGraw-Hill, Inc.
The name "Windcrest" is a registered trademark of TAB Books.

Library of Congress Cataloging-in-Publication Data

Stark, Robin.
dBASE IV: The Master Reference / by Robin Stark and Mason Sharp.
p. cm.
Includes index.
ISBN 0-8306-8332-1 ISBN 0-8306-3332-4 (pbk.)
1. Data base management. 2. dBase IV (Computer program)
I. Sharp, Mason. II. Title. III. Title: Encyclopedia of dBASE 4.
IV. Title: Encyclopedia of dBASE four.
QA76.9.D3S7 1989
005.75′65—dc20 89-5086
CIP

Acquisitions Editor: Stephen Moore
Technical Editor: Sandra L. Johnson
Production: Katherine G. Brown
Book Design: Jaclyn J. Boone
Cover Design: Lori E. Schlosser

Contents

Acknowledgments

THIS BOOK, MORE THAN ANY OF MY OTHERS, HAS TRULY BEEN a group effort. First of all, I must thank Shelley Satonin for jumping in when the going got rough, and as she has done many times before, saving me from a severe case of the ''overwhelms.'' Secondly, I would like to acknowledge David Bright for his help in editing and for his additions. Finally, to the folks at TAB, who have done such a great job at taking a 50 cent floppy disk with a couple of files on it and turning it into a real-life piece of literature — many, many thanks.

— Robin Stark

Introduction

I WILL NEVER FORGET THE DAY THAT MY COPY OF dBASE IV ARRIVED. LIKE MOST dBASE users, I had been anxiously awaiting this new product. The rumors regarding the improvements of dBASE IV over dBASE III were rampant. It was better. It was easier. It was too confusing. The new queries were wonderful; the new queries were useless.

I couldn't wait to try out the program for myself. Then, on that fateful day that the package from Ashton-Tate was dropped off on my doorstep, my heart just sank. Were those really *thirteen* separate users' manuals included in the package!!!? What I had expected to be a fun weekend playing with the new product looked like it might be closer to a year-long project just learning to decipher the documentation!

Fortunately, once I loaded the disks onto my computer and started playing in the program itself, things started to look up. I realized that Ashton-Tate had made some major improvements with this newest member of the dBASE family. The new design of the Control Center is much easier to use. The Query By Example is a welcome addition to the previous methods of selecting records. The addition of Structured Query Language opens up a whole new aspect of database management to dBASE users. And finally, the new commands that create bounce-bar and popup menus are a dBASE programmer's dream.

Well, it didn't take long for me to decide on the goal of this book. *dBASE IV: The Master Reference* is to help anyone who has felt at all intimidated by dBASE's package of thirteen manuals. I realized that there had to be an easier way to explain this program. In many ways, we have attempted to "cut out the fat" from eliminating any of the important aspects of this program.

For instance, in explaining the required syntax of each command, we do not print the command with a long list of optional clauses and arguments. This method of listing all possible options can confuse users, especially those new to dBASE. Instead, we display the simplest syntax of the command, and then list all options along with examples of both simple and complex usage.

The layout of the book is also streamlined. Instead of thirteen sections, *dBASE IV: The Master Reference* is divided into six main sections, namely:

The Control Center
dBASE IV commands including SET commands
dBASE IV functions and system memory variables
Query by Example
Structured Query Language
Programming in dBASE IV

This book contains plenty of reference information regarding each of these topics. In fact, with this book by your computer, you should never again have to wade through the dBASE reference manuals. Our goal was to make a simpler, easier-to-use reference, while still providing all of the information a user would need. If you are new to dBASE, this book should help you move from novice status to confident user. If you are experienced with dBASE products, but just new to dBASE IV, this book will help you get up and running with the new features in no time. And no matter what type of dBASE user you are, *dBASE IV: The Master Reference* will be the easiest way to find the most answers.

With the advent of Version 1.1, dBASE IV became faster, less restrictive, and more powerful. This book will be helpful for users of both version 1.0 and 1.1. In all areas where version 1.1 is less restrictive or there are other differences, the changes are noted.

1

The dBASE IV Control Center

THE dBASE IV CONTROL CENTER IS THE BEST PLACE FOR A BEGINNER TO BECOME familiar with dBASE IV. Because the Control Center operates entirely from menus, you don't have to remember dBASE IV options to perform tasks as you do from the dot prompt. From the Control Center, you can set up your database, design queries, customize your database forms, create reports and labels, and run applications.

Control Center Basics

The Control Center uses two main features to accomplish tasks: work surfaces and menus. A *work surface* is a screen on which you can perform certain tasks. The *menus* let you choose which tasks to perform. *Work surfaces* and menu options change depending on the database file you are working on and what you are doing.

The Control Center Work Surface

The Control Center screen shown in Fig. 1-1 appears when you enter dBASE IV. You can also reach it from the dot prompt by typing Assist or pressing F2.

Menu bar. The menu bar in the upper left corner lets you perform certain tasks on the Control Center work surface. The menu bar changes when your panel selections change.

```
Catalog  Tools  Exit                                              7:00:37 am
                          dBASE IV CONTROL CENTER

                      CATALOG: D:\DBASE\KSCHOOL.CAT

   Data      Queries      Forms      Reports      Labels    Applications

 <create>   <create>    <create>    <create>    <create>    <create>

 KARATE     BBPHONE                 WINREPOR
 TOURNEYS   BBPHONE
            CONGRATS

File:        New file
Description: Press ENTER on <create> to create a new file

 Help:F1  Use:←┘  Data:F2  Design:Shift-F2  Quick Report:Shift-F9  Menus:F10
```

Fig. 1-1. The Control Center work surface.

Catalog name. When you have more than one file pertaining to a single database, it is convenient to be able to handle these files as a group. Creating a catalog lets you list only the files related to the database you want to work on in the six panels. If you don't create catalogs, dBASE IV creates an "Untitled" catalog for your files. When you start dBASE IV the Control Center opens the catalog you were using when you finished your last session.

Panels. The six file panels list the files in the catalog you select. Each panel lists a specific type of file related to the database. For instance, if you customize a form for a database listed in the Data panel, the form filename will appear in the Forms panel in the future. Each panel can contain up to 200 names.

File information. The File and Description lines show the name and the description of the file marked by the cursor.

Navigation Line. The navigation line reminds you of the uses of some of the helpful function keys for the current work surface (see below for a description of work surfaces).

Other dBASE IV Work Surfaces

When you leave the Control Center work surface, a few items are changed on your screen. The catalog name disappears, and the menu bar shows the menus related to your panel selection. Also, the file information is replaced by a *status bar.* A typical status bar displays the current screen (panel name), the current disk drive, abbreviated path and filename, the location of the cursor, the file supplying the data on the screen, and the toggle settings (for instance, Caps when the Caps Lock key is set).

Message line. Most work surfaces display a message line that appears under the navigation line. The message line describes the selected menu option, or gives you information about the highlighted item on the work surface.

Data and Design work surfaces. Most of your database management time is spent either working with data or designing databases, queries, forms, reports, and labels for your data. The Control Center ties together the design and data areas so you can switch back and forth between them.

For instance, if you are designing a label and you want to be sure it has enough space for the addresses in your database, press F2 to see your data. To switch back to design, press Shift – F2.

There are two formats for displaying your data: Edit and Browse. As you can see in Fig. 1-2, Edit shows one record at a time, while Browse lists records in a line. If your database has a large number of fields, they won't show on the Browse screen until you move the cursor to the right. You can toggle between Browse and Edit by pressing F2 from Data mode.

In Design, you often need to see two types of information. If, for instance, you are designing a report that will use specific pieces of data from your database and you change your mind about which data to include, you can toggle from the report work surface to the view query work surface by pressing Shift – F2. To return to the report screen, press Shift – F2 again.

Navigating on a work surface. The cursor allows you to edit and make selections on a work surface. The cursor appears as a small rectangle or as highlighting over a selected area of the screen.

The arrow keys allow you to move the cursor, but there are several other ways to get around the screen. Table 1-1 lists the keys you can use to navigate the work surface, and the movement each key makes on the work surface.

Function keys. Some navigation and menu functions can be performed with function keys. Table 1-2 lists the common function keys and their actions.

```
Records   Fields   Go To   Exit                                    7:03:55 am

LNAME      FNAME     ADDRESS             CITY        ST ZIP   PHONE    RANK
Fuentes    Jose      8934 Collier St.    San Diego   CA 92014 239-6792 -3/Bro
Campbell   Jill      23489 San Vicente   San Diego   CA 92115 453-2349 -1/Bro
Campbell   Phil      23489 San Vicente   San Diego   CA 92115 453-2349 -1/Bro
Smith      Jerry     9633 Cardenas Way   San Diego   CA 92131 693-4721 1 dan
Alvarez    Danny     1326 Oregon St.     El Cajon    CA 92019 297-9812 -5/Gre
Kramer     Carl      9382 Villa View Wy. La Jolla    CA 92037 453-8972 -7/Pur
Martin     Susanna   15571 Fresno St.    San Ysidro  CA 92210 475-4529 -10/Wh
Appleby    Daniella  4465 Convoy St.     San Diego   CA 92119 569-5893 -9/Blu
Fukushima  Jon       3970 Moonlight Way  La Mesa     CA 92041 583-9619 2 dan
Corley     Mason     6227 Verde Rd.      San Diego   CA 92131 493-8932 -4/Gre
Fox        Frank     9370 Wilson St.     La Jolla    CA 92037 456-9873 -2/Bro

Browse  ||D:\dbase\KARATE        ||Rec 1/11       ||File ||       ||
                     View and edit fields
```

```
Records   Go To   Exit                                             7:04:06 am
LNAME      Fuentes
FNAME      Jose
ADDRESS    8934 Collier St.
CITY       San Diego
ST         CA
ZIP        92014
PHONE      239-6792
RANK       -3/Brown
STARTDATE  05/03/87
MEMTYPE    Unlimited
DUES         75
LASTPAYDT  04/03/89
BAL           0
NOTES      memo

Edit    ||D:\dbase\KARATE        ||Rec 1/11       ||File ||       ||
```

Fig. 1-2. The Edit and Browse screens.

Table 1-1. Work surface navigation keys.

Key	Work Surface	Movement or action
→	All	Right one position
←	All	Left one position
↓	Edit	Next field
↓	All others	Down one row
↑	Edit	Previous field
↑	All others	Up one row
PgDn	Browse, Edit, Word wrap, Layout	Display next screen
PgUp	Browse, Edit, Word wrap, Layout	Display previous screen
End	Edit	End of field
	Browse	Last field in record
	Word wrap, Layout	Last text/field on line
	Queries	Last column of skeleton
Home	Edit	Beginning of field
	Browse	Beginning of record
	Layout	Left margin
	Word wrap	Indent (or left margin)
	Queries	First column of skeleton
Backspace	All	Delete previous character
Ctrl – Backspace	Word wrap, Layout	Delete previous word
Tab	Edit, Browse	Next field
	Layout, Word wrap (when Insert is off)	Next tab stop
	Queries, lists, tables	Next column
	Word wrap (when Insert is on)	Insert tab character
	Word wrap (with Enable automatic indent)	Move margin to next tab stop
Shift – Tab	Edit, Browse	Previous field
	Layout, Word wrap	Previous tab stop
	Queries, lists	Previous column
	Word wrap (with Enable automatic indent)	Move margin to previous tab stop
↵	Browse, Edit	Next field
	Word wrap, Layout (when Insert is off)	Move to next line
	Word wrap, Layout (when Insert is on)	Break line, move to new one
Esc	All	Leave, abandon changes (to current record only in Browse or Edit mode); cancel extended selection
Del	All	Delete current selection
Ins	All	Toggle insert/typeover modes
Ctrl – →	All	Beginning of next word or field
Ctrl – →	All	Beginning of previous word or field

Table 1-1. cont.

Ctrl – PgDn	Browse, Edit	Current field in last record
	Layout	Bottom of layout surface
	Word wrap	End of text
Ctrl – PgUp	Browse, Edit	Current field in first record
	Layout	Top of layout surface
	Word wrap	Beginning of text
Ctrl – Home	Memo field	Move into a memo field
Ctrl – End	Memo field	Move out of memo field
	All others	Save work and leave
Ctrl – ↵	Design screens	Save work and remain
Ctrl – T	Browse, Edit	Delete from cursor position to beginning of next word
Ctrl – Y	Browse, Edit	Delete from cursor position to end of current field

Creating files. To create a file in the Control Center, move to the panel you want, highlight <create>, and press Enter. In the form, report and label panels, the new file will use data from the current data file or view. To create a file in a panel other than the Data panel, you must first select a Data file for use (see Selecting Files below). You can use other data or views by choosing the Use different database file or view option from the Layout menu when you get to the design screen.

Selecting files. It is likely that each database you create will have several files related to it. For instance, when you create a custom screen design for displaying your database, that screen design is saved as a separate file with an .scr extension.

All the files in the catalog name displayed are available under the appropriate panel name. To select a file for use, highlight the filename and press Enter. If your Config.db file contains the statement INSTRUCT = ON (this is the default), a prompt box like the one in Fig. 1-3 appears to ask what you'd like to do with the file. If you have changed your Config.db statement to INSTRUCT = OFF, if you have typed Set Instruct Off from the dot prompt, or if you have used the Options to menu to set instruct off, the first option in the prompt box that would have appeared is carried out.

Shortcuts for file selection. You can skip the prompt box if you know what you want to do with your file. If you press Shift – F2 (Design) on a highlighted file, the design screen for the panel appears; this is the second option in the various prompt boxes. Pressing F2 (Data) gives you a Browse/Edit screen (except in Applications), which is the third option in the prompt box. This works with Instruct on or off (to select the first prompt box option with Instruct on, just press Enter twice).

Table 1-2. Common function keys and their actions.

Key	Function
F1 Help	Display on-screen Help
F2 Data	Switch to Browse or Edit Data screens
F3 Previous	Move to previous field (Browse/Edit), object (queries design screen), or page (Help)
F4 Next	Move to next field (Browse/Edit), object (queries design screen), or page (Help)
F5 Field	Add or modify field on layout surface; add or remove field from view skeleton
F6 Extend Select	Select contiguous text and fields; press twice to select word, three times to select paragraph (word wrap edit mode)
F7 Move	Move selected text and fields
F8 Copy	Copy selected text and fields
F9 Zoom	Enlarge/shrink memo fields, condition boxes, some data fill-ins, and file skeletons; show/hide files in DOS utilities directory tree
F10 Menus	Access menus for current screen
Shift – F1 Pick	Display list of items available for current fill-in
Shift – F2 Design	Display design and view query screens
Shift – F3 Find Previous	Locate previous occurrence of search string
Shift – F4 Find Next	Locate next occurrence of search string
Shift – F5 Find	Find search string
Shift – F6 Replace	Replace search string with another string
Shift – F7 Size	Change size of design elements and column widths (Browse)
Shift – F8 Ditto	Copy data from corresponding field of previous record into current field
Shift – F9 Quick Report	Print a Quick Report of data
Shift – F10 Macros	Access macros prompt box

When you select a data file for use, all the other files directly related to it are brought to the top of their panels and separated from the others by a line. The other files are still available for use.

Deleting files. There are two steps to deleting files. When you delete a file from a catalog, it is removed from the catalog list, but it still exists on your disk and can be added to another catalog. Deleting the file from the disk erases the file completely.

You can delete files by highlighting them and pressing Del, or by choosing Remove highlighted file from catalog in the Catalog menu. When you do so, a prompt box asks if you are sure you want to delete the file from the catalog. If

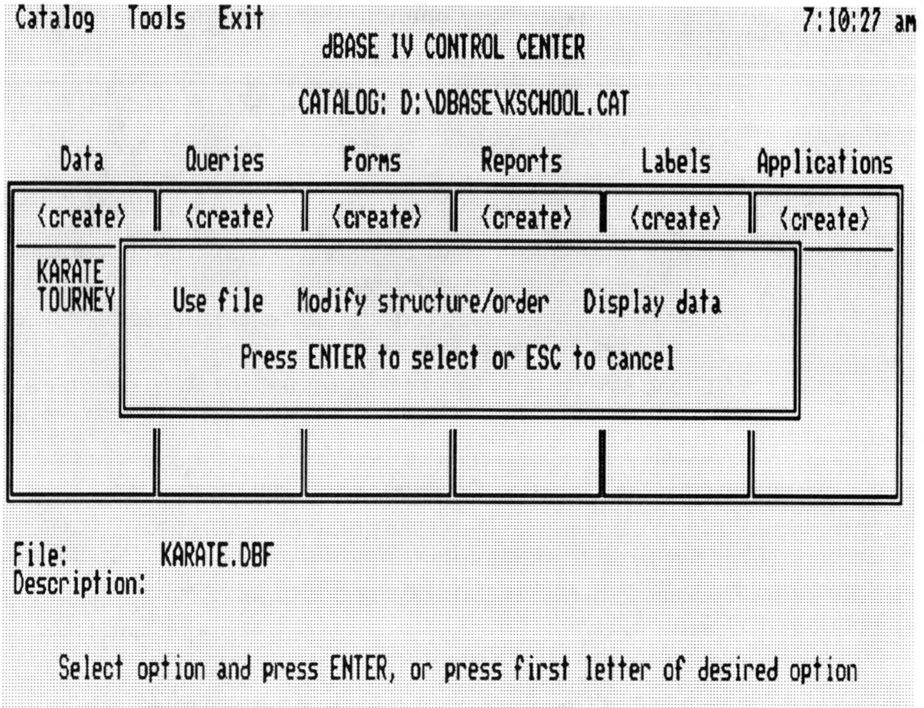

Fig. 1-3. File selection prompt box.

you choose Y (yes), another prompt box asks if you are sure you want to delete the file from the disk. The current database file must be closed before you can delete it from the disk.

Help. There are two ways to get help in the Control Center. When you make an error in choosing menu options or typing filenames, for example, an error box appears. At the top of the box, a message indicates the nature of your error, and the actual option or typed word is shown beneath this message. At the bottom of the box are three options: Cancel, Edit, and Help. If you highlight help, a *context-sensitive* (meaning relevant to your situation) Help box appears.

The other way to get help is to press F1 (Help). Both methods bring up a Help box similar to the one in Fig. 1-4. The title of the information in the Help box is displayed at the top of the box. If you need to see more than the information presented, you can choose Contents for a table of contents for Help, or Related Topics to see information on related topics. The Print option allows you to print the current Help box.

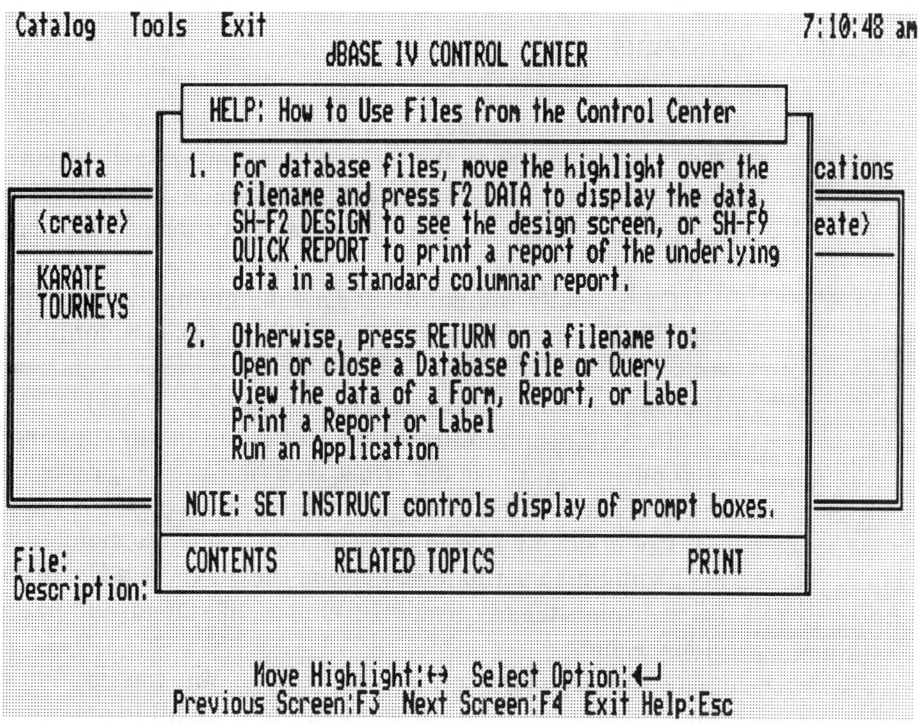

Fig. 1-4. A Help box.

Control Center Menus

Every Control Center work surface contains a menu bar with menus and options appropriate to the task you are performing. When you pull down a menu, you see a list of options that perform tasks. Many of these options have submenus. Options that can be opened to a submenu are marked by a solid triangle.

Occasionally you will notice menu options that are dimmed. This means that they are unavailable. If you are making changes, for instance, to a database structure but have not yet saved the changes, the Organize menu options will be dimmed.

You can open the first menu in a menu bar by pressing F10 (Menus). To view other menus, use the arrow keys. You can pull down a specific menu by pressing Alt plus the first letter of the menu name.

Use the arrow keys to move around inside the menu. Pressing End moves the highlight cursor to the bottom of the menu, and Home moves it to the top. PgDn displays the next section of choices in a menu, and PgUp displays the previous section.

Some lists have columns of choices. You can use Tab and Shift–Tab to move between columns. Other menus provide fill-in options. In this case, press Ctrl–End to accept a fill-in.

To activate a menu option, highlight that option and press Enter. To close a menu without choosing an option, press Esc. The Control Center work surface contains these three menus:

Catalog
Tools
Exit

The Catalog Menu

Before you create a database file, it's a good idea to set up a catalog where that file, and any relating to it, will be listed together. The Catalog menu allows you to do this, and to work with other aspects of your catalogs. The Catalog menu is shown in Fig. 1-5.

Use a different catalog. Choosing this option gives you a list of other catalogs. Select the catalog you want to use, or, if you want to create a new catalog, select the <create> marker and type the new catalog name.

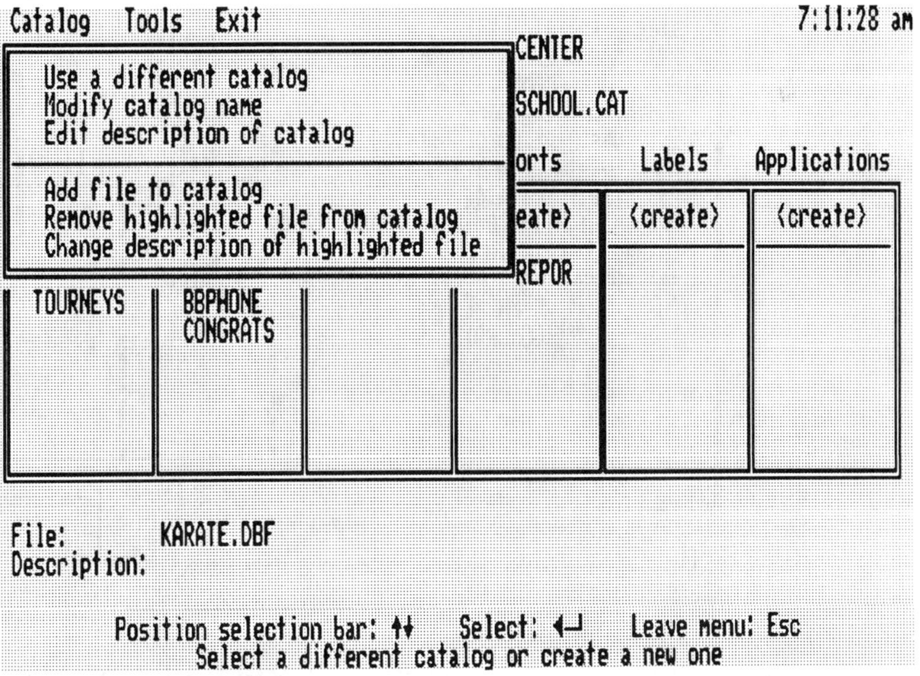

Fig. 1-5. The Catalog menu.

Modify catalog name. When you select this option, the catalog name appears in a text box, and you are prompted to enter a new name. This changes the name of the current catalog.

Edit description of catalog. When you choose this option, you are given an edit box in which to type a brief description of the catalog. This description is displayed only when you choose the Use a different catalog option (see Fig. 1-6).

Add file to catalog. This option lets you add a file to the catalog. When you choose the option, you see a list of all the files and directories in the current panel. Select the file you want to add to the catalog, and it appears in the panel.

When you save a design file, it is saved in a generated code file that consists of dBASE IV code. When you ask to use a file, it cannot be used in generated code. At this point, the file is compiled and given the appropriate file extension. Only certain file extensions can be added to a catalog. Table 1-3 shows these file extensions.

Remove highlighted file from catalog. To remove a file from the current catalog, highlight the file in the Control Center panel, and the Remove option from the Catalog menu. A prompt box asks if you really want to remove the file from the catalog. This does not erase the file from your disk; the catalog is simply a display list.

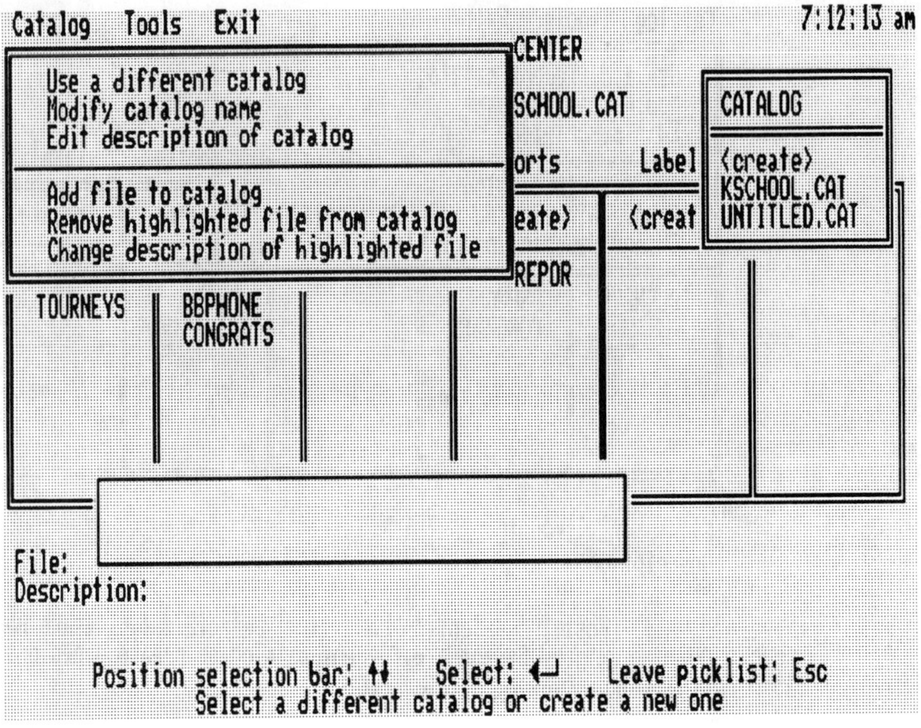

Fig. 1-6. Catalog description edit box.

Table 1-3. Catalog File extensions.

Type of file	Panel	In list	In Untitled.cat
Database	Data	.dbf	.dbf
dBASE III PLUS index	Data		.ndx
View query	Queries	.qbe,.qbo	.qbe
Update query	Queries	.upd,.upo	.upd
dBASE II PLUS view	Queries	.vue	.vue
Form	Forms	.scr,.fmo	.scr,.fmt
Report	Reports	.frm,.fro	.frm,.frg
Label	Labels	.lbl,.lbo	.lbl,.lbg
Program	Applications	.prg,.dbo	
dBASE/SQL program	Applications	.prs,.dbo	
Applications Generator file	Applications	.app,.prg,.app .dbo	
External programs	Applications	.exe,.com	

If you answer Yes, another prompt box asks if you want to remove the file from the disk. If you answer Yes to this prompt, you erase the file from the disk.

Change description of highlighted file. To change the description of a file, highlight that file and then choose this option from the Catalog menu. An edit box appears in which you can type the new description of the file.

The Tools Menu

The Tools menu offers special options that help you manage files, reach DOS, customize DBASE IV, create password protection, and create macros. The Tools menu contains these options:

Macros
Import
Export
DOS utilities
Protect data
Settings

Macros

Macros help you simplify your work in DBASE IV. If you find yourself repeating a sequence of keystrokes frequently, you can write a macro to initiate the sequence with just a few keystrokes. If, for example, you type Empty Checkbook Karate School often, you could write a macro that would type the phrase with only three keystrokes. You can make your work even easier by assigning a function key to your macro. If you assign key F6 to your macro, you can run the macro by pressing Alt – F6.

Because macros play back exactly as you record them, you want to make sure you record the most economical sequence of keystrokes. To do this, you should choose all menus and menus options by pressing their first letter. This is more efficient than using the arrow keys to scroll up and down a menu.

You should also spell out all file or field names to be chosen from lists on the screen. This saves having to choose from a list.

You can store your macros in collections called *libraries*. Each library file can contain up to 35 macros. The size of your macros is limited only by the amount of available space in your computer's memory (RAM).

You can reach the Macros submenu by pressing Shift – F10 (Macros), as well as by opening the Tools menu. The Macros menu contains these options:

Begin recording
End recording

Append to macro
Insert user-input break
Modify
Name
Delete
Copy
Play
Talk
Load library
Save library

Most of these options have submenus.

Begin recording. You create a macro by recording a sequence of actions. Before you record your macro, you need to name it. The Begin recording option opens a display table of function keys and letters before it lets you record your macro.

The top of the display table shows the function keys with any macros assigned to them. The bottom of the list shows the 25 letter keys, and any assigned macros. To record a new macro, press the function key or letter key you want to use to play back the macro. F10 cannot be assigned to a macro because it is the gateway to the letter macros. If you choose a key that is already in use, you are asked if you want to overwrite the current macro.

After you select your macro key, the display table and the macros menu disappear, and any actions you take are recorded in the macro. When you finish recording, press Shift – F10 (Macros), followed by the letter e.

If you want to change the name the macro is saved with, use the Name option of this menu (see below).

To play back a macro, you must be anywhere other than the Macros menu. Press Alt plus the assigned function key, or press Alt – F10 followed by the letter key to play back your macro.

The shortcut for recording a macro is to press Shift – F10 and choose the begin recording option. You can do this from anywhere in the Control Center.

End recording. You can use this option to finish recording a macro. The shortcut is to press Shift – F10 (Macros) and then the letter e.

Append to macro. When you want to add material to an existing macro, choose this option. If you want to work elsewhere than the Control Center, start appending from the Macro menu anyway, and simply move to the work surface you want. You can edit out the extra keystrokes later.

Insert user-input break. You can set up your macros so that the user can input data during the running of the macro. For example, you could write a macro that would set up a complicated calculated field, wait for the user to enter, say, an interest rate, and then continue.

You do this by inserting a user-input break by recording your macro up to the point where you want the inserted data. Then press Shift – F10 (Macros) and select the Insert user-input break option. Now continue recording. You can insert as many breaks as you like.

When you play back the macro, press Shift – F10 after after you have entered the necessary data to resume running the macro.

Modify. You can make changes to your macro with the Modify option. It lets you use a special version of the word wrap editor, or you can use an external editor.

Letters typed from the keyboard appear as regular characters. Special keystrokes, such as the arrow keys, appear inside curly braces. To enter a literal left curly brace, enclose it in a pair of curly braces like this: {{}. The right curly brace does not need special treatment.

Keywords in the macro editor. Table 1-4 lists the keywords for the macro editor. The editor is not case-sensitive.

Table 1-4. Keywords used in macro editor.

Key	Keyword	Key	Keyword
↵	Enter	PgUp	PgUp
Esc	Esc	PgDn	PgDn
Del	Del	Home	Home
PrtSc	PrtSc	End	End
Backspace	Backspace	Shift	Shift
Tab	Tab	Ins	Ins
Shift – Tab	Shift – Tab	Ctrl –	Ctrl –
→	rightarrow	Alt	Alt –
←	leftarrow	Ctrl – -	Ctrl – hyphen
↑	uparrow	Alt – -	Alt – hyphen
↓	downarrow	F1...F10	F1...F10

You can also enter these ASCII numbers inside curly braces: 28, 29, 30, 128, 129,. . .,254. For the user-input break, use the keyword InpBreak.

You can combine Alt- with any number (0 – 9), character (a – z), function key (F1 – F10) or the hyphen keyword.

You can combine Ctrl- with any character (a – z), function key (F1 – F10), or the hyphen keyword, as well as these keywords: Backspace, leftarrow, rightarrow, Home, End, PgDn, PgUp, Enter and PrtSc.

Shift can be combined with any function key (F1 – F10) or with Tab.

Editing macros. The macro for entering the string Empty Checkbook Karate School is shown in Fig. 1-7. This macro was recorded when editing the catalog description of the macro. You can just delete the {Alt–C}e to make the macro enter the string whenever you press Alt–F10, a.

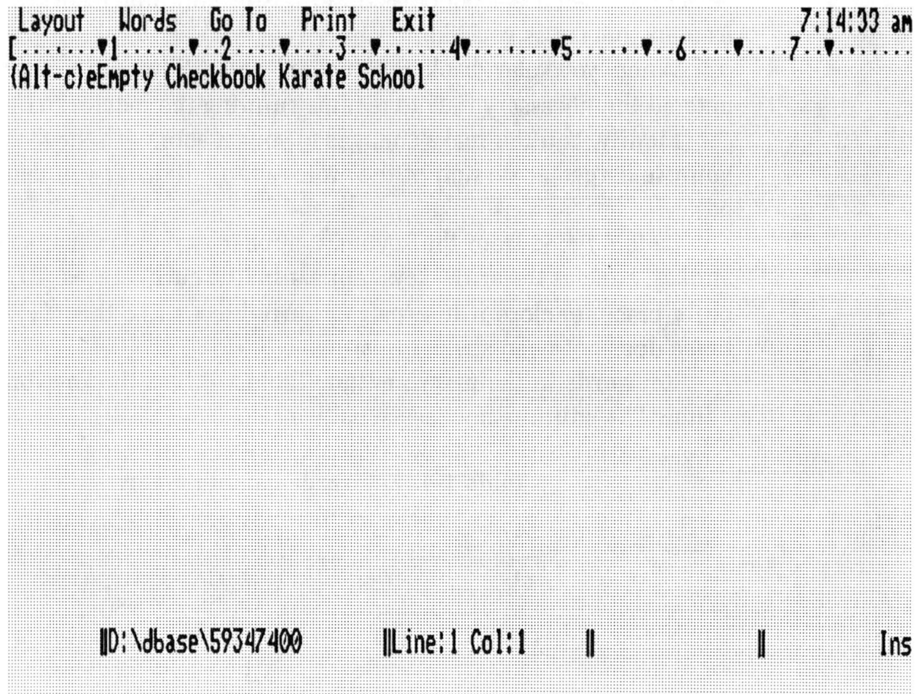

Fig. 1-7. Macro for entering a string.

When you are editing a macro, you can use the Enter key to wrap a string back to the left margin. The Enter key and the Tab key do not become part of the macro when you use them to arrange text.

You can nest one macro inside another by entering the playback keys for that macro. If the macro you want to nest is assigned the playback key k, then {Alt–F10}k would call that macro from within the larger macro.

When you try to save a macro with an incorrect definition, a message displays and you can return to the macro editor to fix the problem. If you choose Abandon edit, your changes are ignored and the original macro remains.

Name. This option lets you change the name of an existing macro. Check the list so you don't choose a name already in use. Press Enter to save the new name.

Delete. To delete a macro, choose this option, and then press the key that activates the macro you want to delete. You are asked to confirm your action. Press Y and Enter to delete the macro.

Copy. To copy a macro to a different slot in the macro display table, choose this option. When the display table for the current library appears, press the key that plays back the macro. Then press the key where you want the macro to be copied.

Play. This option calls up the display table when you can't remember the key for the macro you want to play. Press the key you want to play the macro. You can also press Shift-F10 followed by the function key or letter key of the macro you want to play.

Talk. This option lets you see the macro text as it is being executed. From the Control Center, the macro lines display in the navigation line.

If you want to speed up or slow down the macro, press the < (less than) or > (greater than) key. You do not have to press Shift first.

Load library. When you want to change libraries, choose this option. If you have changed the current library, you are asked if you want to save your changes. After you make your choice, you can select a new library from the list of available libraries.

When you change libraries, any macros in the new library with the same assigned keys as in the previous library overwrite the previous macros. This is a good way to fine-tune your libraries, but be careful that you don't lose valuable macros.

Save library. This option lets you save the current library of macros. Accept the suggested name or enter a new one, and press Enter to save the library.

Import

The Import submenu lets you bring in data from a non-dBASE IV file. The options are:

RapidFile
dBASE II
Framework II
Lotus 1-2-3
PFS:FILE

When you choose Import from the Tools menu, the submenu options listed above are displayed. Choose the type of file you want to import, and then select the filename from the list that appears.

If there is already a file with the same name as the one you want to import, you are asked if you want to overwrite the existing file. If you proceed, the imported file is given a .dbf extension.

In order to import a dBASE II file, you must first change its .dbf extension to .db2.

If you want to bring a Lotus 1-2-3 file with the older .wks extension, use the Copy records from non-dBASE file option on the database design screen's Append menu.

PFS:FILE files have no extensions, so be sure you're choosing an actual PFS:FILE file when you make your selection. When PFS:FILE files are imported, .dbf, .vue, and .fmt files are created.

Export

Use this submenu to export your file to a non-dBASE IV program. When you open this submenu, you see a list of dBASE IV .dbf files. When you choose the file's destination, the appropriate extension is added to the file. The Export options are:

RapidFile
dBASE II
Framework II
Lotus 1-2-3
VisiCalc
PFS:FILE
SYLK-Multiplan
Text fixed-length fields
Blank delimited
Character delimited {"}

When you move a .db2 file to the dBASE II system, rename it to have a .dbf extension, unless there is a chance you might overwrite the original .dbf file.

Text fixed-length fields exports the dBASE IV file to a system data format .txt file.

DOS Utilities

When you choose this option, a new screen appears with the DOS Utilities menu bar and a files list. The DOS Utilities menus can help you manage your files and directories.

Figure 1-8 shows a files list. This is a list of the files in a particular directory, when they were created or last updated, and how large they are.

```
DOS  Files  Sort  Mark  Operations  Exit                              7:16:42 am
                              D:\DBASE
 Name/Extension       Size   Date & Time          Attrs    Space Used

 <parent>            <DIR>   Sep 17,1988 11:07a   ♦♦♦♦
 SOLHOME             <DIR>   Nov  8,1988  9:44a   ♦♦♦♦
 05697000                0   Apr 20,1989  1:12a   a♦♦♦         4,096
 06618200 $ED            0   Mar 17,1989  4:17a   a♦♦♦         4,096
 0713240F                0   Jan 25,1989  7:19a   a♦♦♦         4,096
 07553300 $ED            0   Feb  5,1989  5:07a   a♦♦♦         4,096
 1        DBO          208   Mar 17,1989  4:27a   a♦♦♦         4,096
 1        PRG           46   Mar 17,1989  4:27a   a♦♦♦         4,096
 14108000                0   Apr 20,1989  1:13a   a♦♦♦         4,096
 19284400 $VM            0   May 19,1989  6:50a   a♦♦♦         4,096
 22396400 $VM            0   May 19,1989  7:09a   a♦♦♦         4,096

Total  ◄marked►            0 (   0 files)                           0
Total  ◄displayed► 3,116,429 ( 148 files)                   3,600,384

   Files:*.*                                            Sorted by:  Name

DOS util║D:\DBASE          ║           ║           ║                    Ins
          Position selection bar:↑↓  Mark file:◄┘  Directories:F9
```

Fig. 1-8. DOS Utilities files list.

The Size column shows the amount of space taken up by the data in each file. Directories are indicated by a <DIR> marker in the Size column.

The Attrs column tells you any attributes that have been set for the files. Possible attributes are Archive, Hidden, Read-Only, or System. The diamonds indicate that no attribute has been set. Check your DOS manual for more information on attributes.

The Space Used column shows how much space is needed on the disk to store each file. This depends on the cluster size for the current disk. Values in this column are always equal to or greater than the values in the Size column.

The two Total rows at the bottom show the total number and size of marked files and the total number and size of all files in the list. You mark files by pressing Enter on the filename when you want to work on them as a group. For instance, you might mark five files and delete them all at once. To unmark a marked file, press Enter on the filename.

Navigating the files list. Use the arrow keys, PgUp and PgDn, or the Home and End keys to move around the files list. To display files in another directory, place the cursor on that directory and press Enter.

To see the files in the directory containing the current directory, place the cursor on the <parent> marker and press Enter.

To move from one directory to another more quickly, press F9 (Zoom) from any place in the files list. This replaces the files list with a directory tree containing a diagram of your disks directories and subdirectories.

You can move around the directory tree the same way you would the files list. When you want to see the files in a particular directory, place the cursor in the directory and press Enter.

To change to another disk drive, place the cursor on the drive marker at the top of the tree and press Enter. Choose the drive you want from the list that appears.

DOS Utilities menu bar. The DOS Utilities menu bar consists of these six menus:

DOS
Files
Sort
Mark
Operations
Exit

DOS menu. With the DOS menu you can use DOS commands to manage your files without leaving dBASE IV. The DOS menu contains these options:

Perform DOS Command
Go to DOS
Set Default Drive:directory

Choose the Perform DOS Command option to issue a DOS command directly from dBASE IV. Enter the command you want to use in the prompt box and press Enter. The command is carried out and any screen output is displayed on the screen. Press any key when you finish and the files list reappears.

The Go to DOS option clears the screen and opens a special DOS window where you can perform DOS operations or run other programs without leaving dBASE IV.

If you have marked any files, you are warned that when you return from DOS they will no longer be marked. If you choose to Proceed, the DOS utilities work surface disappears and the DOS dot prompt appears. You can then issue your DOS commands. When you finish, type exit and press Enter to return to dBASE IV.

Use the Set Default Drive:directory option to change the drive and directory that dBASE IV considers the default. Type the new default drive and directory in the prompt box, or press Shift – F1 (Pick) to display the directory tree. Place the cursor on the directory you want and press Enter.

Files menu. The two options that help you see the files you want to mark are Change drive:directory and Display only.

After selecting the Change drive:directory option, press Enter and type the drive and directory you want to see. Press Enter again. You can also use Shift – F1 (Pick) to see the directory tree. Place the cursor on the directory you want and press Enter.

Use the Display only option to filter the files displayed to make it easier to find the ones you want. For instance, if you enter *.fmt in this option, only the files with the .fmt extension will be displayed. To display all files again, type*.* or press Enter if the option is empty. The current Display only choice is shown on the left side of the screen below the files list.

Sort menu. The Sort menu lets you change the order in which files are listed. You can select one of the following four options at a time:

Name
Extension
Date & Time
Size

The current sorting choice is shown on the right side of the screen below the files list.

Mark menu. Use this menu to change file marks. You can only mark files that appear in the list. Files remain marked when you display other lists; only returning to the Control Center or choosing Go to DOS unmarks files.

The Mark menu contains these options:

Mark all
Unmark all
Reverse marks

Choose the Mark all option to mark all files in the list, even those that are scrolled out of view. The Unmark all option clears the marks from all files in the list, even those scrolled out of view. The Reverse marks option switches the marks on all file, marked and unmarked.

Operations menu. This menu contains the options that let you perform operations on the files in the displayed list. The Operations options are:

Delete
Copy
Move

Rename
View
Edit

Each option displays a prompt box asking if you want to apply the operation to the current file, the marked files on the displayed files list, or all the displayed files.

If the cursor is on a directory name when you choose an option (except for Rename, View, and Edit), the operation is performed on the entire directory if you select the Single file option from the prompt box.

When you choose the option to delete files, a prompt box specifies the files that will be deleted. Choose Proceed or Cancel and press Enter. You can also delete the current file by pressing Del. Files cannot be restored after you delete them with this option.

The Copy option lets you copy files to another directory. Choose the files to be copied from the first prompt box, and then accept the suggested drive and directory or enter the destination drive and directory in the second prompt box. You can display the directory tree by pressing Shift – F1 (Pick).

To copy a single file, press Enter to move the cursor to the file name in the prompt box. For marked files, press Enter to move the cursor to the empty filename space in the prompt box. Enter a filename that contains the asterisk (*) wildcard in the basic filename, its extension, or both. Otherwise, the marked files are all copied into the one file named in the prompt box.

For example, if you want to copy Karatel.dbf and Karate2.fmt to a directory named Schools, you could enter the target file name *.* and the files would be copied with the same names. If you enter *.sch, the copied files would be named Karate1.sch and Karate2.sch. If you enter Students, the files will be called Students.dbf and Students.fmt.

When you are ready to carry out the copy operation, press Ctrl – End. If you try to copy a file onto itself, a warning message appears. A shortcut to copying a file is to press F8 (Copy). A prompt box asks you for the path and name for the copy of the current file.

The Move option lets you transfer files from one directory to another. A prompt box like the one for the Copy option appears. You can also move the current file by pressing F7 (Move) and entering the path and name where you want the file transferred. Press Ctrl – End to complete the move.

Choose the Rename option to rename a file or files. You can rename several files with the same name but different extensions by using the asterisk wildcard for the extension. If you try to rename a file to its current name, a warning message appears.

The View option lets you display the contents of the highlighted file. Nontextual characters in a file are filtered out. The display pauses after each screen of data. Press the spacebar to view the next screen, or press Enter to scroll the entire file continuously. Press Enter or the spacebar to stop the scrolling. Press Esc to cancel the display.

Choosing the Edit option lets you use the program editor on the currently selected file. Make sure you are working with an ASCII text file. You cannot edit files with .dbt extensions from this option.

Exit menu. Choosing Exit to Control Center returns you to the Control Center. Any marked files are unmarked.

Protect Data Menus

This option opens a screen with its own menu bar. These menus allow you to control who has access to what files. Before you use the options on this menu you should be very familiar with the dBASE IV security system. This system is described in Chapter 2, under PROTECT (*see p. 137*).

Settings Menus

The Settings option brings up a menu bar with three menus:

Options
Display
Exit

Options menu. The Options menu lets you customize the display and handling of data. It offers the most commonly used setting in dBASE IV (see Fig. 1-9). These settings remain in effect only through the current dBASE IV session. To change settings permanently, modify your Config.db file.

Disable the warning bell by turning Bell off. The Carry and Confirm options affect how data is entered from the Browse/Edit screen. Century, Date order, and Date separator determine how dates are displayed. Enter the number of decimal places you want displayed in Decimal places.

Deleted tells dBASE IV to ignore records marked for deletion. The Exact option requires comparisons to match exactly. Exclusive prevents other users on a network from sharing files. Instruct turns on the panel prompt box. In Margin, enter the amount of space you want your printer to leave before printing unformatted text. Enter the width you want for a memo fields display in Memo width.

Safety gives you warnings before existing files are overwritten by new ones. Talk displays the results of operations, and Trap turns on the Debugger.

See also: SET commands *p. 155*.

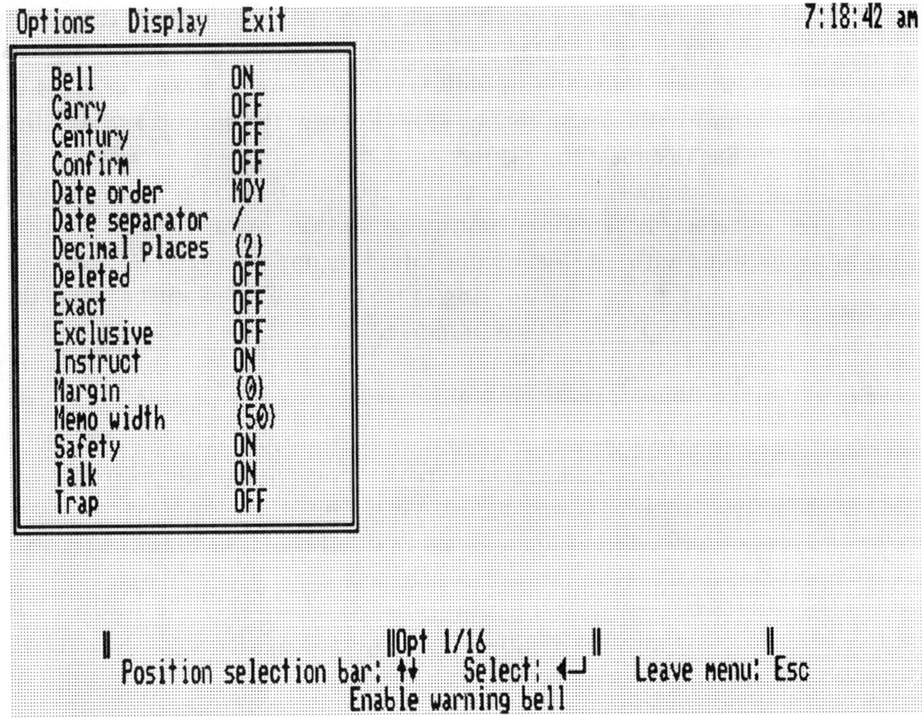

Fig. 1-9. The Options menu.

Display menu. The Display menu options let you assign colors to different parts of your screens. When you select an option on the menu, a lists of colors appears. This palette is the same one used in the Words menu described under Forms *(see p. 58)*.

Exit menu. This option returns you to the Control Center.

Control Center Exit Menu

The Control Center work surface Exit menu (Fig. 1-10) allows you to exit to two places. Choose the Exit to dot prompt option to exit to the dot prompt. Selecting the Quit to DOS option takes you out of dBASE IV and into DOS.

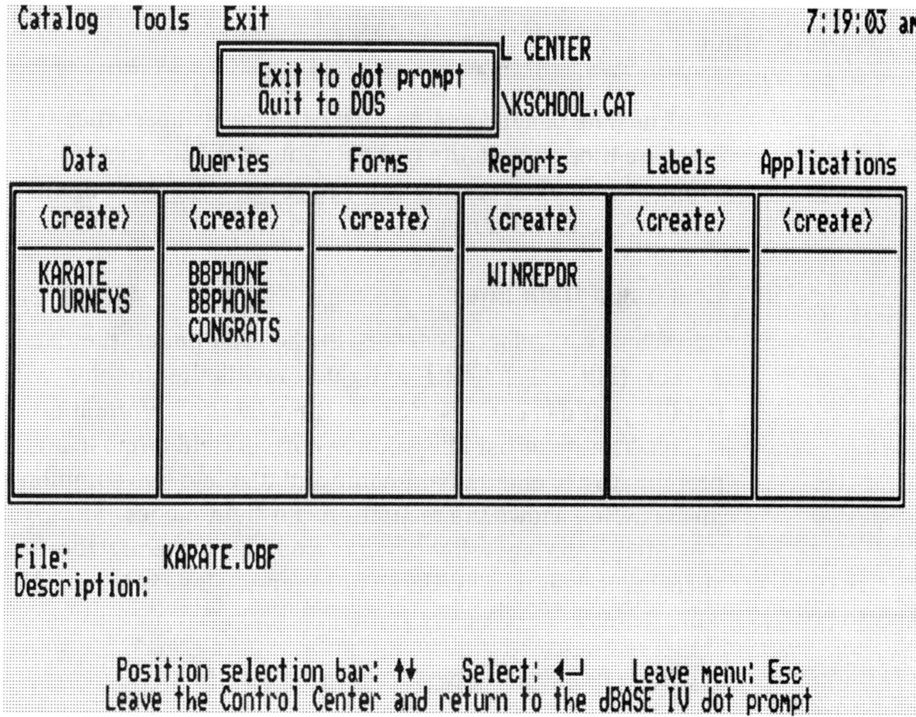

Fig. 1-10. Control Center Exit menu.

The Data Panel

The Data panel contains a list of all the database files in the current catalog. Database files contain the raw data you enter, and they are the basis for the files you create in other panels. You can select a file from the list, or you can select <create> to create a new file.

Creating a Data File

When you select <create> in the Data panel, the database design screen appears (Fig. 1-11). The highlighted row is the line that will describe the first field in your database. Notice the three lines of information at the bottom of the screen. The status bar tells you the current field number, and the navigation line prompts you to enter a field name and displays two common shortcut keys. The message line shows the restrictions for field names.

After entering a field name, you must specify the field type. Press the spacebar to view the available field types. The six types of field are:

```
Layout  Organize  Append  Go To  Exit                          7:20:38 am

                                                 Bytes remaining:   4000
 Num | Field Name | Field Type | Width | Dec | Index
   1 |            | Character  |       |     |   N

Database||D:\dbase\<NEW>          ||Field 1/1        ||                ||
           Enter the field name.  Insert/Delete field:Ctrl-N/Ctrl-U
Field names begin with a letter and may contain letters, digits and underscores
```

Fig. 1-11. Data Design Screen.

Character	Date
Numeric	Logical
Float	Memo

Character fields can hold to 254 ASCII characters or digits.

Numeric fields can be up to 20 spaces wide. Numeric fields store fixed numbers, the kind you use most often for adding and subtracting.

Float fields can also be up to 20 spaces wide. Float fields store floating point numbers, the type often used in scientific applications. If you are working with numbers that are very small or very large, they can speed up multiplication and division.

Date fields use eight spaces. Although dates appear in month, day, year format (for example, 2/14/89), they are stored as eight-digit serial numbers.

Logical fields use one space to indicate either true or false. dBASE IV stores logicals as T or F, but you can enter T, F, t, f, Y, N, y, or n (for yes or no).

Memo fields are 10 characters wide. A memo field does not contain data; it is a window onto a memo file, where you can store large amounts of text. Because you cannot sort on a memo file, you will probably find it useful for storing background information on a client, notes on phone calls, etc. A memo file has the same name as the database file, but with the extension .dbt instead of .dbf. dBASE IV keeps the two files together for you. If you are using version 1.1, you can use any editor for editing the memo file. Define the editor to be used in the CONFIG.DB file.

For each field, you must specify width. Character fields can contain up to 254 characters, and numeric and float fields can take up to 20 digits. Date, logical, and memo widths are entered automatically.

When choosing a field width, you want to enter the longest possible width you might need, but not a width that is longer than necessary. This is because dBASE IV stores the entire width length, even when the field only contains one or two characters.

Fixed and floating fields can use decimal places. Decimal places can be up to 18 characters, but at least two spaces less than the width of the field. This is to allow for the decimal and a minus sign.

You can specify the order your database will be stored in by placing a Y (for yes) next to the field you want the data to be sorted by. For instance, if you want your database to appear in alphabetical order based on last names, place a y next to the LNAME field.

When you indicate indexing for a field, a brief message appears when you leave the screen telling you an index tag has been created for the specified field. In this example, the tag is stored in a file called Names.mdx, and you will need to copy this file as well as your .dbf file if you move your database to another disk or drive.

The Data Design Menus

The Data design screen contains five menus to help you design your database:

Layout
Organize
Append
Go to
Exit

Layout menu. The Layout menu offers three options:

Edit database description
Print database structure
Save this database file structure

Edit database description. When you highlight a file in a Control Center panel, the name of the file and a brief description appear in the lower left corner of the screen (Fig. 1-12). To add a description to a newly created database, or to edit an existing description, select Edit database description. A prompt box asks you to edit the description. Type in a phrase, or edit the existing phrase.

Print database structure. You can print the structure of the current database by selecting this option. The Print menu displays so you can select the settings you want before printing. If you have made changes to the current structure, this option is dimmed until you save your changes.

See also: Reports Print *p. 73.*

Save this database file structure. It's a good idea to save your design changes as you go along, in case of power failure or other electrical problems. When you choose this option, a prompt box gives you the current name of the database file. You can accept this name, or enter a new name. This is a convenient way to create a new database structure without typing all the entries.

Organize menu. The Organize menu (see Fig. 1-13) lets you work directly with the database files. If you have not saved all your changes to the database structure, the options on the menu are unavailable.

Create new index. When you select the Create new index option, a submenu appears, shown in Fig. 1-14.

The submenu contains a list of prompts to help you set up a new index for your database. Select Name of index, and type a name (tag) that is no more than 10 characters long.

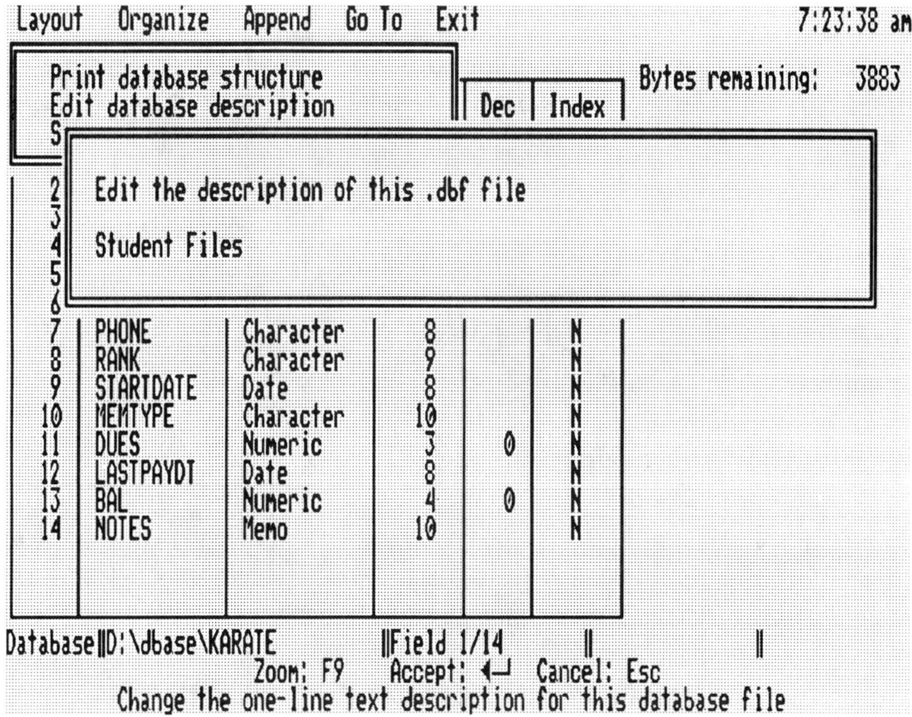

Fig. 1-12. Control Center work surface with file highlighted.

Then select Index expression, and type the expression on which you want the index to be performed. For example, if you want the database to be indexed by city name, enter the City field name here. You can also use complex expressions such as Lastname + City. Press Shift – F1 (Pick) to see a list of possible field names, operators, and functions. If you don't have enough room to enter the expression, press F9 (Zoom) to open more space.

You cannot use the names of logical or memo fields for indexing.

Select Order of index and use the spacebar to toggle between Ascending (Aardvark to zebra) and Descending (zebra to Aardvark). In an ascending index, uppercase letters come before lowercase letters. Zebra comes before aardvark. In descending order, aardvark appears before Zebra.

If your database includes more than one record with the same index expression, you can decide whether to display all of them or just a single record. Select Display first duplicate key only and toggle with the spacebar to Yes if you want to see only the first record found for the index expression.

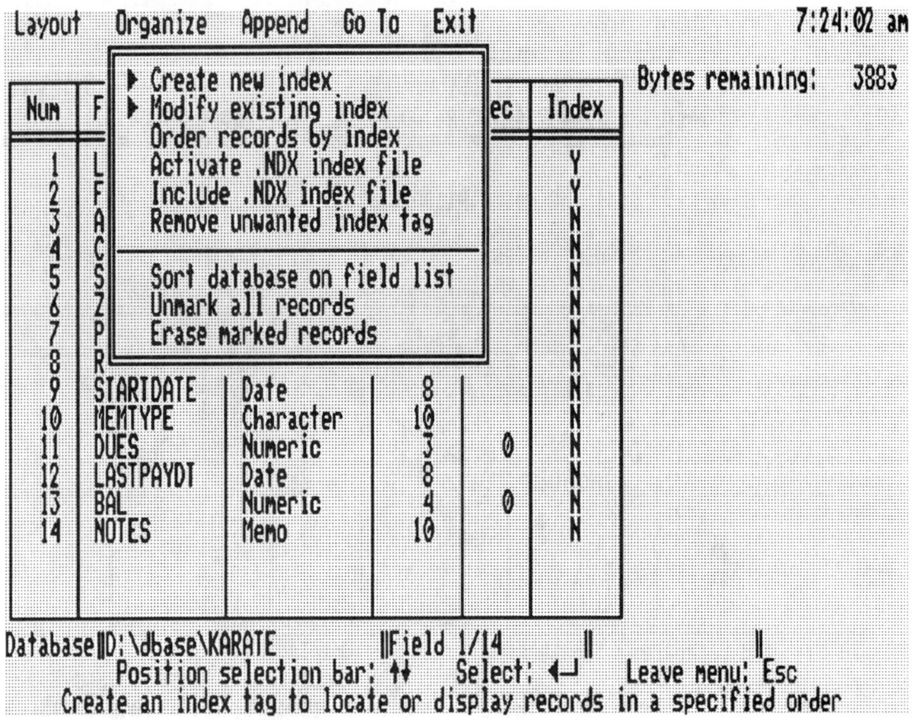

Fig. 1-13. The Organize menu.

When you finish entering information on the Create new index submenu, press Ctrl–End to save your entries. A new index is then created for the current file.

Activate .NDX index file. Index files from earlier versions of dBASE can be used with dBASE IV, but the .mdx index files from dBASE IV cannot be used with earlier dBASE versions. If you plan to switch between the two, you'll need to maintain your .ndx files from the earlier versions as you work in dBASE IV.

To keep your .ndx files up to date, you must activate them before you make changes to the file. Choosing Organize active .NDX index file brings up a list of all .ndx file in the current catalog that apply to the current database file. Highlight the index file you want to activate and press Enter.

You can open up to 10 .ndx and .mdx files at once, in addition to the production .mdx file.

Include .NDX index file. In an open catalog, the Activate .NDX index file option displays only the .NDX files in the current catalog. To add another file to the current catalog, select Include .NDX index file.

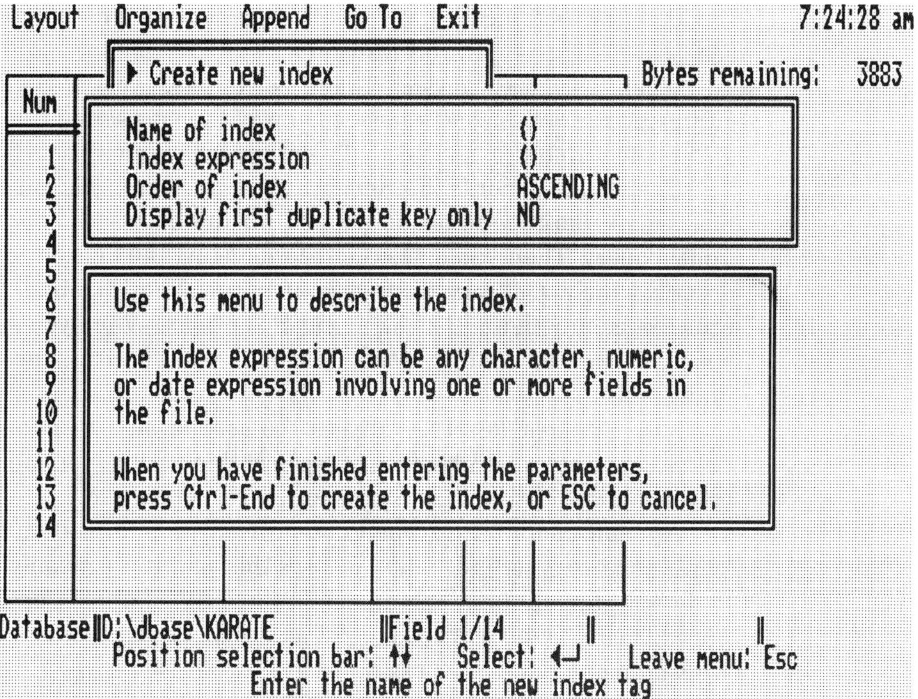

Fig. 1-14. Create new index submenu.

The displayed list includes all the .ndx files in the current directory. Select the index file you want to add to the current catalog, and it appears whenever you use the current database file and choose Activate .NDX index file.

Remove unwanted index tag. If you have created several index files for one database, maintenance for these files can take a good deal of time. When you know you no longer need an index file, it's a good idea to remove it.

Select Remove unwanted index tag and you see a list of the index tags and their expressions. Select the tag you want to delete and press Enter to remove the index from the .mdx file.

Sort database on field list. You can copy data from the current file into a new database file with this option. When you select Sort database on field list, you are prompted to enter the field name to be used for the sort. Type the names, or press Shift – F1 (Pick) to see a list of field names for the current database file. You can select up to 10 field names.

The top field in your sort list is the primary key, the second field the secondary key, and so on. To change the position of a field name, highlight the field name and press F7 (Move). Move the field name and press Enter.

In the right column, you can select the type of sorting by toggling with the spacebar. All four types sort numbers first. Dictionary sorts ignore case.

When you have completed your selections, press Ctrl–End to save your entries. A prompts box asks for the name of the new sorted file. Enter the name, and a new sorted file is created. The original file remains as the current file.

Unmark all records. To delete from a database, you must use two steps. First, mark the records to be deleted on the Browse/Edit screen or with an update query. Then you erase the records using the Erase marked record option described below. If you change your mind about deleting records, you can unmark them with the Unmark all records options. When you select this option, you are asked to confirm your choice. If you confirm, then all records are unmarked.

Erase Marked Records. This is the second step in deleting records (see Unmark all records above). When you select this option, you are asked to confirm your intention. If you do, all marked records are erased.

Append menu. The Append menu lets you add records to your database. While you can enter individual records this way, it is probably more convenient to do that directly on a Browse or Edit screen. The most useful feature of the Append menu is the ability to add records from another file or application. The Append menu contains these options:

Enter records from keyboard
Append records from dBASE file
Copy records from non-dBASE file

Append records from dBASE file. When you select this option, a list of the files in the current catalog is displayed. Choose the file from which you want to copy records. When you press Enter, the records are copied into the current file.

If you want to copy records from a file in another catalog, transfer that file to the current catalog first.

See also: Catalog menu *p. 10*.

Enter records from keyboard. When you select this option the Edit screen appears with a blank record. Usually this record is at the end of the file, but if you have deleted records, the first blank record appears on the Edit screen.

You can switch from Edit to Browse by pressing F2 (*See* Browse/Edit menus *p. 34*). You can also enter records from the Browse screen. Shift – F2, from either the Edit or the Browse screen, takes you back to the Data design screen. If you are using version 1.1, you can access the Organize Menu from Edit or Browse

Copy records from non-dBASE file. You can import non-dBASE IV data into your current file with this option. When you select this option, a list of possible file types appears.

Be sure your source files have the same structure as the current file. They must also have the proper extension, as shown in the list:

RapidFile	.rpd	Lotus 1-2-3	.wks
dBASE II	.db2	VisiCalc	.dif
Framework II	.fw2	Multiplan	no extension

If you choose Text fixed-length fields, Blank delimited, or Character delimited, only files with the .txt extension appear in the list.

To bring data from the new Lotus 1-2-3 files with .wk1 extensions, use the Tools import option.

See also: Tools menu *p. 13.*

Go To menu. This is a very simple menu that allows you to go to a specific field on the database design screen. The Go To options are:

Field number
Last field
Top field

Field number. When you select Field number, you are asked to enter an integer. Then press Enter, and the cursor moves to the field number you specify.

Last field. This option moves the cursor to the last field on the database design screen.

Top field. Top field moves the cursor to the first record in the database.

Exit menu. The Exit menu has two options:

Abandon changes and exit
Save changes and exit

Abandon changes and exit. If you select this option, dBASE IV asks if you are sure. If you press N, you remain on the screen. If you press Y, dBASE IV ignores the changes you have made on the screen and returns you to the Control Center (or the dot prompt, if that's where you came from).

Save changes and exit. If you want to save the changes you have made on the design screen, choose this option. If you are saving a newly created design, you are asked to name the file. If you have modified an existing database field, you are asked if you want to copy the data in the existing database file into this new structure. Choose Yes to maintain the database with the new field name. Be careful! If you choose no, you lose the existing data in the field.

For either choice, a message in the navigation line prompts you to press Enter to confirm your choice. Then you are returned to the Control Center, dot prompt, or program.

The Browse/Edit Screen Menus

The Browse screen lets you view records in a horizontal table, and the Edit screen displays data one record at a time. You can edit, append or delete records from both screens. To switch from Browse to Edit and back, press F2.

The Browse and Edit menus are similar. The Browse screen contains these four menus:

Records
Fields
Go To
Exit

The Edit screen does not contain the Fields menu.

Records Menu

The Records menu (Fig. 1-15) lets you make various changes to entire records.

```
Records     Fields     Go To     Exit                               7:25:43 am
+----------------------------------+  |CITY       |ST|ZIP  |PHONE   |RANK
| Undo change to record            |  |           |  |     |        |
|----------------------------------|  |           |  |     |        |
| Add new records                  |St.   |San Diego  |CA|92014|239-6792|-3/Bro
| Mark record for deletion         |ente  |San Diego  |CA|92115|453-2349|-1/Bro
| Blank record                     |ente  |San Diego  |CA|92115|453-2349|-1/Bro
| Lock record                      | Way  |San Diego  |CA|92131|693-4721|1 dan
| Follow record to new position    |t.    |El Cajon   |CA|92019|297-9812|-5/Gre
+----------------------------------+ew Wy.|La Jolla   |CA|92037|453-8972|-7/Pur
|Martin  |Susanna  |15571 Fresno St.      |San Ysidro |CA|92210|475-4529|-10/Wh
|Appleby |Daniella |4465 Convoy St.       |San Diego  |CA|92119|569-5893|-9/Blu
|Fukushima|Jon     |3970 Moonlight Way    |La Mesa    |CA|92041|583-9619|2 dan
|Corley  |Mason    |6227 Verde Rd.        |San Diego  |CA|92131|493-8932|-4/Gre
|Fox     |Frank    |9370 Wilson St.       |La Jolla   |CA|92037|456-9873|-2/Bro
Browse  ||D:\dbase\KARATE        ||Rec 1/11        ||File ||        ||
        Position selection bar: ↑↓    Select: ←┘    Leave menu: Esc
                  Add records to the end of this database file
```

Fig. 1-15. Records menu.

Undo change to record. You can undo changes to the current record by choosing this option. Once you move the cursor from a record, however, you cannot use this option to undo changes. All changes are saved when you leave a record, or when you leave the screen.

Add new records. Selecting this option is an alternative to moving to the last record, pressing Return, and answering Yes to the prompt. It allows you to add new records to the bottom of the database.

Mark record for deletion/Clear deletion mark. There is a two-process for deleting a record from your database. The first step is to mark the record. To do this, highlight the record you want to delete, and choose Mark record for deletion.

Until you delete the record (choose Erase marked records from the Organize menu), Del appears in the status bar whenever you highlight this record. Also, this menu option changes to Clear deletion mark for marked records.

You can also press Ctrl – U to mark a record for deletion.

Blank record. This option lets you erase the data in a record so you can enter new data. It does not erase the record itself. To erase a record and the space taken up by the record, you must mark the record and delete it. Blanking a record does not remove data from memo fields.

Lock record. If you are working on a network, you might not want someone else to be able to make changes in a record while you are working on it. If you highlight a record and then choose Lock record, the record is locked while the cursor is inside the record, and a lock indicator appears on the screen. When you move the cursor, the record is unlocked.

On a network you can also lock a record by pressing Ctrl – O. RecLock appears in the status bar. To unlock the record, press Ctrl – O again.

The Lock record option is available only if you are on a network.

Follow record to new position. Sometimes the changes you make in a field affect the location of the record in an index. If your current database is organized by an active index, you can use set this option to Yes to move the changed record to its new position in the index.

Fields Menu

The Fields menu (Fig. 1-16) allows you to control the way fields are shown on the Browse screen.

Lock fields on left. If you are working with long records, you won't be able to see all the fields in a record on one screen. It is often useful to be able to see the first field as you scroll across the remaining fields.

If you choose this option, you can type in the number of fields you want to lock at the left of the screen. These fields will remain on screen as you scroll right. Keep in mind that this kind of lock is not the same as locking a record—changes can be made to fields that are locked.

```
Records     Fields     Go To     Exit                                    7:25:59 am

LNAME       Lock fields on left  {0}                  ST ZIP   PHONE    RANK
            Blank field
Fuentes     Freeze field         {}              ego  CA 92014 239-6792 -3/Bro
Campbell    Size field                           ego  CA 92115 453-2349 -1/Bro
Campbell                                         ego  CA 92115 453-2349 -1/Bro
Smith       Jerry      9633 Cardenas Way    San Diego  CA 92131 693-4721 1 dan
Alvarez     Danny      1326 Oregon St.      El Cajon   CA 92019 297-9812 -5/Gre
Kramer      Carl       9382 Villa View Wy.  La Jolla   CA 92037 453-8972 -7/Pur
Martin      Susanna    15571 Fresno St.     San Ysidro CA 92210 475-4529 -10/Wh
Appleby     Daniella   4465 Convoy St.      San Diego  CA 92119 569-5893 -9/Blu
Fukushima   Jon        3970 Moonlight Way   La Mesa    CA 92041 583-9619 2 dan
Corley      Mason      6227 Verde Rd.       San Diego  CA 92131 493-8932 -4/Gre
Fox         Frank      9370 Wilson St.      La Jolla   CA 92037 456-9873 -2/Bro

Browse  ||D:\dbase\KARATE        ||Rec 1/11        ||File ||        ||
        Position selection bar: ↑↓   Select: ←┘    Leave menu: Esc
   Enter the number of fields to remain stationary on the left when scrolling
```

Fig. 1-16. Fields menu.

Blank field. Like the Blank record option, this option blanks a field so you can enter new information. It does not delete the field from the record.

Freeze field. There may be times when you want to specify that only a particular field can be changed. This might be true if a novice were going to work on your database.

To freeze a field, choose this option and type the name of the field you want to freeze. This restricts the cursor to the frozen field. To unfreeze the field, select the option again, and delete the field name.

Size field. There might be times when you don't need to see all the data in some of the fields on the screen. You can change the display size of the fields to make room for other more important fields, or, on the other hand, to increase the space between data.

To size a field, choose Size field and enter a width between the width of the field name and 78 characters. Only logical fields can be less than four characters. You cannot size memo fields and the field at the extreme right of the Browse screen.

You can also size display fields by pressing Shift – F7 (Size) and using the arrow keys to adjust the size of the field. Press Enter to complete the sizing.

Go to Menu

This menu (Fig. 1-17) allows you to go to various specified records in the database.

Top record. Select this option to go to the first record in the current database file. If the file is indexed, this is the first indexed record. If the file is not indexed, it is Record 1.

Last Record. This option takes you to the last record in the database file. If the file is indexed, this is the last record. If it is not indexed, it's the last record number.

Record number. Select this option and type the number of the record you want to go to.

Skip. You can skip up or down in a database with this option. The default number of records to skip is 10, but you can enter another value after you select Skip. Positive numbers skip down, negative numbers skip up.

Index key search. This option allows you to find a record using the field that is the key expression in an index. For example, to find the first record with the last name Martin, you must first index your database on the last name field (select Order records by index from the Organize menu on the Data design screen).

```
 Records    Fields    Go To    Exit                              7:26:24 am
 LNAME      FNAME      Top record                          P   PHONE    RANK
                       Last record
 Fuentes    Jose       Record number           {0}         014 239-6792 -3/Bro
 Campbell   Jill       Skip                    {10}        115 453-2349 -1/Bro
 Campbell   Phil                                           115 453-2349 -1/Bro
 Smith      Jerry      Index key search                    131 693-4721 1 dan
 Alvarez    Danny      Forward search          {}          019 297-9812 -5/Gre
 Kramer     Carl       Backward search         {}          037 453-8972 -7/Pur
 Martin     Susanna    Match capitalization  YES           210 475-4529 -10/Wh
 Appleby    Daniella                                       119 569-5893 -9/Blu
 Fukushima  Jon        3970 Moonlight Way  La Mesa    CA 92041 583-9619 2 dan
 Corley     Mason      6227 Verde Rd.      San Diego  CA 92131 493-8932 -4/Gre
 Fox        Frank      9370 Wilson St.     La Jolla   CA 92037 456-9873 -2/Bro

Browse  ║D:\dbase\KARATE        ║Rec 1/11          ║File ║        ║
          Position selection bar: ↑↓    Select: ←┘    Leave menu: Esc
                Move to the first record in this database file
```

Fig. 1-17. The Go To menu.

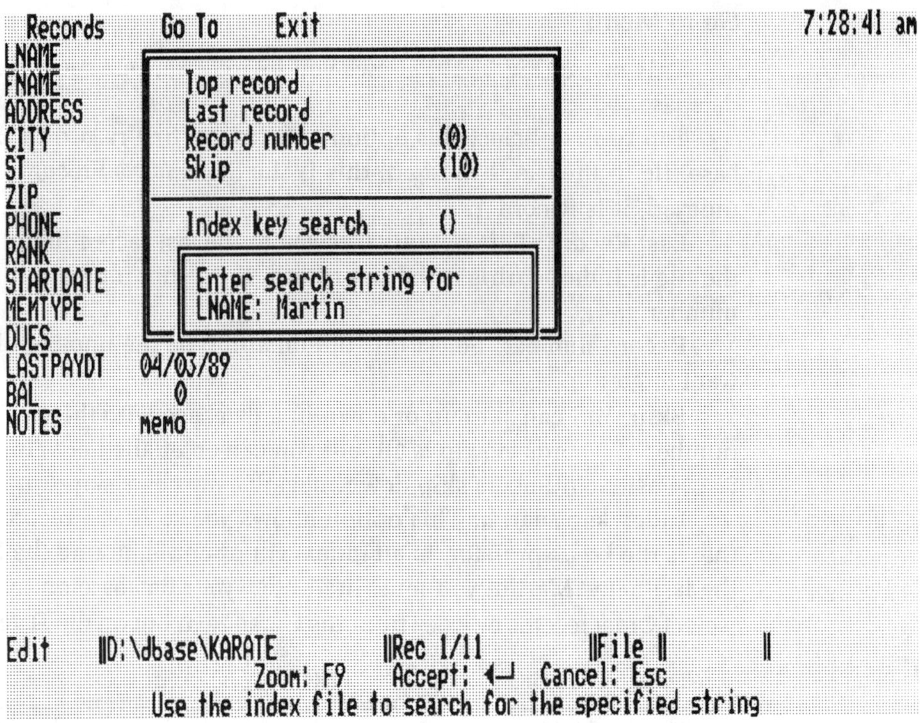

Fig. 1-18. Index key search prompt box.

Return to the Browse screen and choose Index key search. A prompt box like the one shown in Fig. 1-18 displays the index expression and asks for the data you want to find.

The description of your data is called a *search string*. You must use the exact case of the data you want to find. The search will not find Martin if you type martin. You can, however, type Mar. The search will find the first record in the index in which the data in the last name field begins with Mar. This could be Marston or Marford, so be sure you enter enough characters to at least get close to the record you want to find.

The index key search does not use the * and ? as wildcard characters.

Forward search and Backward search. The forward and backward search options allow you to find specific fields without requiring an index key. This is more convenient than the index key search, but it takes more time.

To perform a forward or backward search, place the cursor in the field you want to search. Choose the option and type the search string in the prompt box (see Fig. 1-19). You can use the wildcard characters here. For example, * .Cardenas * will find 3213 Cardenas Rd.

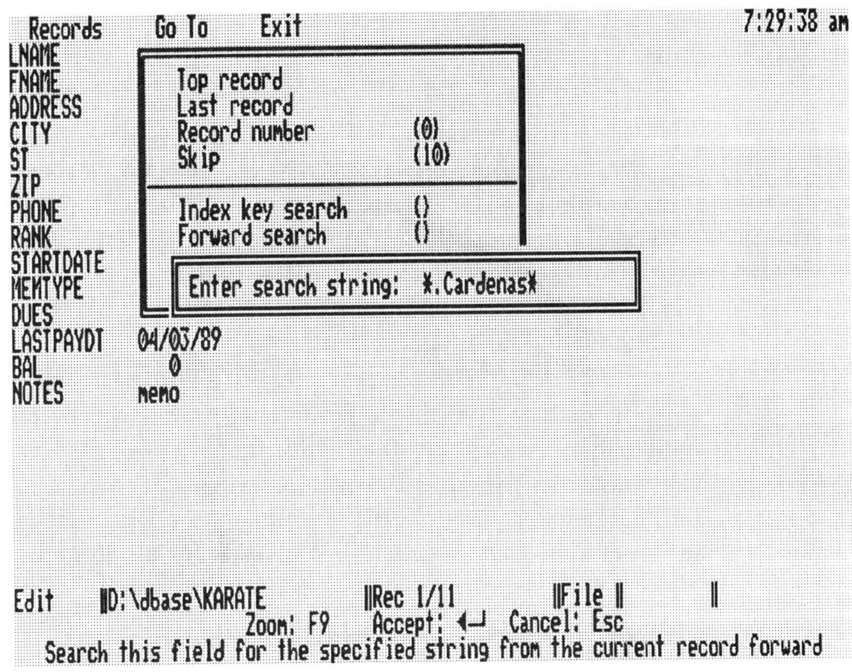

Fig. 1-19. Forward search prompt box.

You can search for the next matching option by using the Search option again, or by pressing Shift – F4 (Find Next). To return to a record already found, press Shift – F3 (Find Previous).

If you start your search from the middle of the database, Forward and Backward search wrap when they reach the end of the file, ending the search at the found record, or the place where you started.

Match capitalization. For forward and backward searches, you can determine whether the search string must have the same capitalization as the data you want to find. By setting Match capitalization to No, a search for Martin would find the record even if you typed martin.

This option does not work with the Index key search option.

Exit Menu

The Exit menu allows you to leave the Browse or Edit screen.

Exit. This option returns you to the Control Center, the dot prompt, or the program that called the Browse/Edit screens. If you have made changes to the design screen you are returned to that screen and asked if you want to save your changes.

Transfer to query design. Select this option to transfer to the queries design screen.

The Queries Panel

The Queries panel menus allow you to retrieve, organize, edit, and display data in a variety of ways. When you select a database for use and choose <create> from the Queries panel, you see a blank design screen (see Fig. 1-20). A file skeleton across the top of the screen shows the fields in your current database. This is where you perform the update query. Under each of the field names you can type conditions that limit the records that will be displayed or modified using the menu options.

At the bottom of the screen, you see a view box. You can use the F5 key to move fields from the update skeleton to the view skeleton. When you move a field to the view skeleton, the field is included in a display of the data (press F2 to see data). For example, the queries design screen in Fig. 1-21 shows the fields in the Karate database in the top skeleton. Under the field Rank, the condition indicates the query wants to see records for all students ranked first dan or higher.

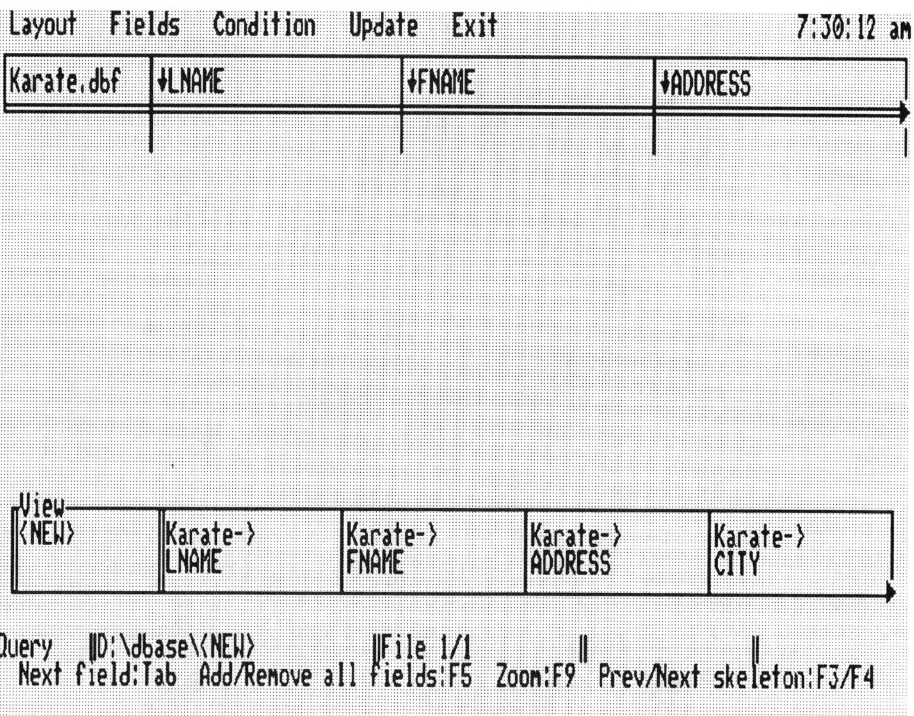

Fig. 1-20. Queries design screen.

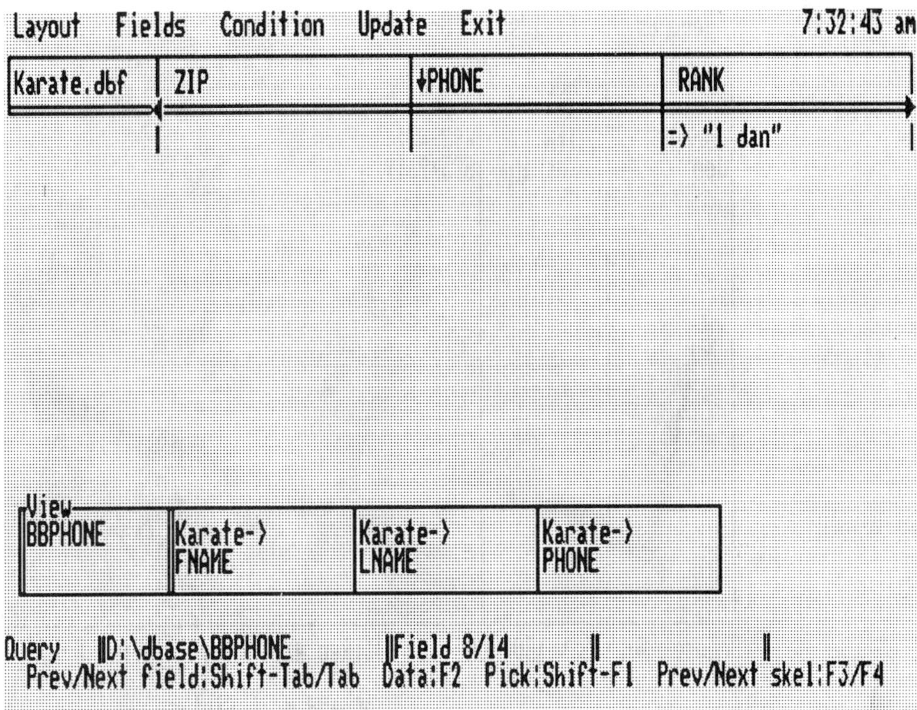

Fig. 1-21. Queries design screen with skeleton.

The view skeleton contains three fields. If you press F2, you see the data screen shown in Fig. 1-22. The screen shows the first and last names and phone numbers (these are the fields listed in the view skeleton) for all black belt students (first dan or higher).

Navigating in the Queries Design Screen

To move between the skeletons and the optional condition box (see Condition menu below), use F3 (Previous) or F4 (Next). Within a field column, use the arrow keys. To move right or left one column, press Tab or Shift – Tab. Press End or Home to move to the far right or far left column. You can use Ctrl – PgUp and Ctrl – PgDn to move to the top or bottom of a file skeleton column. If you have more file skeletons than can fit on one page of the screen (you can place up to eight file skeletons on this screen), you can move to the next or previous page by pressing PgDn or PgUp.

Adding, removing, and moving fields in the view skeleton. To add a field to the View skeleton, place the cursor under the field name in the file skeleton or the calculated field skeleton. Press F5 (Field) or select Add field to view from the Fields menu. This adds the field to the right end of the view skeleton.

```
Records   Fields   Go To   Exit                          7:33:20 am

FNAME     LNAME       PHONE
Jerry     Smith       693-4721
Jon       Fukushima   583-9619

Browse  ||D:\dbase\BBPHONE        ||Rec 4/11        ||View ||      ||
                        View and edit fields
```

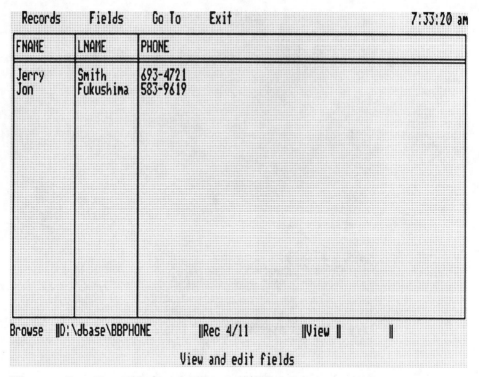

Fig. 1-22. Data Browse screen for Fig. 1-21 skeleton.

You can put all the file skeleton fields in the view skeleton by placing the cursor under the file name and press F5 (Field). If the view skeleton already has some fields, the rest are added. If the view skeleton already contains all the file skeleton fields, pressing F5 (Field) removes all the fields.

To remove a single field from the view skeleton, place the cursor either under the field name in the file skeleton, or over the field name in the view skeleton. Press F5 (Field) or choose Remove field from view from the Fields menu, and the field disappears.

If you want to change the position of a field in the view skeleton, select the field by pressing F6 (Extend Select). You can select more adjacent fields by pressing Tab or Shift–Tab. Now press Enter, F7 (Move), and use the arrow keys to move the field where you want it. Press Enter to finish the move.

Entering Conditions

Conditions are the expression you enter under the field names to filter the specific records you want to see or work on. For a list of field names, operators, and functions, press Shift–F1 (Pick).

To enter a logical condition, enter .t., .f., n., or y., (uppercase is also acceptable) under the logical field name.

To use a date, enter the date inside curly brackets, e.g. {01/23/89}.

If you run out of space when entering conditions, press F9 (Zoom) to see the entire condition. Press F9 (Zoom) again to shrink the column to its original size.

To use a condition in a memo field, you must create a condition box. Then enter the string you want to find in quotation marks, followed by $ Notes.

The $ operator works differently on the rest of the queries design screen. The syntax for $ sign is backwards: to display only records for green belts in the Karate school, type $"Green" under the Rank field.

Two operators not shown in the F1 – Pick list are Like and Sounds Like. Use Like with the wildcards * and ? and a search string in quotes. For example, another way to find all black belts would be to use the expression Like "*dan".

The Sounds Like operator is also followed by a quoted string. For instance, if you know you have a John but you're not sure how he spells his name, you can use Sounds Like "John" under the first name field to find John or Jon.

Combining Conditions

You can use conditions in more than one field at a time. If you place the conditions in the same row of the file skeleton, then all the conditions must be met before the records will be included in the view or update. This is the "and" version of combining conditions.

If you place the conditions in different rows, then only one condition must be met by each record. In other words, the first condition, or the second condition, and so on, must be met.

Combining Skeletons

To filter data from more than one database you must link the two databases or create a condition box (see Condition menu below). Each field name in the condition box must be unique, so you might include the filename for one of the duplicate field names.

Queries Menus

The Queries design screen has five menus:

Layout
Fields
Condition
Update
Exit

Layout menu. The six options on the Layout menu help you add and remove files, link files together, save queries, and save the data generated by view queries:

Add file to query
Remove file from query
Create link by pointing
Write view as database file
Edit description of query
Save this query

Add file to query. You can add a file skeleton for another database to the query screen by choosing this option. The option displays a list of all the database files in the current catalog, or in the current directory if no catalog is open.

Remove file from query. To remove a file skeleton from the design screen, highlight the skeleton and choose this option. Make sure you select the right skeleton—you are not asked to confirm your decision.

Creating link by pointing. Linking databases allows you to combine the skeletons to create a single view. To link two or more files, place the cursor in the column of the field you want to link. This field must have a corresponding field in any database it is to be linked with. After positioning the cursor, choose Create link by pointing. A link marker (Linkl, Link2, etc.) appears in the field.

Now move to the next skeleton and place the cursor in the corresponding field. Press Return, and the same link marker appears. Your databases are linked (see Fig. 1-23).

Another way to create a link is to type an example variable in the corresponding fields. This could be any word, such as Winners, or jabberwocky, or any valid operator. For example, if you want to see a list of winners whose last names start a letter after L, you can use >"L" as the example variable.

When you finish, press F2 to see the data displayed by the link. Figure 1-24 shows the file created by linking the LNAME fields from the Karate and Tourneys databases. Notice that each of the Campbells is listed twice. This is because the link only filtered last names, and any last name in the database file is not necessarily unique. If your databases don't have in common a field in which each record has a unique entry, be sure to create a second link to filter the duplicates that would be displayed. Figure 1-25 shows a queries screen with two links, and the correct list of Las Vegas tournament winners.

Write view as database file. Sometimes you want to use your view to create an entirely new database file. This is not the most efficient use of your memory, but if you need to capture your database as of a certain date for, say, accounting

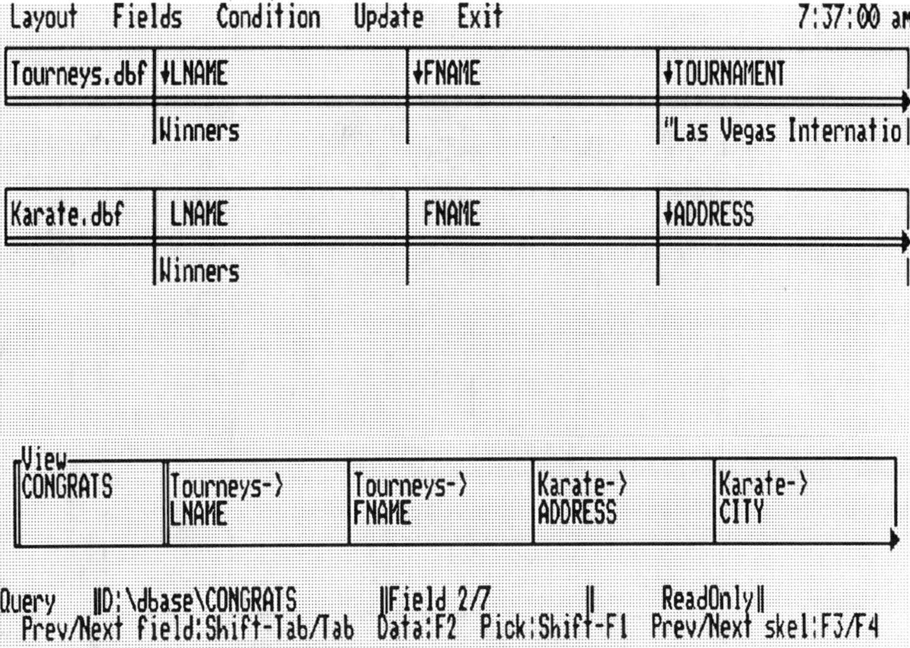

Fig. 1-23. Linked database skeletons.

purposes, or if you want to exchange a portion of your mailing list with another organization, this can be a useful option.

When you select Write view as a database file, the view is saved on disk under the current view name, or the one you enter, with the .dbf extension. You cannot save a view with records longer than 4000 characters.

Saving your view as a database file disconnects it from the original file.

Edit Description of query. This option displays an edit box in which you can type or change the catalog description of the query. If there is no open catalog, this option is not available.

Save this query. Choosing this option brings up a prompt box asking for the name of the query. If the query is already named, you can accept the current name by pressing Enter. If this is a new query, or if you want to edit the current name, type the name you want and then press Enter. This query is saved with the name and .upd extension.

After you have assigned the name, dBASE IV checks the query for errors. If the query is complete and accurate, it is saved to disk. If not, you see a message describing the problem. If the problem is a syntax error, the cursor is positioned on the error.

Records Fields Go To Exit 7:36:46 am

LNAME	FNAME	ADDRESS	CITY	ST	ZIP	TOURNAMENT
Smith	Jerry	9633 Cardenas Way	San Diego	CA	92131	Las Vegas Inter
Campbell	Phil	23489 San Vicente	San Diego	CA	92115	Las Vegas Inter
Campbell	Phil	23489 San Vicente	San Diego	CA	92115	Las Vegas Inter
Campbell	Jill	23489 San Vicente	San Diego	CA	92115	Las Vegas Inter
Campbell	Jill	23489 San Vicente	San Diego	CA	92115	Las Vegas Inter

Browse ‖D:\dbase\CONGRATS ‖Rec 1/5 ‖View ‖ReadOnly‖

View and edit fields

Fig. 1-24. Data list for linked skeletons in Fig. 1-23.

Fields menu. The Fields menu allows you to work with the fields in your view. The menu includes these options:

Add field to view
Remove field from view
Edit field name
Create calculated field
Sort on this field
Include indexes

Add field to view. This option is an alternative to using the F5 (Field) function key. Place the cursor on the field in the file skeleton that you want to include in the view. Choose this option, and the field appears in the view skeleton.

Remove field from view. This option removes the highlighted field from view. You can also remove a field by pressing F5 (Field).

Edit field name. When you use Create calculated field (see below), you must give the calculated field a name. Choose Edit field name, and a prompt box asks you to enter the name of the field.

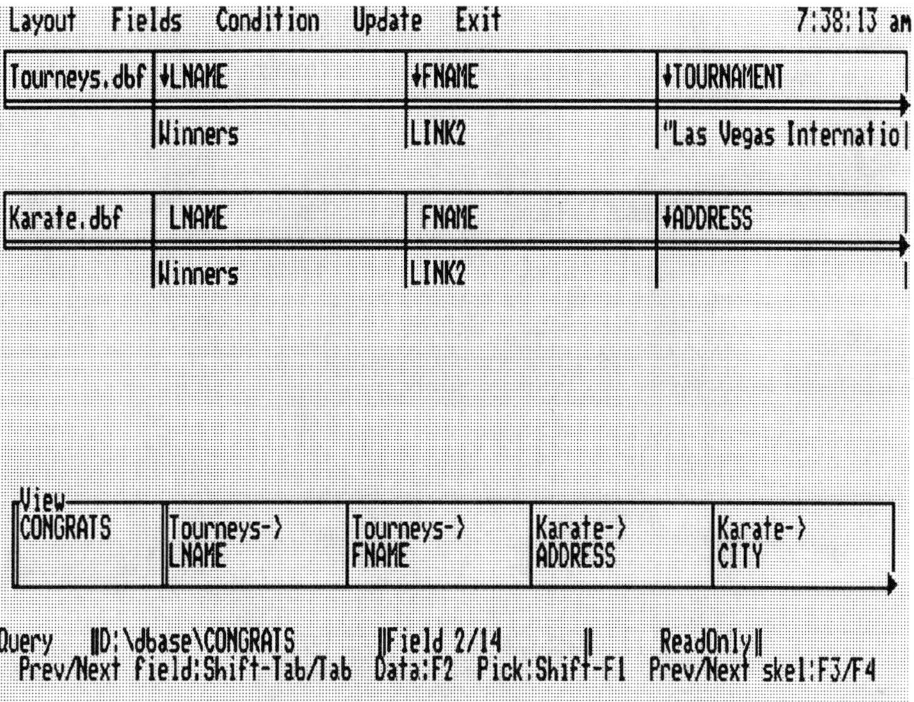

Fig. 1-25. Databases linked by two fields.

Create calculated field. A calculated field performs operations on two or more fields and displays the result. For instance, if you want to know how many years each student has been practicing karate, you can create a field that subtracts the STARTDATE from the LASTPYDT.

When you choose this option, a calculated field skeleton appears on your screen (see Fig. 1-26). To use the field, you must name it, so choose Edit field name. After naming the field, enter the operation you want it to perform. You can select field names, operators, and functions from the list that appears when you press Shift – Fl (Pick).

Now you can add this field to your view as you would a field from the file skeleton.

Sort on this field. This function lets you sort a field in the order you choose from this Sort on this field prompt box. The prompt box includes these choices:

Ascending ASCII (A..Za..z,0..9)
Descending ASCII (z..aZ..A,9..0)
Ascending Dictionary (Aa..Zz,0..9)
Descending Dictionary (zZ..aA,9..0)

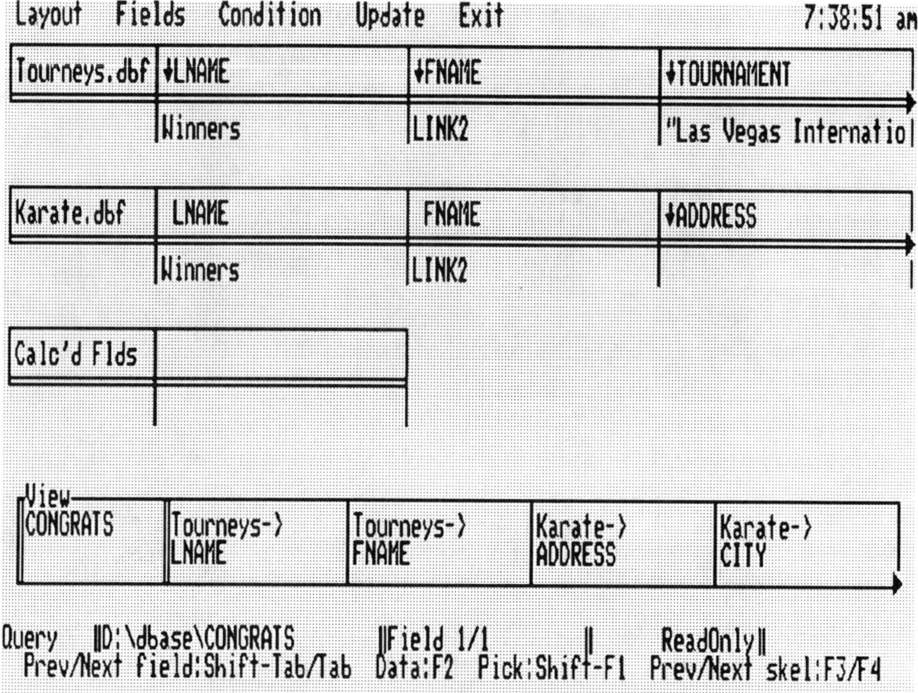

Fig. 1-26. Queries screen with calculated field.

When you choose the type of sort, the operator is placed in the current field. You can add the sort marker to as many fields as you like, including linked fields.

You can also add a sort to a field by typing Asc, Dsc, AscDict, or DscDict in a field (the second sort ends in 2, the third in 3, and so on).

Include indexes. Sometimes the indexing you want is more complicated than sorting on one field. If this is the case, you can use the index from your database file by choosing Include indexes and toggling to Yes.

A crosshatch (#) appears before the name of any field with an index. An index column heading shows a crosshatch and the index expression.

Condition menu. These three options control the display of the condition box on the design screen:

Add condition box
Delete condition box
Show condition box

Add condition box. A condition box allows you to enter a condition that applies to fields in more than one file skeleton, and to specify conditions in a memo field.

When you choose this option, a condition box appears in the lower right corner of the screen. You can use any valid dBASE IV expression in the condition box. Press Shift – F1 (Pick) to see your options. Figure 1-27 shows a condition box that looks for all Las Vegas winners who are color belts (Rank < "1") and who are female ("Wmn" $ Division).

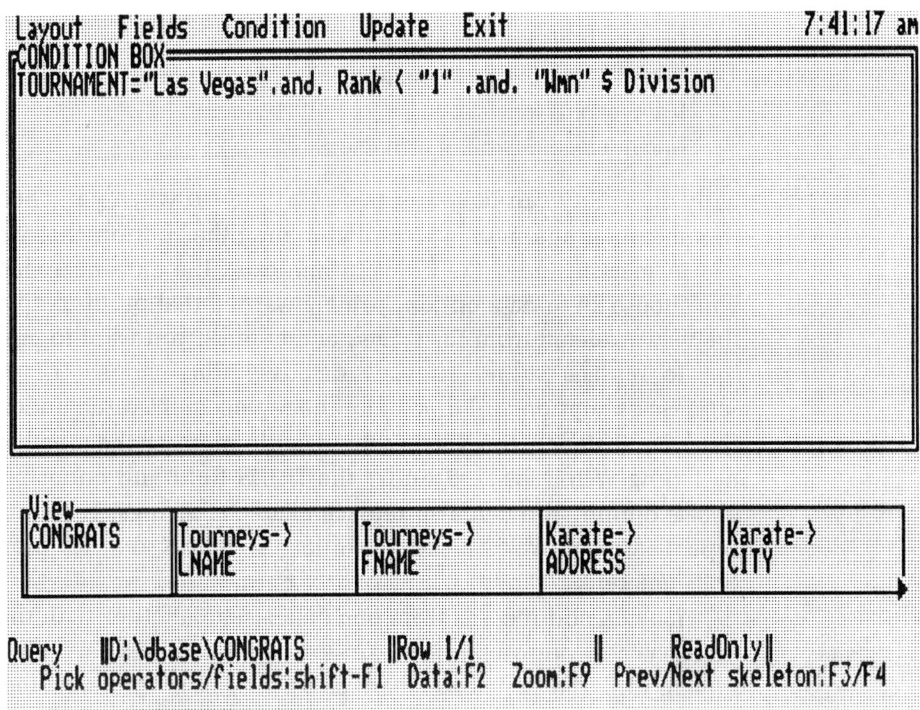

Fig. 1-27. Queries screen with a condition box.

Delete condition box. This option removes the condition box from the screen.

Show condition box. If you have several file skeletons on the screen, it is convenient to hide the condition box so you have room for everything else. The Show condition box option lets you toggle from the box to a marker that displays CONDITION BOX.

To return the condition box to view, place the cursor on the marker and press F3 (Previous) or F4 (Next). To enlarge the condition box, press F9 (Zoom).

Update menu. The Update menu options help you make changes to your database files. The Update options are:

Perform the update
Specify update operation

Perform the update. After you have entered an update query (see Specify update operation next), choose this option to carry out the changes. dBASE IV first checks the query for accuracy. After the changes are made, a message tells you to press F2 to view your new data.

Specify update operation. This option opens a submenu with these four options:

Replace values in <filename>
Append records to <filename>
Mark records for deletion
Unmark records from <filename>

Only one query can be performed at a time, so when you choose an option in this menu, it automatically replaces any other option that was previously in use. A marker under the filename indicates the current update option. When you choose an update option, you are warned that performing an update erases the view skeleton from the screen and asked if you want to proceed.

To replace values in your database file, choose the Replace values in <filename> option and then enter the replacement value under the appropriate field. For instance, the Karate school could increase the membership dues by $5 by typing With Dues + 5 under the DUES field and choosing the Perform the update option. You can also replace character strings. For example, they could type "-6/Green" With "-5/Green" under the RANK field to promote your green belts one rank.

You can add records from one database to another with the Append records to <filename> option. First, make sure both databases have a file skeleton on the screen. Link the skeletons (see Create link by pointing, Layout menu p. 44). Then enter the filter condition under the appropriate field, and place the cursor in the skeleton to which you want to add records. Choose Append records, and that skeleton is marked as the target. Choose Perform the update option to complete the operation.

To delete records, enter the condition under the appropriate field name, and choose the Mark records for deletion option from the menu. When you choose Perform the update, you will see a message that says the records have been deleted, but, actually, you must perform one more step to complete the deletion. Exit the query design screen and open the database design screen for the database file. Choose Erase marked records from the Organize menu, and your records are erased.

If you change your mind about deleting records, choose the Unmark records from <filename> option. The query marker changes to Unmark under the filename in the file skeleton.

Exit menu. Like most exit menus, this one lets you leave the queries design screen and save or abandon your changes.

Save changes and exit. You can use this option to save your changes before leaving the design screen. If this is a new query, you will be asked to give it a name.

If you came from the Control Center, the dot prompt or a program, you are returned there. If you came from the forms, reports or labels design screen, you are returned there and asked if you want to save the new material.

Abandon changes and exit. When you select this option, you are asked if you are sure you want to abandon the operation. If you answer Yes, you are returned to the Control Center, the dot prompt or the program.

Return to report/form/label design. If you came to the queries design screen from one of these screens, this option appears on the Exit menu. You can also return to the design screen by pressing Shift – F2 (Design).

The Forms Panel

The Edit and Browse screens allow you to view data from your database file. The Browse screen always presents the data in table format, but the Edit screen can be customized to display data in other formats than the flush left, line-by-line format it uses by default. Using the forms design screen you can move the fields around on the screen, add lines or boxes, omit certain fields to simplify the display screen, or add calculated fields.

Any time you want to see your format on the Edit screen, press F2 (Data). Press Shift – F2 (Design) to return to the design screen.

Storing Your Custom Screen Formats

When you store a customized screen, the name you give it will appear in the current catalog in the Forms panel on the Control Center screen. You cannot use a form until you have saved it.

Forms are saved with three extensions. The .scr file contain the original forms design that you create. The .fmt files contain dBASE IV code, and the .fmo files are compiled versions of the .fmt files. The only time you need to know this is when you are transferring files from one directory or application to another. If you copy only the .scr file, you can modify the screen, but you cannot use it. Either copy the other files, or save the .scr file to create the format files in the new directory. In another application, you can transfer either the .fmt or the .fmo file without the .scr file.

Forms Menus

The Forms design screen contains five menus:

Layout
Fields
Words
Go To
Exit

Layout menu. The Layout menu works with the general format of the screen. The options on the Layout menu are:

Quick layout
Box
Line

Use different database file or view
Edit description of form
Save this form

Quick layout. When you choose <create> from the Forms panel, you see a blank screen, even if there is an active database file. The Quick layout option lets you see the current layout of the active database file so you can make changes. Each field name appears flush left with its template, the amount of space it uses, to the right.

If no database file is active, you must activate one by using the Use different database file or view option (see below).

Box. You can use this option to draw boxes anywhere on the screen. When you choose Box, a submenu lets you choose whether your box will be constructed of a single line, a double line, or a character. If you choose single or double line, the cursor on the screen highlights a single or double line.

If you choose Using specified character, a list of ASCII characters appear. Highlight the character you want to use and press Enter. Now the cursor highlights the character.

Move the cursor to the position on the screen where you want a corner of the box to appear. Use the arrow keys to expand the box to the right or left, up or down. To fix the box in place, press Enter. To erase the box, press Esc.

Line. The same three choices—single or double line, or character—appear when you choose this option. When you have made your selection, move the cursor to where you want to begin the line, and press Enter. You can use the arrow keys to draw the line in any direction.

If you type text or press the spacebar, the characters will be entered in the direction the line is going. To change direction while typing text, press Tab and the arrow key that points in the new direction you want. Use Backspace to erase in the opposite direction the line is going.

A completed line is treated as text, so you can edit the line. If you want to erase an existing, saved line, choose Use specified character and choose the blank character.

Use different database file or view. This option allows you to activate a file if none is active when you call up the forms design screen, or to change files or views from the screen. This is convenient when you want to modify an existing form for one database or view and then save the form another database or view.

Edit description of form. This option lets you edit the description of the screen in the catalog.

Save this form. When you choose this option, you can accept the suggested name or type in a new name.

Fields menu. The Fields menu lets you work with field arrangement and display on the design screen. Most of the Fields menu options contain extensive submenus. The Field options are:

Add field
Remove field
Modify field
Insert memory variable

Add field. You will use this option when you want to add a field to the screen that you previously removed, or when you want to create a calculated field. Before you choose Add field, position the cursor where you want the field added on the screen. When you choose this option, a box appears with two lists. The left column is a list of all the fields in the database file. To add one of these files, highlight the field and press Enter. A field description menu like the one in Fig. 1-28 appears.

The top half of the menu contains information about the field from the database file or view definition. You cannot modify this information from the

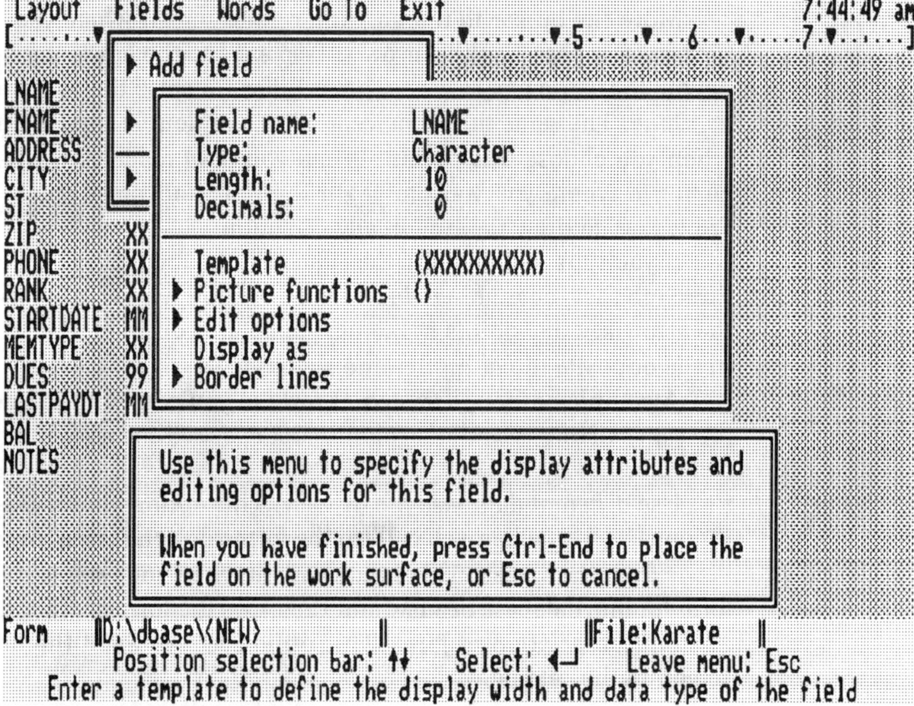

Fig. 1-28. Field description menu.

design screen. The bottom half of the menu contains options that allow you to modify the field.

The Template option lets you determine how a field accepts and displays data (in Reports and Labels you can specify how data is printed, but not how it is entered). The field template shows the width of the field and the specifications for characters entered and displayed.

For example, you might want to specify that the last name field accepts only letters, and that the first letter be converted to uppercase. To do this, after selecting the LNAME field from the list, you would place an exclamation mark in the first position of the template, and As in the remaining positions, as shown in Fig. 1-29. The table at the bottom of the screen shows the choices for specifying entries in the selected field.

You cannot use the Template option for date fields, because the date format is already specified. You can change date display formats with the Date order and Date separator options from the Settings submenu from the Tools menu.

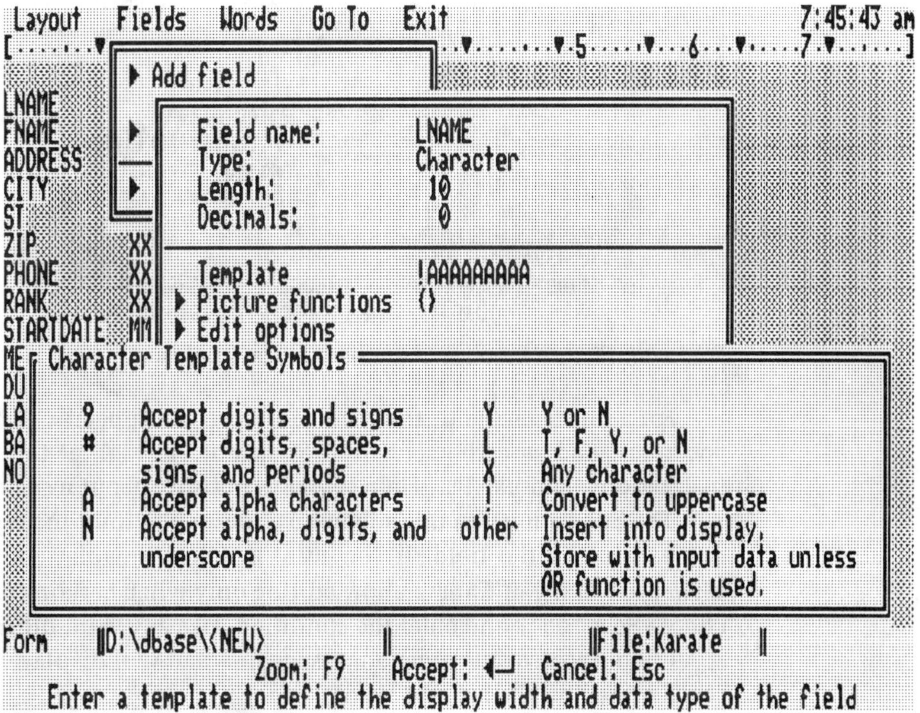

Fig. 1-29. *Template specifications.*

The Picture functions option helps you specify the data displayed in your fields. When you select this option, a menu of attributes is displayed, and you can toggle the ON/OFF switches for one or more options.

For a numeric field, the menu in Fig. 1-30 appears. Turn on the options you want and press Ctrl – End to save your selection.

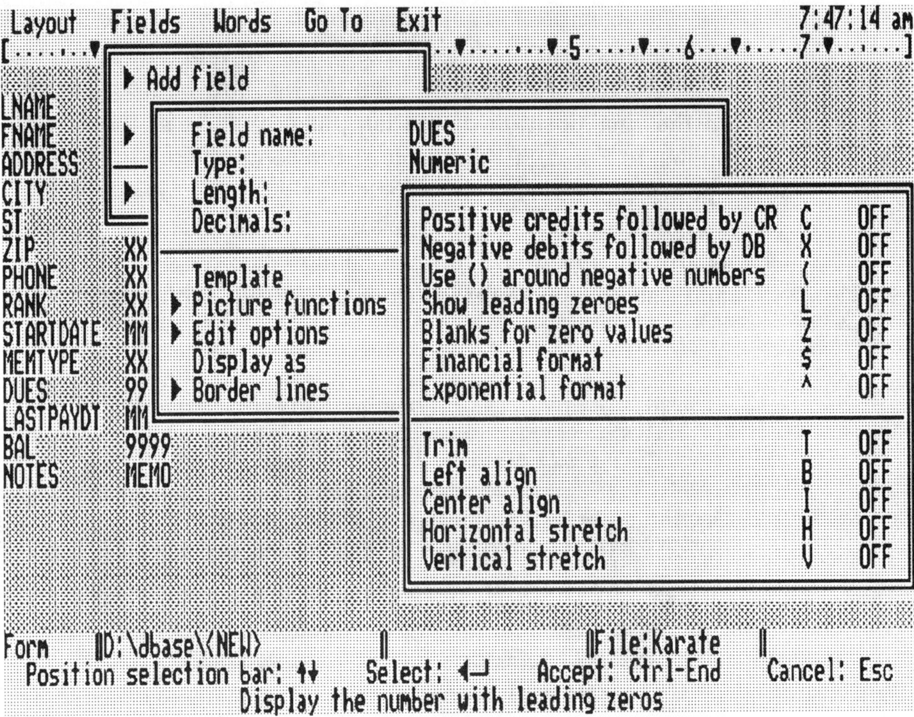

Fig. 1-30. Picture function menu for numeric fields.

For a character field, the menu in Fig. 1-31 appears. Turn on the options you want, and save the selection. Remember to look at the message line for instructions, and use F1 – Help if you're not sure about a selection.

The Edit options on this submenu allow you to limit the types of values that can be used in the field. If you want a field to display only, change Editing allowed to No. If you want to allow editing only when certain conditions are met, choose Permit edit if and enter the condition. Use any valid dBASE IV expression.

Choose Message to enter a message line that will display whenever the cursor is placed on the current field.

Carry forward fills in the data from this field in the previous record when you add a record to the database.

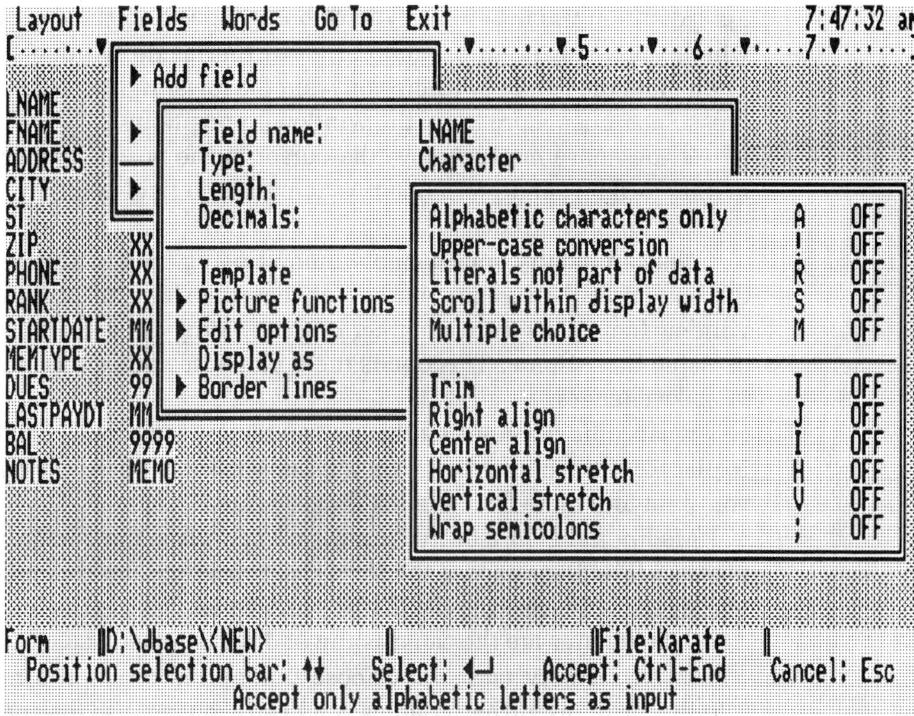

Fig. 1-31. Picture function menu for alpha fields.

You can display an initial value in this field by choosing default value and entering the value. This value can be edited.

You can limit the range of a value by choosing Smallest allowed value or Largest allowed value and entering the limiting values. Then, if you try to enter a value outside the range, a message will appear showing the acceptable range.

Accept value when is another condition option. You could use the same condition that you use in the Smallest allowed value, for example, but with Accept value when, you can use Unaccepted message to display a message when the required condition is not met.

A memo field can be identified on the screen by a marker (MEMO) or by a window. A *window* is a small box that allows you to edit memo data inside memo fields without leaving the form. This is convenient, although it takes up more space on your screen.

When you select the Display as option, you can toggle the display from marker to window. If you choose window, you need to specify the type of border with the Border option and its submenu. Press Ctrl–End to save the selection.

After you've chosen the type of border, position the cursor on the screen where you want the upper left corner of the memo window and press Enter. Then move the cursor to where you want the lower right corner, and press Enter. Press Enter once more to fix the window in position.

If you chose marker, move the cursor to the position where you want the marker to show, and press Enter. When a memo field is empty, the marker displays in lowercase letters.

You can modify your memo windows using the function keys displayed at the bottom of the screen. You can change the size and position of the memo window that opens from a marker by positioning the cursor on the marker and pressing Ctrl–Home. This opens the window so you can use the function keys to make changes.

Remove field. Choosing this option removes the field on which the cursor is placed. If the cursor is not on a field, you can choose the name of the field you want to remove from the list that appears.

Modify field. To modify a field, you can place the cursor on the field and press F5 (Field), or choose the Modify field option. If the cursor is not on a field, choose the field from the list that appears when you use the function. The Modify field submenus are the same as the Add field submenus.

Insert memory variable. Choose this option to insert a memory variable into the form. Insert the variables you need. You can use the spacebar to toggle. Press Ctrl–End to save your selections.

Words menu. The Words menu appears in the Reports, Labels, and Programs design screens as well as on the Forms screen. Each menu option, even those that do not pertain to forms, are described below. The Words menu includes these options:

Style
Display
Position
Modify ruler
Hide ruler
Enable automatic indent
Add line
Remove line
Insert page break
Write/read text file

Style. There are two ways to look at data: on the screen, and on the printed page. The Style option determines how the data is printed, and thus is not available from the Forms screen.

When you position the cursor at the location of the text you are about to type and choose the Style option, you are given six toggle options. Turn on as many options as you want. If your printer does not support italic, superscript, or subscript, these styles are underlined when printed.

On a color screen, bold material is bolded and other print styles are shown in the bright version of the titles color. On a monochrome monitor, underlined material is shown underlined.

Beneath the style options is a list of numbers next to which you can type special user fonts, such as Helvetica or Courier. You can establish special fonts in your Config.db file.

Display. You can assign color and other attributes to text, fields or boxes with this option. If you want to assign colors to material on the screen, select the data by placing the cursor on it. Use F6 (Extend Select) to make an extended selection. Then choose the Display option.

To assign colors to data you are about to enter, make your selection from the Display submenu and then enter the data. Everything you enter will be assigned that color.

When you choose Display, you are shown one of two submenus, depending on the type of monitor you have. For a monochrome monitor, the menu includes these options:

Intensity
Underline
Reverse video
Blink

When you turn on the Intensity option, characters are boldfaced. Reverse video switches your foreground and background colors.

With a color monitor, the Display submenu contains two lists of colors, one for the foreground and one for the background, and a Blink option. Each foreground color name is displayed in that color. When you move the greater than sign to a foreground color name, you'll see the color names in the background column change to that color.

The background color names are displayed on the background color named. So, for example, if you select Red as your foreground color, all the background names are shown in red. Now, use the arrow key to put the greater than sign in the background column. As you move up and down the list, you'll see the background colors change behind the red foreground. The background colors also change behind the foreground list, allowing you to try the background colors with all the foreground colors. To toggle the Blink on and off, press b.

Save your selection by pressing Ctrl – End.

Position (forms, reports (layout bands), and labels design). This option lets you align text within the current margins. When you choose Position, a submenu gives you the options of Left, Centered, and Right.

If you select just one character before you choose Position, the entire line will be positioned. If you make an extended selection, the selection is positioned in relation to the nearest text or field to the margins.

Modify ruler (forms, reports, and labels design). Choosing Modify ruler puts the cursor in the ruler line so you can change margins, paragraph indentation, and tab stops. To move in the ruler, use the spacebar or the arrow keys. Ctrl–arrow moves the cursor right or left eight spaces. Tab and Shift–Tab move the cursor right or left one tab stop. To move to the extreme right or left of the ruler, press End or Home.

To set margins, press [where you want the left margin and] where you want the right margin.

In word wrap bands, set the paragraph indentation by pressing #. The margins, indentation, and tabs in word wrap bands are always set by paragraph. The paragraph indentation point is relative to the left margin so if you change the left margin, the paragraph indentation changes accordingly. To reset both the left margin and the indentation point to zero, enter 0. The widths for word wrap objects are:

Object	Width
Memo field	65
Report word wrap band (variable)	255
Program editor (MODIFY COMMAND)	1,024
Text editor (MODIFY FILE)	1,024
Command line window (dot and SQL prompt)	80
Macro editor	80

To set tabs, press !. You can also set tabs at equal intervals by typing = in the ruler. A prompt will ask you to enter the number of spaces you want between tabs. If you enter 0, there will be no tabs.

Del or Backspace clears tabs, margins and indentation markers and return them to the default.

You can enter more than one marker in a position, but only one marker shows at a time. The order of precedence is margin, indentation, tab, column number. For example, if you set a tab and a margin in the same place, only the margin will show. If you later move the margin, the tab will be displayed, and will still be in effect.

To save your changes, press Ctrl–End or Enter. To abandon your changes, press Esc.

You cannot use the ruler for editing memo fields, programs, or text files. To change tab settings for these situations, modify the tab settings in your Config.db file.

Hide ruler. If you choose this option, the ruler is not displayed. Choosing Modify ruler returns the ruler to the screen.

Enable automatic indent (programs and word wrap bands). When you place the cursor at the beginning of a paragraph in a word wrap band or program and turn on Enable automatic indent, Tab and Shift – Tab reset the left margin to the next or previous tab stop. If there are no available tab stops, the margin is unchanged.

When this option is off, Shift – Tab moves the cursor to the previous tab stop. With Insert off, Tab moves the cursor to the next tab stop. If Insert is on, however, Tab inserts a tab character, which moves the cursor to the next available tab stop.

Add line. Choose this option to add a new line following the current line. In word wrap, choosing Add line closes the current paragraph and moves the cursor to the beginning of the next line. In layouts, Add line adds a new line to the layout and moves the cursor to the beginning of the new line. This option is not available on the Labels design screen.

Remove line. This option removes the current line.

Insert page break. Choose this option to insert a page break into word wrap text just above the current line. Insert page break is not available for layout editing.

Write/read text file. You can exchange text between a design surface and other files with these options. Write selection to file prompts you for a filename, and writes the current selection to that file. If you don't make a selection before you choose this option, the entire text or layout is written to the disk file.

You can insert the contents of another file with this option. Type the filename at the prompt, or choose a filename from the Shift – F1 (Pick) list. The text from the file is inserted at the current cursor position.

Go To menu. The Go To menu contains options described above under the Browse/Edit Screens. *See p. 34.*

Exit menu. Like the other Exit menus, the Forms Exit menu allows you to save your changes and enter a filename (if none exists), or leave the screen without saving your changes.

The Reports Panel

The Reports design screen helps you group the data from your database files, perform statistical operations on that data, print fields where you want them, and insert data from records into standard text.

To get to the Reports design screen, select a database file for use, then highlight <create> in the Reports panel and press Enter. If you want to modify an existing report, highlight that report name and press Enter. Choose Modify layout from the prompt box. If you choose Modify layout for a report that is not normally used with the current database file, you are prompted to choose between the current database file and the one normally used with this report.

The Reports Screen

When you choose <create> from the Reports panel, the screen shown in Fig. 1-32 appears. The work surface contains five bands:

Page Header
Report Intro
Detail
Report Summary
Page Footer

Under the Page Header band, you typically enter information such as the page number and date, or column titles.

The Report Intro usually contains descriptive material. For example, the Report Intro might be a summary of the purpose of the report.

The Detail band shows the data from the records. This band is different from the others because it lists the contents of every record for each field displayed. For example, the detail band might list the last names of all students who have green belts combined with the medals they had won at tournaments.

The Report Summary appears at the end of the report. It can contain either text that, for example, draws conclusions about the report, or gives final totals for specific fields.

The Page Footer band is similar to the Page Header band. You could use this band for the name of the Karate school, or a satellite school.

Layout and wrap modes. You can use one of two editing modes to design a band. Layout mode lets you do such things as move fields around the screen, add boxes and lines. Word wrap mode wraps text within margins. You would probably use word wrap mode for the Report Intro, or to create a form letter. Each band can use only one of these modes.

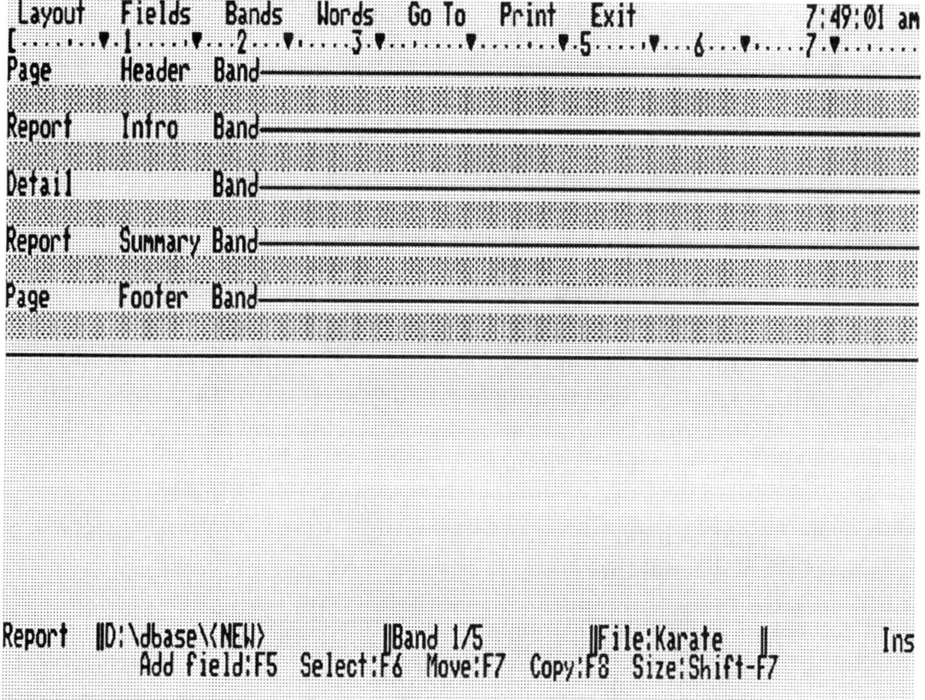

Fig. 1-32. Reports design screen.

Reports menus. There are seven Reports menus:

Layout
Fields
Bands
Words
Go To
Print
Exit

The Words menu is explained under Forms panel (*see p. 58*). The Go To menu is described under the Browse/Edit menus (*see p. 37*).

When you choose an existing report in the Reports panel, a prompt box asks if you want to print the report, modify its structure, or display data.

Layout Menu

When you choose <create> under the Reports panel, the reports design screen appears with the Layout menu open and the Quick layouts option highlighted. The other Layout options are:

Box
Line
Use different database file or view
Edit description of report
Save this report

Quick layout. The Quick layout option gives you a submenu with three types of report design choices: Column layout, Form layout, and Mailmerge layout.

The Column layout option places all fields in the current view in a row under the Page Header band (see Fig. 1-33) with a marker for the date and page number. The field templates are displayed under the Detail band beneath the corresponding field names. Numeric fields have summary fields placed below them in the report summary band.

The report surface is 255 characters wide. If your field line is longer than 255 characters, dBASE IV beeps, displays an error message, and truncates the material that won't fit.

```
Layout  Fields  Bands  Words  Go To  Print  Exit                    7:49:36 am
[.......▼.1.....▼...2...▼.....3.▼.......▼.......▼.5....▼...6...▼.....7.▼......
Page     Header  Band──────────────────────────────────────────────────────────

Page No. 999
MM/DD/YY

LNAME       FNAME       ADDRESS              CITY        ST  ZIP    PHONE     R

Report   Intro   Band──────────────────────────────────────────────────────────
Detail           Band──────────────────────────────────────────────────────────
XXXXXXXXXX  XXXXXXXXXX  XXXXXXXXXXXXXXXXXXXX XXXXXXXXXX  XX  XXXXX  XXXXXXXX  X
Report   Summary Band──────────────────────────────────────────────────────────

Page     Footer  Band──────────────────────────────────────────────────────────

────────────────────────────────────────────────────────────────────────────────

Report  ║D:\dbase\<NEW>        ║Band 1/5        ║File:Karate  ║             Ins
          Add field:F5  Select:F6  Move:F7  Copy:F8  Size:Shift-F7
```

Fig. 1-33. Quick Layout column report screen.

You can use the function keys to move fields around and the Del key to delete fields and field names.

The Form layout option is similar to the Edit screen. The date and page number appear under the Page Header band, and the fields and templates appear flush left under the Detail band just as they do on the Edit screen. The report intro band is closed in this layout, and the detail band begins with a blank line so each record is distinguished from the next.

The Mailmerge layout option is what you choose to create form letters. In Mailmerge layout, the Detail band is the only open band. No fields are displayed on the screen—you will add fields where they are appropriate in the text (see Fig. 1-34).

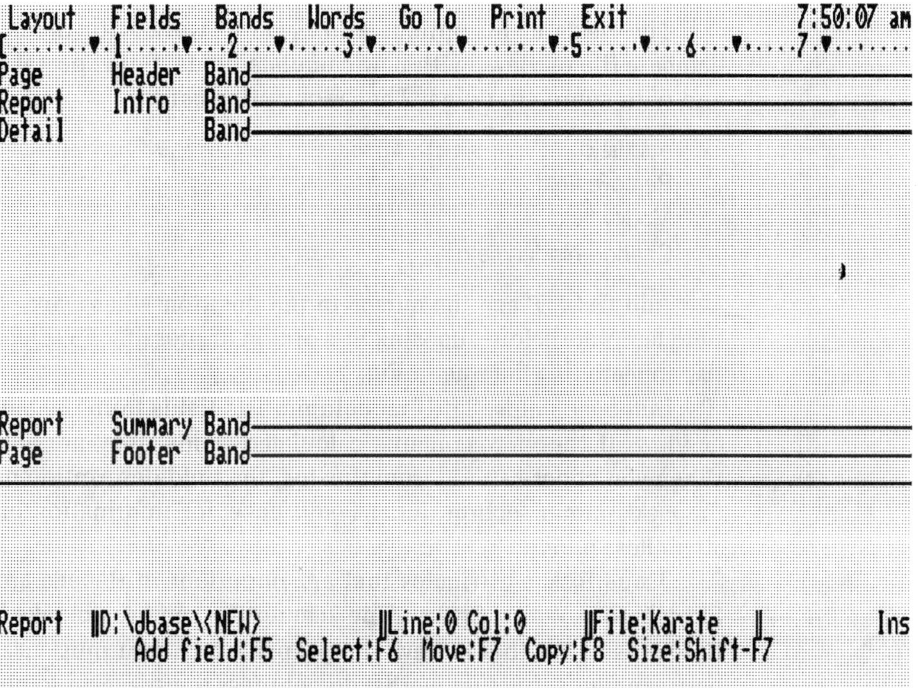

Fig. 1-34. *A Mailmerge Reports layout.*

Box. This option lets you draw boxes on the screen. It is described under Forms menus (*see* p. 52).

Line. This option helps draw lines. It is also described under Forms menus (*see* p. 52).

Use different database file or view. This option allows you to use fields from another database file or view. If the different file or view you choose does not contain all the fields in the current file, a message box tells you the missing fields.

Edit description of report. Use this option to edit the catalog description of this report.

Save this report. It's a good idea to save your report periodically as you work on it, in case of power failure or other electronic problems. You can enter the name of the report or accept the suggestion.

The report is assigned to the current catalog when you save it. The current print form file is always saved with the report file, and they remain together even if the report is assigned to a different catalog.

Fields Menu

The Fields menu options allow you to work with fields from the current database file or view, with new calculate fields, with special predefined fields, and with summary fields. The Fields options are:

Add field
Remove field
Modify field
Change hidden field

Add field. Place the cursor in the position where you want to add a new field template before choosing this option or pressing F5 (Field). A four-column list appears like the one in Fig. 1-35.

Database fields. The first column lists fields from the current database file or view. If the view contains calculated fields, they are also displayed here. When you choose a field from this list, the field description menu appears. See the Fields menu section under Forms panel for information on modifying field attributes (p. 54).

Three Picture attributes that are important in Reports are Trim, Horizontal Stretch, and Vertical Stretch. The Trim option removes blanks before and after a field's data. For this to have the proper effect, you must use character blanks between fields. In other words, do not press the spacebar to put a space between text and a field. The character blanks glue the fields and the text together, so that the extra spaces allowed for, say, a long name, can be trimmed and the first name and last name can be printed with only one space between them.

Vertical stretch wraps a field's data within a specified width. Fields with vertical stretch are represented by VVVVV templates. The number of Vs indicates the width in number of characters of the template. The number Vs that initially appear is determined by the default width of the field. Use Shift – F7 (Size) to adjust the width of a vertical stretch template.

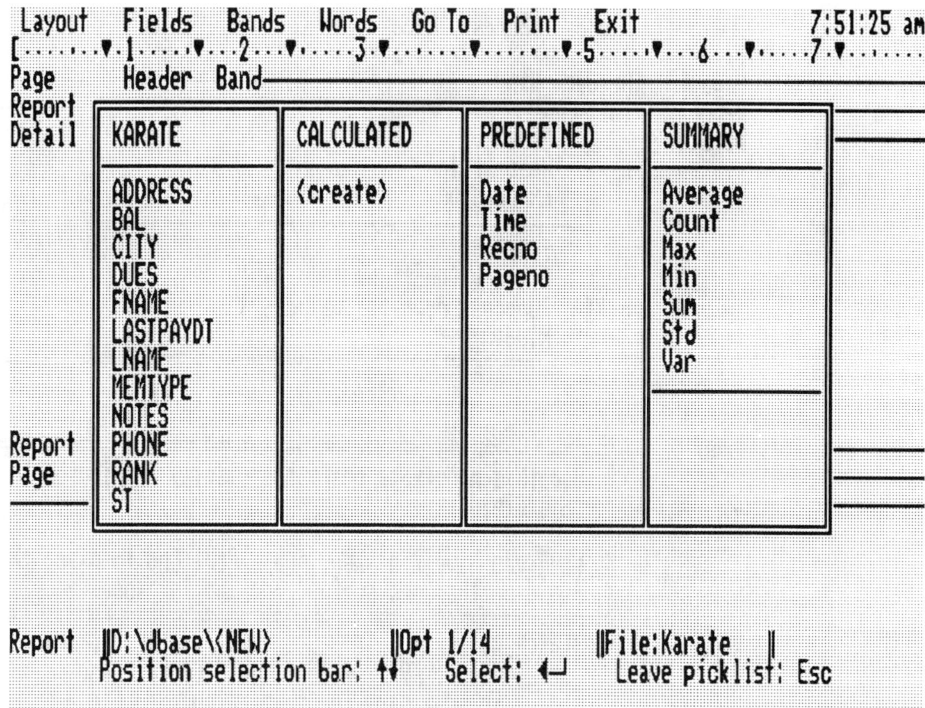

Fig. 1-35. Add Field field list.

For memo fields, the width is determined by the MEMWIDTH setting in the Settings option of the Tools menu (see *p. 13*). Memo fields in a report are automatically assigned a vertical stretch template.

Horizontal stretch allows the space in which a field to stretch so that excess data is not truncated. Fields with horizontal stretch are shown as HHHHH templates. These templates cannot be edited.

The Wrap semicolon picture function can be used for character and memo fields. This option interprets a semicolon as a carriage return and begins a new line in the column where the field template begins. This function is applied automatically when you import dBASE II PLUS report forms (.frm files) to the reports design screen.

Calculated fields. Use the right arrow key to move to the next column. This column lists any calculated fields created so far in this report. When you choose <create> to create a new calculated field, or when you choose a calculated field created in this report, a field definition menu like the one in Fig. 1-36 appears.

Enter the name and description of the field after press Enter on those options. The Expression option requires that you enter a valid dBASE IV expression. Press Shift–F1 to display a list of field names, operators, and functions

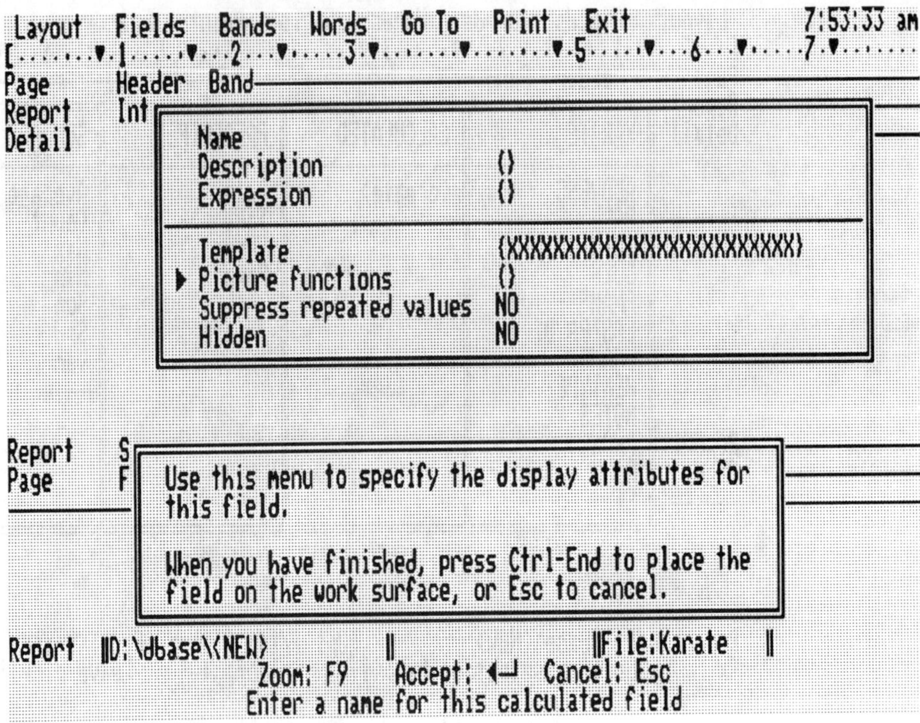

Fig. 1-36. Field definition menu.

you can use. The expression can include predefined memory variables and user-defined functions as well. The Template and Pictures options are described under the Fields menu section of Forms panel (*see* p. 54).

You can hide the field on the report by toggling the Hidden option to yes. A field must have a name to be hidden.

Predefined fields. The third column lists predefined fields. When the report is printed, these fields show the current date, time, record number, and page number. When you select a predefined field, the field description menu appears. You can change the type of predefined field by placing the cursor on the Name option and pressing Enter until the field name you want appears. The Pictures option is the @SAY . . . GET command under Forms panel (*see* p. 87). Press Ctrl – End to add the field to the work surface.

Summary fields. The fourth column lists the seven generic summary fields, followed by any field names specifically defined in this report. These fields can be used to summarize the values of a group (see Bands menu below). You can also place them in the Report Summary band or the Detail band, where they show a running result.

When you choose a field, the field description menu appears. You can choose the Operation option to call up a list of summary operations and change the type of operation to be performed in the field.

The Field to summarize on options displays a list of fields. It is not available when you use Count as the summary field.

The Reset every options lets you reset the current summary field to zero at the end of every page or at the end of every report (this is the default).

You can also reset a summary field every time a new group begins. If your work surface contains group bands, the list includes field names, expressions or record counts used to form all the groups in your report. Choose the item that describes the group for which you want the summary field reset. For instance, if you grouped the karate students by belt color, you might want the count to reset after every group.

When you have specified the field description, press Ctrl – End to place the field at the current cursor position.

Remove field. There are three ways to remove field templates from the report screen. To remove a single field, you can place the cursor on the template and press Del, or choose Remove field from the menu. If you want to remove more than one instance of a field, or if you want to remove several fields, position the cursor so that it does not mark any fields, and choose Remove field. A list of fields will be displayed, and you can choose the field to remove. You'll notice that removing a field does not remove the field name. Use Del or Backspace to remove field names from the screen.

Modify field. This option lets you change the field definitions for a field.

Change hidden field. If you previously hid a field and you decide you want it to print on the report, place the cursor where you want the field to appear, choose Change hidden and change the attribute on the menu. You can choose the hidden field from a list displaying all hidden fields. Only calculated and summary fields can be hidden.

Bands Menu

The Bands menu (Fig. 1-37) lets you add and remove bands, and assign special characteristics to bands.

Add a group band. A group band lets you list data in groups on your report. Before you choose this option, place the cursor above the detail band; either in the page header band, the report intro band, or an existing group intro band.

A group band actually consists of two bands: the group's intro band (above the detail band) and the group's summary band (below the detail band). You

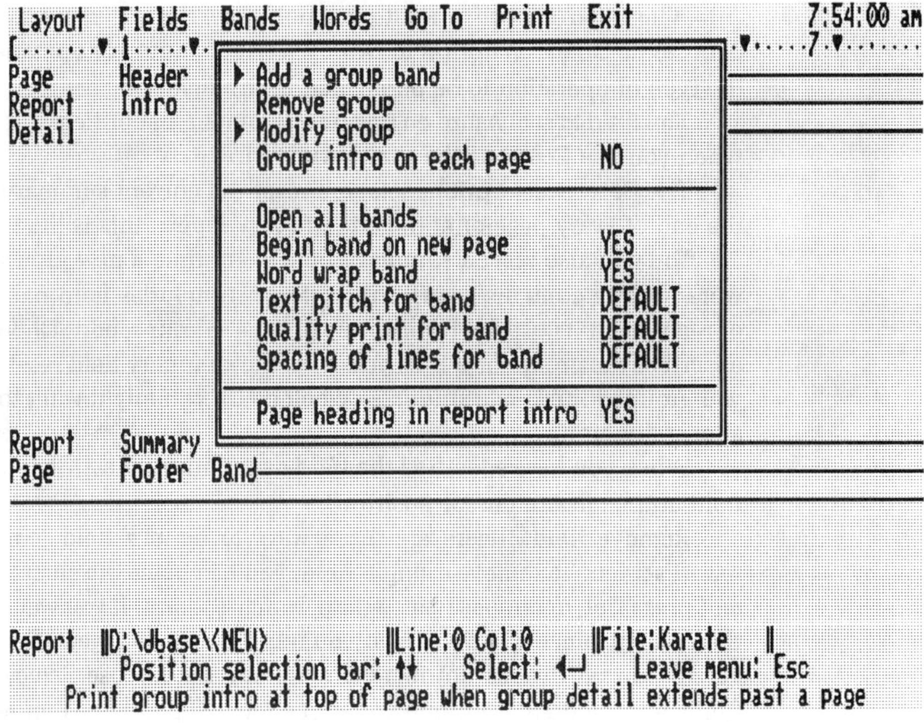

Fig. 1-37. The Bands menu.

can use the intro band for column headings or titles to clarify the grouping procedure. You can use the standard summary operators in the summary band, just as you would at the end of the report. Subtotaling is one of the most common reasons for grouping records in a report.

If you want to create subgroups within groups, you can nest a group band by placing the cursor beneath the current band. To make the existing band a subgroup, place the cursor above the existing band before adding the new band. When you choose Add a group band, a submenu appears so you can specify one of three conditions that you can use to separate groups.

Field value. This option lets you start a new group each time the value in that field changes. For example, to group students by rank, you would enter rank in the field value option. In order for this to work, you must first index your database on the field you plan to specify for grouping.

Expression value. You can define your group with any valid dBASE IV expression. Press Shift – F1 (Pick) for a list of field names, operators and functions, or type the expression into the menu.

Record count. If you want to separate records for visual purposes, you can specify a number of records that equals one group. This option can be combined with others. For instance, you could group on the field value City and create a subgroup with a record count of 10.

Remove group. Place the cursor on the group you want to remove and choose this option to delete both the group intro band and the group summary band from the report.

You can quickly remove a group band by highlighting the group's border line and pressing Del. If the group you remove has a subgroup, that subgroup becomes the main group.

Modify group. If you change your mind about the specifications you want for your group, choose this option. The submenu of field groups described above appears. Enter your new conditions.

Group intro on each page. If your group runs over onto the next page, you can use this option to reprint the group intro (for example, column headings) on the second page for the group.

You can print a group intro that describes the information on the subgroups on each page, and have column headings for each group as well. Use a subgroup created by the same group value as the main group, put the column headings in this group and turn on the Group intro on each page option. For example, Fig. 1-38 shows the layout for a report on tournament wins. Both

```
Layout  Fields  Bands  Words  Go To  Print  Exit                 7:55:17 am
[.......▼.1.....▼...2...▼.....3.▼.......▼.......▼.5.....▼...6...▼.....7.▼.......
Page      Header  Band
Page No. 999
MM/DD/YY
Report    Intro   Band
Group  1  Intro   Band
Below are students who won medals in 1989:
Group  2  Intro   Band
Last Name  First Name  Rank       Tournament                      Place
Detail            Band
XXXXXXXXXX  XXXXXXXXXX  XXXXXXXXX  XXXXXXXXXXXXXXXXXXXXXXXXXXXXXX  99
Group  2  Summary Band
Group  1  Summary Band
Report    Summary Band
Report  ‖D:\dbase\WINREPOR        ‖Band 1/9         ‖File:Karate  ‖         Ins
             Add field:F5  Select:F6  Move:F7  Copy:F8  Size:Shift-F7
```

Fig. 1-38. A report with a group band.

groups are grouped by rank, and the column headings will appear at the top of every page because the Group intro on each page option is turned on.

Open all bands. You might want to close some bands to make it easier to focus on one band at a time. Because closed bands are not printed, this is also a convenient way to customize your reports.

To close an open band, or to open a closed band, place the cursor on the border of a band and press Enter. To reopen all closed bands, choose the Open all bands option.

Begin band on new page. Turn this option on when you want each new group in a band to start at the top of a new page.

Word wrap band. Except on a mailmerge layout, new bands are automatically created as layout bands. If you want to be able to wrap text, change this option to Yes.

Be careful switching back and forth from one mode to another in a band. If, for example, you change from word wrap back to layout, make sure you finish entering your text first, because although it looks the same, it no longer wraps in layout mode. When you change from layout to word wrap, space are inserted to preserve the appearance of the text. Hard carriage returns are placed at the end of every line, and each line becomes a paragraph.

Text pitch for band. This option works together with the Text pitch option on the Print menu's Control of printer submenu (*see p. 75*).

Most of the print settings are supplied on the Print menus, but you can specify pitch for the current band with the Text pitch for band option. This setting will have priority over the Print menu settings when the report is printed. If you want the band to print at the pitch set on the Print menu, choose the DEFAULT option.

When you specify a band pitch, the report screen does not display differently. All screen characters are shown with the same width, no matter what the band settings.

Quality print for band. You can specify print quality for a band the same way you specify text pitch. Using this option overrides the settings on the Print menu, unless you choose the Default option.

Spacing of lines for band. This option also allows you to specify the print setting for the current band. Choose DEFAULT to use the Print menu setting.

Page headings in report intro. Normally the report intro band prints information from the page header and page footer bands. If you do not want this information in the report intro, set this option to No. This is useful when, for instance, you want a cover letter at the beginning of a report. To start the report on a new page, use the Insert page break option from the Words menu (*see p. 58*).

Setting Page headings in report intro to No moves the report intro to the top of the layout and the report summary to the bottom.

Print Menu

You can reach a Print menu in the Control Center in several ways. When you press Enter on a filename in the Reports or Labels panel, the prompt box gives you a Print option. You can also open a Print menu from the Report, Label, or Application design screens.

If you press Shift–F9 (Quick Report) from a filename in any Control Center panel except the Applications panel, the Print menu appears on screen. Shift–F9 (Quick Report) also brings up a Print menu from the Browse/Edit screen or the Queries design screen. A Quick Report produces a series of field columns, listing the information from each record of the current database file or view.

The Reports, Labels, and Applications screens have slight variations in the Print menus. Options for all three are discussed. The Print menus contain these options:

Begin printing
Eject page now
View report/labels on screen (Reports and labels)
Generate sample labels (Labels only)
Line numbers (Applications only)
Use print form {<filename>}
Save settings to print form
Destination
Control of printer
Output options
Page dimensions

Most of the settings that affect the look of your reports or labels are specified in the screen design menu options. You can specify character attributes such as boldface type or italics, with the Style submenu of the Words menu (*see p.* 58).

Begin printing. Once you have chosen the settings you want, choose this option to print. If you want to pause printing temporarily, press Ctrl–S. If you want to stop printing entirely, press Esc. If you have a print buffer, it might take a few moments for the buffer to empty.

Eject page now. Use this option to make the printer eject a page so you can start and end pages at their perforations. You can also eject pages by selecting the New page option from the Control of printer submenu (see below).

Line numbers (Applications). Toggle to YES if you want the lines numbers to print at the left of every line. This helps you keep track of where you are in the program you are writing.

View report/labels on screen. This option lets you view your report or labels as they will look when they are printed. This is a good way to make sure all fields are properly defined. If the report is wider than your screen, the text wraps to the next line.

Generate sample labels. It's a good idea to check your label settings before printing a large number of labels. When you choose this option, a sample label is sent to the printer. If you are printing more than one label in a row, the sample includes one row of labels.

You are then asked if you want to print another sample. You can keep printing samples until your alignment is correct.

Use print form. When you select settings to print, you can save those settings in a print form file with a .prf extension, allowing you to use the same settings for printing later.

When you can select the Use print form option, a list of print forms appears. Choose the form you want and use Begin printing to print with those settings.

Save settings to print form. This option lets you save or modify a collection of print settings to a print form with a .prf extension. Enter the new name of the form or accept the suggestion, and the form is saved for future use.

Destination. This option displays a submenu that lets you determine where to send the output.

Write to. This option lets you print the report immediately, or send it to another DOS file for printing later. Toggle from Printer to DOS file with the spacebar.

Name of DOS file. If you choose DOS File in the Write to option, a file is created that meets the requirements of the printer shown in the Printer model option. The option usually suggests the name of the current file with a .prt extension.

If you choose ASCII text with the Printer model option, the suggested extension is .txt. You can press Enter and type the name and extension you want to use.

Printer model. Your toggle choices in this option depend on the printers you installed when you put dBASE IV on your computer, or when you installed a printer driver by setting the _pdriver memory variable at the dot prompt. Your choice will determine the printer control codes embedded in the file.

The ASCII text option lets you send a file by a form of electronic mail that cannot handle printer control codes, as well as when you want to produce an ASCII file. Generic creates a file that uses only the most common printer codes.

Echo to screen. You can set this option to YES to watch the report or label on your screen as it is being sent to an electronic file or printer. The display with Echo to screen is only an approximation of the printed material.

Control of printer. The options on this submenu let you specify the size and quality of printing, the way new pages are handled, and special codes required to initiate the printer.

Text pitch. Toggle to the text pitch you want. Pica prints 10 characters per inch, while Elite prints 12 characters per inch. Condensed prints even smaller, with the exact number of characters per inch depending on your printer. Default prints with the current printer pitch.

Quality print. YES prints the best quality your printer can print (nearest letter quality). NO prints the fastest (draft) quality. DEFAULT prints the current printer quality setting.

New page. Toggle through these options to choose whether you want pages to be ejected before printing, after printing, or both before and after. Choose NONE if you want no pages ejected.

Wait between pages. If you need to insert paper after each page, you can use this option to tell the printer to wait after each page.

Advance page using. You might need to use this option if your paper length is not one of the standard form length supported by your printer. Form feeds tells the printer to move to the top of the next form. Line feeds lets you specify the number of lines needed to fill the page length.

Starting control codes . Before you print labels or reports you can send control codes to your printer telling it to do things not on the Print menus.

When you choose this option, you are prompted to enter a string. Characters with ASCII codes less than 32 cannot be entered simply by pressing their keys on the keyboard. You can, however, type the codes inside curly braces, like this: {27}. Characters entered without curly braces are sent directly to the printer.

Some codes can be typed inside curly braces with their everyday names. For example, Esc can be sent to the printer either by its ASCII code {27} or by the mnemonics {esc} or {escape}.

Below is a list of control codes allowed inside curly braces:

Code	ASCII Number
Null	0
Bell	7
Backspace	8
Tab	9
Return	13
Esc	27
{	123
Del	127
0 through 255	0 through 255

Ending control codes. After you print reports or labels, you can reset your printer by entering codes the same way you did in the Starting control codes option.

Output options. The options on this submenu let you choose the number of copies printed and which pages are printed.

Begin on page. Enter the page number you want to begin printing on. The maximum setting is 32,767. After you print, this number automatically resets to the starting number stored in the current print form. This is usually 1.

End after page. Enter the last page number you want printed. The printer stops after printing this page. The maximum, and default, number is 32,767. After printing, this number resets to the number stored in the current print form.

First page number. You can specify the page number printed on the first page with this option. You might do this if you have a document composed of several reports.

Number of copies. This option lets you indicate the number of copies to print. The maximum setting is 32,767. After printing, the number of copies automatically resets to the number stored in the current print form. The default setting is 1.

Page dimension. This submenu lets you determine placement of text on the page.

Length of page. Enter the length of the page in single spaced lines. An 11 inch page is 66 lines long (the default). The maximum page length setting is 32,767 lines.

Offset from left. This option determines where printing begins on the left edge of the page. This is column zero for report layout bands and labels. In word wrap mode, the first printed column begins at the position of the sum of the offset setting and the left margin setting. For instance, if you want word wrap text to begin 10 spaces from the left edge of the paper, you could set the margin to 10 and the offset to zero, or the margin to five and the offset to 5.

Spacing of lines. Choose single, double, or triple to indicate the spacing between lines.

Other Menus

The Words menu is explained under Forms panel (*see p. 58*). The Go To menu is described under the Browse/Edit menus (*see p. 37*).

The Exit menu allows you to save your changes and leave the Report screen, or to leave the screen without saving your changes.

The Labels Design Panel

In dBASE IV, you can design labels for everything from mailing to name tags. Labels are designed in layout editing mode, the same way you would design a form or a report with layout bands. While a standard label looks like the one shown in Fig. 1-39, labels can be up to 255 lines tall and 255 characters wide.

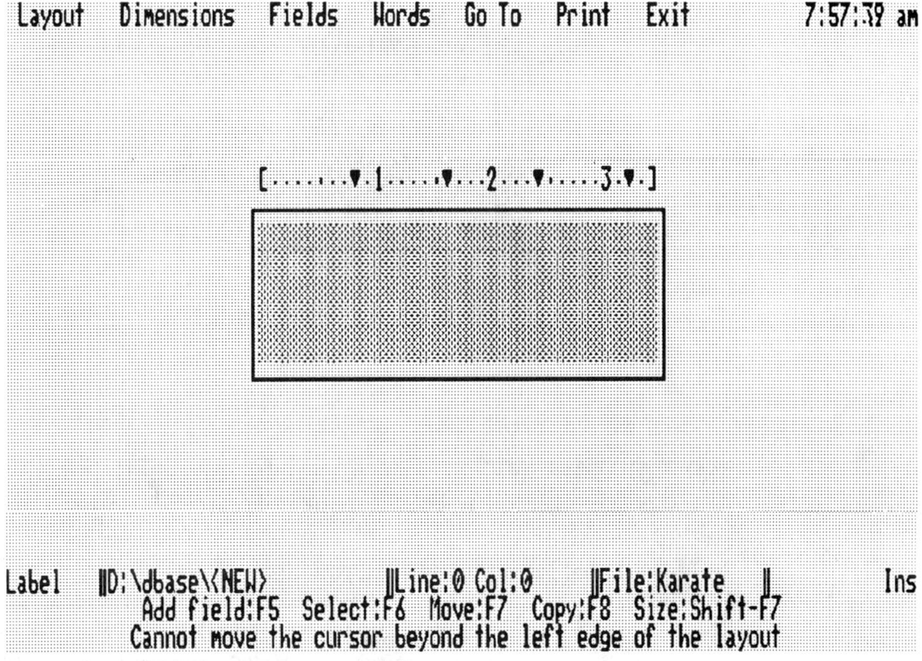

Fig. 1-39. The Label design screen.

You can enter fields on a label design screen two ways. You can make use of the Trim function, which is automatically applied to labels. This function trims excess spaces from the beginning or end of a field, so, for example, a first and last name can appear with only one space between them, instead of the entire number of unused spaces in the first name field. To do this, use the arrow keys to move from one field entry to the next.

If you use the spacebar between fields, the fields line up as though the total number of field spaces is in use. In Fig. 1-40, the first and last name are separated without blank characters, but the city and state were separated with the spacebar. You can see in the labels in Fig. 1-41 that the state always prints in the same place, regardless of how short the city name is. The first and last name, however, always print with one space between them.

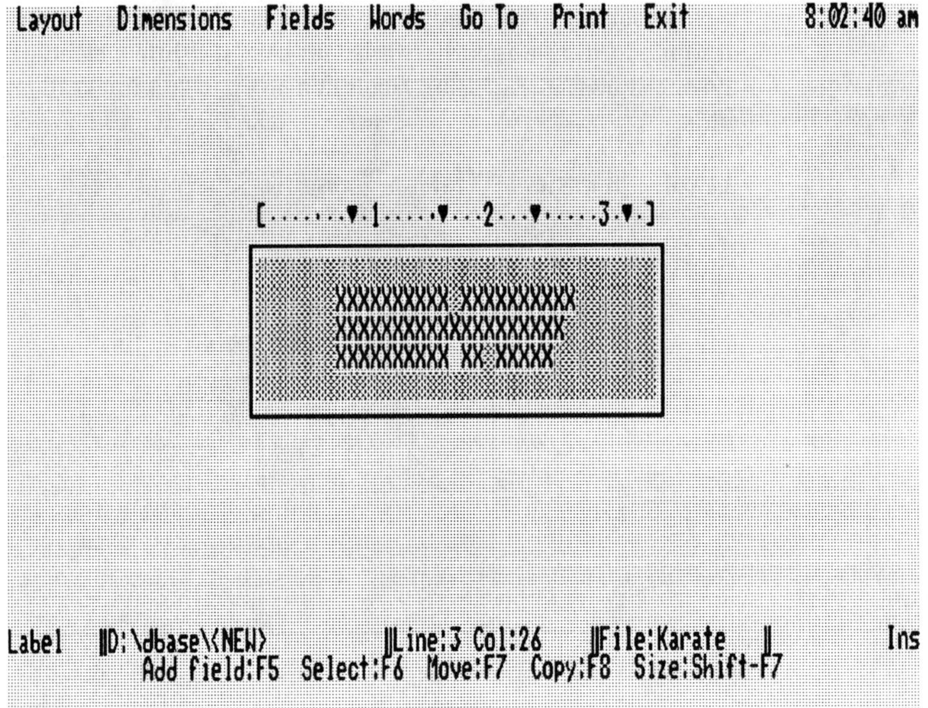

Fig. 1-40. Label layout using Trim function.

Fig. 1-41. Labels printed from label layout in Fig. 1-40.

```
Jon Fukushima
33970 Moonlight Way
La Mesa,       CA 92041
```

From the Labels panel, you can highlight <create> to create a new label form, or you can select a file from the panel. When you select an existing file, a prompt box asks if you want to print the label, modify its layout, or display the data.

Labels Menus

The Labels menu bar consists of seven menus: Layout, Dimensions, Fields, Words, Go To, Print, and Exit. Several of these menus are described earlier in this chapter. The Fields and Go To menus are described under the Browse/Edit menus (see p. 37). The Words menu is explained under the Forms menu (see p. 58). The Print menu is presented under Reports (see p. 73).

Layout Menu

The Labels Layout menu contains three options:

Use different database file or view
Edit description of label design
Save this label design

Use different database file or view. When you design a label, it is initially associated with a particular database file or view. You can use the label form with other files or view by choosing this option and making your selection.

The label form lets you print labels for a number of files without creating a separate label format for each one. When you use a different file or view, the label remains ''attached'' to the original file or view, unless you save it with the change.

If you try to use a file or view that doesn't contain the necessary fields for the label design, a message appears. If this happens, you need to select a different file or create a view of the file with the necessary fields.

Edit description of label design. This option lets you enter or change the description in the catalog of the current label.

Save this label design. When you choose this option, you can accept the suggested filename or enter a new one.

Dimensions Menu

The Dimensions menu lets you define the shape and spacing of your label. The menu contains these options:

Predefined size
Width of label
Height of label
Indentation
Lines between labels
Spaces between label columns
Columns of labels

Predefined size. When you choose this option, the submenu shown in Fig. 1-42 displays a list of common label sizes. The first two dimensions are height and width in inches. If there is a third dimension, it refers to columns. Option 1, for instance, prints 1 label in a row. Option 4 prints 3 labels in a row.

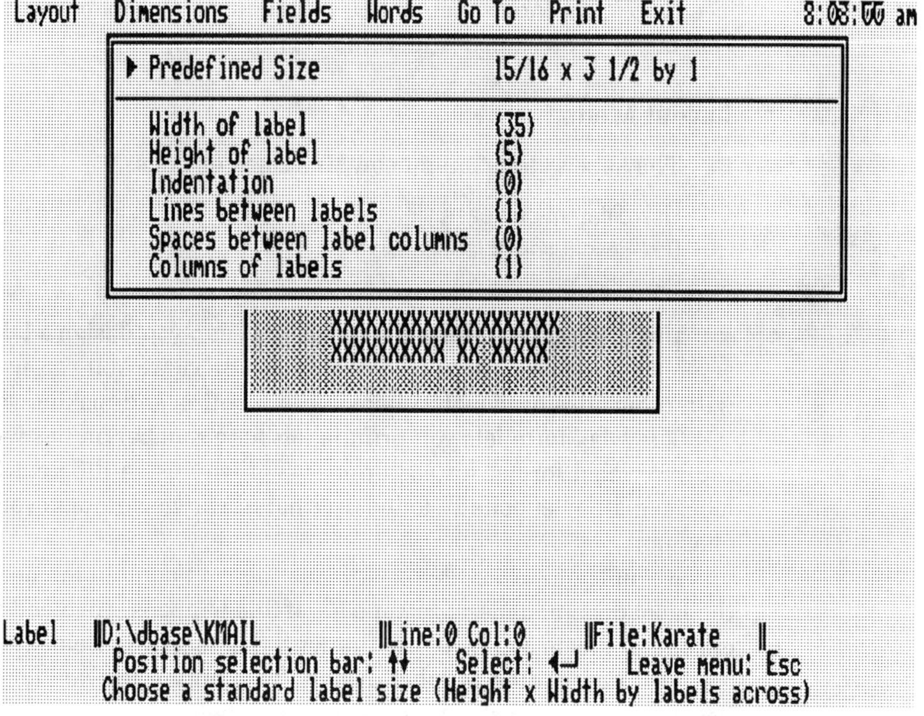

Fig. 1-42. Predefined label menu.

If you change your print settings, the label settings do not automatically change.

Width of label. This option specifies the width of the label in characters. This number can be up to 255, but it must match the space needed for the text and field templates already on the work surface. If not, a warning message appears.

Height of label. Specify the label's height in lines with this option. If your printer prints six lines per inch, a 15/16 inch label can take five lines of print. The maximum number you can enter is 255.

Indentation. This option works with the Offset from left option from Print menu's Page dimensions submenu. In other words, if your offset setting if 5 and you want the printer to begin printer at position 5 of your label, you don't need to use the Indentation option. But if the offset is set to 5 and you want the printer to start at position 10, set the indentation to 5. The two values are added together to get the starting position. You can enter any value from 0 to 250.

Lines between labels. Enter the number of blank lines you want from the bottom of one label to the top of the next. The range of this setting is 0 to 16 lines.

Spaces between label columns. Specify the number of spaces between the right side of one label and the left side of the next with this option. You can enter any number from 0 to 120.

Columns of labels. This option lets you specify the number of labels to print in each row. Enter any number from 1 to 15. The total width of your label design cannot exceed 255 characters.

Other Menus

The Fields and Go To menus are described under the Browse/Edit menus (*see* p. 34). The Words menu is explained under the Forms menu (*see* p. 52). The Print menu is presented under Reports (*see* p. 73).

The Exit Menu

Before leaving the Labels design screen, you can save your changes with the Exit and save option, or you can abandon your changes without saving them.

The Applications Panel

If you have created custom programs in dBASE IV, you can place them in the Applications Panel for easy access. In most cases, you will want to group your programs together into one application which can call the smaller programs. This way you can avoid difficulties in locating the application in a long list in the panel.

You can also place DOS programs in the Applications panel, which can be convenient if you want to be able to execute, for instance, an .exe or .com program from the Control Center.

To create a custom program from the Applications panel, you can select <create> and press Enter. Then choose to use either the program editor from the Tools menu (*see p. 13*), or the dBASE IV Applications Generator (*see p. 385*). (If you create a program outside dBASE IV, save it in ASCII format and use the TEDIT setting in your Config.db file to tell dBASE IV you want to use an external editor for programs.)

If you want to modify an existing application, highlight the name of that application and press Shift – F2 (Design). This takes you to the program editor or the dBASE IV Applications Generator, whichever was used to make the application.

Applications Menus

The Applications menus are similar to the menus described earlier in this section. Only the Layout and Exit menus differ greatly. For a description of the Words menu, *see p. 58* in the Forms section. The Go To menu is explained under the Browse/Edit menus (*see p. 34*). The Print menu is described under Reports (*see p. 62*).

The Layout Menu

The Layout menu consists of these options:

Modify a different program
Edit description of program
Save this program

Modify a different program. If you want to modify a program other than the current program, choose this option. If you have made changes to the current program, you are given the opportunity to save the changes before the new program is called up. You can enter the name of the program or ASCII file you want to work on, or choose it from the Shift – F1 (Pick) list.

Edit description of program. This option lets you edit the catalog description of the current program. It is only available if a catalog is open.

Save this program. When you choose this option, you can enter a new name to save a new program, or to create a new program from a modified one, or you can accept the suggested name. It is a good idea to save your changes as you work, in case of power outages.

Exit Menu

The Applications Exit menu lets you leave or test your program. The Exit options are:

Save changes and exit
Abandon changes and exit
Run program
Debug program

Save changes and exit. Choose this option to save your changes and leave the program editor. You are returned to the Control Center, the dot prompt or the program you came from.

Abandon changes and exit. If you choose this option, you are asked to confirm your choice. If you do, you are returned to the Control Center, the dot prompt or the program you came from.

Run program. This option lets you run the program from which you are working. It automatically saves any changes you have made. When the program is finished running, you are returned to the Control Center or the dot prompt, whichever you came from.

Debug Program. This option saves the current program, turns on the debugger and displays the debugger screen. You can enter a list of parameters that will be passed to the program (*see p. 133*). When the program finishes, you are returned to the Control Center or the dot prompt, depending on where you came from.

2

dBASE IV Commands

dBASE IV COMMANDS CAN BE ISSUED FROM THE DOT PROMPT OR FROM WITHIN programs. Each option from the Control Center has a corresponding command that can be issued outside of the Control Center. However, many additional commands cannot be issued from the Control Center. Many of these commands (such as DO WHILE, and IF) are used only within programs.

In this chapter, the commands are listed in alphabetical order. Each command is followed by a short description and then details for using it. In situations where variable information must be provided, the argument is placed within angle brackets (< >). In cases where optional clauses may be used, examples show the command with and without the clause.

? and ??

Description. The ? and ?? commands display the contents of the expression list.

Operational rules. The ? command issues a carriage return before printing the expression list, so it is one line below the previous item displayed. The ?? command prints at the current screen or printer position. The ? command by itself displays a blank line.

The following optional functions can be used with the FUNCTION keyword to format the display output:

@B Left-aligns the field display (default).
@C Centers a field display.
@J Right-aligns the field display.

- @T Trims leading and trailing blanks from the field.
- @H A long field will push additional expressions on to the next line.
- @V A long field will wrap vertically in column format.

Use the PICTURE option to change displays such as uppercase conversion and comma mode. See the @ command for a list of PICTURE templates.

Use the AT function to define the column where the expression will display.

The following optional fonts can be used with the STYLE keyword to format the display output:

- B Bold
- I Italic
- U Underline
- R Superscript
- L Subscript

Not all styles can be displayed on all monitors and printers.

Examples.

```
? Fname FUNCTION "@T", Lname STYLE "U" PICTURE  "@!"
John SMITH

? Fname FUNCTION "@T", Lname AT 50
John                                             Smith
```

See also: @...SAY... *p. 87*

??? <expression>

Description. The ??? sends an expression to the printer without changing the position of the printer head.

Operational rules. This command is helpful to use when you need to send printer control codes at the beginning of a printout. The ? and ?? commands can be used to perform the same function, but they can move the printer head, disturbing the layout of the printout.

Control codes can be designated in several ways, namely:

- The CHR( ) function Example: CHR(27) + "E"
- The ASCII number Example: "{27}{69}"
- The character Example: "{ESC}{69}"
- A combination Example: "{27}E"

See also: @...SAY...GET *p. 87.*
CHR( ) *p. 185.*

@ <row>, <col> SAY <expression> GET <expression>

Description. The @...SAY...GET command displays and receives information formatted on the screen.

Operational rules. The @ command allows you to designate the row and column where the expressions will be displayed. The SAY argument is used for displaying an expression, while the GET argument allows editing of the expression. The READ command must follow the list of @...GETs for a screen.

The following optional functions can be used with the FUNCTION keyword to format the display output:

- @B Left-aligns the field display (default).
- @C Centers a field display.
- @J Right-aligns the field display.
- @T Trims leading and trailing blanks from the field.
- @H A long field will push additional expressions on to the next line.
- @V A long field will wrap vertically in column format.

Use the PICTURE option to change displays such as uppercase conversion and comma mode. Below are a list of picture template symbols. If your template is not as long as the GET variable, or the variable is truncated to the length of the template.

- ! Converts to uppercase.
- # Allows only digits, blanks and + or –.
- $ Displays a "$" in place of leading zeroes.
- * Displays a "*" in place of leading zeroes.
- , Displays commas between thousands.
- A Allows only letters.
- N Allows letters or digits.
- X Allows any character.
- Y Allows only Y or N.

The $, COL( ), and ROW( ) functions allow you to use relative row and column referencing. Each represents the current position of the cursor.

Examples.

```
@ 5,1 SAY "Enter Last Name" GET Lname PICTURE "!XXXXXXXXXXXXXXX"
@ 5,50 SAY "First Name" GET Fname PICTURE "!XXXXXXXXXXXXXXX"
READ
@ 10,1     SAY "   Name: " GET Name FUNCTION "@!"
@ $+1,1    SAY "   Address: " GET Address
@ $+1,1    SAY "   City: " GET City
READ
```

See also: READ *p. 138.*

@ <row 1>, <col 1> CLEAR <row 2>, <col 2>

Description. The @...CLEAR command clears a rectangular area of the screen.

Operational rules. This command erases the rectangular area made up of corner <row 1>, <col 1> through the opposite corner or <row 2>, <col 2>.

See also: @...SAY *p. 87.*

@ <row 1>, <col 1> TO <row 2>, <col 2>

Description. The @...TO command creates a box on the screen.

Operational rules. This command draws a box in the rectangular area made up of corner <row 1>, <col 1> through the opposite corner or <row 2>, <col 2>.

The optional arguments DOUBLE, PANEL, or <character string> define the character to be used in drawing the box. The default is a single line. The optional argument COLOR <attribute> defines the color of the box. The attribute codes are listed under the SET COLOR TO command.

Examples.

```
@ 10, 1 TO 15, 75

@ 1, 1 TO 5, 30 DOUBLE COLOR b/r
```

The first example draws a single line box at the bottom half of the screen. The second example draws a colored double line box.

See also: @...SAY *p. 87.*

@ <row 1>, <col 1> FILL TO <row 2>, <col 2>

Description. The @...FILL TO command colors in a rectangular area of the screen.

Operational rules. This command colors in a rectangular area made up of corner <row 1>, <col 1> through the opposite corner or <row 2>, <col 2>.

The optional argument COLOR <attribute> defines the color of the box. The attribute codes are listed under the SET COLOR TO command.

Examples.

```
@ 1, 1 FILL TO 5, 30 COLOR r/b
```

See also: @...SAY *p. 87.*

ACCEPT <prompt> TO <mem variable>

Description. The ACCEPT command displays the prompt and pauses until the user enters something.

Operational rules. This command is most often used in programs where few questions are to be prompted on the screen. Each ACCEPT command halts the program until the user types in an answer and presses Enter. The ACCEPT command is easier to use than full-screen editing commands such as @...GET, because the memory variable does not have to be initialized before issuing the command and screen coordinates do not have to be set (ACCEPT displays the prompt in the same manner as the ? command).

However, the ACCEPT command is not as powerful as the full-screen editing commands, especially because the entry cannot be formatted. Memory variables created by the ACCEPT command are always of the character type. The variable becomes the length of the entry typed in.

If the optional <prompt> is not used, the ACCEPT command simply pauses and waits for the user to enter something.

Examples.

```
.ACCEPT "Enter Your Name " TO MNAME
? "Hi there ", MNAME
```

The preceding program prompts the user to enter his or her name. The memory variable MNAME becomes the length of the entry.

See also: @...SAY...GET *p. 87.*

ACTIVATE MENU <menu name>

Description. ACTIVATE MENU displays a bounce-bar menu on the screen.

Operational rules. Bounce bar menus are menus that show a list of options. The user can navigate through the options with the arrow keys. To choose an option, the user highlights it with the cursor and presses Enter.

Menus are designed with the DEFINE MENU and DEFINE PAD commands. The ON PAD and ON SELECTION PAD commands define the operations to be performed when a pad is selected. Once the definitions are set, you can use ACTIVATE MENU to call it up. Use DEACTIVATE MENU to erase a menu from the screen.

See DEFINE MENU for a program that creates a bounce-bar menu.

See also: DEFINE MENU *p. 109.*

ACTIVATE POPUP <popup name>

Description. ACTIVATE POPUP displays a popup menu on the screen.

Operational rules. Popup menus are menus that appear on the screen, often as a "menu within a menu" that displays as bounce-bar options are highlighted. Popup menus can have their own options listed, and the user can navigate through these options with the arrow keys. To choose an option, the user highlights it with the cursor and presses Enter.

Although bounce-bar menus can be vertically or horizontally oriented, popup menus are always vertical.

Popup menus are designed with the DEFINE POPUP and DEFINE BAR commands. The ON SELECTION POPUP command defines the operations to be performed when a bar from the popup menu is selected. Once the definitions are set, you can use ACTIVATE POPUP to call it up. Use DEACTIVATE POPUP to erase a popup menu from the screen.

See DEFINE BAR for a program that creates a popup menu within a bounce-bar menu.

See also: DEFINE BAR *p. 108.*

ACTIVATE SCREEN

Description. ACTIVATE SCREEN "zooms" into a window, displaying it on the entire screen.

Operational rules. Windows are designed with the DEFINE WINDOW command. Use ACTIVATE WINDOW to then display it. The window must be displayed on the screen before ACTIVATE SCREEN is issued.

Example.

```
DEFINE WINDOW Wind1 FROM 3,3 TO 10,30
ACTIVATE WINDOW Wind1
? "This is Window 1"
ACTIVATE SCREEN
```

The preceding program displays a window on the screen, and then expands it to the entire screen.

See also: DEFINE WINDOW *p. 111.*

ACTIVATE WINDOW

Description. ACTIVATE WINDOW displays a window.

Operational rules. Windows are designed with the DEFINE WINDOW command. Use ACTIVATE WINDOW to then display it.

See also: DEFINE WINDOW *p. 111.*

APPEND

Description. The APPEND command allows the user to add new records to the database.

Operational rules. This command brings up the editing screen. Each new record is added on to the bottom of the file.

See also: EDIT *p. 116.*

APPEND BLANK

Description. The APPEND BLANK command adds one more record to the database without going into the full-screen edit mode.

Operational rules. The new record added with the APPEND BLANK command will have no entries in any of the fields, hence the BLANK argument.

Example.

```
USE Maillist
APPEND BLANK
SET FORMAT TO Mailedit
READ
CLOSE FORMAT
```

The program adds a record to the file using APPEND BLANK. This method is advantageous to the full-screen APPEND command because the user cannot scroll to any other records, and the program regains control after the entry of this one record.

See also: APPEND *p. 91.*

APPEND FROM <data file> or <array>

Description. The APPEND FROM command adds records from a database or array to the current file.

Operational rules. When appending from a file, the optional file types are:

Type	**Description**
DBASEII	dBASE II database file
SDF	fixed length fields ASCII file
DELIMITED	variable length fields separated with commas
DELIMITED WITH <expC>	variable length fields separated with <expC>
DIF	VisiCalc format
FW2	Framework

RPD	RapidFile
SYLK	MultiPlan
WKS	Lotus 1-2-3

The optional FOR <conditional> argument appends only the records that match a certain criteria.

When appending from an array, each array element represents a field.

Example.

USE Maillist	
APPEND FROM Mail	(add records from another dBASE file)
APPEND FROM Mail FOR State = "CA"	(add records that match criteria)
APPEND FROM Mail SDF	(add records from ASCII file)
APPEND FROM Mail DELIM WITH /	(add records with fields separated with /)

See also: APPEND *p. 91.*

APPEND MEMO <memo field> FROM <file name>

Description. The APPEND MEMO command reads the memo field from <file name> into the specified memo field of the current file.

Operational rules. The optional OVERWRITE argument replaces the value of the memo field. If this option is not used, the command simply appends the memo data to the end of the current memo.

You can read memo from a text file when running this command from the control center.

Example.

USE Maillist	
APPEND MEMO Comments FROM Mail	(adds memos from Mail)

ASSIST

Description. The ASSIST command accesses dBASE IV Control Center.

Operational rules. Many dBASE commands can be run through the Control Center, which provides full screen editing with pull-down menus and function key support. These same commands can be run from the dot prompt when not in ASSIST mode. Some dBASE commands can only be run from the dot prompt.

AVERAGE

Description. AVERAGE provides the arithmetic mean of the numeric fields of a data file.

Operational rules. If no arguments are provided, dBASE displays the average of each numeric field in the database. You can provide a field list to specify the field(s) to be summed.

To create memory variables whose values are the averages, use the TO <memory variable list> or TO ARRAY. When calculating to an array, the array must be declared as single dimension, and each field in the field list updates the next row of the array.

You can use the optional FOR <condition>, WHILE <condition>, and <scope> arguments to include only a subset of the records in the calculation.

Examples.

```
AVERAGE
AVERAGE Wage, Bonus to Awage, Abon
AVERAGE Wage TO Awage FOR State = "CA"
AVERAGE Wage, Bonus, Commsion TO ARRAY Mamount
```

The last example assumes that Mamount has been declared as a one dimensional array. After the AVERAGE, Mamount(1) is equal to the average of the Wage field.

See also: DECLARE *p. 107.*

BEGIN TRANSACTION
<commands>
END TRANSACTION

Description. Use BEGIN TRANSACTION to begin processing in a situation where you might want to abort the results.

Operational rules. When the BEGIN TRANSACTION command is given, dBASE places a special mark in the database. This mark is not released until the END TRANSACTION or ROLLBACK command has been issued. At any time during the transaction, all updates to the file can be aborted with the ROLLBACK command.

Changes made by the following commands can be rolled back are APPEND, BROWSE, CHANGE, DELETE, EDIT, RECALL, REPLACE, and UPDATE. Commands that cannot be issued during a transaction are CLEAR ALL, CLOSE, DELETE FILE, ERASE, INSERT, MODIFY STRUCTURE, PACK, RENAME, and ZAP.

Example.

```
BEGIN TRANSACTION
USE Maillist
SCAN FOR .NOT. State = "CA"
      REPLACE Tax with 0
```

```
        IF Active = "N"
          DELETE
        ENDIF
    ENDSCAN
    END TRANSACTION
```

In the example, certain changes are made to the file. If an error occurs during the transaction, all changes can be aborted with the ROLLBACK command.

See also: ROLLBACK *p. 143.*

BROWSE

Description. The BROWSE mode allows the user to add/edit records in the current file.

Operational rules. When browsing a file, the records appear in list format, one record per row. Full screen editing is in effect with the addition of the following keys:

Ctrl – Left arrow	Horizontally scroll left
Ctrl – Right arrow	Horizontally scroll right

The optional NOAPPEND, NOEDIT, NODELETE, NOCLEAR, NOMENU, NOFOLLOW, and NOINIT arguments restrict the capabilities of the BROWSE command.

The optional FIELDS <field name list> arguments restrict the fields or field order displayed in the BROWSE command. The SET FIELDS TO command can also set the order.

The other optional arguments are COMPRESS, FORMAT, LOCK <expN>, WIDTH <expN>, FREEZE <field name>, WINDOW <window name>. The LOCK and FREEZE options prevent changing of a particular field.

Example.

```
BROWSE
BROWSE NOAPPEND NODELETE
BROWSE FIELDS Lname,Fname,City,Zip
```

See also: APPEND *p. 91.*
EDIT *p. 116.*

CALCULATE <option list>

Description. The CALCULATE command performs a calculation of all or a subset of records in the current database.

Operational rules. The command displays the answer to the calculations. Valid calculations for the <optional list> are AVG( ), CNT( ), MAX( ), MIN( ), NPV( ), STD( ), SUM( ), and VAR( ).

Keep in mind that if the talk is set OFF, the calculation will not display on the screen. The optional TO <memory variable> initializes a memory variable that is equal to the calculation. Use a <memory variable list> or <<array name> if more than one calculation is in the <option list>. The array must already be declared, and must be one dimensional.

The optional FOR <condition> and WHILE <condition> and <scope> arguments are used to calculate only records that match a specified criteria.

Example.

```
CALCULATE MAX(Grade)
CALCULATE MIN(Sales) FOR Salesman = "JONES"
CALCULATE STD(Grade) TO Stdgrad
CALCULATE MAX(Grade), MIN(Grade), STD(Grade) to Mxgrad, Mngrad, Sdgrad,
CALCULATE MAX(Grade), MIN(Grade), STD(Grade) to Mxgrad
```

The last example assumes that Mxgrad is a one-dimensional array that has been declared.

See also: RECCOUNT( ) *p. 243.*

CALL <module name>

Description. The CALL command runs a binary program loaded into memory.

Operational rules. dBASE can run binary (assembly language and machine language) programs. To do this you must:

1. Load the program into memory with the LOAD command
2. Run the program with the CALL command
3. Release it from memory with the RELEASE MODULE command

Binary programs are useful in instances where a function must be performed that dBASE cannot do. For instance, certain screen graphics manipulation and file maintenance on non-dBASE files can be done only through binary programs.

You can pass variables to the program using the WITH <expression list> option. You can pass up to seven expressions.

See also: LOAD *p. 126.*

CANCEL

Description. The CANCEL command halts a program and returns to the dot prompt.

Operational rules. This command stops a program without exiting the dBASE system. The user is exited to the dot prompt. All data files remain open, while all private memory variables are released.

This command is equivalent to choosing the Cancel option from the prompt Cancel, Suspend, Ignore which is displayed when an error is encountered in a program, or when the user presses Esc while running a program.

CHANGE

The CHANGE command is equivalent to EDIT.

See: EDIT *p. 116.*

CLEAR

Description. The CLEAR command is used to clear the screen, the memory, the open databases, or other elements from dBASE.

Operational rules. The CLEAR command without any arguments clears the screen. The optional argument MEMORY clears all memory variables. The arguments MENUS, POPUPS, and WINDOWS clear those on-screen options. GETS removes the ability to move into fields currently displayed with the @...GET command. TYPEAHEAD clears the keyboard buffer.

The CLEAR ALL command removes everything currently in memory, although it does not close files and indexes.

Examples.

```
CLEAR                  (clears the screen)
CLEAR MEMORY           (clears all memory variables)
CLEAR MENUS, POPUPS    (clears all menus and popup menus)
CLEAR TYPEAHEAD        (clears the keyboard buffer)
```

See also: CLOSE *p. 96.*

CLOSE

Description. The CLOSE command is used to close any file currently open.

Operational rules. The CLOSE command ensures that the contents of a currently open file have been saved. To close one database file, issue the USE command while in that SELECT area.

The optional arguments ALTERNATE, DATABASES, FORMAT, INDEX, and PROCEDURE close only files of each particular type. The argument ALL closes files of all types.

Examples.

CLOSE DATABASES	(close all databases)
CLOSE INDEX	(closes all index files)
CLOSE ALL	(closes all files)

See also: CLOSE *p. 96.*

COMPILE <filename>

Description. The COMPILE command is used to compile a source code program file to a .dbo object code file.

Operational rules. dBASE IV requires that program files are compiled into object code before running. Object code files allow the programs to run much faster. These files, unlike source code, cannot be edited with MODIFY COMMAND.

dBASE IV automatically recompiles programs when DO <program name> is issued. The date and time stamp on the source code (.PRG) file is compared to the object code (.DBO) file. If the two are different, then it recompiles the object code. Use SET DEVELOPMENT OFF to turn off automatic compiling.

The COMPILE command checks for errors in the source code. If an error is found, the command displays the line number of the error and aborts the compile.

If the optional argument RUNTIME is used, dBASE will print out a list of any commands in the source code that cannot be used in the runtime version.

See also: SET DEVELOPMENT *p. 161.*

CONTINUE

Description. The CONTINUE command is used to locate the next record that matches the criteria used in the LOCATE command.

Operational rules. The LOCATE command is used to find the first record that matches a specified criteria. If the criteria is based on a field that is indexed, the SEEK command will find the record much faster than the LOCATE command.

To find the next record that matches the criteria, use the CONTINUE command. If no other records match the criteria, the record pointer moves to the end of file, and EOF( ) will be true (.T.).

Example.

```
 . USE Maillist
 . SET EXACT OFF
 . LOCATE FOR Lname = "SMITH"
 . ? Lname, Fname
SMITH          JOHN
 . CONTINUE
 . ? Lname, Fname
SMITHSON       ANDY
```

See also: LOCATE *p. 126.*

CONVERT

Description. The CONVERT command changes a single-user database to a multi-user user database.

Operational rules. dBASE IV multi-user databases must have a character field named _dbaselock. The CONVERT command adds this field. _dbaselock consists of four sections:

- Count A 2-byte hexadecimal number that tracks the number of times the record has ben changed
- Time A 3-byte hexadecimal number that tracks the time that the record was locked.
- Date A 3-byte hexadecimal number that tracks the date that the record was locked.
- Name A 0 to 16 character name of the person that locked the record.

The length of the _dbaselock field can be changed with the optional TO <expN> argument. The default length of the field is 16 characters, making the Name portion 8 characters. The length of _dbaselock can be anywhere from 8 to 24. Use the LKSYS( ) function to display the contents of the _dbaselock field for the current record.

The CONVERT command makes a backup copy of the single-user database to a file with the extension .cvt.

See also: LKSYS( ) *p. 218.*

COPY TO <filename>

Description. The COPY TO command copies the records from the current file to <filename>.

Operational rules. Unless a type is specified, the new file is a dBASE IV database with a .DBF extension. When copying to a file, the optional file types are:

Type	Description
DBASEII	dBASE II database file
DBASEIII	dBASE III (dBASE III cannot read dBASE IV memo fields)
SDF	fixed length fields ASCII file
DELIMITED	variable length fields separated with commas
DELIMITED WITH <expC>	variable length fields separated with <expC>
DIF	VisiCalc format
FW2	Framework
RPD	RapidFile
SYLK	MultiPlan
WKS	Lotus 1-2-3

The optional FOR <condition> and WHILE <condition> and <scope> arguments are used to copy only records that match a specified criteria. The optional FIELDS <field list> argument copies only the specified fields to the new database.

Examples.

COPY TO Mail2 FOR LNAME = "S"	(copies for specified criteria)
COPY TO Mail2 NEXT 100	(copies next 100 records)
COPY TO Mail2 SDF	(copies to a fixed ASCII file)
COPY TO Mail2 DELIMITED WITH /	(copies to a variable length file)
COPY TO Mail2 Fields Lname, Fname, City	(copies to a three-field file)

See also: APPEND *p. 91.*

COPY FILE <filename> TO <filename>

Description. The COPY FILE command makes a duplicate copy of any type of file.

Operational rules. This command is equivalent to the COPY command from DOS. The DOS command is actually faster than COPY FILE, and it can be accessed from dBASE through the RUN command. However, some users cannot access the RUN command because they do not have enough memory. In this case, COPY FILE can be substituted.

Example.

```
COPY FILE Mail.Frm TO Mail2.Frm
```

See also: RUN *p. 144.*

COPY INDEXES <index file list> TO <multiple index file>

Description. The COPY INDEXES command copies a list of index files into a new or existing multiple index file.

Operational rules. Multiple index files can include up to 47 separate index tags. The default extension is .mdx, where .ndx is the extension for an index file.

If the multiple index file does not exist, it is created. If it does exist, the new index tag is simply added to the current list of tags. If the optional TO <multiple index file> clause is not used, dBASE automatically copies the file to a file with the same name as the .dbf file but with a .mdx extension.

Example.

```
USE Maillist
COPY INDEX Mailzip              (adds Mailzip.ndx to Maillist.mdx)
COPY INDEX Mailzip TO Mail2     (adds Mailzip.ndx to Mail2.mdx)
```

See also: INDEX *p. 121.*

COPY MEMO <memo field> TO <filename>

Description. The COPY MEMO command copies the text from a memo file to another file.

Operational rules. If <filename> does not exist, dBASE creates it with a .txt default extension. If the file does exist, it will be overwritten unless the optional ADDITIVE argument is used. This appends the memo field text to the bottom of <filename>.

Example.

```
COPY MEMO Comment TO Narrative
COPY MEMO Comment TO Narrative ADDITITVE
```

See also: APPEND MEMO *p. 92.*

COPY STRUCTURE TO <filename>

Description. The COPY STRUCTURE command copies only the structure of the current file to <filename>.

Operational rules. The new file is a dBASE IV database with a .dbf extension. It will not contain any records. The optional FIELDS <field list> argument copies only the specified fields to the new database.

Example.

```
COPY STRUCTURE TO Mail2
COPY STRUCTURE TO Mail2 FIELDS Lname,Fname,City
```

See also: APPEND *p. 91*

COPY TO <filename> STRUCTURE EXTENDED

Description. The COPY TO STRUCTURE EXTENDED command copies structure of the current file to a special type of file that contains the structure in its records.

Operational rules. The new file is made up of five fields: FIELD_NAME, FIELD_TYPE, FIELD_LEN, FIELD_DEC, and FIELD_IDX. There is one record in this database for each field in the current file.

This command can be used to create structures of new files within programs. The program can make decisions on the structure (such as adding or deleting fields, or changing names and lengths) through editing the extended file, and then issuing the CREATE FROM command. This allows the user to create or modify a structure without using the full-screen CREATE or MODIFY STRUCTURE commands.

See also: MODIFY STRUCTURE *p. 128.*

COPY TAG <tag name> TO <index file name>

Description. The COPY TAG command copies a tag from a multiple index file to a .ndx index file.

Operational rules. Multiple index files can include up to 47 separate index tags. The default extension is .mdx, where .ndx is the extension for an index file.

If the optional OF <multiple index file> clause is not used, dBASE automatically copies from a multiple index file with the same name as the .dbf file but with a .mdx extension. The .mdx file must be open when this command is issued.

Example.

COPY TAG Zip TO Mailzip	(creates Mailzip.ndx)
COPY TAG Zip OF Mail2 TO Mzip	(creates Mzip.ndx from Mail2.mdx)

See also: INDEX *p. 121.*

COPY TO ARRAY <array name>

Description. The COPY TO ARRAY command copies the records from the current file an array.

Operational rules. The array must be declared before running this command. If the array is two-dimensional, each record is given a row in the array. If the array is one-dimensional, then dBASE simply adds in each field from each record. The copying stops at the last field and record, or when all dimensions are filled, whichever comes first.

The optional FOR <condition> and WHILE <condition> and <scope> arguments are used to copy only records that match a specified criteria. The optional FIELDS <field list> argument copies only the specified fields to the array.

Example.

```
 . USE Maillist
 . DECLARE Mail[5,6]
 . COPY TO ARRAY Mail FOR ZIP = "92111"
   5 records copied
 . ? Mail[1,1] + Mail[1,2]
John            Smith
 . ? Mail[2,1] + Mail[2,2]
Joe             Schmo
```

See also: APPEND FROM ARRAY *p. 91.*

COUNT

Description. The COUNT command counts the number of records in the current database.

Operational rules. The command displays the number of records counted. Keep in mind that if the talk is set OFF, the count will not display on the screen. The optional TO <memory variable> initializes a memory variable that is equal to the number of records counted. The optional FOR <condition> and WHILE <condition> and <scope> arguments are used to count only records that match a specified criteria.

Example.

```
COUNT FOR Zip = "92111"
COUNT TO Zcount
COUNT TO Zcount WHILE Lname = "SMITH"
```

See also: RECCOUNT( ) *p. 243.*

CREATE

Description. The CREATE command creates the layout for a dBASE IV database file.

Operational rules. A dBASE database file is defined by its field names, the type of each field, the length of each field, and whether the field is to be indexed. The default extension for a database file is .dbf. A database can have up to 255 fields. Field names can be from 1 to 11 characters, and can contain letters, numbers and the underline character (_). Field names must begin with a letter. Each field must be one of the following types: Character, Numeric, Floating Point Number, Logical, Date, or Memo.

Character field widths can be from 1 to 254 in length. Numeric fields can be up to 20 digits. Date fields are automatically 8, Memo fields are 10, and Logical fields are 1. Data entered in a memo field is not stored in the .dbf file, but it a second file with the extension .dbt. Each memo entry can be up to 512K.

When using the CREATE screen, you can use the following key combinations:

Ctrl – N	inserts a field at the cursor position
Ctrl – U	deletes a field at the cursor position
Ctrl – End	saves the file

See also: MODIFY STRUCTURE *p. 128.*

CREATE <filename> FROM <structure extended file>

Description. The CREATE FROM command creates a database file from a special type of file that contains the structure in its records.

Operational rules. The structured file is made up of five fields: FIELD_NAME, FIELD_TYPE, FIELD_LEN, FIELD_DEC, and FIELD_IDX. There is one record in this database for each field in the current file. These files can be created from the COPY TO STRUCTURE EXTENDED command.

Structure Extended files can be used to create structures of new files within programs. The program can make decisions on the structure (such as adding or deleting fields, or changing names and lengths) through editing the extended file, and then creating the file with CREATE FROM. This allows the user to create or modify a structure without using the full-screen CREATE or MODIFY STRUCTURE commands.

See also: COPY TO STRUCTURE EXTENDED *p. 101.*

CREATE VIEW <.vue filename> FROM ENVIRONMENT

Description. The CREATE VIEW command creates a view (.vue) file from the current settings.

Operational rules. A view file saves information regarding the following settings:

- ☐ Open data and index files and their work areas
- ☐ Current selected work area
- ☐ Relationships set between files
- ☐ Open format files
- ☐ Current filter conditions

To quickly restore all these settings with one command, use SET VIEW TO <.vue filename>. The CREATE VIEW command creates the .vue file from the current settings.

See also: SET VIEW TO *p. 173.*

CREATE APPLICATION <filename>

Description. The CREATE APPLICATION command uses the dBASE IV Applications Generator to create programs.

Operational rules. The applications generator creates programs automatically. Program can be created that open and set relationships between files, run reports, queries, menus, and lists.

When in the Applications Generator, you first set the Application name, Database/View, and Index/Order information. You can then define screen, reports, label formats, and main menus. The optional "?" argument can be used in place of <filename>. dBASE will then provide a list of all .app files from which you can choose. If <filename> already exists, the CREATE APPLICATION command does not overwrite it. Instead, it allows you to modify the file.

You can further edit on programs created with the Applications Generator with MODIFY COMMAND.

See also: MODIFY COMMAND *p. 127.*

CREATE LABEL <filename>

Description. The CREATE LABEL command uses the dBASE IV Label generator to create a label format (.lbl) file.

Operational rules. When in the label generator, you set the dimensions of the label, the number of labels to print across the page, and then the contents of each label (fields and templates).

The optional ? argument can be used in place of <filename>. dBASE will then provide a list of all .lbl files from which you can choose. If <filename> already exists, the CREATE LABEL command does not overwrite it. Instead, it allows you to modify the file.

Use LABEL FORM to print the labels. Labels printed with this command automatically omit blank lines for records that have no contents in particular fields.

See also: LABEL FORM *p. 124.*

CREATE QUERY/VIEW <filename>

Description. The CREATE QUERY command calls up the query design screen, which generates a file that extracts records that match a criteria.

Operational rules. Two types of query files can be defined. Query (.qbe) files set a filter condition using a full-screen editor, so that only records that match the condition will display. Update query (.upd) files modify records in the database according to a criteria.

When in the query design screen, you define the field to select by, the comparison operator (< >, =, >, <, etc.) and the comparison. You can enter multiple criteria by connecting them with .AND. or .OR..

The optional ? argument can be used in place of <filename>. dBASE will then provide a list of all .qbe and .upd files from which you can choose. If <filename> already exists, the CREATE QUERY/VIEW command does not overwrite it. Instead, it allows you to modify the file.

Activate query conditions using the SET FILTER TO or SET VIEW commands.

See also: SET FILTER TO *p. 164.*
SET VIEW TO *p. 173.*

CREATE REPORT <filename>

Description. The CREATE REPORT command uses the dBASE IV Report generator to create a report format (.frm) file.

Operational rules. When in the report generator, you set the dimensions of the report, headings, contents of the body of the report, and subtotal groupings. Three types of reports can be created: Mailmerge, Columnar, and Free Form.

The optional ? argument can be used in place of <filename>. dBASE will then provide a list of all .frm files from which you can choose. If <filename> already exists, the CREATE REPORT command does not overwrite it. Instead, it allows you to modify the file.

Print reports using the the REPORT FORM command.

See also: REPORT FORM *p. 141.*

CREATE SCREEN <filename>

Description. The CREATE SCREEN command uses the dBASE IV Screen generator to create a custom screen format (.scr) file that is used with the EDIT and APPEND commands.

Operational rules. When in the screen generator, you can position each field on the screen, and add prompts, templates, and boxes. The custom screen can then be used with either the APPEND or EDIT commands for a better looking entry screen than the dBASE default.

The optional ? argument can be used in place of <filename>. dBASE will then provide a list of all .scr files which you can choose from. If <filename> already exists, the CREATE REPORT command does not overwrite it. Instead, it allows you to modify the file.

Call the screen before the EDIT or APPEND commands with the SET FORMAT TO command.

See also: CREATE SCREEN *p. 106.*

DEACTIVATE MENU

Description. DEACTIVATE MENU erases a bounce-bar menu from the screen.

Operational rules. Menus are designed with the DEFINE MENU and DEFINE PAD commands. Use ACTIVATE MENU to then display them. DEACTIVATE MENU erases the current menu from the screen, but does not clear it from memory.

See DEFINE MENU for a program that creates a user-defined menu.

See also: DEFINE MENU *p. 109.*

DEACTIVATE POPUP

Description. DEACTIVATE POPUP erases a pop-up menu from the screen.

Operational rules. Popup menus are designed with the DEFINE POPUP and DEFINE BAR commands. Use ACTIVATE POPUP to then display them.

DEACTIVATE POPUP erases the current popup menu from the screen, but does not clear it from memory.

See DEFINE BAR for a program that creates a user-defined popup menu.

See also: DEFINE BAR *p. 108.*

DEACTIVATE WINDOW

Description. DEACTIVATE WINDOW erases a window from the screen.

Operational rules. Windows designed with the DEFINE WINDOW command. Use ACTIVATE WINDOW to then display it. DEACTIVATE WINDOW erases the window from the screen, but does not clear it from memory.

See also: DEFINE WINDOW *p. 111.*

DEBUG <filename>/<procedure name>

Description. The DEBUG command uses the dBASE IV full-screen debugger to help detect bugs in programs.

Operational rules. The debugger allows you to step, command by command, through a program. When in the debugger, there are four windows of the screen:

1. The top left window displays the program. Th next command to be performed is highlighted.
2. The top right window is the command box for you to enter commands.
3. The DISPLAY box is where you can display fields and variables as they are changed through the program.
4. The DEBUGGER box displays information about current file and program status.

The optional argument WITH <parameter list> allows you to pass parameters.

See also: MODIFY COMMAND *p. 127.*

DECLARE <array name> [<number of rows>,<number of columns>]

Description. Use DECLARE to establish an array.

Operational rules. You must declare arrays before using them. Arrays are special memory variables that have multiple values. An array is set up like a table. When storing values to an array, you define which number of the table you are storing to. The DECLARE statement declares the maximum number of values to be stored in each dimension of the array.

An array may be single or multi-dimensional. The first number is called the *row* number. If the array is two-dimensional, the second number is called the *column number*. You can declare more than one array at a time.

Example.

```
. DECLARE Subtotal[5,2]    & declare an array named Subtotal
. Subtotal[1,1] = 100
. DECLARE Marray[3,3], Marray2[4,2], Marray3[6,6]
```

See also: STORE *p. 149.*

DEFINE BAR <line number> OF <popup name> PROMPT <expC>

Description. DEFINE BAR sets the contents of a popup menu.

Operational rules. Each option in a dBASE-designed menu is called a bar. It is possible to design a popup menu that is displayed whenever one of the bars in the main menu is highlighted with the cursor. DEFINE BAR allows you to define the options that exist within the popup menu. Once the popup menu is displayed, the user can move the cursor to any of the options in the popup, creating a "menu within a menu."

Each popup option is given a <line number> starting with 1. The <popup name> is defined with the DEFINE POPUP command. The actual option is defined as <expC>.

To define a menu that contains options with popup menus that contain additional options, the following commands must be issued:

1. DEFINE MENU to name the menu.
2. DEFINE PAD to name and position each option in the menu.
3. ON PAD to activate each popup for each pad.
4. DEFINE POPUP to name and position each popup menu.
5. DEFINE BAR to position each option within the popup menu.

Use the optional MESSAGE <expC> to display a message at the bottom of the screen when this particular option is highlighted.

Example. The program creates the menu and popup options:

```
DEFINE MENU Mail
DEFINE PAD Adit OF Mail PROMPT "Add " AT 2,2
DEFINE PAD Edit OF Mail PROMPT "Edit" AT 2,20
DEFINE PAD List OF Mail PROMPT "List" AT 2,38
```

```
DEFINE PAD Exit OF Mail PROMPT "Exit" AT 2,56
ON PAD Adit OF Mail ACTIVATE POPUP Whch_file
DEFINE POPUP Whch_file FROM 3,2
DEFINE BAR 1 OF Whch_file PROMPT "Members"
DEFINE BAR 2 OF Whch_file PROMPT "Guests"
DEFINE BAR 3 OF Whch_file PROMPT "Prospect"

ACTIVATE MENU Mail
```

See also: DEFINE POPUP *p. 156.*

DEFINE BOX FROM <print col1> TO <print col2> HEIGHT <expN>

Description. DEFINE BOX sets coordinates and borders of a box to be printed.

Operational rules. The default border of the box is a single line box. The optional DOUBLE, and <border definition string> allow you to change the border characters. See SET BORDER regarding the layout of the <border definition string>. To print the box, the system variable _box must be set to true (.T.).

Examples.

```
DEFINE BOX FROM 2 TO 60 HEIGHT 10
```

See also: SET BORDER *p. 156.*

DEFINE MENU <menu name>

Description. DEFINE MENU assigns the name of a bounce-bar menu.

Operational rules. Before a menu can be designed, it must be named. DEFINE MENU simply allows you to name the menu. Use DEFINE PAD to set each of the options and their coordinates.

To define and run a bounce-bar menu, the following commands must be issued:

1. DEFINE MENU to name the menu.
2. DEFINE PAD to name and position each option in the menu.
3. ON SELECTION PAD to assign the commands that will be run when a pad is selected.
4. ACTIVATE MENU to run the menu.

Use the optional MESSAGE <expC> to display a message at the bottom of the screen when the menu is displayed.

Example.

The following program creates the menu and activates the options.

```
DEFINE MENU Mail
DEFINE PAD Adit OF Mail PROMPT "Add " AT 2,2
DEFINE PAD Edit OF Mail PROMPT "Edit" AT 2,20
DEFINE PAD List OF Mail PROMPT "List" AT 2,38
DEFINE PAD Exit OF Mail PROMPT "Exit" AT 2,56

ON SELECTION PAD Adit OF Mail APPEND
ON SELECTION PAD Edit OF Mail EDIT
ON SELECTION PAD List OF Mail DO Lister
ON SELECTION PAD Exit OF Mail QUIT

ACTIVATE MENU Mail
```

See also: DEFINE PAD *p. 110.*

DEFINE PAD <pad name> OF <menu name> PROMPT <expC> AT <row>, <col>

Description. DEFINE PAD sets the options that display in a bounce-bar menu.

Operational rules. Use DEFINE PAD to set each of the options and their coordinates of a menu that has been named with DEFINE MENU. The coordinates are optional. If you do not include them, dBASE will place the first option in the left corner of row one. Each subsequent option is one space to the right.

There is no limit to the pads that can be defined, other than the computer's memory limits.

Use the optional MESSAGE <expC> to display a message at the bottom of the screen when the menu is displayed.

See DEFINE MENU for a program that creates a bounce-bar menu.

Examples.

```
DEFINE PAD Adit OF Mail PROMPT "Add " AT 2,2
DEFINE PAD Adit OF Mail PROMPT "Add "
DEFINE PAD Adit OF Mail PROMPT "Add " MESSAGE "Add Records To Mail.dbf"
```

See also: DEFINE MENU *p. 109.*

DEFINE POPUP <popup name> FROM <row>, <col>

Description. DEFINE POPUP sets the placement and name of a popup menu.

Operational rules. DEFINE POPUP designs a popup menu that is displayed vertically. You can call popup menus that display whenever an option from a bounce-bar menu is highlighted. This creates a "menu within a menu." The coordinates <row> and <col> define the placement of the top left corner of the popup.

See DEFINE BAR for a complete program that displays a bounce bar menu with popup menus.

Use the optional MESSAGE <expC> to display a message at the bottom of the screen when the popup is displayed. You do not need to provide the optional TO <row2>, <col2> for the bottom corner coordinates of the menu. dBASE will choose a "best fit" determined by the number and width of bars within the popup menu, set with the DEFINE BAR command.

The PROMPT FIELD <field name>, PROMPT FILES, and PROMPT STRUCTURE clauses are used when you want the options of the popup to be files or fields. You cannot use DEFINE BAR if you are going to use any of the PROMPT options. PROMPT FIELD displays the contents of <field> in each record of the file in the popup window. PROMPT FILES displays a list of the files (you may use the optional LIKE <skeleton> clause) contained in the current catalog. PROMPT STRUCTURE displays all fields in the active database.

Examples.

```
DEFINE POPUP Whch_file FROM 3,2
DEFINE POPUP Whch_file FROM 3,2 TO 8,12
DEFINE POPUP Whch_file FROM 3,2 PROMPT FILES LIKE M*
DEFINE POPUP State_pop FROM 3,2 PROMPT FIELD States
```

See also: DEFINE BAR *p. 108.*

DEFINE WINDOW <window name> FROM <row1>, <col1> TO <row2>, <col2>

Description. DEFINE WINDOW sets coordinates, borders, and colors of a user-defined window.

Operational rules. The default border of the window is a single line box. The optional DOUBLE, NONE, and <border definition string> allow you to change the border characters. See SET BORDER regarding the layout of the <border definition string>.

The COLOR option allows you to define two sets of foreground/background color combinations, one for <standard>, one for <enhanced>. You can include a different color for <frame>.

To display a defined window, use the ACTIVATE WINDOW command. You can store up to 20 window definitions in memory at a time.

Examples.

```
DEFINE WINDOW Wind1 FROM 3,2 TO 10,78
DEFINE WINDOW Wind1 FROM 3,2 TO 10,78 COLOR GR/B, B/GR, W
DEFINE WINDOW Wind1 FROM 3,2 TO 10,78 "#","#","#","#","$","$","$","$"
```

See also: SET BORDER *p. 156.*

DELETE

Description. The DELETE command marks a record for deletion from the current database file.

Operational rules. To delete a record from the database file mark all records to be deletedand then issue the PACK command. The PACK command actually removes the records. It makes a copy of the data file without the old records, so it can take a while to run, and it does renumber the records.

The DELETE command is equivalent to pressing ^U while editing or browsing. Records marked for deletion display an asterisk when listed. The SET DELETED ON command tells dBASE to ignore deleted records when displaying, editing, and listing. This allows deleted records to appear removed without having to PACK.

You can make global deletions with the optional FOR <condition>, WHILE <condition>, and <scope>.

Example.

```
DELETE
DELETE FOR State = "NY"
DELETE NEXT 5
```

See also: PACK *p. 133.*

DELETE FILE <filename>

Description. DELETE FILE removes an entire file from the disk.

Operational rules. This command is equivalent to the ERASE command. You cannot erase a file that is currently open. The DELETE FILE command does not allow wildcards (? and *) to delete multiple files at one time, so you might prefer to use the DEL command from DOS. To run a DOS command while at the dot prompt, use ! or RUN.

The optional ? argument can be used to get a listing of files from which you can choose.

Example.

```
DELETE FILE Maillist.dbf
ERASE Maillist.dbf
DELETE FILE ?
! DEL Maillist.*
```

See also: RUN *p. 144.*

DISPLAY COMMANDS

Each DISPLAY command is equivalent to a LIST command. The only difference is that when DISPLAY is issued, only one screen is displayed at a time, and the user is requested to Press a key to continue.... The LIST commands list the entire contents without pausing between screens. For information about each DISPLAY command, see its LIST companion. The commands are:

```
LIST/DISPLAY
LIST/DISPLAY FILES
LIST/DISPLAY HISTORY
LIST/DISPLAY MEMORY
LIST/DISPLAY STATUS
LIST/DISPLAY STRUCTURE
LIST/DISPLAY USERS
```

See also: LIST *p. 124.*

DO <program or procedure name>

Description. The DO command calls a program or procedure.

Operational rules. From the dot prompt, call the master module of the program. Use DO <program> within a command file to call other programs. Each program that is called extends one level lower. Use the RETURN command to return to the calling program. The program then continues processing at the line below the DO command.

Use DO <procedure> to a call a procedure, which is a subroutine placed within the program file or in a procedure file. See the PROCEDURE command regarding details of procedures.

Lower level programs can access memory variable initialized in upper level programs. However, memory variables initialized in lower level programs are local to that program, and cannot be accessed to higher levels.

To change a variable's value in a lower level program (or procedure) and pass that value back to the calling program, set the variable as a parameter. Include the WITH <parameter list> clause in your DO statement.

Examples.

```
DO Mainmenu
DO Heading WITH Title, Pageno
```

See also: PARAMETER *p. 133.*
PROCEDURE *p. 136.*

DO CASE
CASE <condition>
<commands>
•
•
•
OTHERWISE
<commands>
ENDCASE

Description. The DO CASE command is used within programs to provide conditional processing.

Operational rules. If the <condition> is true (.T.), then the program will process all commands between the CASE and next CASE statement. The program only processes the first condition that is true. The DO CASE command must end with an ENDCASE statement. It is good programming technique to indent all commands within the CASE statements. For example:

```
DO    CASE
      CASE Choice = "1"
           DO Addit
      CASE Choice = "2"
           DO Prnit
      CASE Choice = "3"
           QUIT
      OTHERWISE
           CANCEL
ENDCASE
```

The DO CASE command is best used in situations where each case is mutually exclusive. In other words, instances where only one of the CASES can be true. The CASE statement above is an example.

You can use the OTHERWISE command as the last case to handle situations when none of the cases are true.

See also: IF *p. 120.*

DO WHILE <condition>
<commands>
ENDDO

Description. The DO WHILE command is used within programs to provide a looping capability with conditional processing.

Operational rules. If the <condition> is true (.T.), then the program will continue processing all commands between the DO and ENDDO statement until <condition> is not true. It is good programming technique to indent all commands within the DO and ENDDO statements. For example:

```
DO WHILE Mem < 10
    ? Mem
    Mem = Mem + 1
ENDDO
```

The LOOP command can be used within a DO WHILE to return to the beginning of the loop. Use the EXIT command to exit the loop and continue processing the program at the command line below ENDDO.

Example.

```
USE Maillist
DO WHILE .NOT. EOF()
    IF Active = "N"
       SKIP
       LOOP
    ENDIF
    CLEAR
    ? Fname, Lname, Phone
    ACCEPT "Display another? " TO Cont
    IF Cont = "N"
       EXIT
    ENDIF
    SKIP
ENDDO
```

The command skips through the Maillist database, and displays one record at a time. If a record has N in the Active field, the record is not displayed. Although this is a valid program, a simpler program could be written that performs the same function with the SCAN FOR command.

See also: DO CASE *p. 114.*

EDIT

Description. The EDIT mode allows the user to add/edit records in the current file.

Operational rules. When editing a file, the records appear one record at a time on the screen. The full-screen editing commands are in effect. If a custom format (.fmt) file is active, the screen displays using its definitions.

The optional NOAPPEND, NOEDIT, NODELETE, NOCLEAR, NOMENU, NOFOLLOW, and NOINIT arguments restrict the capabilities of the EDIT command. The optional FIELDS <field name list> arguments restrict the fields or field order displayed in the EDIT screen.

The other optional arguments are COMPRESS, FORMAT, LOCK <expN>, WIDTH <expN>, FREEZE <field name>, WINDOW <window name>. The LOCK and FREEZE options prevent changing of a particular field.

The optional FOR <condition> and WHILE <condition> and <scope> arguments are used to edit only records that match a specified criteria.

You can supply a <record number>, otherwise EDIT will edit the current record. The scope RECORD causes EDIT to edit only one record. Otherwise you can move to other records in the file with PgDn and PgUp.

Example.

```
EDIT
EDIT 5
EDIT RECORD 5
EDIT FOR State = "CA"
EDIT NOAPPEND NODELETE
EDIT FIELDS Lname,Fname,City,Zip
```

See also: APPEND *p. 91.*

EJECT

Description. EJECT advances the paper to the next page.

Operational rules. This command sends a form feed (ASCII character 12) to advance the paper to the top of the next page. However, if the system memory variable _padvance has been set to LINEFEEDS, the correct number of linefeeds to advance the page will be sent instead.

EJECT will reset PROW( ) and PCOL( ) to zero. EJECT PAGE, unlike the EJECT command, affects the _pageno and _plineno system variables. Use EJECT PAGE when the ON PAGE handler is in effect.

See also: EJECT PAGE *p. 117.*

EJECT PAGE

Description. EJECT PAGE advances the paper to the next page, and takes in consideration printer system variables.

Operational rules. This command sends a form feed unless the system variable _padvance has been set to LINEFEEDS, in which case the correct number of linefeeds will be sent to advance the paper to the top of the next page.

EJECT PAGE, unlike the EJECT command, affects the _pageno and _plineno system variables. Use EJECT PAGE when the ON PAGE handler is in effect.

See also: ON PAGE *p. 131.*

ERASE

The ERASE command is equivalent to the DELETE FILE command.

See: DELETE FILE *p. 112.*

EXPORT TO <filename> <file type>

Description. The EXPORT TO command copies the records from the current dBASE file to <filename> in a format other than dBASE IV.

Operational rules. When copying to a file, the optional file types can be:

Type	**Description**
DBASEII	dBASE II database file
PFS	PFS File
FW2	Framework
RPD	RapidFile

The optional FOR <condition> and WHILE <condition> and <scope> arguments are used to copy only records that match a specified criteria. The optional FIELDS <field list> argument copies only the specified fields to the new database.

This command can be run from the ASSIST menu, where there are some additional file types not available from the dot prompt. The COPY TO command also allows exporting to some additional file types.

Examples.

```
EXPORT TO Mail2 PFS FOR LNAME = "S"
EXPORT TO Mail2 RPD
EXPORT TO Mail2 FW2 FIELDS Lname, Fname
```

See also: COPY TO *p. 98.*

FIND <literal>

Description. The FIND command moves to the first record in the index that matches <literal>.

Operational rules. FIND searches the master index for <literal>. This command is very much like the SEEK command, except that SEEK searches for an expression instead of a literal. When the argument is a literal, you do not place quotes around it. Therefore, if it is a character memory variable, it should be preceded with an ampersand (&). There is no way to use FIND with a numeric memory variable.

If a match is found, the record pointer moves to that record. Use SKIP to find the next record that matches. If no records match, FOUND( ) will be set to false, and the record pointer will be moved to the end of the file (EOF( ) is true).

Example.

```
  . USE Maillist index Mlname
  . Find Smith
Record 2
  . Mname = "Brown"
  . Find &Mname
Record 7
```

See also: SEEK *p. 146.*

FUNCTION <procedure name>

Description. FUNCTION allows you to create user-defined functions that perform like dBASE IV's built-in functions.

Operational rules. If there is a certain function that must be performed more than once in a program, it is easier to create a user-defined function with the FUNCTION command. User-defined functions are created just like procedures, except that they are used within commands, instead of performing a separated command.

Functions begin with the FUNCTION command, and end with RETURN( ). A user-defined function can have multiple arguments.

Example.

```
Mhead = "Income Analysis"
? CENTERIT(Mhead,75)
    .
    .
    .
```

```
FUNCTION CENTERIT( )
    PARAMETERS Heading, Width
    MCENTER = SPACE(Width/2 - LENGTH(Heading)/2)) + Heading
    RETURN(MCENTER)
```

In the program, the heading program calls a user-defined function that prints the heading centered on the page, depending on the width of the paper.

See also: PARAMETER *p. 133.*

GOTO <record number>

Description. The GOTO command moves to the specified record.

Operational rules. The alternate arguments are BOTTOM and TOP. GOTO TOP moves to the top record, which is record number 1 in a non-indexed file, or the first record in an indexed file. GOTO BOTTOM moves to the bottom record, which is the last record number in a non-indexed file, or the last record in an indexed file. To reach the end of the file (where EOF( ) is true), issue GOTO BOTTOM, and then SKIP. The record number will display as one more than RECCOUNT( ).

The optional argument IN <alias> allows you to move the record pointer in a file other than the current file.

The GO command is equivalent to GOTO.

Example.

```
GOTO BOTTOM
GO 5
GO 5 IN Maillist
```

See also: SEEK *p. 146.*

HELP

Description. The HELP command brings up the dBASE IV help screens.

Operational rules. When in the help screens, you will get a screenfull of help regarding a particular subject. You can then highlight additional keywords, and press ENTER to get screens of information regarding other topics.

The optional argument <keyword> allows you to get a screen of information regarding a particular topic.

Example.

```
HELP
HELP INDEX
```

IF <condition>
<commands>
ENDIF

Description. The IF command is used within programs to provide conditional processing.

Operational rules. If <condition> is true (.T.), then the program will process all commands between the IF and ENDIF statement. If <condition> is false (.F.), then the program continues processing after the ENDIF statement. It is good programming technique to indent all commands within the IF and ENDIF statements. For example:

```
IF MPRN = "P"
      SET PRINT ON
      EJECT
ENDIF
```

An alternate IF structure is IF-ELSE-ENDIF. This is useful in situations where one procedure should be performed if the condition is true, with a different procedure if the condition is false. Although IF statements can be nested (just remember each IF must have a companion ENDIF), it is often better to use the DO CASE command if there are many conditions to be tested.

Example.

```
IF MPRN = "P"
      SET PRINT ON
      EJECT
ELSE
      IF MPRN = "F"
         SET ALTERNATE TO PRNFILE
         SET ALTERNATE ON
      ELSE
           SET CONSOLE ON
      ENDIF
ENDIF
```

See also: DO CASE *p. 114.*

IMPORT FROM <filename> <file type>

Description. The IMPORT FROM command copies the records from a non-dBASE IV file to the current dBASE IV file.

Operational rules. When copying from a file, the optional file types can be:

Type	**Description**
DBASEII	dBASE II database file
PFS	PFS File
FW2	Framework
RPD	RapidFile

If the dBASE IV file exists, the records are simply appended. If a file has not been created, one is created named <filename> with the .dbf extension.

This command can be run from the ASSIST menu, where there are some additional file types not available from the dot prompt. The APPEND FROM command also allows importing from some additional file types.

Example.

```
USE Maillist
IMPORT FROM Mail2.PFS PFS
```

See also: APPEND FROM *p. 91.*

INDEX ON <key expression> TO <index file name>FOR<criteria>

Description. Puts the data in order by <key expression>.

Operational rules. When copying from a file, the optional file types can be:

- ☐ An index (.ndx) file is smaller than the datafile
- ☐ The index file does not affect the .dbf file, so the record numbers remain intact
- ☐ As long as the index file is opened along with the datafile, new records will maintain the sorted order.

You can index a file on one field, multiple fields, or by fields within functions. If you will be combining character fields and numeric fields, you must convert the numeric field to a string with the STR function. Below are examples of each:

```
INDEX ON Lname TO Mname                (sorts by LNAME field)
INDEX ON UPPER(Lname) TO Mname         (sorts ignoring case)
INDEX ON Lname+Fname TO Mname          (sorts by Fname within Lname)
INDEX ON STR(Dept,2)+Lname TO        Mname
```

To create a multiple (.mdx) index file, use the TAG <tag name> argument. You do not have to provide a filename with the OF <.mdx filename> command, because it automatically makes a .mdx file with the same name as the .dbf file. Multiple indexes can contain up to 47 tags. This allows you to have all indexes in one file.

The FOR argument (version 1.1) only indexes records that match the criteria. This can greatly improve the speed of searching through an indexed file.

The UNIQUE argument only includes the first records that contains a particular key. For instance, if the file is indexed on CITY, it will only place in the first entry for each city. This is helpful when getting lists of all unique entries for a certain field.

The DESCENDING argument will sort the expression in descending order. The default order is ascending.

Examples.

```
INDEX ON Amount TO Mamt FOR State = "CA"
INDEX ON Amount TO Mamt DESCENDING
INDEX ON Amount TAG Mamt
INDEX ON Amount TAG Mamt OF Multi
```

See also: USE *p. 153.*

INPUT <prompt> TO <mem variable>

Description. The INPUT command displays the prompt and pauses until the user enters something.

Operational rules. This command is most often used in programs where few questions are to be prompted on the screen. Each INPUT command halts the program until the user types in an answer and presses Enter. The INPUT command is easier to use than full-screen editing commands such as @...GET, because the memory variable does not have to be initialized before issuing the command and the screen coordinates do not have to be set (ACCEPT displays the prompt in the same manner as the ? command).

However, the INPUT command is not as powerful as the full-screen editing commands, especially because the entry cannot be formatted. Memory variables created by the INPUT command are numeric if a number is entered, otherwise they are of the character type. The variable becomes the length of the entry typed in.

The ACCEPT command is just like INPUT, except the memory variable is always a character.

See also: ACCEPT *p. 89.*

INSERT

Description. The INSERT command allows the user to add new records to the database at the position of the current record.

Operational rules. This command brings up the full-screen edit mode, just like the APPEND command. The record is added one below the current record. For instance, if the pointer is at record 10, the new record is inserted as record 11, and the numbers of all record below are increased by one.

Use the BEFORE clause to insert records at the current record number instead of one record below. Use BLANK to insert a record without going into the full-screen edit mode. When inserting a blank record, all fields of the record will be blank.

See also: EDIT *p. 116.*

JOIN WITH <alias> TO <new filename> FOR <condition>

Description. The JOIN command makes a new file out of two files.

Operational rules. The new file is made up of all of the fields in the active file, plus all of the names in the joined file. There will be one record in the new file for every time a record in the active file matches a record in the second file. The JOIN command can take a very long time to run if both files are large.

The field order of the new file will be all of the fields from the first file plus all of the fields from the second file, up to the 255 field limit. To change the field order or restrict the fields in the new file, use the optional argument FIELDS <field list>.

Example.

```
. USE Maillist IN 1
. USE Sales IN 2
. SELECT 1
. JOIN WITH Sales TO Salename FOR A->CLICODE = B->CLICODE FIELDS;
  A->CLICODE, A->NAME, B->DATE, B->AMOUNT
```

In this example, a new file named Salename is made up of each sales record which includes the sales information from Sales and the name of the client from Maillist.

See also: SELECT *p. 146.*

KEYBOARD (version 1.1 only)

Description. The keyboard command allows you to enter a "keyboard macro" in a program. The program performs the character keystrokes as if someone were typing them in.

LABEL FORM <label filename>

Description. The LABEL FORM command prints labels for a data file. The label format must already be created with the CREATE LABEL command.

Operational rules. The CREATE LABEL command allows you to set the label dimensions, number of labels across, and contents of the label within a label (.lbl) file. To run the labels, make sure the datafile is your current file, and issue the LABEL FORM command.

The argument ? can be used in place of the <label filename>. dBASE displays a list of .lbl files to choose from. Use the optional FOR <condition>, WHILE <condition>, and <scope> arguments to print labels for a subset of the data file.

Labels default to printing on the screen. Use the TO PRINTER option to print to the printer, or the TO FILE <filename> to print to an ASCII file.

Example.

```
LABEL FORM Mlabel
LABEL FORM Mlabel TO PRINT
LABEL FORM Mlabel FOR State = "CA"
LABEL FORM Mlabel NEXT 100 TO FILE Labels
```

See also: CREATE LABEL *p. 104.*

LIST

Description. LIST displays a list of the records in a file.

Operational rules. The list is not formatted. It simply displays a row of field names, and then lists the records. If the fields are wider than the screen, each record will wrap on the screen and use multiple rows.

The optional <field list> argument allows you to specify which fields, and in which order they will display. The default order is file structure order. The optional OFF argument will not display the field names. Use the optional FOR <condition>, WHILE <condition>, and <scope> arguments to list records for a subset of the data file.

Lists default to printing on the screen. Use the TO PRINTER option to print to the printer, or the TO FILE <filename> to print to an ASCII file.

The DISPLAY command is much like the LIST command, except than it pauses the screen at each screenfull of information. To pause the LIST command, you must press the PAUSE key, (or Ctrl – S) as it is scrolling.

Examples.

```
LIST
LIST OFF FOR State = "CA"
LIST NEXT 100 TO PRINT
```

```
LIST Lname, Fname, City
LIST Lname, Fname WHILE Zip = "9"
```

See also: DISPLAY *p. 113.*

LIST FILES

Description. LIST FILES lists all files in a directory that match a parameter.

Operational rules. The default list is a list of .dbf files, along with their size, number of records, and last update date. Use the LIKE <skeleton> option to get a list of files other than the *.dbf default. Skeletons follow the wildcard conventions of DOS: asterisk (*) represents any combination of characters, while question mark (?) represents any one character.

The file list defaults to printing on the screen. Use the TO PRINTER option to print to the printer, or the TO FILE <filename> to print to an ASCII file.

Examples.

```
LIST FILES
LIST FILES LIKE *.prg
LIST FILES LIKE *.* TO PRINTER
```

See also: DISPLAY FILES *p. 113.*

LIST HISTORY

Description. This command lists the last set of commands issued at the dot prompt.

Operational rules. dBASE IV keeps a history of the commands last entered at the dot prompt. Press the up arrow to scroll back through the commands, and the down arrow to scroll forward. This useful when you want to repeat a command already given, or to make slight changes in a command. It is also handy if you have entered a command with a syntax error in it. Instead of typing the command over again, use the up arrow to retrieve it, and then edit it.

The optional LAST <expN> allow you to specify the number of commands you wish to print. The list defaults to printing on the screen. Use the TO PRINTER option to print to the printer, or the TO FILE <filename> to print to an ASCII file.

Examples.

```
LIST HISTORY
LIST HISTORY LAST 5
LIST HISTORY TO FILE Histfile
```

See also: DISPLAY HISTORY *p. 113.*

LIST STATUS

Description. This command lists the current work environment status.

Operational rules. LIST STATUS will display a list of all open files, indexes, format files, and their respective work areas. It also displays all filter conditions, file relationships, and other information such as settings for the printer, function keys, and other SET commands.

The status list defaults to printing on the screen. Use the TO PRINTER option to print to the printer, or the TO FILE <filename> to print to an ASCII file.

See also: DISPLAY STATUS *p. 113.*

LIST STRUCTURE

Description. This command lists the structure of the current database file.

Operational rules. LIST STRUCTURE will display a list of all field names, their lengths, and types. This command also lists the name of the file, last date updated, total number of records, and total bytes in a record.

See also: DISPLAY STRUCTURE *p. 113.*

LOAD <binary file name>

Description. The LOAD command loads a binary program into memory.

Operational rules. dBASE can run binary (assembly language and machine language)programs. To do this you must:

1. Load the program into memory with the LOAD command
2. Run the program with the CALL command
3. Release it from memory with the RELEASE MODULE command

Binary programs are useful in applications where a function must be performed that dBASE cannot do. For instance, certain screen graphics manipulation and file maintenance on non-dBASE files can be done only through binary programs.

You should always release the program from memory once it is no longer needed, otherwise you may get memory error messages.

See also: CALL *p. 95.*

LOCATE FOR <condition>

Description. The LOCATE command moves to the first record in the datafile where <condition> is true (.T.).

Operational rules. LOCATE searches the file sequentially, starting from the top. This command is very much like the SEEK command, except that SEEK searches on an indexed file, so it is much faster, especially with large files. Use the alternative WHILE <condition> and <scope> in place of FOR <condition>.

If a match is found, the record pointer moves to that record. Use CONTINUE to find the next matching record. If no records match, FOUND( ) is set to false, and the record pointer will be moved to the end of the file (EOF( ) is true).

Example.

```
 . USE Maillist
 . LOCATE FOR Lname = "Smith"
Record =          5

 . LOCATE FOR Lname = "Smith" .AND. State = "CA"
Record =          7
 . CONTINUE
End of LOCATE scope
 . ? EOF( )
.T.
```

See also: SEEK *p. 146.*

LOGOUT

Description. The LOGOUT command quits dBASE and returns to the sign-on screen when using a networked version of dBASE.

Operational rules. Only networked versions of dBASE use the sign-on screen. The PROTECT command should be issued at the beginning of the dBASE session (usually through a program) to establish the user's access level. If PROTECT was not issued, then LOGOUT returns to the dot prompt.

See also: PROTECT *p. 137.*

MODIFY APPLICATION <filename>

Description. MODIFY COMMAND allows you to edit program files with the text editor.

Operational rules. For more details, see Chapter 8, dBASE IV Programming.

See also: CREATE APPLICATION *p. 104.*

MODIFY LABEL <filename>

Description. MODIFY LABEL command changes the setting of a label format (.lbl) file.

Operational rules. For more details, see CREATE LABEL.

See: CREATE LABEL *p. 104.*

MODIFY QUERY/VIEW <filename>

Description. MODIFY QUERY command allows you to make changes in a query design screen.

Operational rules. For more details, see CREATE QUERY/VIEW.

See: CREATE QUERY *p. 105.*

MODIFY REPORT <filename>

Description. MODIFY REPORT is used for editing the settings in a report format (.frm) file.

Operational rules. For more details, see CREATE REPORT.

See: CREATE REPORT *p. 105.*

MODIFY SCREEN <filename>

Description. MODIFY SCREEN is used for editing the settings in a custom screen format (.scr) file.

Operational rules. For more details, see CREATE SCREEN.

See: CREATE SCREEN *p. 106.*

MODIFY STRUCTURE

Description. MODIFY STRUCTURE allows you to change the layout for a dBASE IV database file.

Operational rules. This command is the same as CREATE, except it is used on existing file structures. Make sure that there is enough room on your disk for the new file plus the space used by the old file (roughly double the .dbf file space).

When using the MODIFY STRUCTURE screen, you can use the following key combinations:

Ctrl–N	inserts a field at the cursor position
Ctrl–U	deletes a field at the cursor position
Ctrl–End	saves the file

For more details, see CREATE.

See: CREATE *p. 103.*

MOVE WINDOW <window name> TO <row>, <column>

Description. Use MOVE WINDOW to move a window to a new location on the screen.

Operational rules. Use this command to reposition a window on the screen. You can issue the new coordinates of the window with <row>, <column>. An alternate method is to move the window relative to its current position. To do this, replace TO <row>, <column> with BY <change in row>, <change in column>.

Example.

```
MOVE WINDOW Mwind TO 5, 20
MOVE WINDOW Mwind BY 1, 0
```

The first example moves the window to row 5, column 20. The second example moves the window up two rows from its current position.

See also: DEFINE WINDOW *p. 111.*

NOTE

Description. NOTE allows the user to type lines of comment in a program file.

Operational rules. It is always a good practice to place notes and comments in program files. This documents the program and makes it easier to understand if you must go back to it to make changes, or for someone else who looks at it.

When dBASE encounters the NOTE command, it ignores the rest of the text on that line. The asterisk (*) can be used in place of NOTE.

The other comment command is two ampersands (&&). These can be placed after a command, on the same line. Enter the text after the ampersands.

Examples.

```
****************************************
* Maillist.prg — Mailing List Program
* Last Updated: 5/1/89

NOTE — Maillist.prg prints selected records in a name & phone format

USE Maillist INDEX Mzip        && open file and index
DO WHILE .NOT. EOF()
    etc.
```

ON ERROR <command>

Description. ON ERROR calls <command> if an error occurs within a program.

Operational rules. Use this command to trap errors so that the program does not fall out with the dBASE error message. This command should be placed at the beginning of the program, and it remains effective until an error or another ON ERROR command is encountered. Disable the trap by issuing ON ERROR without the <command> argument.

Example.

```
SET PROCEDURE TO Mailpro
ON ERROR DO Errmess
USE Maillist INDEX Mzip
    etc.
```

The program assumes that there is a procedure in the Mailpro procedure file named ERRMESS.

See also: ON KEY *p. 130.*

ON ESCAPE <command>

Description. ON ESCAPE calls <command> if the Esc key is pressed within a program.

Operational rules. Use this command to trap when the user presses the Esc key, so the program does not fall out with the dBASE abort message. This command has precedence over any ON KEY traps that have been set. SET ESCAPE OFF disables this command. You can also disable the trap by issuing ON ESCAPE without the <command> argument.

Example.

```
SET PROCEDURE TO Mailpro
ON ESCAPE DO Escmess
USE Maillist INDEX Mzip
    etc.
```

The program assumes that there is a procedure in the Mailpro procedure file named ESCMESS.

See also: ON KEY *p. 130.*

ON KEY <command>

Description. ON KEY calls <command> if a key is pressed within a program.

Operational rules. The optional LABEL argument is used to set a trap for a particular key. Because you can set ON KEY for separate keys, you might have more than one ON KEY in effect. If there is no LABEL argument, ON KEY checks for the pressing of any key.

Example.

```
SET PROCEDURE TO Mailpro
? "Press F2 to abort printing"
ON KEY LABEL F2 DO Keyabort
USE Maillist INDEX Mzip
    etc.
PROCEDURE Keyabort
SET PRINT OFF
RETURN TO MASTER
```

See also: ON ERROR *p. 130.*

ON PAD <pad name> OF <menu name>

Description. ON PAD displays a popup menu when the user is highlighting <pad name>.

Operational rules. This command is used in conjunction with a menu created with the DEFINE MENU and DEFINE PAD commands. When the user highlights a particular option, the ON PAD command calls a popup menu to appear.

The optional ACTIVATE POPUP <popup name> argument allows the user to then use the arrow keys to move among the bars of the popup menu.

See also: DEFINE POPUP *p. 110.*

ON PAGE AT LINE <expN> <command>

Description. ON PAGE calls <command> when line <expN> is reached on a printed page.

Operational rules. This command can be used to print page breaks and headers after every <expN> number of lines. Previous versions of dBASE did not have this command, and users were forced to check for line numbers using memory variables.

Set ON PAGE before turning on the printer with SET PRINT ON or SET DEVICE TO PRINT. To disable the ON PAGE trap, issue the ON PAGE command without an argument.

Example.

```
USE Maillist INDEX Mzip
SET PRINT ON
ON PAGE AT LINE 58 DO Header
DO Header
DO WHILE .NOT. EOF( )
   ? Lname,Fname
   SKIP
ENDDO
ON PAGE

PROCEDURE Header
EJECT PAGE
? "Mailing List by Zip Code"
RETURN
```

See also: SET PRINTER *p. 169.*

ON READERROR <command>

Description. ON READERROR calls <command> if an error occurs on an entry screen.

Operational rules. The errors that occur on edit screens are invalid data entries, entries outside of the RANGE specification, and entries that do not meet the VALID conditions. dBASE automatically provides an error message for these instances, but ON READERROR allows you to run your own error handling routines.

This command should be placed at the beginning of the program, and it remains effective until an error or another ON READERROR command is encountered. Disable the trap by issuing ON READERROR without the <command> argument.

See also: ON KEY *p. 130.*

ON SELECTION PAD <pad name> OF <menu name> <command>

Description. ON SELECTION PAD calls <command> when the user has selected <pad name>.

Operational rules. This command is used in conjunction with a menu created with the DEFINE MENU and DEFINE PAD commands. When the user selects a particular option from the pad, ON SELECTION defines the command or procedure that will then be performed.

The <command> can utilize the MENU( ) or PAD( ) functions which determine the last selected option. Disable the branching by issuing ON SELECTION PAD without the <command> argument.

See also: DEFINE MENU *p. 109.*

ON SELECTION POPUP <popup name> <command>

Description. ON SELECTION POPUP calls <command> when the user has selected <popup name> from a popup menu.

Operational rules. This command is used in conjunction with a menu created with the DEFINE POPUP command. When the user selects a particular option from the popup menu, ON SELECTION POPUP defines the command or procedure that will then be performed.

You can use ALL in place of <popup name> to select the same command for all popups. Disable the branching by issuing ON SELECTION POPUP without the <command> argument.

See also: DEFINE POPUP *p. 110.*

PACK

Description. The PACK command permanently deletes all records marked for deletion from the current database file.

Operational rules. To delete a record from the database file, mark all records to be deleted and issue the PACK command. PACK makes a copy of the datafile without the old records, so it might take a while to run. PACK will renumber the records as deleted records are removed. Make sure that there is enough room on your disk for the new file plus the space used by the old file (roughly double the .dbf file space).

The SET DELETED ON command tells dBASE to ignore deleted records when displaying, editing, and listing. This allows deleted records to appear as if they have already been removed without having to PACK.

See also: DELETE *p. 112.*

PARAMETERS <parameter list>

Description. PARAMETERS is used to pass memory variables to a procedure or function, where those variables can be changed and passed back.

Operational rules. If the PARAMETERS command is not used in procedure or function, any variables changed will not retain their new values after returning back to the calling program.

When using PARAMETERS, call the procedure, program, or function by defining the parameter list using WITH <parameter list>. The variables in the calling parameter list must match the number of items in the PARAMETERS parameter list. The names of the variables need not match.

Example.

```
USE Maillist INDEX Mzip
SET PRINT ON
Line = 99
DO WHILE .NOT. EOF( )
   IF Line > 60
      DO Header with Line, "Mailing List by Zip Code"
   ENDIF
   ? Lname,Fname
   Line = Line+1
   SKIP
ENDDO

PROCEDURE Header
PARAMETERS Lineno, Title
EJECT PAGE
?
? Title
?
? REPLICATE("-",75)
Line = 5
RETURN
```

See also: PROCEDURE *p. 136.*

PLAY MACRO <macro name>

Description. PLAY MACRO performs a macro.

Operational rules. Macros are sets of keystrokes that dBASE automatically performs for you. Macros are created through the Control Center using Tools/ Macros.

Macros are created on the keys Alt–F1 through Alt–F9. Alt–F10 macros are then followed by a letter. Therefore, you can define up to 35 macros. To run the macro, simply press the Alt key combination. To call a macro from a program, use PLAY MACRO. This causes the keystrokes to perform as if someone had pressed the Alt combination.

You can keep separate sets of macros in a macro library file. To make a macro library current, use the RESTORE MACROS command.

See also: RESTORE MACROS *p. 142.*

PRINTJOB <commands> ENDPRINTJOB

Description. PRINTJOB utilizes dBASE IV system memory variables while printing.

Operational rules. Examples of some of the system memory variables are printer setup codes (_psetup), number of copies (_pcopies), page eject controls (_peject) and beginning page number (_pbpage). These variables can only be utilized with dBASE built-in reporting capabilities (such as the REPORT FORM), or within programs that call PRINTJOB.

System variables should be defined before the PRINTJOB command is issued. Print jobs can work in conjunction with reports printed through SET PRINT ON or SET FORMAT TO PRINT. At the end of the reporting commands, finish with ENDPRINTJOB.

Example.

```
USE Maillist INDEX Mzip
SET PRINT ON
_pcopies = 3
_peject = "both"
PRINTJOB
ON PAGE AT LINE 58 DO Header
DO WHILE .NOT. EOF()
    ? Lname,Fname
    SKIP
ENDDO
ENDPRINTJOB
SET PRINT OFF
```

See also: RESTORE MACROS *p. 142.*

PRIVATE <memvar list>

Description. PRIVATE is used to declare a private memory variable in a lower level program. This prevents changes from being passed back to the calling program.

Operational rules. Private memory variables allow you to have two variables with the same name in a lower level program and the program that called it. If the value of the variable in the lower level program is changed, it will not affect the value of the variable in the calling program. Memory variables created in programs default to being private variables.

The keywords ALL or LIKE <skeleton> can be used in place of <memvar list>.

Examples.

```
PRIVATE Date, Amount, Time
PRIVATE ALL
PRIVATE LIKE D*
```

See also: PUBLIC *p. 137.*

PROCEDURE

Description. The PROCEDURE command must be at the beginning of each subroutine.

Operational rules. A program calls a procedure with the DO <procedure name> command. Procedures are best utilized for parts of a program that will be called more than once. Procedures run faster than if they were their own separate command (.prg) files.

Procedures can be placed in the program file (usually at the bottom), in a procedure file, in any program file that called the current file, in a file (.obj or .prg) with the procedure name, or in an SQL program file. Procedure names may be up to eight characters (no spaces allowed).

A procedure file can hold up to 1,170 procedures. Use SET PROCEDURE TO <procedure file> at the top of your main program to open the procedure file. Procedures that will be called from more than one program should be placed in the procedure file. Procedures that will only be called from one program should be placed at the bottom of that file.

Procedures must begin with PROCEDURE and end with a RETURN. Memory variables that are changed within the procedure will not retain the changes in the calling program unless they have been declared public or have been passed through the PARAMETER keyword.

Examples.

```
USE Maillist INDEX Mzip
SET PRINT ON
Line = 99
DO WHILE .NOT. EOF()
    IF Line > 60
       DO Header
    ENDIF
```

```
        ? Lname,Fname
        Line = Line+1
        SKIP
ENDDO

PROCEDURE Header
EJECT PAGE
? "MAILING LIST PRINTOUT FOR",DATE( )
?
? REPLICATE("-",75)
Line = 5
RETURN
```

See also: PARAMETER *p. 133.*

PROTECT

Description. The PROTECT command assigns a users access level.
Operational rules. PROTECT allows three types of protection to be set:

Login	access to the dBASE IV program itself.
File/Field	which files and fields within files that can be accessed.
Data	encrypts dBASE files so they cannot be read by unauthorized.
Encryption	users.

Not all types of protection must be set. The login security simply provides password protection for entering dBASE. File/field security is set for each user. You must create a user profile for each user which holds that user's access level regarding adding, deleting and updating records. Levels are between 1 and 8, where 1 has the most privilege. Passwords are stored in the DBSYSTEM.DB file.

PUBLIC <memvar list>

Description. PUBLIC is used to declare a public memory variable in a lower level program. This allows changes to the variable to be passed back to the calling program.

Operational rules. Public memory variables allow you to make changes to a memory variable in a lower level program or subroutine and pass those changes back to the calling program. Variables created at the dot prompt are automatically PUBLIC variables, while variables created in programs default to PRIVATE variables. Public memory variables are logicals until they are initialized to some other type.

The argument ARRAY <array list> can be used in place of <memvar list> if you are declaring array memory variables.

See also: PRIVATE *p. 135.*

QUIT

Description. QUIT ends the current dBASE session.

Operational rules. QUIT closes all files before exiting. dBASE files can be damaged or destroyed if the computer is turned off or reset without quitting dBASE. To help prevent this from happening, close files with the CLOSE commands once you no longer need them during a dBASE session.

See also: CLOSE *p. 96.*

READ

Description. The READ command allows you to edit variables with the @...GET command.

Operational rules. The @...GET command allows you to display more than one variable or field on the screen for editing. Use the @...GET and @...SAY command to "paint" the screen. The READ command must follow the list of @...GET's for a screen. The user can then move back and forth while editing the GET variables.

READ will allow editing of all @...GET statements made since the last READ, CLEAR GETS, or CLEAR command. The optional SAVE argument prevents gets from being cleared after the last READ command. When you use READ SAVE, make sure that you CLEAR GETS when you do want to remove them.

The screen generator creates a format file of @...GET statements, so the READ command can be used in conjunction with SET FORMAT TO when using custom screen layouts.

Examples.

```
@ 5,1 SAY "Enter Last Name" Lname
@ 5,50 SAY "First Name" GET Fname
READ
```

See also: @...GET *p. 87.*

RECALL

Description. The RECALL command "unmarks" records marked for deletion.

Operational rules. To delete a record from the database file, mark all records to be deleted and issue the PACK command. The RECALL command reinstates the current record. Use the optional FOR <condition>, WHILE <condition>, and <scope> arguments to recall records for a subset of the datafile. To reinstate all records, use the ALL argument.

Examples.

```
RECALL
RECALL FOR State = "CA"
RECALL NEXT 100
RECALL ALL
```

See also: DELETE *p. 112.*

REINDEX

Description. REINDEX recreates all open index and multiple index files.

Operational rules. Index files usually must be reindexed if they were not closed properly. This occurs when the computer is turned off or reset without using the QUIT command. Index files will also need to be reindexed if they were not open when records were added or edited in the database.

See Also: DELETE *p. 112.*

RELEASE <memory variable list>

Optional. The optional syntax is RELEASE MODULE <module name list>, RELEASE MENUS <menu name list>, RELEASE POPUPS <popup name list>, or RELEASE WINDOWS <window name list>.

Description. The RELEASE command erases certain variables from memory, opening up space for new variables.

Operational rules. To delete select memory variables use RELEASE with the memory variable list, or with the ALL, ALL LIKE <skeleton>, or ALL EXCEPT <skeleton> argument.

RELEASE MODULE erases a binary file that has been loaded with the LOAD command. You cannot erase menus, popups or windows unless they are no longer in use.

Examples.

```
RELEASE ALL
RELEASE ALL LIKE S*
RELEASE MENUS Main, Edit
```

See also: CLEAR MEMORY *p. 96.*

RENAME <old name> TO <new name>

Description. RENAME changes the name of a file.

Operational rules. You cannot rename a file that is currently open. The RENAME command does not allow wildcards (? and *) to rename multiple files at one time, so you might prefer to use the REN command from DOS. To run a DOS command while at the dot prompt, use ! or RUN.

Example.

```
RENAME Maillist.dbf TO Mail.dbf
RENAME C:\DATA\Maillist.dbf TO C:\DATA\Mail.dbf
```

See also: RUN *p. 144.*

REPLACE <field> WITH <expression>

Description. The REPLACE command performs global finds and replaces in the current database.

Operational rules. Use the optional FOR <condition>, WHILE <condition>, and <scope> arguments to perform the operation for a subset of the datafile. To replace a field in all records, use the ALL argument. Without one of these clauses, REPLACE will only replace the contents in the current record.

You can provide a list of fields to be replaced in one command. Replacing several fields at one time is faster than issuing separate REPLACE commands.

Use the ADDITIVE clause when replacing a memo field with an expression. This is only relevant when <field> is a memo field.

Do not perform a global replace on the key field of the current index. All the records might not be replaced because each record is reindexed as its key changes.

Examples.

```
REPLACE ALL Wages with Wages * 1.1
REPLACE City with "San Jose", State with "CA" FOR City = "SJ"
REPLACE NEXT 100 City with UPPER(City)
REPLACE Narrative WITH Comment1 + Comment2 ADDITIVE
```

REPLACE FROM ARRAY (version 1.1 only)

Description. This command updates current records with values from an array.

See also: APPEND FROM ARRAY *p. 91.*

REPORT FORM <report form filename>

Description. REPORT FORM prints a formatted report for a datafile. The report format must already be created with the CREATE REPORT command.

Operational rules. The CREATE REPORT command allows you to set the report dimensions, headings, groupings, and contents of the report within a report (.frg) file. To run the report, make sure the data file (or multiple files) is your current file, and issue the REPORT FORM command.

The argument ? can be used in place of the <report filename>. dBASE will display a list of .frg files from which to choose. Use the optional FOR <condition>, WHILE <condition>, and <scope> arguments to print the report for a subset of records from the data file.

Reports default to printing on the screen. Use the TO PRINTER option to print to the printer, or the TO FILE <filename> to print to an ASCII file.

The PLAIN clause prevents the headers from printing on pages other than the first. HEADING <expC> causes an additional line of text to print on the top of each page. NOEJECT prevents the initial form feed even if it has been set to Yes in the CREATE REPORT generator. SUMMARY prints a summary report (subtotals only) even if has been set to No in the CREATE REPORT generator.

The primary file should be index by the field(s) to be grouped on, if there will be grouping in the report.

Example.

```
REPORT FORM Mlist
REPORT FORM Mlist TO PRINT
REPORT FORM Mlist TO PRINT HEADING "Rotary Club Mailing"
REPORT FORM Mlist FOR State = "CA" PLAIN NOEJECT
REPORT FORM Mlist NEXT 100 TO FILE Mreport
```

See also: CREATE REPORT *p. 105.*

RESET

Description. The RESET command removes the integrity tag from a file.

Operational rules. When the BEGIN TRANSACTION command is given, dBASE places an integrity tag in the database header record. This mark is not released until the END TRANSACTION or ROLLBACK command has been issued. The BEGIN TRANSACTION command, like the file locking commands, marks a file as being updated; unlike the file locking commands, at any time during the transaction all updates to the file can be aborted with ROLLBACK.

In an unusual circumstance, such as the computer being reset in the middle of a transaction the tag can be left on the file. Remove the tag with RESET. RESET will reset the current file, unless an argument is provided.

See also: BEGIN TRANSACTION *p. 93.*
ROLLBACK *p. 143.*

RESTORE FROM <filename>

Description. The RESTORE command reads a memory (.mem) file, and loads all variables into memory.

Operational rules. Memory files are created with the SAVE TO command, which saves all or a subset of current variables to a file. RESTORE causes all current variables to be deleted unless the ADDITIVE option is included. If there are current memory variables with the same name, they will be overwritten with the new values. When variables are restored from within a program, they will automatically become PRIVATE unless they were previously declared PUBLIC in the program.

Examples.

```
RESTORE FROM Memfile
RESTORE FROM Memfile ADDITIVE
```

See also: SAVE TO *p. 144.*

RESTORE MACROS FROM <macro file>

Description. The RESTORE MACROS command reads a macro (.key) file, and loads all macros into memory.

Operational rules. Macro files are created with the SAVE MACROS command, which saves all macros to a file. If there are current macros with the same name, they will be overwritten with the new values.

See also: SAVE MACROS *p. 144.*

RESTORE SCREEN FROM <screen name> (version 1.1 only)

Description. This command restores a screen image previously saved with the SAVE SCREEN command.

See also: SAVE SCREEN *p. 145.*

RESTORE WINDOW <window name list> FROM <filename>

Description. The RESTORE WINDOW command reads a window (.win) file, and loads the window into memory.

Operational rules. Window files are created with the SAVE WINDOWS command, which saves the currently defined window to a file.

See also: SAVE WINDOW *p. 145.*

RESUME

Description. The RESUME command causes a program to resume processing after it has been suspended.

Operational rules. When a program encounters an error, it will ask the user whether they want to Cancel, Suspend, or Ignore. If the user chooses Suspend, the program will drop out to the dot prompt. All memory variables will still exist, as will file status. At this point, files and variables can be manipulated. If the user then chooses RESUME, the program will resume processing at the next command line. If the user chooses Cancel, memory variables will be erased and the program can not resume processing. SUSPEND can also be placed within a program to make it return to the dot prompt.

See also: SUSPEND *p. 150.*

RETRY

Description. RETRY repeats a command after an error has caused it to abort.

Operational rules. Use this command with ON ERROR to repeat the command after the error is trapped.

Examples.

```
ON ERROR DO ERRTRAP
SET PRINT ON
? "HI THERE"

PROCEDURE
     IF ERROR( ) = 125 .OR. ERROR( ) = 126
        ? "Fix printer connection and then press a key to continue."
        WAIT
        SET PRINT ON
        RETRY
        RETURN
     ENDIF
```

RETURN

Description. The RETURN command causes a program or subroutine to return to the calling program.

Operational rules. If RETURN is placed in the master program, it will drop out to the dot prompt. When placed in any other program, RETURN returns to the calling program, one line below the line that made the call.

The TO MASTER clause causes a return to the highest level calling program (usually the main menu in menu-based systems). The TO <procedure> clause allows you to choose the program to return to.

See also: DO *p. 113.*

ROLLBACK

Description. The ROLLBACK command causes all changes made in a transaction to be rolled back.

Operational rules. ROLLBACK is used in conjunction with BEGIN TRANSACTION. The BEGIN TRANSACTION command is like the file locking commands, in that it marks a file as being updated, but unlike the file locking commands at any time during the transaction all updates to the file can be aborted with the ROLLBACK command.

In an unusual circumstance, such as the computer being reset in the middle of a transaction the tag can be left on the file. Remove the tag with RESET.

See also: BEGIN TRANSACTION *p. 93.*

RUN <DOS commands>

Description. The RUN command calls any program available from the DOS prompt.

Operational rules. RUN calls any program that can be run from the DOS prompt. However, some programs use up too much memory to be called from dBASE. The ! command is equivalent to the RUN command.

The COMMAND clause will cause dBASE to return to the DOS prompt. You can then type in commands from there. Type EXIT to return to dBASE.

Examples.

```
RUN DATE
! CHKDSK
RUN COMMAND
```

SAVE TO <filename>

Description. The SAVE command create a memory (.mem) file of current memory variables and their values.

Operational rules. Memory files are created with the SAVE TO command, which saves all or a subset of current variables to a file. Use the ALL LIKE <skeleton> or ALL EXCEPT <skeleton> clauses to save a subset of current memory variables. Use the RESTORE command to load the variables into memory.

Examples.

```
SAVE TO Memfile
SAVE TO Memfile ALL LIKE S*
```

See also: RESTORE FROM *p. 142.*

SAVE MACROS TO <macro file>

Description. The SAVE MACROS command saves currently defined macros to a macro (.key) file.

Operational rules. Macro files are created with the SAVE MACROS command, which saves all macros to a file. Load these macros with the RESTORE MACROS command.

See also: RESTORE MACROS *p. 142.*

SAVE SCREEN TO <screen name> (version 1.1 only)

Description. This command saves the current screen image to an area of memory designated by < screen name >. This command is very useful for applications where a help screen is displayed over the current screen, and then the current screen must be restored.

See also: RESTORE SCREEN *p. 142.*

SAVE WINDOW <window name list> TO <filename>

Description. The SAVE WINDOW command saves the current window settings to a window (.win) file.

Operational rules. Window files are created with the SAVE WINDOWS command, which saves the currently defined window to a file. You can substitute ALL in place of <window name list>.

See also: RESTORE WINDOW *p. 142.*

SCAN
<commands>
ENDSCAN

Description. SCAN processes all or selected records of a database.

Operational rules. SCAN is much like the DO WHILE command when processing a database. However SCAN, unlike DO WHILE, automatically advances the record pointer with each loop, eliminating the need for the SKIP command.

You can use the optional FOR <condition>, WHILE <condition>, and <scope> arguments to process only a subset of the datafile.

As with the DO WHILE command, you can use the LOOP to loop back to SCAN and begin processing the next record. You can use the EXIT command to end the SCAN process.

Example.

```
USE Maillist
SCAN FOR State = "CA"
      IF Active = "N"
         LOOP
      ENDIF
```

```
        ? Lname, Fname
        REPLACE Printed with "Y"
    ENDSCAN
```

See also: DO WHILE *p. 115.*

SEEK <expression>

Description. The SEEK command moves to the first record in the index that matches <expression>.

Operational rules. SEEK searches the master index for <expression>. The expression must be of the same type as the key expression of the master index. If a match is found, the record pointer moves to that record. Use SKIP to find the next record that matches. If no records match, FOUND( ) will be set to false, and the record pointer will be moved to the end of the file (EOF( ) is true).

If SET EXACT is OFF, the expression does not have to be complete. For instance, the command SEEK "S" will find the first record in the index that begins with S. If SET EXACT is ON, the expression must match exactly. If SET NEAR is ON and no match is found, the record pointer is placed at the first record whose key follows <expression>.

Example.

```
 . USE Maillist index Mlname
 . SEEK "Smith"
Record 2
 . Mname = "Brown"
 . SEEK Mname
Record 7
```

See also: FIND *p. 118.*

SELECT <work area>

Description. The SELECT command specifies the current work area to open files in.

Operational rules. Up to 10 work areas can be opened at a time. Each area may have only one data (.dbf) file, but multiple index (.ndx and .mdx) files may be open in it. Work areas may be identified by numbers (1 through 10) or letters (A through J).

The usual process for working with multiple files is to SELECT each area and open the files in it with the USE command. Then, to change the current work area, simply call the SELECT command. When selecting the current work area, you can use the alias name in place of the number or letter.

To access fields from a file not in the current work area, proceed the field name with the work area letter or alias name and an arrow (->).

Example.

```
. SELECT A
. USE Maillist
. SELECT B
. USE States
. ? A->LNAME, A->FNAME, State
Smith         Joe          California
. SELECT A
. SKIP
. ? LNAME, FNAME, B->State
Brown         Sue          California
```

See also: USE *p. 153.*

SHOW MENU <menu name>

Description. SHOW MENU displays the currently defined menu without activating it.

Operational rules. The menu will display on the screen, but you cannot move the cursor through it or make selections. The optional PAD <pad name> defines the pad that will be highlighted.

See also: DEFINE MENU *p. 109.*

SHOW POPUP <popup name>

Description. SHOW POPUP displays the currently defined popup menu without activating it.

Operational rules. The menu will display on the screen, but you cannot move the cursor through it or make selections. This command is most often used when designing menus so you can test the appearance of your popup menu.

See also: DEFINE POPUP *p. 110.*

SKIP

Description. SKIP is used to move to the next record in a database.

Operational rules. If the database is not indexed, SKIP simply moves to the next record number. If the database is indexed, this will be the next record in the index.

The optional <expN> causes the pointer to skip <expN> records. The number can be either positive, which will cause it to move forward, or negative, which will cause it to move backwards.

If the pointer is at the bottom record and a SKIP is issued, the record pointer will move to the end of file, and EOF( ) will be true (.T.). If the pointer is at the top record and a SKIP -1 is issued, the record pointer will move to the beginning of file, and BOF( ) will be true (.T.).

The SET FILTER and SET DELETED ON commands are honored by SKIP.

Example.

```
 . USE Maillist
 . SKIP
Record 2
 . SKIP 2
Record 4
 . SKIP -1
Record 3
```

See also: CONTINUE *p. 97.*

SORT TO <filename> ON <field>

Description. SORT creates a new database file with the records in order by <field>.

Operational rules. The SORT command copies the datafile, so it will use up the same amount of space. If records are added to the new sorted file they will not maintain the sorted order.

You can sort a file on multiple fields by providing a field list in place of <field>. Fields may be followed the following arguments:

/A sort in ascending order
/D sort in descending order
/C ignore differences between upper and lower case

To combine these arguments use only one slash (for example, /DC). The arguments ASCENDING and DESCENDING are then used for all fields that do not have a slash argument.

Examples.

```
SORT TO Mname ON Lname
SORT TO Mname ON Lname, Fname /C
SORT TO Mname ON Zip /A, Amount /D
SORT TO Mname ON Lname FOR State = "CA"
```

See also: INDEX *p. 121.*

STORE <expression> TO <memory variable>

Description. STORE creates and/or changes the value of a memory variable.

Operational rules. Memory variable are most often used in programs, although they can be used from the dot prompt. Memory variables are much like fields, in that they may be character, numeric, logical, or date type. A variables name can be from 1 to 10 characters. However, memory variable are not stored in a file, so they are lost when the dBASE session is over. The data type of a memory variable is established by its value.

The "=" command is equivalent to the STORE command, except you can only store a value to one memory variable at a time with "=". STORE will accept either a memory variable or memory variable list.

These commands are also be used to set the values of array elements. However, the array must already have been initialized with the DECLARE command.

Examples.

```
Mtot = 0
Mtot = Mtot + 1
STORE "Smith" TO Mname
STORE Lname TO Mname
STORE 0 TO Gtot, Mtot, Ltot
STORE 500 TO Marray(1,2)
```

See also: DECLARE *p. 107.*

SUM

Description. SUM provides the totals of the numeric fields of a datafile.

Operational rules. If no arguments are provided, dBASE displays the sum total of each numeric field in the database. You can provide a field list to specify the field(s) to be summed.

To create memory variables whose values are the sums, use the TO <memory variable list> or TO ARRAY. When summing to an array, the array must be declared as single dimension, and each field in the field list updates the next row.

You can use the optional FOR <condition>, WHILE <condition>, and <scope> arguments to include only a subset of the records in the calculation.

Examples.

```
SUM
SUM Wage, Bonus to Mwage, Mbon
SUM Wage TO Mwage FOR State = "CA"
SUM Wage, Bonus, Commsion TO ARRAY Mamount
```

The last example assumes that Mamount has been declared as a one-dimensional array. After the SUM, Mamount(1) is equal to the total of the Wage field.

See also: DECLARE *p. 107.*

SUSPEND

Description. The SUSPEND command drops the current program out to the dot prompt.

Operational rules. When a program encounters an error, it will ask the user whether they want to Cancel, Suspend, or Ignore. The SUSPEND command is equivalent to when the user chooses Suspend. All memory variables will still exist, as will file status. At this point, files and variables can be manipulated. If the user then chooses RESUME, the program will resume processing at the next command line.

SUSPEND can be placed within a program to make it return to the dot prompt. The CANCEL command also halts the program, but memory variables will be erased and the program cannot resume processing.

See also: RESUME *p. 143.*

TEXT
<text characters>
ENDTEXT

Description. This displays all text entered between the TEXT and ENDTEXT commands.

Operational rules. TEXT is the easiest command for printing text on the screen or to a printer. Simply enter the text as you want it displayed. You do not need to surround character strings with quote marks, as you do with the ? command.

You cannot display memory variables in the text output, because all entries are interpreted literally.

Examples.

```
TEXT
     This is information that will display
     just as it looks. Notice that there are no
     quote marks around the strings or commands
     such as ? or ??.

ENDTEXT
```

See also: ? *p. 85.*

TOTAL ON <key field> TO <filename>

Description. TOTAL copies a database to a second file that contains subtotals of each numeric field.

Operational rules. Unless the optional FIELDS <fields list> clause is included, the new file will have the same structure as the active file. There will be one record in the new file for each unique <key field> record in the active file. The active file must be indexed by <key field> before issuing the command.

The numeric fields in the new file will contain the sum totals for each particular key. Character, date and logical fields will contain the information of the first record that matches the unique key. Memo fields are not copied to the new file.

You can use the optional FOR <condition>, WHILE <condition>, and <scope> arguments to include only a subset of the records in the new file.

Examples.

```
. USE Dues INDEX Member
. ? RECCOUNT()
          20
. TOTAL ON Membcode TO Totdues
. USE Totdues
. LIST Membcode, Dues
Record #     MEMBCODE          DUES
      1           A01        200.00
      2           A02        150.00
      3           A12         50.00
      4           B03        100.00
      5           B05        150.00
```

See also: SUM *p. 149.*

TYPE <filename>

Description. TYPE displays the contents of <filename>.

Operational rules. The TYPE command works just like the TYPE command from DOS. It is most often used when displaying the contents of a program (.prg) or format (.fmt) file. Files that are not standard ASCII will not display clearly with the TYPE command.

The output defaults to printing on the screen. Use the TO PRINTER option to print to the printer, or the TO FILE <filename> to print to an ASCII file.

The NUMBER clause will number each line in the program. Page numbers, the current date, and the name of the program will display at the top unless SET HEADING is off.

Examples.

```
TYPE Maillist.prg
TYPE Maillist.prg TO PRINTER
TYPE Maillist.prg TO PRINTER NUMBER
```

See also: LIST FILES *p. 125.*

UNLOCK

Description. UNLOCK releases the last lock set.

Operational rules. Use FLOCK( ) and RLOCK( ) to place locks on files and records. Release the lock with UNLOCK. Some commands automatically lock files and records, and they automatically unlock when finished.

Use the ALL option to release locks in all files and records. Use the IN <alias> option to release locks in a particular file.

Examples.

```
. USE Maillist
. ? RLOCK( )
          .T.
. REPLACE Wage with Wage*1.1
. UNLOCK
```

See also: RLOCK( ) *p. 247.*

UPDATE ON <key field> FROM <alias> REPLACE <field name> WITH <expression>

Description. The UPDATE command performs a global find and replace on <field name> while relating two files.

Operational rules. The update command sets a relationship between the active file, where the replace will occur, and <alias>. The two files must each have <key field>, and <alias> must be indexed on that field. The current file must also be indexed on the field unless the RANDOM clause is included. If there are multiple records with the same key in the active file, then only the first record that matches is updated.

Example.

```
. SELECT 1
. USE Dues INDEX Member
. LIST
Record #    MEMBCODE      DUES
       1         A01     40.00
       4         A01     60.00
```

```
         2            A02          50.00
         3            A12          50.00
         5            A12          50.00
     . SELECT 2
     . USE Members INDEX Membcode
     . UPDATE ON Membcode FROM Dues REPLACE Totdues WITH Totdues + Dues
     . LIST
   Record #     MEMBCODE        DUES
         1            A01         100.00
         4            A02          50.00
         2            A12         100.00
```

See also: SET RELATION *p. 170.*

USE <filename>

Description. The USE command opens a database (.dbf) file in a work area.

Operational rules. The file will be opened in the current work unless the IN <work area> option is included. If a file is already open in that area, it will be closed so that the new one can be opened. To close a file in a work area without opening a new file, issue USE without a <filename>.

The INDEX <.ndx or .mdx file list> clause allows you to open an index files with the database file. The first index in the <.ndx file list> is the master index. When using multiple index files, use the ORDER clause to set the order of the tag that will be the master index. If the ORDER clause is issued without the INDEX clause, dBASE assumes an .mdx file with the same name as the .dbf file.

The optional ? argument can be used in place of <filename>. dBASE will then provide a list of all .dbf files, which you can choose from.

In multi-user applications, use the EXCLUSIVE clause to prevent other users from accessing it until you close it. The NOUPDATE clause prevents any changes to file, although it can be displayed.

Example.

```
. USE Maillist INDEX Zips, Memcode
. USE Maillist ORDER Zip, Amount, Code
. USE Maillist IN 3
. USE Maillist IN 3 EXCLUSIVE
```

See also: INDEX *p. 121.*

WAIT

Description. WAIT pauses the processing until a key is pressed.

Operational rules. WAIT halts the program until the user presses a key. Use the TO <memory variable name> clause to create a character memory variable which stores the keyboard entry. If the optional <prompt> is not used, dBASE displays Press any key to continue as the default message.

Examples.

```
WAIT
WAIT "Do you want to print (Y/N) " TO PRN
```

See also: ACCEPT *p. 89.*

ZAP

Description. ZAP erases all records from the database file.

Operational rules. Use ZAP in place of the commands DELETE ALL and PACK. ZAP is much faster, and provides the verification question Zap?.

See also: DELETE *p. 112.*
PACK *p. 133.*

3

dBASE IV Set Commands

THE SET COMMANDS ARE A SPECIAL GROUP OF COMMANDS THAT CHANGE MANY OF the default settings of dBASE. The SET commands can be issued from the dot prompt or from a program. In addition, the command SET, by itself, provides a full-screen menu for changing many of the settings such as screen colors, function keys, default disk drives, and many other options.

In this chapter, the commands are listed in alphabetical order. Each command displays the possible options. The option in capital letters is the default dBASE IV setting. For instance.

```
SET PRINT on/OFF
```

Shows that the default setting for this command is OFF. Variable options are placed in angle brackets (< >), such as,

```
SET MARGIN TO <expN>
```

which shows that a numeric expression must be used as the option. Any optional clauses are placed in square brackets.

SET ALTERNATE on/OFF
SET ALTERNATE TO [<filename>][ADDITIVE]

Description. SET ALTERNATE stores all output to a text file except full screen commands.

Operational rules. There is a two-step process for the SET ALTERNATE command. First, create a text file using MODIFY FILE <filename> by SET

ALTERNATE ON. This output overwrites any data previously in the file of that name, however, this can be avoided by following SET ALTERNATE TO <filename> with

Through the command SET ALTERNATE OFF, the text file can remain open, though no output is saved to it. The command CLOSE ALTERNATE closes the text file. Be sure to close the text file before using the file. The text file is a standard ASCII file that can be modified via MODIFY COMMAND or a word processor.

SET AUTOSAVE on/OFF

Description. The SET AUTOSAVE command saves each record to the disk after alterations have been made, thus reducing possibility of lost data. When AUTOSAVE is OFF, records are saved to the disk as the buffer is filled.

Operational rules. AUTOSAVE can be activated (or deactivated) by the command SET AUTOSAVE ON (OFF) from the dot prompt or the SET menu.

SET BELL ON/off

Description. The SET BELL command controls the audible tone that is heard when an error is made or when a field is filled.

Operational rules. From dot prompt, enter SET BELL OFF, or from SET menu, select OFF. When SET BELL is OFF, no tone is heard.

SET BLOCKSIZE TO <expN>

Description. This command enables the memo fields to be enlarged by a factor of 512 bytes. The default setting is 1.

Operational rules. The range of the numerical expression is 1 to 32; the memo size increases by a factor of <expN> times. For example, if 3 is chosen for the expN, then the size of the memo is increased to 1536 bytes.

The SET BLOCKSIZE command must be performed prior to creating, changing the structure of, or copying a file containing memo fields for the expansion or reduction in memo field size to be effective. To enlarge memos of existing files, use the SET BLOCKSIZE command, then copy the database file to a new filename. The new file will contain the new block size.

SET BORDER TO <SINGLE/DOUBLE/PANEL/NONE> <border definition string>

Description. SET BORDER changes the border of windows, menus, and @...SAY commands from a single line box to a variety of styles via user-defined options.

Operational rules. The available border choices are single line or double line, and reverse video display. By using SET BORDER in conjunction with the @...SAY and @...TO commands, borders can vary in size and combine double lines and single lines.

DOUBLE changes the border to double line, and PANEL displays the border in reverse video format. To return to the single lined box, use the command SET BORDER TO followed by Enter.

SET CARRY on/OFF
SET CARRY TO [<field list>][ADDITIVE]]

Description. SET CARRY carries forward all changes made in a record to proceeding records when using APPEND, INSERT, or BROWSE. SET CARRY TO brings the contents specified fields forward to the next record when using the aforementioned commands.

Operational rules. SET CARRY TO <field list> specifies fields that will be updated while SET CARRY ON will update all fields. The use of ADDITIVE adds the field list to the existing list that has already been specified. SET CARRY TO without an argument restores the default condition where all fields are updated. If SET CARRY is OFF, the SET CARRY TO will automatically SET CARRY ON as well as define the field list.

SET CATALOG on/OFF
SET CATALOG TO [<filename>/?]

Description. When SET CATALOG is ON, all files created are added to the catalog. You can also use SET CATALOG to create new catalogs.

Operational rules. SET CATALOG TO <filename> opens the specified catalog file or creates a catalog file if one of the specified name does not exist. SET CATALOG TO? displays a master catalog of catalog files with accompanying descriptions.

When SET CATALOG is on, the catalog is updated when commands like CREATE, INDEX, AND CREATE/MODIFY REPORT are used. When the CATALOG command is OFF, the catalog file is not updated, but the catalog file is still open. This allows extraneous files in the catalog to be created, modified, etc., without closing the catalog file.

SET CENTURY on/OFF

Description. This command allows for the input and display of the century prefixes in the year portion of dates.

Operational rules. The CENTURY command can be activated (deactivated) from the dot prompt, SET CENTURY ON (OFF), or from the SET menu, select ON (OFF).

SET CLOCK on/OFF
SET CLOCK TO [<row], [column>]

Description. The CLOCK command determines if the clock will be displayed, and its position on the screen.

Operational rules. Select SET CLOCK ON for the clock's display on the screen. To align its position, use the SET CLOCK TO command with the appropriate coordinates. SET CLOCK TO without any coordinates following reverts the clock back to its default position.

SET COLOR ON/OFF
SET COLOR TO [<standard>], [<enhanced>], [<perimeter>], [<background>]
SET COLOR OF NORMAL/MESSAGES/TITLES/BOX/HIGHLIGHT/INFORMATION/FIELDS TO [<COLOR ATTRIBUTE>]

Operational rules. SET COLOR ON/OFF is used to select between color and monochrome display. The default is dependent upon the particular default of the system dBASE IV is run on.

SET COLOR TO allows the color of the standard text, highlighted areas, borders, and backgrounds to be changed. SET COLOR TO not followed by an argument resets display to default setting in the Config.db file. The option <standard> denotes the color of the background and the standard text. [enhanced] is the color of the text and background of the highlighted areas. [perimeter] is the color of the border. The colors are represented by:

Color	Symbol	Color	Symbol
Black	N or blank	Red	R
Blue	B	Magenta	RB
Green	G	Brown	GR
Cyan	BG	Yellow	GR+
Blank	X	White	W
Gray	N+		

Example.

```
SET COLOR TO B/G, GR+/R, R
```

This command will produce blue text on a green background; the highlighted areas will be yellow text with a red background and a red border.

SET COLOR OF...TO enables the colors of particular screen area groupings to be changed while the rest of the screen remains in its assigned colors. NORMAL refers to unselected items of menus, layout editor design surface, calculated field expressions, and output from @...SAY commands. MESSAGES is the interior of error, help, and prompt boxes, unavailable or unselected menu or list choices, field window contents, and message lines. TITLES included headings and underlined text, and BOXES encompasses borders. HIGHLIGHT is all highlighted material. INFORMATION refers to the clock, status line, and the selected button in the help and error box. Finally, FIELDS comprises data entry areas and all highlighted field areas.

SET CONFIRM on/OFF

Description. CONFIRM, when activated, holds the cursor at a field that has been filled until Return is pressed.

Operational rules. CONFIRM is activated from the dot prompt or the SET menu. When CONFIRM is set OFF, then the cursor automatically advances to the next field when a field is filled.

SET CONSOLE ON/off

Description. The SET CONSOLE command can be used within a program to turn the screen display on and off.

Operational rules. Working only within a program, SET CONSOLE is used to prevent display of output to the screen. It cannot be used from the dot prompt. Input is accepted through such commands as WAIT and ACCEPT, but neither the prompts nor what is being typed will display to the screen.

@...SAY...GET overrides the console setting as well as all error messages and safety prompts.

SET CURRENCY TO [<exp>]
SET CURRENCY LEFT/right

Description. This command changes the character symbolizing currency and positions the currency symbol on either the left or right.

Operational rules. SET CURRENCY TO accepts a currency symbol of up to nine characters in length. The SET CURRENCY TO command allow dBASE IV to work with currencies with right-side conventions like the French franc.

SET CURSOR ON/off (version 1.1 only)

Description. This command can be used to hide the cursor in situations where you do not want it to show.

SET DATE [TO] AMERICAN/ansi/british/german/italian/japan/usa/mdy/dmy/dmy/ymd

Description. SET DATE determines the convention for date display.

Operational rules. This date allow quick change of date convention to aid in date output and date input. The date conventions available are:

AMERICAN	MM/DD/YY
ANSI	YY.MM.DD
BRITISH/FRENCH	DD/MM/YY
GERMAN	DD.MM.YY
ITALIAN	DD-MM-YY
JAPAN	MM/DD/YY
USA	MM-DD-YY
MDY	MM/DD/YY
DMY	DD/MM/YY
YMD	YY/MM/DD

SET DEBUG on/OFF

Description. SET DEBUG is used to locate errors in programs in conjunction with SET ECHO by determining if output from SET ECHO is sent to the screen or printer.

Operational rules. SET DEBUG is activated from the dot prompt. When ON, the output of SET ECHO is directed to the printer, otherwise this output is sent to the screen. The effect is of SET DEBUG ON is to prevent output of the debugging process to interfere with the output of the program.

SET DECIMAL TO <expN>

Description. The number of significant digits to the right of the decimal point in the display of numeric functions and calculations is determined by the <expN> of the SET DECIMAL TO command.

Operational rules. The maximum number of decimal places that can be displayed is 18. The default is two decimal places.

SET DEFAULT TO <drive> [:]

Description. SET DEFAULT specifies the drive where all dBASE IV operations take place and files are stored.

Operational rules. The default drive is the drive that dBASE IV was started on. dBASE IV does not check if the specified drive exists and does not return to the previous drive after quitting dBASE IV.

SET DELETED on/OFF

Description. SET DELETED mandates whether deleted files are recognized by other dBASE IV commands.

Operational rules. This command affects commands such as BROWSE, LOCATE, LIST, REPORT and EDIT. If SET DELETED is on, all records marked for deletion are not displayed, as if they have been removed. However, you can GOTO a deleted record, or display it within a scope even if SET DELETED is ON.

SET DELIMITERS on/OFF
SET DELIMITERS TO <expC>/DEFAULT

Description. SET DELIMITERS command allows characters to define field widths.

Operational rules. The default for DELIMITERS is OFF. Because the SET INTENSITY is ON, the default display is for fields to appear reverse video with no delimiters. When SET DELIMITERS is ON, the default delimiters are colons (:).

SET DELIMITERS TO reads one or two characters in the <expC>, all others are ignored. If one character is entered, that character will appear at the beginning and end of the field entry width. If two characters are entered in the character string, the first character will mark the beginning of the field, and the second will mark the end. SET DELIMITERS must be ON in order for the delimiters defined to appear.

SET DESIGN ON/off

Description. SET DESIGN prevents the user from entering the design mode from the dot prompt or the control center.

Operational rules. The command denies access into Database, Report, Form, Label, Query, and Applications from the Control Center. This allows the user only limited access, thus protecting all files.

SET DEVELOPMENT ON/off

Description. This command runs a checking program that updates the object file (.dbo) every time a program (.prg) is modified.

Operational rules. The object file is a file containing an execute-only form of dBASE IV commands: object files cannot be modified. Every time a dBASE IV program is modified, an updated version of this executable object replaces the previous object file. If SET DEVELOPMENT is OFF, an updated object file will not be created; moreover, the modifications of the program won't register.

SET DEVICE TO SCREEN/printer/file <filename>

Description. The SET DEVICE command determines the destination of output from @...SAY commands to the screen, printer, or a file.

Operational rules. When SET DEVICE is set to the PRINTER, the output form @...SAY commands goes directly to the printer, and all @...GET commands are ignored.

SET DIRECTORY TO <drive> <path> (version 1.1 only)

Description. This command allows you to set the default drive letter and path.

SET DISPLAY TO MONO/COLOR/EGA43/MONO43

Description. SET DISPLAY specifies either monochrome or color display, and determines the number of lines displayed.

Operational Usage. This command can only be used if the operating hardware can support monochrome and/or color display and an equivalent graphics card that can support a 43-line display. If these requirements are not met and the command is used, an error message is given.

SET DOHISTORY on/OFF

Description. This command is included only to retain compatibility with dBASE III + ; it is not used in dBASE IV.

SET ECHO on/OFF

Description. SET ECHO is used in debugging programs by displaying commands as they are executed.

Operational rules. SET ECHO is used only during debugging and can be used in conjunction with the three other debugging commands, SET DEBUG, SET STEP, and SET TALK.

SET ENCRYPTION on/OFF

Description. This command is used with *encrypted* files, those with data that is coded into another form to hide its contents. SET ENCRYPTION ON is used to copy these protected files into a decrypted form.

Operational rules. Access to an encrypted file is granted only after a valid user name, password, a group name are entered at the login screen. Authorization and access levels determine if an encrypted file can be copied.

SET ENCRYPTION OFF to copy a decrypted form of the file after accessing the file. Encryption works only with PROTECT.

SET ESCAPE ON/off

Description. SET ESCAPE ON allows the execution of a program to be stopped via the Esc key.

Operational rules. With SET ESCAPE OFF, the Esc key will no longer operate. SET ESCAPE OFF should only be used with tested programs, for the only other way to halt execution is rebooting computer. This can result in lost data.

SET EXACT on/OFF

Description. SET EXACT ON requires an exact match in length and contents when comparing strings in searches.

Operational rules. When SET EXACT is OFF, a character string matches another as long as the comparison string is the same length or longer and contains the same characters as the model string. With EXACT ON, the comparison string must match the model string character for character. For instance, if SET EXACT is OFF, the command is

```
LIST FOR Lname = "S"
```

will list all records with a Lname that begins with an S in Lname and nothing else.

SET EXCLUSIVE on/OFF

Description. For use on multi-user systems, SET EXCLUSIVE ON restricts use of database file to the user that opened the file.

Operational rules. No other user can write to nor read a file that has been opened for exclusive use. The CREATE and SAVE commands activate SET EXCLUSIVE ON whenever used.

SET FIELDS on/OFF
SET FIELDS TO [<field>][/R]/<calculated field id>...] [,<field>[/R]/<calculated field id>...]
SET FIELDS TO ALL [LIKE/EXCEPT <skeleton>]

Description. SET FIELDS is used define a list of fields that can be accessed by one or more files. The defined field list is used by all commands that have a field list option available in their use.

Operational rules. A field list must be identified before SET FIELDS is activated. Use of the /R denotes read-only flag, telling dBASE IV that data is to be read only, not accepted. Calculated fields can be defined within the statement, for instance,

TAX = PRICE*.07

using any valid dBASE IV expression.

The skeleton is used to include or exclude fields of similar name via the wildcard character(*). dBASE IV accepts any character that appears in the space with the wildcard. ALL LIKE includes all fields that match the skeleton while ALL EXCEPT excludes them.

SET FIELD TO followed by a Return strikes all fields from the active database from the field list, and SET FIELDS TO ALL includes all fields from the active database.

SET FILTER TO [FILE <filename>/?][<condition>]

Description. SET FILTER TO only displays those records that meet a specified condition.

Operational rules. SET FILTER TO alone deactivates filter for the active database file. SET FILTER TO FILE adds a query file to a catalog if one is open. SET FILTER TO FILE <filename> reads the filter condition that has been created by CREATE/MODIFY QUERY. If a catalog is open, the query file of the active database file can be displayed.

SET FILTER TO <condition> specifies a condition for displaying records. The condition can be any valid dBASE IV expression like CITY = "Los Angeles" or BDAY = {09/12/68}. Filters are activated when the record pointer is moved; use of SKIP or GOTO can be used to begin use of filter.

SET FIXED on/OFF

Description. This command is not used in dBASE IV; it is included to preserve compatibility with dBASE III.

SET FORMAT TO [<format file>/?]

Description. SET FORMAT TO selects the format file (.fmt) to be used with the APPEND, BROWSE, CHANGE, EDIT, INSERT, or READ commands.

Operational rules. Format files are created with CREATE/MODIFY SCREEN. If SET FORMAT TO is not activated, then the standard display and entry form are used. SET FORMAT TO? will display a menu of format files. CLOSE FORMAT or SET FORMAT TO closes the format file.

SET FULLPATH on/OFF

Description. The SET FULLPATH command makes dBASE III programs that contain the functions MDX( ), NDX( ), or DBF( ) compatible to dBASE IV by removing the path names from the above functions' output.

Operational rules. Because MDX( ), NDX( ), and DBF( ) do not return the full file name in dBASE IV specification, it is necessary to SET FULLPATH ON when using dBASE III programs that use these functions, which display full file and path name.

SET FUNCTION <expN>/<expC>/<key label> TO <expC>

Description. SET FUNCTION allows the function keys to be programmed with up to 238 characters per function key to be used in data entry operations. The default key assignments are as follows:

Key	Assignment	Key	Assignment
F1	HELP;	F6	DISPLAY STATUS;
F2	ASSIST;	F7	DISPLAY MEMORY;
F3	LIST;	F8	DISPLAY;
F4	DIR;	F9	APPEND;
F5	DISPLAY STRUCTURE	F10	EDIT;

Operational rules. The function keys may be set in three ways from the set menu, the dot prompt, or the config.db file. Shift - F1 through Shift - F9, and Ctrl - F1 through Ctrl1 - 10 can be programmed with functions as well. The Alt keys, Shift - 10, and the F11 and F12 keys cannot be programmed. When programming function keys, a semicolon denotes a Return causing dBASE IV to execute the command. Quotes can be used to denote text strings.

SET HEADING ON/off

Description. With SET HEADING ON, the column titles of the fields are displayed using the command DISPLAY, LIST, SUM, and AVERAGE.

SET HELP ON/off

Description. SET HELP ON summons a pop-up window listing dBASE IV help options when a command is entered incorrectly at the dot prompt.

Operational rules. When an error is made and the help window appears, the options of CANCELing or EDITing the command, or using the help system to find appropriate command usage are offered.

SET HISTORY ON/off
SET HISTORY TO <expN>

Description. With SET HISTORY ON, commands previously made from the dot prompt can be edited, executed, or displayed using the up and down arrow keys.

Operational rules. When SET HISTORY is off, previous commands cannot be accessed. The numerical string determines how many of the commands made from the dot prompt are saved to the buffer with a range of 0 to 16000. The default number is 20. To clear the contents of the buffer SET HISTORY TO 0.

SET HOURS TO [12/24]

Description. This command determines the time format of the clock to either twelve or twenty-four hour cycle. The default is set to 12.

SET INDEX TO [?/<filename list>
[ORDER <.mdx tagname>] OF <.mdx filename>]

Description. SET INDEX TO is used to open index and multiple index files. It allows for the option of specifying the controlling index or tag for an active database file.

Operational rules. SET INDEX TO ? displays a catalog of index and multiple index files. If the ? is replaced by a list of filenames, those files are opened to be used with the active database file. ORDER can be used following the field list to specify a controlling index file. This is not necessary with a .ndx <filename list>, because the first index in the list automatically becomes the master index.

If a file extension is not specified, first an attempt to open a multiple index (.MDX) file is made, followed by an index (.NDX) file.

The OF clause is optionally used to specify the source multiple index file from where the index files are to be found. Alterations to the active database are made to all open index files as well.

SET INSTRUCT ON/off

Description. SET INSTRUCT allows for the display of prompts.

Operational rules. With SET INSTRUCT ON, prompts appearing in the use of full screen commands, like APPEND, BROWSE, and EDIT are displayed.

SET INTENSITY ON/off

Description. SET INTENSITY determines whether the field widths of input areas when using APPEND or edit, or @...SAY...GET commands are highlighted. Input areas are highlighted with SET INTENSITY ON.

SET LOCK ON/off

Description. SET LOCK applies multi-user systems to prevent a record from being updated by more than user at a time.

Operational rules. When commands that update or edit records or files are executed by a user, all other users on the system can only read that file or record. After the command is completed, the file is unlocked.

SET MARGIN TO <expN>

Description. SET MARGIN is used to adjust the left margin of the printer. It does not affect the screen. The left margin default setting is 0.

SET MARK TO [<expC>]

Description. SET MARK changes the delimiter of the day, month, and year of date displays.

Operational rules. A new delimiter can be set by enclosing the desired character in quotes. For example, SET MARK TO "-" will separate the month, day, and year by dashes.

SET MEMOWIDTH TO <expN>

Description. SET MEMOWIDTH allows for the alteration in the widths of memo field output.

SET MENU ON/off

Description. SET MENU is a dBASE III PLUS command that has no effect in dBASE IV.

SET MESSAGE TO [<expC>]

Description. When SET STATUS is ON, a statement or character string defined by the user via SET MESSAGE is displayed on the bottom line of the screen. With version 1.1, you can make the message print anywhere on the screen when SET STATUS is OFF.

Operational rules. The MESSAGE length can be a maximum of 79 characters consisting of a phrase surrounded by quotes or the contents of a field denoted by a field name. The MESSAGE appears centered on line 23 of the screen. The default setting is the display of dBASE IV messages.

SET NEAR on/OFF

Description. SET NEAR positions the database record pointer to the record following that which is most similar to the search criteria in database file searches that fail to find an exact match. The default setting is off.

SET ODOMETER TO <expN>

Description. For commands that display a record count, SET ODOMETER determines the interval that the record count is updated.

Operational rules. The update interval can be in the range of 1 through 200. The default is set to 1.

SET ORDER TO
SET ORDER TO <expN>
SET ORDER TO [Tag] <filename> / < .mdx tagname> [OF <.mdx filename>]

Description. SET ORDER is used to change the controlling index or tag without closing any index or multiple index files.

Operational rules. SET ORDER TO without an argument restores the database file to its natural order; it can be used with.ndx and .mdx files. SET ORDER TO <expN> can only be used with .ndx files when no .mdx files are open. The argument can be between 0 and 10 depending on the number of .ndx files open. The argument determines the order of index files in a list. This order is important when using the SET INDEX TO and USE commands.

When using both .ndx and .mdx files, the order must be specified by index filename. Changing the order of the index files causes dBASE IV to update all index files. The TAG option allows the master index to be changed to a new index file. A multiple index contains tags, which are different orders of index files. If there exist two tags of the same name, it is recommended, to avoid confusion, to use the [OF <.mdx filename>] option to specify the correct .mdx file.

SET PATH TO [<path list>]

Description. dBASE IV does not use the DOS path command; the SET PATH command establishes a path for dBASE IV to use when searching for files that are not in the current directory.

SET PAUSE on/OFF

Description. SET PAUSE stops the display of data after each screenful.

Operational rules. The SET PAUSE command enables multi-screen output to be displayed with a pause between each screenful of data, similar to output of the DISPLAY command. If SET PAUSE is OFF, then the output scrolls down the screen without a pause, like the output of the LIST command.

SET POINT TO [<expC>]

Description. SET POINT specifies the character denoting the decimal point.

Operational rules. Any single alphanumeric character can be specified for the decimal point; a space cannot be used for the decimal. The default can be restored by entering SET POINT TO without an argument. The default character is a period (.).

SET PRECISION TO [<expN>]

Description. SET PRECISION determines the number of significant digits dbase IV uses in mathematical operations. The default setting is 16 digits.

Operational rules. The numeric expression can range from 10 to 20 digits.

SET PRINTER on/OFF
SET PRINTER TO <DOS device>
SET PRINTER TO \\<computer name> \<printer name> = <destination>
SET PRINTER TO \\SPOOLER
SET PRINTER TO\\CAPTURE
SET PRINTER TO FILE <filename>

Description. SET PRINTER ON routes all output except output specified by the @...SAY command to the printer of a file. Output can be redirected via the SET PRINTER TO commands to a file or other printer.

Operational rules. With SET PRINTER ON, output previously mentioned is routed to the printer. Another printer can be specified via the SET PRINTER TO command. The parallel ports (LPT1, LPT2, LPT3) or the serial ports (COM1 and COM2) represent alternate destinations for printer output. SET PRINTER TO FILE <filename> directs the printer output to a file; if a file is produced with the print driver ascii.pr2, the file is transformed to an ASCII file.

SET PROCEDURE TO [<procedure filename>]

Description. This command is used to open procedure files.

Operational rules. A procedure file is a file that performs a basic task and can be called from any program or another procedure. Procedures are used widely in programming for this reason. Only one procedure file can be open at a time.

If a file extension is not specified, dBASE IV will search for and compile, if necessary, the desired file with the .dbo extension.

SET REFRESH TO <expN>

Description. SET REFRESH is used on networks to determine the time interval between checks to see if a record has been changed in a file where the EDIT or BROWSE command are being used.

SET REFRESH is designed to be used before using BROWSE or EDIT by displaying alterations to records in a file being made in the network. The interval, 1 second to 1 hour, can range from 1 to 3600, the units being seconds. At the default value, the system does not refresh. Furthermore, SET REFRESH works only with files that have been converted via the CONVERT command. The default is setting is 0.

SET RELATION TO
SET RELATION TO <exp>
SET RELATION TO <expN> INTO <alias>

Description. SET RELATION allows use of two database files by linking them via a key expression that occurs in both files.

Operational rules. An active database file is linked to an open database file in another work area via a common field. The <alias> database must be index on the common field. SET RELATION without an argument removes the relation in use.

The following program sets a relationship between two files. The common field is Clicode:

```
.SELECT 1
.USE Sales
.SELECT 2
.Use Clients INDEX Code
.SELECT 1
.SET RELATIONSHIP TO Clicode INTO Clients
.LIST OFF Clicode, Amount, Date,B->Name

CLICODE  AMOUNT    B->Name
 A01       50.00   JIM JONES
 A02      150.00   RUTH DOE
 A01      200.00   Jim Jones
 A03      100.00   Harry Carey
 A02       50.00   RUTH DOE
```

SET REPROCESS TO<expN>

Description. SET REPROCESS is a network command that limits the number of attempts to access a file or record before an error message is produced.

Operational rules. On a network, files and records can be locked by users, thus denying access to others who want to use that record or file. SET REPROCESS limits the number of attempts made to access the locked file. The numeric expression range is – 1 to 32000; – 1 permits an infinite number of attempts to access the file.

The default setting is 0. This also makes an infinite number of attempts to access the record or file with no ON ERROR command. Esc can be used to exit the loop.

SET SAFETY ON/off

Description. SET SAFETY prevents accidental overwriting of files by requiring a verification that the file is to be overwritten.

Operational rules. With SAFETY ON, if a file of the same name as the file being created exists or if the ZAP command is used, the message

```
File already exists
Overwrite    Cancel
```

appears on the screen. Note that an acknowledgment is necessary to overwrite the file. When SET SAFETY is OFF, files can be overwritten without a warning message.

SET SCOREBOARD ON/off

Description. With SET SCOREBOARD ON and SET STATUS OFF, dBASE IV indicates the status of the Num lock and Caps lock keys by displaying Num and Caps when these functions are activated as well as display Del for deleted records.

Operational rules. If SET STATUS is ON, SET SCOREBOARD has no effect. The indicators are displayed on line 0.

SET SEPARATOR TO [<expC>]

Description. SET SEPARATOR allows the numeric separating conventions of other countries to be used in the display of numbers.

Operational rules. The separator character can be only one character long. The default setting is the comma (,).

SET SKIP TO [<alias> [,<alias>]...]

Description. SET SKIP is used to handle updating records in database files linked with the SET RELATION command.

Operational rules. SET SKIP determines the sequence of the record pointer in updating records contained in the files of the relationship chain. Records of the last file in the argument are updated first followed by the preceding files in the list. The active database file will automatically be updated, so it is unnecessary to include it in the argument.

SET SPACE ON/off

Description. SET SPACE ON causes a space to be printed between expressions when using the ? or ?? commands.

Operational rules. The SPACE command prints a space between expressions separated by a comma in the ? or ?? command.

SET SQL on/OFF

Description. SET SQL ON takes dBASE IV into the SQL interactive mode.

Operational Rules. SET SQL can be entered from the dot prompt. Once in SQL mode, only a subset of dBASE IV commands and SQL commands can be used. SET SQL OFF can be issued from the SQL mode; it returns dBASE IV to the dot prompt. SET SQL cannot be used in programs.

SET STATUS on/OFF

Description. SET STATUS ON specifies that the status bar displays at the bottom of the screen using full screen commands and within programs.

Operational rules. The status bar displays the command name, active file, and the record number in fraction form with the number of records. This is only displayed with SET STATUS ON.

SET STEP ON/off

Description. This command is a debugging tool that executes a program line by line, pausing after each task.

Operational rules. After executing a task with SET STEP ON:

```
Press SPACE to Step, S to Suspend, or Esc to Cancel...
```

Execution stops, and the system pauses until one of the three responses are entered.

SET TALK ON/off

Description. SET TALK ON displays the responses of dBASE IV commands.

Operational rules. Memory variables, record numbers, and output from commands like APPEND FROM, COPY, PACK, STORE, and SUM are displayed with TALK ON. It is recommended that SET TALK be ON when working from the dot prompt. In programs, many times this information is not desired output; it is this situation when SET TALK is OFF.

SET TITLE ON/off

Description. SET TITLE controls the catalog file title prompt.

Operational rules. Files are automatically added to the catalog when SET CATALOG is ON. When SET TITLE is ON, a prompt requesting a catalog title appears after creating a file not in the active catalog file.

SET TRAP on/OFF

Description. SET TRAP calls the debugger when an error occurs or when Esc is pressed.

Operational rules. If SET TRAP is ON and there is no ON ERROR condition, when an error occurs or Esc is pressed, program execution stops and the debugger is called.

SET TYPEAHEAD TO <exp>

Description. SET TYPEAHEAD determines the number of keystrokes dBASE IV will save in its buffer. It is useful for fast typists who type faster than a program executes commands.

Operational rules. The numeric expression can be within the range of 0 to 32000. The default setting is 20 characters. SET TYPEAHEAD works only when SET ESCAPE is ON.

SET UNIQUE on/OFF

Description. When SET UNIQUE is ON, only the first record of those with the same key value will be included in index files created.

Operational rules. An index file created while SET UNIQUE was ON will retain its UNIQUE form when reindexed whether SET UNIQUE is ON or OFF. Furthermore, records added to the database file will not be added to the index file if they include a key value already residing in the index file. A UNIQUE index file can be changed to a standard index file by the commands SET UNIQUE OFF, INDEX ON, and to restore the duplicate records, REINDEX.

SET VIEW TO <query>/?

Description. SET VIEW executes a query.

Operational rules. SET VIEW executes a query, a file with the extension control center. The ? argument will call a catalog of query files to the screen.

SET WINDOW OF MEMO TO <window name>

Description. SET WINDOW allows the use of windows to edit memos when using the commands APPEND, BROWSE, CHANGE, EDIT, and READ.

Operational rules. The window name is defined prior to using SET WINDOW via the DEFINE COMMAND.

4

dBASE IV Functions

dBASE IV FUNCTIONS ARE USED WITHIN COMMANDS. EACH FUNCTION RETURNS A value, in the same way that a formula returns a value. There are many functions of many types, but in general they fall into one of the following categories:

string functions
arithmetic functions
date functions
screen handling functions
file handling functions

In this chapter, the functions are listed in alphabetical order. Each function is followed by a short description. Most functions have at least one argument within the parentheses. Variable options are placed in brackets (< >). For instance,

```
ABS(<expN>)
```

shows that a numeric expression must be used as the argument.

&

Description. & is called the macro substitution function. Include it any time that you are using a string memory variable with a command that doesn't expect quotes around the string. Examples of these commands are FIND, USE, and other commands that expect a filename.

This function can also be used for referencing fields or memory variables, because field and variable names do not have quotes around them.

Operational rules. The macro substitution can be used with a character memory variable, or as a prefix or a suffix to a literal string. When the macro is used as a prefix, it must be followed by a period (.) to show where the macro ends and the literal begins.

Examples.

```
.Mfile = "MAILLIST"
.USE &Mfile
```

The first example shows a macro being used with a memory variable to open a file. The macro must be used because otherwise the command would be given as USE Mfile, and dBASE would look for a file named MFILE instead of MAILLIST.

Beginning with dBASE version 4.0, there is another way that you can open a file with a memory variable that is faster than macro substitution. If you begin the filename with the character string of the drive, and/or the directory, you can simply use the memory variable. The following command is valid:

```
USE "C:\" + Mfile
```

The second example shows the function used for referencing fields in a database:

```
. ACCEPT "Enter the field to list:" TO Mfield
Enter the field to list: LNAME
. LIST &Mfield
Smith
Jones
Miller
```

The third example shows the function used as a prefix and a suffix to a literal:

```
. WCH  = "STR"
. MSTR = "Hi There"
. STR1  =  "ByeNow"
. ? M&WCH
Hi There
.? &WCH.1
Bye Now
```

See also: USE *p. 153.*

ABS(<expN>)

Description. ABS displays the positive value of X, whether X is a positive or negative number.

Operational rules. This function can be used to circumvent an ERR from occurring when taking the square root of a negative number, showing the number of days between two dates, or to display a negative number as positive, as in an outstanding balance on a bill.

Examples.

```
. Mem = -64
. ? SQRT(ABS(Mem))
8

. ? ABS({9/9/89} - {12/25/89})
```

See also: SQRT *p. 257.*

ACCESS( )

Description. The ACCESS( ) functions shows the *access level* of the user. Access levels are only used in networked systems. A user's access level is anywhere between 1 and 8. The lower the access level, the more privileges the user has. You set each user's access level with the PROTECT command.

PROTECT is also the command you use to set the privilege schemes that define what each access level may do. There are two types of privileges: file and field.

File privileges assign which access level can delete, append, read, and edit a file. For instance, if your application has two files, Journal.DBF and Accounts.DBF, you can set Journal to have all four privileges at access level 4, but set Accounts to read/only at that level. This way, users that are level 4 can change the Journal file, but only look at the Accounts file. Of course, level 1 is given all privileges on all files.

All levels less than the specified one have the privilege, and all levels greater do not. For instance, if 4 is the UPDATE privilege for the Journal file, 1 through 3 automatically have that privilege, and 5 through 8 do not.

Field privileges are of three types: full, read-only, and none. This allows you to restrict access to certain fields in a database. For instance, even though the file CUSTOMER might have complete file privileges at access level 3, you can set the field named COMMENTS to read-only at that same level.

Operational rules. There are three cases where the ACCESS function returns 0:

- ☐ The system is single-user.
- ☐ The user entered the system without using the login screen.
- ☐ The file DBSYSTEM.DB was not found by dBASE IV during startup.

When writing programs on network systems, it is a good idea to check the access level of the current user in the beginning of the program.

Examples.

```
DO CASE
    CASE ACCESS( ) > 4
      ? "You will be able to look at the fields, but not edit them."
    OTHERWISE
      ?"You will be able to add, update, and delete records."
      ?"Do not abuse this privilege!"
ENDCASE
WAIT
DO Mailedit
```

The program informs the user as to how much file privilege they will have, and keeps out any users with access level 0.

See also NETWORK( ) *p. 230.*
PROTECT *p. 137.*
USER( ) *p. 263.*

ACOS(<expN>)

Description. ACOS(X) returns the arccosine (the inverse cosine) of an angle. This trigonometric function is used in calculating the degrees of an angle when the lengths of two of the sides are known. The RTOD function converts the answer, which is given in radians, to degrees. Therefore, the function RTOD (ACOS(x)) is equal to ACOS(x)*180/P1.

Operational rules. Figure 4-1 shows a circle with points marked in radians (0 to PI) to illustrate the limits of the ACOS and other trigonometric functions. The argument x, must be between -1 and 1. Keeping in mind that the cosine represents the x-axis value at any point, the ACOS function will always return a value between 0 and PI (3.1416).

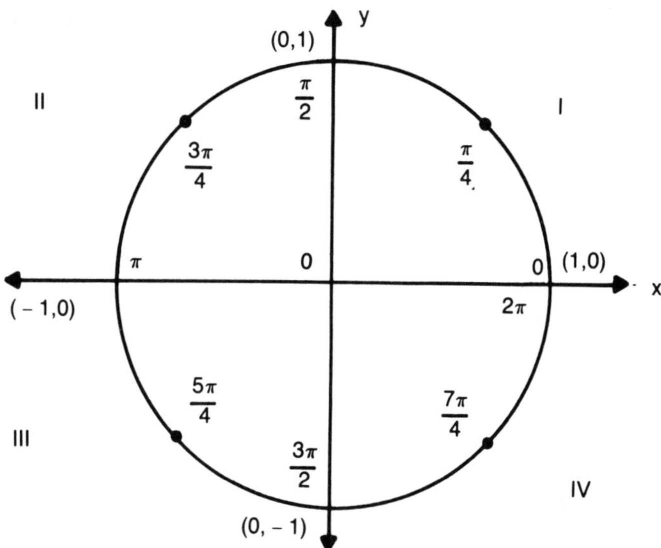

Fig. 4-1. This circle with points marked in radians shows the limits of the ACOS and other trigonometric functions.

If you use memory variables as the argument, the function will then use 20-place numeric accuracy. You can change the number of decimal points displayed in the answer with the SET DECIMALS command.

Examples.

```
.?ACOS(1)
        0

.? RTOD(ACOS(0))
        90
```

See also: ASIN( ) *p. 180.*
COS( ) *p. 189.*
PI( ) *p. 234.*
SET DECIMALS *p. 160.*
SIN( ) *p. 256.*

ALIAS(<expN>)

Description. ALIAS returns the alias name of a specified work area.

Operational rules. Use the IN keyword with the USE command to choose the work area before opening a file. The valid work areas are 1 through 10, or A through J. The filename is the default alias, although you can provide a different one by using the ALIAS keyword with the USE command.

If you do not specify an area when using the ALIAS function, it returns the name of the current work area.

Examples.

```
. USE Journal IN 1
. USE Account IN 2 ALIAS Coa
. ? ALIAS(1)
Journal
. ?ALIAS(2)
COA
```

See also: SELECT *p. 254.*
USE *p. 153.*

ASC(<expC>)

Description. The ASC function is used to show the ASCII number of a character. If the argument is a string of more than one character, the function return the number of the first character of the string.

Each key on a computer keyboard has a number that corresponds to it. These numbers are called ASCII codes (pronounced ASK-key), which stands for American Standard Code for Information Interchange. Almost all microcomputers use the ASCII codes when storing information.

Operational rules. See the CHR( ) section (*p. 185*) for a table of ASCII codes. Following this chart, "A" is number 65, while "a" is number 97. The first 32 numbers represent characters such as the backspace (BS) and escape (ESC) which cannot be entered as a character expression.

Examples.

```
. ?ASC("a")
        97
. Mem = "A"
. ?ASC(Mem)65
```

See also: CHR( ) *p. 185.*

ASIN(<expN>)

Description. ASIN( ) returns the arcsine (the inverse sine) of an angle. This trigonometric function is used in calculating the degrees of an angle when the lengths of two of the sides are known. The RTOD function converts the answer, which is given in radians, to degrees. Therefore, the RTOD(ASIN(x)) is equal to ASIN(x)*180/PI.

Operational rules. The ACOS( ) section shows a circle with points marked in radians. This illustrates the limits of the ASIN function. The argument x, must be between − 1 and 1. Keeping in mind that the sine represents the y − axis value at any point, the ASIN function will always return a value between − PI/2 to PI/2.

If you use memory variables as the argument, the function will then use 20-place numeric accuracy. You can change the number of decimal points displayed in the answer with the SET DECIMALS command.

Examples.

```
? ASIN(PI( ))
          0

? RTOD(ASIN(PI( )))
           90
```

See also: ACOS( ) *p. 178.*
PI( ) *p. 234.*
SET DECIMALS *p. 160.*
SIN( ) *p. 256.*

AT(<expC>, <expC>)

Optional. The optional syntax is AT(<expC>, <expC> or <memofield name>).

Description. The AT function returns the position where one string appears within another.

Operational rules. The arguments are entered as: AT (''substring'', ''string to search''). The function is very useful for finding key words within comments or addresses, or for finding the first space in a full name or address. If the substring does not exist in the string, the function returns 0.

Example.

```
. ? AT("Street","5 Main Street")
          8
```

The example below shows how the AT can be used in conjunction with the SUBSTR function to extract last names from fields that contain both the first and last names. The arguments of the SUBSTR are SUBSTR(*string, start number,n*). Therefore, the function in D1 states, ''extract part of the NAME field, starting at the position of the space, and going until the field ends.''

```
. USE CLIENTS
. LIST OFF NAME
```

```
NAME
John Smith
Bonnie Miller
Tom Jones

. LIST SUBSTR(NAME, AT("    ",NAME))
Smith
Miller
Jones
```

See also: SUBSTR *p. 259.*

ATAN(<expN>)

Description. ATAN ( ) returns the arc tangent (the inverse tangent) of an angle.

Operational rules. This trigonometric function is used in calculating the degrees of an angle when the lengths of two of the sides are known. The RTOD function converts the answer, which is given in radians, to degrees. Therefore, the RTOD(ATAN(x)) is equal to ATAN(x)*180/PI( ).

The tangent represents the sin/cos value at any point on a circle. Therefore, the ATAN function will always return a value between −PI/2 to PI/2, representing a quadrant I or IV angle.

Examples

```
? ATAN(0)
        0            (radians)

? ATAN(1)*180/PI( )
        45           (degrees)
```

See also: COS( ) *p. 189.*
SIN( ) *p. 256.*

ATN2(<expN>, <expN>)

Description. ATN2(X,Y) returns the arc tangent (the inverse tangent) of an angle whose tangent is y/x.

Operational rules. Because both y and x are given, the quadrant can be calculated. Therefore, unlike the ATAN( ) function, the result can be between −PI and PI.

Examples.

```
? ATN2(1,0)
            0        (radians)
```

```
? RTOD(ATN2(1, -1))
        -45        (degrees)
```

See also: ATAN *p. 182.*
RTOD( ) *p. 252.*

BAR( )

Description. BAR( ) returns the bar number of the most recent selection from a pop-up menu.

Operational rules. Each bar in a pop-up menu is numbered using the DEFINE BAR command. BAR( ) will return zero if there is no pop-up menu active.

See also: ACTIVATE POPUP *p. 90.*
DEFINE POPUP *p. 110.*

BOF( )

Optional. The optional syntax is BOF(<alias>or<expn>).

Description. BOF returns a logical true (.T.) when the record pointer is at the top of a file and is then moved one record back. This function is useful in programs where the database is being read in reverse order.

Operational rules. The SKIP command moves the record pointer forward on record, and SKIP -1 moves the pointer backward one record. The top record in a non-indexed file is record number one.The top record in an indexed file is the first record in the index.

The two situations where the BOF ( ) will return .T. are:

- ☐ When the pointer is at the top record, and SKIP -1 is issued.
- ☐ When the top record is being edited, and the user presses PgUp.

If no file is opened in the current work area, BOF( ) returns a logical false (.F.).

The optional alias can be either the alias name, or work area. Work areas are designated from 1 through 10, or A through J.

Examples.

```
. USE MAILLIST
. GOTO TOP
. SKIP -1
. ? BOF( )
.T.

GOTO BOTTOM
DO WHILE .NOT. BOF( )
```

```
? LNAME
SKIP – 1
ENDDO
```

See also: EOF( ) *p.* 197.
SKIP *p.* . .

CALL(<expC>,<expC>

Description. CALL( ) is used to run a binary (assembly language) program from dBASE IV.

Operational rules. CALL( ) performs the same function as the CALL command, except that it is issued as a function. For details regarding this function, see CALL under the commands chapter.

The first argument is the name of the program. The second argument is a memory variable that can be passed to the program and returned with a new value.

See also: CALL *p.* 95.

CDOW(<expD>)

Description. CDOW returns the name of the day, given a date expression.

Operational rules. You can enter a date as an argument in three ways:

Enclose the date in curly brackets: {12/5/89}.
Use the CTOD function: CTOD("12/5/2010").
Use a field name or memory variable.

The date is assumed to be in the 1900s when two digits are used for the year. An invalid date as the argument will generate an error message.

Examples.

```
. CDOW({9/6/60})
  Tuesday
. CDOW(CTOD("12/25/89"))
  Monday
```

See also: CTOD( ) *p.* 189.
DTOC( ) *p.* 195.

CEILING(<expN>)

Description. CEILING returns the argument, rounded up with 0 decimal places. In other words, this function always returns an integer that is greater than the argument, unless the argument is an integer.

Operational rules. If the argument is a negative number, it will return a number closer to zero. This function is useful in cases where must round up all numbers that have decimal places.

Examples.

```
.? CEILING(5.2)
      6
. ? CEILING(5.6)
      6
. ? CEILING(-5.2)
      -5
. ? CEILING(-5.6)
      -5
```

See also: FLOOR( ) *p. 204.*
ROUND( ) *p. 250.*

CERROR( ) (version 1.1 only)

Description. CERROR( ) returns the number of the last compiler-time error.

CHANGE( )

Optional. The optional syntax is CHANGE (<alias>).

Description. CHANGE( ) returns true (.T.) if a record has been changed since the file was opened.

Operational rules. This function is only valid in network environments on files that have been updated with the CONVERT command.

See also: CONVERT *p. 98.*

CHR(<expN>)

Description. CHR( ) shows the character that corresponds to the number in the argument.

Operational rules. Each key on a computer has a number that corresponds to it. These numbers are called ASCII codes (pronounced ASK-key). Almost all microcomputers use ASCII codes when storing information.

The CHR( )function is useful for displaying special characters on the computer and printer, such as graphics characters, the bell tone, and printer control codes.

Table 4-1 shows the codes for the numbers 0 through 127, which are standard among all ASCII computers. Following this chart, you can see that CHR(65) is an "A", while CHR(97) is "a". The first 32 numbers represent characters, such as the backspace (BS)and Escape (Esc), which cannot be printed.

Table 4-1. The standard ASCII codes.

<table>
<tr><td>0 NUL</td><td>16 DLE</td><td>32 SP</td><td>48 0</td><td>64 @</td><td>80 P</td><td>96 '</td><td>112 p</td></tr>
<tr><td>1 SOH</td><td>17 DCI</td><td>33 !</td><td>49 1</td><td>65 A</td><td>81 Q</td><td>97 a</td><td>113 q</td></tr>
<tr><td>2 STX</td><td>18 DC2</td><td>34 "</td><td>50 2</td><td>66 B</td><td>82 R</td><td>98 b</td><td>114 r</td></tr>
<tr><td>3 ETX</td><td>19 DC3</td><td>35 #</td><td>51 3</td><td>67 C</td><td>83 S</td><td>99 c</td><td>115 s</td></tr>
<tr><td>4 DOT</td><td>20 DC4</td><td>36 $</td><td>52 4</td><td>68 D</td><td>84 T</td><td>100 d</td><td>116 t</td></tr>
<tr><td>5 ENQ</td><td>21 NAK</td><td>37 %</td><td>53 5</td><td>69 E</td><td>85 U</td><td>101 e</td><td>117 u</td></tr>
<tr><td>6 ACK</td><td>22 SYN</td><td>38 &</td><td>54 6</td><td>70 F</td><td>86 V</td><td>102 f</td><td>118 v</td></tr>
<tr><td>7 BEL</td><td>23 ETB</td><td>39 '</td><td>55 7</td><td>71 G</td><td>87 W</td><td>103 g</td><td>119 w</td></tr>
<tr><td>8 BS</td><td>24 CAN</td><td>40 (</td><td>56 8</td><td>72 H</td><td>88 X</td><td>104 h</td><td>120 x</td></tr>
<tr><td>9 HT</td><td>25 EM</td><td>41)</td><td>57 9</td><td>73 I</td><td>89 Y</td><td>105 i</td><td>121 y</td></tr>
<tr><td>10 LF</td><td>26 SUB</td><td>42 *</td><td>58 :</td><td>74 J</td><td>90 Z</td><td>106 j</td><td>122 z</td></tr>
<tr><td>11 VT</td><td>27 ESC</td><td>43 +</td><td>59 ;</td><td>75 K</td><td>91 [</td><td>107 k</td><td>123 {</td></tr>
<tr><td>12 FF</td><td>28 FS</td><td>44 ,</td><td>60 <</td><td>76 L</td><td>92 \</td><td>108 l</td><td>124 |</td></tr>
<tr><td>13 CR</td><td>29 GS</td><td>45 -</td><td>61 =</td><td>77 M</td><td>93]</td><td>109 m</td><td>125 }</td></tr>
<tr><td>14 SO</td><td>30 RS</td><td>46 .</td><td>62 ></td><td>78 N</td><td>94 ^</td><td>110 n</td><td>126 ~</td></tr>
<tr><td>15 SI</td><td>31 US</td><td>47 /</td><td>63 ?</td><td>79 0</td><td>95 _</td><td>111 o</td><td>127 DEL</td></tr>
</table>

Therefore the CHR( ) of numbers between 1 and 32 are blank.

```
. ? CHR(65)
A
```

```
. ? CHR(7) + "That answer is invalid, try again." (with a beep)
That answer is invalid, try again.
```

See also: ASC( ) *p. 180.*

CMONTH(<expD>)

Description. CMONTH returns the name of the month, given a date expression.

Operational rules. You can enter a date as an argument in three ways:

- ☐ Enclose the date in curly brackets: {12/5/89}.
- ☐ Use the CTOD function: CTOD("12/5/2010").
- ☐ Reference a field name or memory variable.

The date is assumed to be in the 1900s when two digits are used for the year, otherwise you must enter four digits for the year. An invalid date as the argument will generate an error message.

Examples.

```
. ? CMONTH({9/6/60})
September
```

```
. ? CMONTH(CTOD"12/25/89"))
December
```

See also: CTOD( ) *p. 189.*
DOW( ) *p. 194.*
DTOC( ) *p. 195.*

COL( )

Description. COL( ) returns the current column number position of the cursor.

Operational rules. The COL( ) function is used in conjunction with the @...SAY...GET command that places a display in a particular position on the screen or printed page. The @ command places the display on the screen using the following syntax:

```
@ <row> <col> SAY <expression>
```

For instance, the command

```
@5,30 SAY "HI THERE"
```

would display the words HI THERE on the fifth row on the screen, in column 30. The cursor is then positioned at the end of the expression, so the COL( ) function would return 38 after printing the expression in the example above. This allows you to use the COL( ) function to display an expression on the screen relative to another expression.

Examples. The following program prints a message after the expression Mstring (assuming it is of variable lengths). If Mstring places the cursor too far to the right, the program places the message on the next line, otherwise it is placed right next to Mstring:

```
@ 5,30 SAY Mstring
IF COL( ) > 68
   @5, COL( ) SAY "Y)es or N)o"
ELSE
   @ 6, 30 SAY "Y)es or N)o"
ENDIF
```

This program prints a string continuously until it reaches the end of the screen:

```
DO WHILE COL( ) <75
   @10, COL( ) SAY Mstring
ENDDO
```

The operator $ can also be used with the @...SAY...GET command interchangeably with COL( ). For instance, the following commands are valid:

```
@5,30 SAY Mstring
@5, $ SAY "Y)es or N)o"
```

The difference between COL( ) and $ is that COL( ) can also be used in a conditional statement, as in the two examples given.

See also: PCOL( ) *p. 233.*
PROW( ) *p. 238.*
ROW( ) *p. 251.*

COMPLETED( )

Description. The COMPLETED( ) function returns .T. if all lines of the last transaction were completed successfully.

Operational rules. This function is used in conjunction with the BEGIN TRANSACTION command. When BEGIN TRANSACTION is issued, dBASE creates a log file that tracks all further changes in the file(s). The ROLLBACK command can undo changes in all files changed, or just in selected files.

COMPLETED( ) will return a logical true (.T.) if the last transaction (in the current session) was successful. Otherwise, the command returns logical false (.F.).

The companion function is ROLLBACK( ), which tests whether the ROLLBACK command was performed successfully.

The two most common reasons why a transaction is not completed are:

- ☐ The user pressed Esc while the command(s) were processing.
- ☐ An error occurred during the processing.

Examples.

```
.USE MAILLIST
.LIST FNAME, LNAME

RECNO     FNAME      LNAME
   1      John       Smith
   2      Joe        Brown

BEGIN TRANSACTION
REPLACE ALL LNAME WITH UPPER LNAME
? COMPLETED( )
.T.
```

Next is an example of a program that increases the prices in a file by 10%. The transaction can be aborted in the middle of the process if the user presses Esc (and then chooses Ignore at the prompt), or if an error occurs while the command is running. The program checks whether this has happened.

```
USE PRICES
BEGIN TRANSACTION
```

```
REPLACE ALL PRICE WITH PRICE * 1.1
END TRANSACTION
IF .NOT. COMPLETED ( )
     ? "The prices have been corrupted. Please use the backup"
     ? "Copies from your data disks."
     WAIT
ENDIF
RETURN
```

See also: BEGIN TRANSACTION *p. 93.*
ROLLBACK *p. 143.*

COS(<expN>)

Description. COS returns the cosine of an angle, given in radians.

Operational rules. The cosine represents the x-axis value at any point on a circle, so it will always be between −1 and 1. See the ACOS( ) section for a figure of a circle with quadrants marked.

In Quadrant I: cos(x) decreases from 1 to 0
In Quadrant II: cos(x) decreases from 0 to −1
In Quadrant III: cos(x) increases from −1 to 0
In Quadrant IV: cos(x) increases from 0 to 1

The argument <expN> must be between 0 and 2PI.

Examples.

```
? COS(PI( ))
     0
? COSN(0)
       1
```

Both examples are in radians.

See also: SIN( ) *p. 256.*
TAN( ) *p. 261.*

CTOD(<expC>)

Description. CTOD converts the expression, entered as a string that looks like a date, into a date that can be used for calculations.

Operational rules. Variables that are date type can be used to calculate the difference between two dates. For instance, subtracting 5/1/89 from 5/20/89 will give you 19, the number of days between the two dates. This type of calculation is often used in accounts aging reports and with personnel database applications.

The character expression in the arguments must be MM/DD/YY, unless the format has been changed with SET DATE or SET CENTURY. The date is assumed to be in the 1900s when two digits are used for the year, otherwise you must enter four digits for the year. Any date between January 1, 100, and December 31, 9999, can be used.

Beginning with dBASE version 4.0, you can substitute the curly brackets ({}) for the CTOD function.

Examples.

```
. ? CTOD("12/25/89")  -  CTOD("9/6/89")
110
.?{12/25/89} - {9/6/89}
110
```

The following program used the CTOD function to create a blank date for input with the @...SAY...GET function.

```
Bdate = CTOD(" / / ")
@ 5,1 SAY "Enter Date:" Get Bdate
```

See also: DATE( ) *p. 190.*
DTOC( ) *p. 195.*

DATE( )

Description. DATE returns the system date as a date that can be used for calculations.

Operational rules. Variables that are date type can be used to calculate the difference between two dates. For instance, subtracting 5/1/89 from 5/20/89 will give you 19, the number of days between the two dates.

The system date is kept through DOS, and can be set with the DATE command at the DOS prompt. Many computers come with battery clocks that keep the system date current at all times.

The SET CENTURY and SET DATE commands will change the way that the date is displayed. The default is MM/DD/YY.

Examples.

```
. ? {12/25/89} - DATE()
210
```

The following program uses the DATE( ) function to create a date for input with the @...SAY...GET function:

```
Mdate = DATE()
@ 5,1 SAY "Enter Date:" GET Mdate
```

See also: SET DATE *p. 160.*
SET CENTURY *p. 157.*
CTOD( ) *p. 189.*

DAY(expD)

Description. DAY returns the number of a day of the month, given a date expression.

Operational rules. You can enter a date as an argument three ways:

- ☐ Enclose the date in curly brackets: {12/5/89}.
- ☐ Use the CTOD function: CTOD("12/5/2010").
- ☐ Reference a field name or memory variable.

The date is assumed to be in the 1900s when two digits are used for the year, otherwise you must enter four digits for the year.

Examples.

```
. ? DAY({9/6/89})
6
. ? DAY(CTOD("12/25/89"))
25
```

See also: CTOD( ) *p. 189.*
DOW( ) *p. 194.*
MONTH( ) *p. 229.*

DBF( )

Optional. The optional syntax is DBF(<alias>).

Description. DBF returns the name of the database file in the current work area or a specified work area.

Operational rules. Use the IN keyword with the USE command to choose the work area before opening a file. The valid work areas are 1 through 10, or A through J. The filename is the default alias, although you can provide a different one by using the ALIAS keyword with the USE command.

Examples.

```
.SELECT 1
. USE Journal IN 1
. USE Account IN 2 ALIAS COA
. ? DBF( )
C:JOURNAL.DBF
. ? DBF(COA)
C:COA.DBF
```

See also: USE *p. 153.*
NDX( ) *p. 229.*

DELETED( )

Optional. The optional syntax is DELETED(<alias>).

Description. DELETED returns .T. if the current record in a specified file is marked for deletion.

Operational rules. A record can be marked for deletion in one of two ways:

- ☐ By using the DELETE command.
- ☐ By pressing ^U while in EDIT or BROWSE.

While there are deleted records in a database, the SET DELETED ON command can be used so that all deleted records are ignored when listing, reporting, editing, etc.

Examples.

```
. SELECT 1
. USE Journal
. USE Coa IN 2
. GOTO 5
. ? DELETED( )
.F.
. ? DELETED(COA)
.T.
```

See also: PACK *p. 133.*
RECALL *p. 138.*
SET DELETED *p. 161.*

DIFFERENCE(<expC>, <expC>)

Description. DIFFERENCE returns a number that estimates how much two strings sound alike. The SOUNDEX( ) code (described next) is used to calculate the difference.

Operational rules. In brief the SOUNDEX( ) code is a four-digit code, made up of the following:

- ☐ The first digit is the first character of the string.
- ☐ After the first digit of the string, all occurrences of the letters a,e,h,i,o,u,w, and y are ignored.
- ☐ It assigns a number to the remaining letters. For example, the letters b, f, p, and v equal 1. c,g,j,k,q,s,z, equal 2, and so forth.

For example, the word *humbug,* is coded as H512. Additional rules to soundex coding are described under the SOUNDEX( ) section.

The DIFFERENCE( ) function compares the SOUNDEX codes of two strings. If the SOUNDEX codes are the same, DIFFERENCE returns a 4. If none of the characters in the SOUNDEX codes match, DIFFERENCE returns a 0. Each character in common returns a 1.

Examples.

```
. ? DIFFERENCE("HUMBUG","HAMBURGER")
    3
. ? DIFFERENCE("TINY","LITTLE")
    1
. USE CLIENTS
. LIST Lname FOR DIFFERENCE("BALISTRERI", LNAME) > 3
      4 Balistreros
      8 Balistreri
     10 Balosteri
     20 Balestri
```

See also: SOUNDEX( ) *p. 256.*

DISKSPACE( )

Description. DISKSPACE returns the number of bytes available on the current disk drive.

Operational rules. Certain file operations in dBASE require as much free space on disk as there is room in the file. Two of these functions are the PACK command and the MODIFY STRUCTURE command. Use DISKSPACE( ) before running either of these two commands.

Additional functions that can be used to calculate disk space are RECCOUNT( ) (number of records in the file) and RECSIZE (number of bytes used by each record). When using these functions, keep in mind that the header record uses up an additional 2000 bytes at the top of the file.

The current drive can be changed with the SET DEFAULT TO command.

Examples.

```
IF DISKSPACE( ) < (RECCOUNT( ) * RECSIZE( )) + 2000
   ? "There is not enough room to run the PACK routine"
   WAIT
ELSE
   PACK
ENDIF
```

This example shows a program that checks whether there is room on the disk to run the PACK routine before executing the command.

See also: RECCOUNT( ) *p. 243.*
RECSIZE( ) *p. 245.*

DMY(expD)

Description. DMY converts a date to the character string of DD Month YY, where the month is spelled out.

Operational rules. The DMY conversion shows the day as a one or two digit number, the month is spelled out, and the year is two digits. To show the year as four digits, use the SET CENTURY ON command. For example, the date 5/15/89 would be displayed 15 May 89 in the DMY format.

Examples.

```
. ? DMY({9/6/89})
 6  September 89

. ? DMY(CTOD("12/15/89"))
25 December 89
```

See also: CTOD( ) *p. 189.*

DOW(expD)

Description. DOW returns the numeric value of the day of the week of the date expression.

Operational rules. You can enter a date as an argument three ways:

- ☐ Enclose the date in curly brackets: {12/5/89}.
- ☐ Use the CTOD function: CTOD("12/5/2010").
- ☐ Reference a field name or memory variable.

The DOW will return a number with two decimal places. To change the number of decimals, use the SET DECIMAL TO command.

Examples.

```
. ? DOW( ){12/9/89})
   9.00

. ? This contract, commencing" , CMONTH(DATE( )), STR(DOW(DATE( )),2) . . .
This contract, commencing January 12 . . .
```

See also: CTOD( ) *p. 189.*
DATE( ) *p. 190.*

DTOC(<expD>)

Description. DTOC converts the expression, entered as a date, to a string that looks like a date in MM/DD/YY format.

Operational rules. The date is assumed to be in the 1900s when two digits are used for the year, otherwise you must enter four digits for the year. Any date between January 1, 1000, and December 31, 9999, can be used.

Examples.

```
. ? DTOC(DATE( ))

. HEADING = "Date : " + DTOC(DATE( )) + "                MONTHLY REPORT"
. ? HEADING
Date: 02/20/89                         MONTHLY REPORT"
```

See also: SET DATE *p. 160.*
CTOD( ) *p. 189.*

DTOR(<expN>

Description. DTOR converts a number, representing an angle measured by degrees, into radians.

Operational rules. Fractions of a degree, usually represented by minutes and seconds, must be represented by decimals. For instance, 45 minutes should be depicted as .75 degrees.

The figure in the ACOS( ) section on *p. 178* shows a circle with points marked in radians (0 to PI). This helps illustrate the conversion of degrees to radians.

Use the SET DECIMALS command to change the number of decimals which appear in the answer. The RTOD( ) function is used to conversely change radians to degrees.

Examples.

```
. ? DTOR(50)
   .87

. ? DTOR(PI( )/2)
   .03
```

See also: ACOS( ) *p. 178.*
RTOD( ) *p. 252.*

DTOS(<expD>)

Description. DTOS converts a date to a character expression, but unlike the DTOC function, which returns a character in MM/DD/YY format, the DTOS character can be used for sorting because it is in the format YYYYMMDD.

Operational rules. The DTOS( ) function, introduced in dBASE version 4, is useful when you need to index on both a date and character string added together. The DTOS( ) function will return a character in the YYYYMMDD format regardless of the SET CENTURY COMMAND.

When entering the expression, you can use a field, memory variable, or date entered using {}.

Examples.

```
. ? DTOS({12/25/89})
19891225

. USE CHECKS
. INDEX ON DTOS(Chk_date) + Acct
. LIST Chk_date, Acct
```

Record #	Chk_date	Acct
3	12/27/89	A1001
4	12/27/89	A1001
1	12/27/89	B2000
5	12/29/89	A2001
2	01/03/90	A1005
7	01/03/90	B2002
6	01/05/90	A1001
8	01/05/90	A2001

Notice that the DTOC function could not be used in place of DTOS for this index, because the dates in January would precede the dates in December.

See also: CTOD( ) *p. 189.*
DTOC( ) *p. 195.*

EOF( )

Optional. The optional syntax is EOF(<alias> or <expN>).

Description. EOF returns a logical true (.T.) when the record pointer is at the end of a file and is then moved one more record forward. This function is useful in programs where the database (either indexed or non-indexed) is being read sequentially.

Operational rules. The SKIP command moves the record pointer forward one record. The last record in a non-indexed file is the record number returned by RECCOUNT( ). The last record in an indexed file is the record reached with the command GO BOTTOM. When SKIP is used to go one record past this record, the record number becomes RECCOUNT( ) + 1, and EOF( ) is set to .T.

The two situations where the EOF( ) will return true are:

- ☐ When the pointer is at the bottom record, and SKIP 1 is issued
- ☐ When the bottom record is being edited, and the user presses PgDn

If the pointer is already at the end of file, and the SKIP command is issued again, dBASE returns an End of File Encountered error message.

If no file is opened in the current work area, EOF( ) returns a logical false (.F.).

The optional alias can be either the alias name, or work area. Work areas are designated from 1 through 10, or A through J.

Examples.

```
. USE MAILLIST
. GOTO BOTTOM
. SKIP 1
. ? EOF()
.T.
```

```
GOTO TOP
DO WHILE .NOT. BOF()
    ? LNAME, FNAME
    SKIP 1
ENDDO
```

See also: BOF( ) *p. 183.*
RECCOUNT( ) *p. 243.*
SKIP *p. 147.*

ERROR( )

Description. ERROR returns the number corresponding to the error that has just occurred. The ON ERROR command must be active for this function to work.

Operational rules. The ON ERROR command is given at the beginning of a program, but waits until an error occurs before performing. When ON ERROR is triggered by an error, the command can call a program, a procedure, or a user-defined function. The syntax for the command is ON ERROR <command>.

The ERROR( ) function can be used in conjunction with the program that ON ERROR branches to. The program can display different directions to the user, depending on the error that has occurred. The MESSAGE( ) function can also be helpful in this routine, as it displays the error message that would appear if the ON ERROR( ) command was not present.

If the ON ERROR command is not active, errors in programs display the Cancel, Suspend, Ignore? error message.

To clear the number returned by ERROR( ), use the RETURN or RETRY command.

Examples.

Mailprog.PRG

```
ON ERROR DO Errtrap
USE MAILLIST
SET PRINT ON
DO WHILE .NOT. EOF( )
    ? LNAME, FNAME
    SKIP
ENDDO
```

The program called an error routine command named ERRTRAP.

Errtrap.PRG

```
DO CASE
    SET PRINT OFF
    CASE ERROR( ) = 126 .OR. ERROR( ) = 125
          ? "Please put your printer on line. "
          WAIT
          SET PRINT ON
          RETRY
CASE ERROR( ) = 114
          ? "The index is corrupted, please reindex the file"
          RETURN TO MASTER
```

```
        OTHERWISE
            ? "The following error has occurred: ", MESSAGE( )
            WAIT
            RETURN TO MASTER
    ENDCASE
```

The routine Errtrap checks for a printer error (126 or 125) that signifies that the printer is off-line. If that is the case, the program pauses until the user sets the printer on. Error 114 reports a corrupted index file, so the user is instructed to reindex the file. All other error codes return the user to the main program that called Mailprog.PRG.

See also: ON ERROR *p. 130.*
MESSAGE( ) p. 225.
RETRY *p. 143.*

EXP(<expN>)

Description. The EXP( ) function returns the number e raised to the expN power.

Operational rules. The value of e is approximately 2.7182818. The EXP function is the inverse of the natural logarithm LOG( ). The expN may be a numeric field or memory variable, or the actual value.

Examples.

```
. ? EXP(1)
  2.72

. SET DECIMALS TO 6
. ? EXP(1)
  2.718282
```

See also: SET DECIMALS *p. 160.*
LOG( ) *p. 218.*

FIELD(<expN>)

Optional. The optional syntax is FIELD(<expN>,<alias>).

Description. The FIELD( ) function returns the name of the specified field, designated by the number. Each field is numbered sequentially in the data file structure.

Operational rules. You can see the number of each field when creating, modifying, or displaying the structure. The FIELD( ) returns the name as an uppercase string. If the number in the argument is greater than the number of fields in the database, FIELD( ) returns a null string (""). If no file is opened in the current work area, FIELD( ) returns a null string.

The optional alias can be either the alias name or work area. Work areas are designated from 1 through 10, or A through J.

Examples.

```
.USE MAILLIST
. ? FIELD(1)
LNAME
```

Showfld.PRG

```
SET TALK OFF
USE Maillist
Rnd = 1
DO WHILE ""<> FIELD(Rnd)
    ? FIELD(Rnd)
    RND = Rnd + 1
ENDDO
```

Showfld output

```
LNAME
FNAME
ADD
CITY
ST
ZIP
```

See also: RECSIZE( ) *p. 245.*
RECCOUNT( ) *p. 243.*

FILE(<expC>)

Description. The FILE( ) function returns a logical true (.T.) when a file with the name <expC> exists on the disk. The name is not case sensitive, but the extension must be included.

Operational rules. Unless the drive and directory are entered in the character expression, the function searches the default drive and directory. This is the drive that the user was on when going into dBASE. The default drive can be changed after entering dBASE, using SET DEFAULT, and the default directory can be changed using SET PATH.

Examples.

```
. ? FILE("Maillist.DBF")
.T.
. ? FILE("d:\FILES\Journal.DBF")
.T.
```

Openfile.PRG

```
SET TALK OFF
IF FILE("MAILLIST.DBF")
  USE Maillist
ELSE
  ? "The MAILLIST.DBF file is not found on the disk."
  WAIT
  QUIT
ENDIF
```

See also: SET DEFAULT *p. 160.*
SET PATH *p. 168.*

FIXED(<expN>)

Description. The FIXED( ) function returns a long, real floating point number to a binary coded decimal number (used in machine programming languages).

Operational rules. The expN can be a numeric field or memory variable, or the actual value. dBASE can convert any number between 10^{308} and 10^{-308}.

The FIXED( ) function is the inverse of the function FLOAT( ), which converts from binary to floating point decimal.

See also: FLOAT( ) *p. 202.*

FKLABEL(<expN>)

Description. The FKLABEL( ) returns the name that has been given to the specified function key.

Operational rules. SET FUNCTION (or the full-screen SET command) allows you to program the function keys. You may program 9 function keys (F2 through F10), 9 Shift–function keys, and 10 Ctrl–function keys.

The SET FUNCTION command can be issued one of two ways. The more common is SET FUNCTION <key label>. (For instance, SET FUNCTION F2 TO "Modify Command".) The second way is SET FUNCTION <expN>,. where each key is designated by a number. (For instance, SET FUNCTION 1 TO "Modify Command".) The FKLABEL( ) function returns the function key assigned to each number.

The F1 key is not assignable, because it is used as the HELP key. Therefore, the numbers start with F2 = 1, F3 = 2, and so forth.

Examples.

```
. ? FKLABEL(1)
F2
```

See also: SET FUNCTION *p. 165.*

FKMAX( )

Description. The FKMAX( ) returns the number of keys on the current keyboard that can be programmed.

Operational rules. SET FUNCTION (or the full-screen SET command) allows you to program the function keys. The maximum number of programmable keys is 28: 9 function keys (F2 through F10), 9 Shift–function keys, and 10 Ctrl–function keys. Function keys F11 and F12 are not programmable through dBASE.

This command is used primarily with applications that are not going to be run on typical IBM-compatible keyboards.

Examples.

```
. ? FKMAX( )
28
```

See also: SET FUNCTION *p. 165.*

FLOAT(<expN>)

Description. The FIXED( ) function returns a binary coded decimal number (used in machine programming languages) converted from a long, real floating point number.

Operational rules. The expN can be a numeric field or memory variable or the actual value (type N). dBASE can convert any number between 10^{308} and 10^{-308}.

The FLOAT( ) function is the inverse of FIXED( ), which converts from floating point decimal to binary.

See also: FIXED ( ) *p. 201.*

FLOCK( )

Optional. The optional syntax is FLOCK(<alias> or <expN>).

Description. The FLOCK( ) function performs a file lock on a database file.

Operational rules. The FLOCK( ) function locks all records in a database, so that other users cannot make any updates to the file. File locking is only performed on multi-user systems running on networks.

When the SET LOCK command is on, many commands automatically lock the file without using FLOCK( ). Some commands lock the file regardless of whether the SET LOCK is on or off. These commands include: APPEND FROM, REPLACE <scope>, DELETE <scope>, and UPDATE. See the SET LOCK section for a list of all commands that explicitly lock the file, and/or records.

The FLOCK( ) function is still useful, however, because it can be used to check whether the file is currently locked, and it can lock the file before issuing the command. FLOCK( ) returns a logical false (.F.) if the file is already locked.

Although a locked file cannot be updated by other users, it can be opened on a read-only basis.

FLOCK( ) will lock the current file, unless an argument is provided. The optional alias can be either the alias name or work area. Work areas are designated from 1 through 10, or A through J.

You can unlock a file three ways:

- ☐ Use the UNLOCK command.
- ☐ Close the file with the USE or CLOSE command.
- ☐ Quit dBASE.

FLOCK( ) will return a logical true (.T.) and lock the file, if the file is not currently locked. On single-user systems, FLOCK( ) always returns true (.T.). The RLOCK( ) function is used to lock records in a database.

If relationships have been set with other files, these other files will also be locked. Once you unlock one of the related files, all others will be unlocked also.

Examples.

```
USE Maillist
IF .NOT. FLOCK( )
     ? "This process cannot be run now, because the file is locked."
     ? "Try again later."
     WAIT
     RETURN
ENDIF
DELETE FOR Active = "N"
PACK
```

This program checks whether a file is locked before running a command which will automatically lock the file.

This variation on the program will keep attempting to lock the file if it finds it locked to begin with. After 1000 attempts, it will return to the master if unsuccessful.

```
USE Maillist
SET REPROCESS TO 1000
IF .NOT. FLOCK( )
    ? "This process cannot be run now, because the file is locked.
    "Try again later.".
    WAIT
    RETURN
ENDIF
```

See also: SET LOCK *p. 167.*
SET REPROCESS *p. 170.*
UNLOCK *p. 152.*
RLOCK( ) *p. 247.*

FLOOR(<expN>)

Description. FLOOR returns the argument, rounded down to 0 decimal places. In other words, this function always returns an integer that is less than or equal to the argument.

Operational rules. This function is useful in cases where you must round down all numbers that have decimal places. Negative numbers will return a number less than the argument by rounding to the next smaller number.

Examples.

```
. ? FLOOR(5.2)
         5
. ? FLOOR(5.6)
         5
. ? FLOOR(-5.2)
        -6
. ? FLOOR(-5.6)
        -6
```

See also: CEILING( ) *p. 184*
ROUND( ) *p. 250.*

FOUND( )

Optional. The optional syntax is FOUND(<alias> or <expN>).

Description. The FOUND( ) function returns a logical .T. if the most recent positioning command (FIND, SEEK, LOCATE, or CONTINUE) was successful.

Operational rules. The FOUND( ) function can be used at the dot prompt or in programs, to show whether a record that matches the search criteria has been found. All of the positioning commands move the record pointer to the first record that matches the criteria. The FIND and SEEK commands require the database to be indexed on the search criteria, and are much faster than the LOCATE command.

FOUND( ) will return the search status of the current file, unless an argument is provided. The optional argument can be either the alias name, or work area. Work areas are designated from 1 through 10, or A through J.

When searching for a record, the entire key field does not have to match. For instance, the command SEEK "SM" will find the first occurrence of a name beginning with SM (for instance, SMITH). The SET EXACT ON command turns off this ability to check only the number of characters in the comparison string. With the EXACT on, the criteria must be the exact length of the key field(s) in question. For instance, if the Last Name field is a length of 12 characters, only SEEK "SMITH   " will return FOUND( ).

Examples.

```
USE Maillist
LOCATE FOR Lname = "SMITH"
? FOUND()
    .T.
CONTINUE
? FOUND()
    .F.
```

These commands perform a search on a non-indexed file. In the first example, only one record matches the criteria. The following program performs a search and edit on an indexed file:

```
USE Maillist INDEX Mailname
ACCEPT "Enter Name to edit" TO Mname
SEEK Mname
IF FOUND()
   EDIT
ELSE
   ? "Name not found"
   WAIT
ENDIF
```

See also: CONTINUE *p. 97.*
FIND *p. 118.*
LOCATE *p. 126.*
SEEK *p. 147.*

FV(<payment>,<rate>,<term>)

Description. The FV( ) function returns the future value of fixed periodic payments with a compounded interest rate. This is the function that will answer the question, "If I put $250 a month in an account that pays 10 percent interest, how much will I have at the end of 10 years?"

Operational rules. As with all of the dBASE financial functions, keep in mind that if the rate is given as an annual percentage rate (as it most often is), and the periods are monthly (as they most often are), then the interest rate must be divided by 12, and the term must be in months (years time 12).

Payments are assumed to be made at the end of each period. The formula to calculate the future value if the payments are made at the beginning of each period is:

```
FV(pmt,rate,term) * (1 + rate)
```

The term must be at least one. The following formula is used to calculate the future value:

```
pmt *(((1 + rate) ^term) – 1/rate)
```

Examples.

```
.? FV (250,.1/12,10*12)
      51,211.24
```

See also: PAYMENT( ) *p. 232.*
PV( ) *p. 239.*

GETENV(<expC>)

Description. The GETENV( ) returns the status of current DOS settings such as PATH, PROMPT, and COMPSPEC.

Operational rules. DOS has a group of commands that change the DOS working environment. These commands include PROMPT, which changes the appearance of the DOS system prompt, and PATH, which tracks the subdirectories that should be searched when a command is issued. Your DOS manual has a list of these commands. They are often automatically issued through the AUTOEXEC.BAT file.

The argument must be given as a string or string variable. It may be uppercase or lowercase, but must match the particular DOS system command.

Examples.

```
? GETENV("PATH")
C:\;C:\DOS;C:\WP
```

The function in the example checks the existing path set up in the DOS working environment.

See also: OS( ) *p. 231.*

IIF(<condition>,<x>,<y>)

Description. The IF( ) function tests a condition, returning x if the condition is true, and y if the condition is false.

Operational rules. A simple explanation of this function is to use the English translation, "If this condition is True, do this (x), otherwise do this (y)." The condition must be a logical formula, or logical variable.

Conditional statements will usually use one or more of the following operators:

=	equal
<	less than
< =	less than or equal
>	greater than
> =	greater than or equal
< >	not equal
$	substring search
.AND.	both conditions must be true
.OR.	either condition can be true

For instance, IIF (Sex = "F", "FEMALE","MALE") states, "If the variable Sex equals F, then display FEMALE, otherwise display MALE."

The expressions, x and y can be character, numeric, logical, or date. However, both expressions must be of the same type.

The IIF( ) function can save you space in your programs, because in one line it can take the place of the five-line IF-ELSE-ENDIF command. However, in many cases the IF command must be used, because the IIF( ) function cannot be used to issue commands based on a condition. Following is an example of the IF command replaced by the one-line IIF( ) function.

```
IF Results = "P"
   ? "Positive"
```

```
ELSE
   ? "Negative"
ENDIF
```

or as an IIF function:

```
? IIF (Results = "P","Positive","Negative")
```

The IIF function can also be used in the contents of a report created with the report generator, or a label created with the label generator.

In instances where more than two conditions must be run, you can nest IIF( ) functions. An example is a grading application where (in English): "If score >= 90, then return A, otherwise, if score >= 80, then return B, otherwise return a C." (In this case, "C" is the lowest grade possible.) The comparable dBASE function for this case is:

```
IIF(Score >= 90, "A",IIF(Score >= 80, "B","C"))
```

Examples.

`IIF(Grade > 70, "PASS","FAIL")` (contents of a report column)

```
? IIF(Sex = "M","Male",IIF(Sex = "F","Female",""))

Tax = IIF(State = "CA" .AND. Taxable = "Y",Price*.06,0)
```

See also: IF *p. 120.*

INKEY( )

Optional. The optional syntax is INKEY(<expN>).

Description. INKEY( ) returns a number that represents the most recent key pressed on the keyboard. Unlike the INKEY function in some other programming languages such as BASIC, the dBASE INKEY does not pause and wait for the user to type something unless the optional argument is used.

Operational rules. When the INKEY( ) function is used, the key that the user presses is not displayed on the screen, as with all other interactive commands. Also, INKEY( ) can detect the exact keystroke pressed, such as a Ctrl key combination or an arrow key, unlike the other commands.

If the user has typed several characters, the INKEY( ) function returns the first character in the type-ahead-buffer, and removes it from the buffer.

The optional numeric argument determines how long INKEY( ) will pause to receive the keystroke. If there is no argument, INKEY reads the most recent key pressed.

INKEY does not return the values of Alt function key combinations because these keystrokes are handled by the macro interpreter.

For values 0 through 255, the number is the ASCII value that corresponds to the keystroke. Function keys and their Ctrl and Shift combinations are represented by negative numbers. Alt key combinations with letters are also negative, and there is no differentiation between uppercase and lowercase with Alt keys.

If the key pressed is between 40 and 126, the CHR( ) function of the INKEY will display the character pressed. For instance, the function

```
CHR(INKEY(20))
```

will return the letter "A" if uppercase A (INKEY value 65) is pressed.

Examples.

```
Pressed = INKEY(20)
DO CASE
        CASE Pressed = 5
            ? "Going UP!"

        CASE Pressed = 24
            ? "Going DOWN!"

     Otherwise
            ? "Please press the up or down arrow!"
ENDCASE
```

The program pauses and waits for the user to press a key. The program responds with three different displays depending if the up arrow, down arrow, or other key is pressed.

See also: ON KEY *p. 130.*
CHR( ) *p. 185.*
READKEY( ) *p. 241.*

INT(<expN>)

Description. The INT( ) function returns the numeric expression, truncated at the decimal point.

Operational rules. The INT( ) function ignores all numbers that are right of the decimal point, and returns the integer value of the number. To round numbers to zero decimal places, use the ROUND( ) function with zero decimal places. The INT(5.6) is equal to 5, while the ROUND(5.6,0) is equal to 6.

Examples.

```
. ? INT(5.2)
       5
. ? INT(5.6)
       5
```

```
. ? INT(-5.6)
        -5
```

See also: CEILING( ) *p. 184.*
FLOOR( ) *p. 204.*
ROUND( ) *p. 250.*

ISALPHA(<expC>)

Description. The ISALPHA( ) function returns logical true (.T.) if the character expression in the argument begins with a letter.

Operational rules. The ISALPHA( ) function returns true if the first character of the string is an uppercase or lowercase letter, a through z. All other cases return logical false (.F.)

The function that tells whether a variable is a character string or a numeric (or other type), is the TYPE( ) function.

Examples.

```
ACCEPT "Enter a name or record number" TO Search
IF ISALPHA(Search)
    SEEK Search
ELSE
    GOTO VAL(Search)
ENDIF
EDIT
```

The program allows the user to edit a record. The user can pull up the record by entering the record number, or a last name for seeking. The ISALPHA( ) functions checks whether the first character of the seek string begins with a letter or a number. If it is a number, the GOTO <record number> command is used, otherwise a SEEK is performed.

See also: TYPE( ) *p. 262.*

ISCOLOR( )

Description. The ISCOLOR( ) function returns logical true (.T.) if the computer has the ability to display color.

Operational rules. The ISCOLOR( ) function checks whether the computer has a color graphics adapter. This function can be used in programs that will be run on several computers. By checking if ISCOLOR is true, the program can set screen colors on or leave them off. The command to change the colors is SET COLOR TO.

There is one problem with changing the colors even if a color graphics adapter is present. Sometimes the computer will have the adapter, but not a color terminal. In these cases, when the colors are turned on, the screen can become unreadable.

Examples.

```
IF ISCOLOR( )
   ACCEPT "Can this console display colors?" TO Colorit
   IF UPPER(Colorit) = "Y"
      SET COLOR TO G/B, GR+/N
   ENDIF
ENDIF
```

The program checks whether there is a color adapter. If there is, it then asks the user whether the console is a color console (in case there is a monochrome console on a color graphics computer).

See also: SET COLOR *p. 158.*

ISLOWER(<expC>)

Description. The ISLOWER( ) function returns logical true (.T.) if the character expression in the argument begins with a lowercase letter.

Operational rules. The ISLOWER( ) function returns true if the first character of the string is a lowercase letter, a through z. All other cases return logical false (.F.)

Example.

```
? ISLOWER("John")
.F.
. ? ISLOWER("john")
.T.
. ? ISLOWER("")
.F.
. ? ISLOWER("55")
.F.
```

See also: ISUPPER( ) *p. 212.*

ISMARKED( )

Optional. The optional syntax is ISMARKED(<alias> or <expN>).

Description. The ISMARKED( ) function checks whether a file is currently being used in a transaction.

Operational rules. The ISMARKED( ) returns logical true if the database is currently marked as being in the middle of a transaction. The only way to mark a database file this way is with the BEGIN TRANSACTION command.

When the BEGIN TRANSACTION command is given, dBASE places a mark in the database header record. This mark is not released until the END TRANSACTION command has been issued. The BEGIN TRANSACTION command is like the file locking commands, in that it marks a file as being updated, but unlike the file locking commands in that:

- ☐ At any time during the transaction, it can be aborted with the ROLLBACK command.
- ☐ The file can be marked sooner that with the commands that implicitly lock a file, such as APPEND FROM or UPDATE.

ISMARKED( ) will lock the current file, unless an argument is provided. The optional alias can be either the alias name or work area. Work areas are designated from 1 through 10, or A through J.

ISMARKED( ) will return a logical true (.T.), if the file is currently marked. When a file is marked, commands such as PACK, MODIFY STRUCTURE, and REPLACE are not allowed and will return an error 108 or 109. Command that do not alter the file, such as COPY TO <filename> and TOTAL, are allowed.

Examples.

```
USE Maillist
IF ISMARKED( )
    ? "This process cannot be run now, because the file is being"
    ? "used in a transaction. Try again later."
    WAIT
    RETURN
ENDIF
DELETE FOR Active = "N"
PACK
```

This program checks whether a file is marked for a transaction before running a command that will automatically lock the file!

See also: BEGIN TRANSACTION *p. 93.*
ROLLBACK *p.143.*

ISUPPER(<expC>)

Description. The ISUPPER( ) function returns logical true (.T.) if the character expression in the argument begins with a uppercase letter.

Operational rules. The ISUPPER( ) function returns true if the first character of the string is an uppercase letter, A through Z. All other cases return logical false (.F.).

Examples.

```
. ? ISUPPER("John")
.T.
. ? ISUPPER("john")
.F.
. ? ISUPPER("")
.F.
```

See also: ISLOWER( ) *p. 211.*

KEY(<expN>)

Optional. The optional syntax is KEY(<expN>,<alias>) or KEY(<.mdx filename>,<expN>) or KEY (<expC>).

Description. The KEY( ) function returns the expression that the specified index file was keyed on.

Operational rules. KEY( ) returns the key expression of the current index file. This is the same expression displayed in DISPLAY STATUS.

KEY( ) will display for the numbered index of the current file, unless an argument is provided. The optional alias can be either the alias name or work area. Work areas are designated from 1 through 10, or A through J.

See also: ORDER( ) *p. 231.*

LASTKEY( )

Description. LASTKEY( ) returns a number that represents the most recent key pressed on the keyboard in response to an interactive command.

Operational rules. LASTKEY( ), like the INKEY( ) function, can detect the exact keystroke pressed (such as a Ctrl key combination, or an arrow key), unlike other interactive commands such as READ and ACCEPT.

The LASTKEY function is different than INKEY( ), however, in that it reads the key pressed in the last interactive command (such as READ, or ACCEPT), while INKEY( ) pauses to receive the keystroke (or captures it during a non-interactive command). The READKEY( ) function, which also captures keystrokes, is different in that it is only used with full screen commands, and it returns a different value depending on whether data was changed or not.

For a list of the LASTKEY values, see the INKEY section. For values 0 through 255 the number is the ASCII value that corresponds to the keystroke.

Function keys and their Ctrl, Shift and Alt combinations are represented by negative numbers.

Examples.

```
*    Mailing List Program
PRN = "P"
ZSORT = "A"
@ 1,1 SAY "Press ESC to Return to Main Menu"
@ 3,1 SAY "Display on Printer or Screen? (P/S) " GET PRN
@ 5,1 SAY "Sort by Zip or Alpha? (A/Z) " GET ZSORT
READ
IF LASTKEY() = 27
     CLEAR
     ? " Returning to Master Menu"
     RETURN
ENDIF
DO MAILLIST
```

The program instructs the user to press Escape to abort the program and return to the main menu. The LASTKEY function reads whether that key was pressed. The following keys (and their LASTKEY values) can be used to exit a full screen command without the user having to press Enter through each field: PgDn (3), PgUp (18), Ctrl–End (23), and Esc (27).

See also: ON KEY *p. 130.*
INKEY( ) *p. 208.*
READKEY( ) *p. 241.*

LEFT(<expC>,<expN>)

Description. The LEFT( ) function returns the first <expN> letters of a string.

Operational rules. The LEFT( ) function returns a substring of <expC>. This can be helpful in retrieving first initials of names, or printing variables on forms where there is not enough room for the entire string to print. There is no difference between the LEFT( ) function and the SUBSTR(string,start-number,length) function where the start-number is 1.

If the number <expN> is larger than the length of the string, the result will be the string itself. If the number is 0, the function will return the null string.

dBASE IV, unlike previous versions, allows you to perform the LEFT( ) function on a memo field.

Example.

```
? LEFT("California",5)
Calif

? LEFT("California",0)
                        (a null string)

MM = "11-Nov-89"
? LEFT(MM,2)
11

? LEFT("Hello",9)
Hello
```

See also: SUBSTR( ) *p. 259.*
RIGHT( ) *p. 246.*

LEN(<expC>)

Description. The LEN function returns the number of letters in a string.

Operational rules. The LEN( ) function is often used with coding schemes such as product codes, where codes of one length are treated differently than codes of another length. LEN( ) can also be used to check data entry that should be a certain length, such as zip codes or employee numbers.

A null string returns the length of 0. The LEN( ) of a database field will always be the length of the field itself. To calculate the length of the entry, take the LEN( ) function of the TRIM( ) of the field.

dBASE IV, unlike previous versions, allows you to perform the LEN( ) function on a memo field. LEN( ) returns the exact length of the memo field entry without having to use the TRIM( ) function.

Example.

```
? LEN("John")
        4
```

The following example assumes that Lname is the name of a field that is 25 characters long:

```
? Lname
Smith

? LEN(Lname)
       25
```

```
? LEN(RTRIM(Lname))
          5
```

See also: TRIM( ) *p. 253.*

LIKE(<expC>,<expC>)

Description. LIKE returns a .T. if the two character expressions match. The first expression, however, can contain wild card operators.

Operational rules. The first character expression can include any combination of the two wildcards:

- * represents any group of characters
- ? represents any one character

For instance, the string SM?TH represents SMITH, SMOTHERS, SMITHSONIAN, and SMYTHE.

Unlike DOS, which uses the same wildcard operators, the asterisk (*) can be placed anywhere within the string. DOS only allows the asterisk at then end of the string. For instance, SM*TH represents both SMITH and SMOOTH.

The LIKE( ) function returns logical true (.T.) if the two strings match. The function is case sensitive, so SM?TH will not match Smith. The SOUNDEX( ) function is like this function, except it compares the SOUNDEX codes attributed to each character expression to estimate how much the two strings sound alike.

Examples.

```
? LIKE("Go?f*","Golfing")
.T.
? LIKE("GO?F*","GOOFIER")
.T.
? LIKE("GO?F?","GOOFIEST")
.F.
? LIKE("Go?f*","GOOFIER")
.F.

. USE Clients
. LIST LNAME, FNAME FOR LIKE("J*NSON*",LNAME)
      4 JOHNSON   JILL
      8 JONSON    JANE
     10 JANSONS   JAMES
     20 JENSON    JULIE
```

See also: SOUNDEX( ) *p. 256.*

LINENO( )

Description. LINENO returns the number of the next line of a program that is about to occur.

Operational rules. The LINENO( ) function is useful with the ON ERROR command and the DEBUG window. Use LINENO( ), the error routine can display the line number where the error occurred.

DEBUG is a full-screen environment that can be displayed while running a program. DEBUG displays a variety of information, and can be very helpful in catching programming errors. When the LINENO( ) functions is used in the Breakpoint window of the DEBUG environment, control is returned to the debug window at the bottom of the screen.

Examples.

```
Mailprog.PRG
ON ERROR DO Errtrap
USE Maillist
DO While .NOT. EOF( )
      ? Lname, Fname
      SKIP
ENDDO
```

The program calls an error routine command named ERRTRAP.

```
Errtrap.PRG
CLEAR
? "An error has just occurred. The error is:",MESSAGE( )
? "and it occurred on line", LINENO( )
WAIT
RETURN TO MASTER
```

The routine Errtrap is automatically called any time an error occurs. The MESSAGE( ) function displays the error message, while LINENO( ) shows the line number that the error occurred in. The user then returns to the main program that called Mailprog.PRG.

See also: DEBUG *p. 107.*
ON ERROR *p. 130.*

LOCK( )

Description. For a full description, see RLOCK( ) *p. 247.*

LKSYS(<expN>)

Description. The LKSYS function returns information regarding the user who has locked the the current record.

Operational rules. The argument <expN> can be 0, 1, or 2. Zero returns the time of the lock, one returns the date, and two returns the name of the user.

This function will return a null string if the database file has not been converted to multi-user status. This function is useful when a record is locked and you want to get information about who locked it and when.

See also: RLOCK( ) *p. 247.*

LOG(<expN>)

Description. The LOG function returns the number e base x, or natural logarithm.

Operational rules. e is approximately 2.7182818. The LOG( ) function returns e^x or, in English: e, raised to the x power. A zero or negative value will return an error message. The EXP( ) function is the inverse of the natural logarithm.

Examples.

```
. ? LOG(5)
    1.61

. ? LOG(-5)
  you get an appropriate error message

. ? LOG(2.7182818)
    1.02
```

See also: EXP( ) *p. 199.*

LOG10(<expN>)

Description. The LOG10( ) function returns the base 10 exponent of the numeric expression x. This is called the command logarithm.

Operational rules. The LOG10( ) function returns x in the formula <expN> = $1.0^{<x>}$ For instance, the logarithm of 100 is 2, because 10^2 is 100.

A zero or negative value will return an error message.

Examples.

```
. ? LOG10(5)
    0.70

. ? LOG10(100)
    2.00
```

To calculate the antilog of an expression:

```
Mem = LOG10(3) + LOG10(3)
  .95
. ? 10^Mem
  9
```

See also: EXP( ) *p. 199.*

LOWER(<expC>)

Description. The LOWER( ) function converts all the letters in a string to lowercase letters.

Operational rules. The companion function is UPPER( ), which converts all letters in the expression to uppercase. Numbers and other nonalphabetical characters are not affected.

Examples.

```
? LOWER("Hello")
hello
? LOWER("HELLO")
hello
```

To convert a string to proper case (first letter uppercase, and all other letters lowercase):

```
Fname = "JOHN"
? UPPER(LEFT(Fname,1)) + LOWER(SUBSTR(Fname,2))
John
```

The following program converts a field (or memory variable) that contains more than one word to uppercase. This is useful in converting databases where the addresses or cities have been entered in all uppercase letters:

Proper.prg

```
Mcity = "SAN JUAN CAPRISTANO"
Mcity = Trim(Mcity) + " "
Newc = " "
Do WHILE .T.
   Mfind = AT(" ", (Mcity))
   Newc = Newc + UPPER(LEFT(Mcity,1)) +
   LOWER(SUBSTR(Mcity,2,Mfind – 1))
   IF Mfind = LEN(Mcity)
      EXIT
```

```
    ENDIF
    Mcity = SUBSTR(Mcity,Mfind+1)
ENDDO
? Newc
```

The pseudocode for this program is:

1. Add a one space to the end of the string Mcity.
2. Create a null string memory variable named Newc.
3. Set Newc to Newc + the upper of the first character of Mcity + the lower of the characters up to the first space.
4. Take off the characters up to and including the first space in Mcity.
5. Repeat steps 3 and 4 until there is only one space left in Mcity.

See also: SUBSTR( ) *p. 259.*
UPPER( ) *p. 262.*

LTRIM(<expC>)

Description. The LTRIM( ) function removes all leading spaces from a string.

Operational rules. The companion function is TRIM( ), which removes all trailing blanks from an expression. The LTRIM( ) function is often used to trim off leading spaces created by the STR( ) function which converts numbers to a character string.

Examples.

```
? LTRIM("   Hello")
Hello

? LEN(TRIM(LTRIM("   Hello   ")))
       5

Donation = 500
? "Thank you for the donation of $" + LTRIM(STR(Donation)) + " to us."
  Thank you for the donation of $500 to us.
```

See also: RTRIM( ) *p. 253.*
STR( ) *p. 258.*

LUPDATE( )

Optional. The optional syntax is LUPDATE(<alias> or <expN>).

Description. The LUPDATE( ) function returns the date that the file was last updated.

Operational rules. The LIST FILES command shows the last date that a database file was updated (as well as the number of records and byte size of the database). The DIR command from DOS shows the same date.

Because the date is based on the DOS system date, the computer must have a battery clock, or the date must be set with the DATE command. Otherwise, the date will reflect the DOS BIOS date, which is January 1, 1980 in many computers.

LUPDATE( ) will return the last update date of the current file, unless an argument is provided. The optional alias can be either the alias name or work area. Work areas are designated from 1 through 10, or A through J. If no file is open in the designated area, LUPDATE( ) returns a blank date.

Examples.

```
USE Maillist
? "This file was last updated on ", LUPDATE()
WAIT
DO Mailedit
```

This program displays the last date that the file was updated, and verifies it with the user, before continuing the program.

See also: DBF( ) *p. 191.*
RECCOUNT( ) *p. 243.*

MAX(<exp>,<exp>)

Description. The MAX( ) function compares two expressions and returns the larger value. The two arguments may be numeric, character, or date.

Operational rules. The MAX ( ) is equivalent to the following IIF( ) function:

```
IIF(<exp1> > <exp2>, <exp1> , <exp2>)
```

When the arguments are dates, the later date is considered greater. When the arguments are strings, its value is designated by its ASCII code value. Therefore, "S" is greater than "A", and "a" is greater than "Z".

To calculate the maximum value of a field in a dBASE file, use the MAX argument of the CALCULATE command.

Examples.

```
MAX_wage = 45000
Income = 60000
? MAX(Max_wage,Income)
   60000
```

```
? MAX("Apple","Banana")
Banana
```

```
? MAX("Pear","banana")
banana
```

The following function will display 12/25/89 until the system date is set to a date later than December 25, 1989:

```
? MAX(DATE( ),{12/25/89})
12/25/89
```

See also: MIN( ) *p. 226.*

MDX(<expN>)

Optional. The optional syntax is MDX(<expN>,<alias>).

Description. MDX returns the name of the multiple index file in the current work area or a specified work area. The argument <expN> designates the index order number.

Operational rules. A multiple index file is created with the INDEX ON command, in conjunction with the TAG keyword. Multiple indexes end with the extension .MDX, and can maintain up to 47 different key expressions. Each expression must be given a tag name. Tag names follow the convention of field names (up to 10 characters, etc.).

Each index file is given an order number, depending on the order that it was opened in, with the first file in the list being the master index. The SET ORDER TO command can be used to change the order of currently opened index files.

MDX( ) will return the name of appropriately numbered index in the current file, unless a second argument is provided. The optional alias can be either the alias name or work area. Work areas are designated from 1 through 10, or A through J. If no file is open in the designated area, or multiple index in the specified numeric order, MDX( ) returns a null string.

See also: SET ORDER TO *p. 168.*
USE *p. 153.*
DBF( ) *p. 191.*
NDX( ) *p. 229.*

MDY(<expD>)

Description. MDY converts the expression, entered as a date, to a string that looks like a date in the written format Month Day, Year (such as September 16, 1989).

Operational rules. The character string returned by the MDY function will only show two digits for the year, unless the SET CENTURY command is ON.

You can enter a date as an argument three ways:

- ☐ Enclose the date in curly brackets: {12/5/89}.
- ☐ Use the CTOD function: (CTOD("12/5/2010").
- ☐ Reference a field name or memory variable.

The date is assumed to be in the 1900s when two digits are used for the year, otherwise you must enter four digits for the year. Any date between January 1, 100, and December 31, 9999 can be used.

Examples.

```
. ? MDY(DATE( ))
September 16, 89
. SET CENTURY ON
. ? MDY({09/16/89})
September 16, 1989

. HEADING = "Date: " + MDY(Repdate) "        MONTHLY REPORT"
. ? HEADING
Date: February 20, 1989        MONTHLY REPORT
```

See also: SET CENTURY *p. 157.*
CTOD( ) *p. 189.*
DATE( ) *p. 190.*

MEMLINES(< memo field >)

Description. MEMLINES returns the number of lines in a the memo of the current record.

Operational rules. The argument is the name of the memo field and can include an alias. MEMLINES( ) returns the number of lines of the memo at the current record, so the pointer must be set at the desired record.

The command SET MEMOWIDTH TO determines the width of the memo display. dBASE automatically word wraps the memo according to the MEMOWIDTH. The default is 50 characters. When the memowidth is changed, the memo is automatically displayed with the new margin, so the MEMLINES( ) might also change.

Notice that the argument is not a character expression. It is the name of a field, so it does not have to be surrounded by quotes. Therefore, if you are using a memory variable as the expression, you can use the macro substitution sign (&).

Example.

```
USE MAILLIST
. ? Comments
   Joe's Garage is one of our happiest clients.
They may always be used as a referral, although try not to give their name out more
than once a month.

. ? MEMLINES(Comments)
4
. SET MEMOWIDTH TO 30
    Joe's Garage is one of
our happiest clients. They may
always be used as a referral,
although try not to give their
name out more than once a
month.

 . ? MEMLINES(Comments)
6
 . Mfield = "Comments"
 . ? MEMLINES(&Mfield)
6
```

See also: SET MEMOWIDTH *p. 167.*

MEMORY( )

Optional. The optional syntax is MEMORY(0).

Description. MEMORY returns the number of RAM that is available in the current application.

Operational rules. The MEMORY( ) function returns the amount of RAM available in units of 1,024 bytes (or 1 kilobyte). For instance, a MEMORY( ) of 5 is equal to 5 kilobytes, or 5125 RAM.

The three instances where dBASE might need additional RAM are when:

- ☐ Applications use menus and windows.
- ☐ Extra memory must be allocated for some arrays.
- ☐ The RUN/! command, which loads COMMAND.COM, needs an additional 25 kilobytes of memory.

The optional argument of 0 does not affect the MEMORY( ) function, the companion function to MEMORY( ) is DISKSPACE, which returns the disk space available.

Example.

```
. ? MEMORY()
60
```

See also: DISKSPACE( ) *p. 193.*

MENU( )

Description. MENU returns the name of the most recent menu activated.

Operational rules. The command that activates a bar menu is ACTIVATE MENU. A bar menu is a menu that pops up on the screen and the user chooses the desired option by navigating through menu with the arrow keys, and pressing Enter at the desired pad. The MENU( ) function returns the name of only the most recent menu activated.

To create a bar menu, you must use the commands DEFINE MENU and DEFINE PAD. DEFINE MENU assigns a name to the menu, and DEFINE PAD is used to define the prompt and coordinated of each pad within the menu.

The companion function, PAD( ) returns the name of the pad most recently chosen.

Example.

```
. ? MENU()
Main
```

See also: ACTIVATE MENU *p. 89.*
DEFINE MENU *p. 109.*
DEFINE PAD *p. 110.*

MESSAGE( )

Description. MESSAGE returns the message corresponding to the error that has just occurred. The ON ERROR command must be active for this function to work.

Operational rules. The ON ERROR command is given at the beginning of a program, but waits until an error occurs before performing. When ON ERROR is triggered by an error, the command may call a program, a procedure, or a user-defined function. The syntax for the command is ON ERROR <command>.

The MESSAGE( ) function can be used in conjunction with the program that ON ERROR branches to. The program can display directions to the user, including the error that occurred. The ERROR( ) function is similar to MESSAGE( ), except it returns the error number.

If the ON ERROR command is not active, errors in programs behave like errors at the dot prompt, with the Cancel, Edit, Help message. To clear the message returned by MESSAGE( ), use the RETURN or RETRY command.

Examples.

Mailprog.PRG

```
ON ERROR DO Errtrap
USE MAILLIST
DO WHILE .NOT. EOF()
    ? Lname, Fname
    SKIP
ENDDO
```

The program calls an error routine command named ERRTRAP.

Errtrap.PRG

```
CLEAR
? "The following error has occurred. Please call your service "
? "representative if you do not understand it."
?
? "Error Message: " +MESSAGE()
?
? "You will be returning to the main menu."
WAIT
RETURN TO MASTER
```

See also: ON ERROR *p. 130.*
RETRY *p. 143.*
RETURN *p. 143.*
ERROR( ) *p. 198.*

MIN(<exp>,<exp>)

Description. The MIN( ) function compares two expressions and returns the smaller value. The two arguments can be numeric, character, or date.

Operational rules. The MIN( ) is equivalent to the following IIF( ) function:

```
IIF(<exp1> < <exp2>, <exp1> , <exp2>)
```

When the arguments are dates, the less recent date is considered less. When the arguments are strings, its value is designated by its ASCII code value. Therefore, "A" is less than "K", and "Z" is less than "a".

Examples.

```
Min_wage = 45000
Income = 60000
? MIN(Max_wage,Income)
   45000

? MIN("Apple","Banana")
Apple

? MIN("apple","Banana")
Banana
```

The following function will display today's date until the system date is set beyond December 25, 1989. It will display that date from then on:

```
? MIN(DATE( ),{12/25/89})
09/16/89
```

See also: MAX( ) *p. 221.*

MLINE(<memo field>,<expN>)

Description. MLINE returns a specific line of text in the memo of the current record.

Operational rules. The arguments are: 1) the name of the memo field and, 2) the line number to be returned. MLINE returns a character string. As always when working with MEMO fields, the pointer must be set at the desired record.

The command SET MEMOWIDTH TO determines the width of the memo display. dBASE automatically word wraps the memo according to the MEMOWIDTH. The default is 50 characters. When the memowidth is changed, the memo is automatically displayed with the new margin, so the contents of each line will be altered, changing the value returned by MLINE.

Examples.

```
USE MAILLIST
. ? Comments
          . ? Joe's Garage is one of our happiest clients.
They may always be used as a referral, although
try not to give their name out more than once a
month.

  . ? MLINE(Comments,2)
  They may always be used as a referral, although
```

```
. SET MEMOWIDTH TO 30
. ? Comments
. ? Joe's Garage is one of
our happiest clients. They may
always be used as a referral,
although try not to give their
name out more than once a
month.

. ? MLINE(Comments,2)
our happiest clients. They may
```

The following program allows the user to print a memo field on a 4 inch long index card. If the field is too long, it pauses and lets the user put a new card in the printer:

```
USE Maillist
SET MEMOWIDTH TO 55
Line = 1
SET PRINT ON
DO WHILE Line < MEMLINES(Comments)
    ? MLINE (Comments,Line)
    Line = Line + 1
    IF Line = 20
        EJECT
        SET PRINT OFF
        ? Put a new index card in
        WAIT
        SET PRINT ON
        Line = Line + 1
    ENDIF
ENDDO
```

See also: SET MEMOWIDTH *p. 167.*
MLINE( ) *p. 227.*

MOD (<expN>,<expN>)

Description. The MOD(x,*y*) function returns the remainder of x/y (modulo). For instance, the MOD(5,2) is 1 because 5 divided by 2 equals to 2 with 1 left over.

Operational rules. The MOD function can be helpful in finding every **n**th occurrence of a number. For instance, in the sequence 1, 6, 11, 16, etc, each of the number have to modulo of 1 when y is 5. y might not be a 0 because a denominator of zero is an infinite number. If y is negative, then the MOD( ) will return a negative answer.

Example.

```
. ? MOD(5,2)
   1

. ? MOD(11, -3)
  -1
```

See also: FLOOR( ) *p. 204.*

MONTH(expD)

Description. MONTH returns the number of the month, given a date expression.

Operational rules. You can enter a data as an argument three ways:

- ☐ Enclose the date in curly brackets: {12/5/89}.
- ☐ Use the CTOD function: CTOD("12/5/2010").
- ☐ Reference a field name or memory variable.

The date is assumed to be in the 1900s when two digits are used for the year, otherwise you must enter four digits for the year.

Examples.

```
. ? MONTH({9/6/89})
9
. ? MONTH({12/25/89})
12
```

See also: CTOD( ) *p. 189.*
DAY( ) *p. 191.*

NDX(<expN>)

Optional. The optional syntax is NDX(<expN>,<alias>).

Description. NDX returns the name of the index file in the current work area, or a specified work area. The argument <expN> designates the index order number.

Operational rules. Each index file is given an order number, depending on the order that it was opened. The SET INDEX TO and USE INDEX commands open the indexes. The first file in the list is the master index, or 1. The SET ORDER TO command can be used to change the order of currently opened index files.

If the number in the argument is larger than the number of index files open, then NDX( ) returns a null string.

A multiple index file is created with the INDEX ON command, in conjunction with the TAG keyword. Multiple indexes end with the extension .MDX and can maintain up to 47 different key expressions.

NDX( ) will return the name of appropriately numbered index in the current file, unless a second argument is provided. The optional alias can be either the alias name or work area. Work areas are designated form 1 through 10, or A through J. If no file is open in the designated area, NDX( ) returns an error message.

The companion function MDX( ) returns the name of the multiple index file in the current work area or a specified work area.

Examples.

```
. USE Maillist INDEX Name,Zip,Code
. ? NDX(1)
NAME.NDX
. SET ORDER TO 2
. ? NDX(1)
ZIP.NDX
```

See also: SET ORDER TO *p. 168.*
USE *p. 153.*
MDX( ) *p. 222.*

NETWORK( )

Description. NETWORK returns logical true (.T.) if the system is running on a network.

Operational rules. This function can be used to determine whether record and file locking will be needed in an application. A computer can be hooked to a network, but can be booted up with a single-user system disk. The NETWORK( ) function will only return .T. if the computer is booted up with the network system.

Example.

```
. ? NETWORK( )
.T.
```

See also: OS( ) *p. 231.*

ORDER( )

Optional. The optional syntax is ORDER(<alias>).

Description. ORDER returns the name of the master index file (or multiple index tag) in the current work area, or a specified work area.

Operational rules. Each index file is given an order number, depending on the order that it was opened. The SET INDEX TO and USE INDEX commands open the indexes. The first file in the list is the master index, or 1. The SET ORDER TO command can be used to change the order of currently opened index files.

A multiple index file is created with the INDEX ON command, in conjunction with the TAG keyword. Multiple indexes end with the extension .MDX and can maintain up to 47 different key expressions.

ORDER( ) will return the name of the primary index or tag in the current file, unless a second argument is provided. The optional alias can be either the alias name or work area. Work areas are designated from 1 through 10, or A through J. If no file is open in the designated area, ORDER( ) returns a null string. If the designated alias name does not exist, ORDER( ) returns an error message.

Examples.

```
 . USE Maillist INDEX Name,Zip,Code
 . ? ORDER()
Name
 . SET ORDER TO 2
 . ? ORDER("Maillist")
Zip
```

See also: SET ORDER TO *p. 168.*
USE *p. 153.*

OS( )

Description. OS returns the name and version of the operating system that dBASE is running on.

Operational rules. This function can be used to determine whether certain DOS operations can be performed with the RUN/! command. A companion function is VERSION( ), which gives the number of the current dBASE running.

Examples.

```
. ? OS()
DOS 3.10
```

See also: VERSION( ) *p. 265.*

PAD( )

Description. PAD returns the name of the pad most recently selected from a bar menu.

Operational rules. The command that activates a bar menu is ACTIVATE MENU. A *bar menu* is a menu that pops up on the screen and the user chooses the desired option by navigating through the menu with the arrow keys and pressing Enter at the desired pad. The PAD( ) function returns the name of only the most recent pad activated.

To create a bar menu, you must use the commands DEFINE MENU and DEFINE PAD. DEFINE MENU assigns a name to the menu, and DEFINE PAD is used to define the prompt and coordinates of each pad within the menu.

The companion function, MENU( ) returns the name of the menu most recently activated.

Examples.

```
. ? PAD()
Labels
```

This example assumes that a bar menu has been recently activated. The options are Print Report, Listing, and Labels.

See also: ACTIVATE MENU *p. 89.*
DEFINE MENU *p. 109.*
DEFINE PAD *p. 110.*

PAYMENT(<principal>,<rate>,<term>)

Description. The PAYMENT function returns the fixed payment on a loan of principal at a rate of interest rate for term periods. This is the function that will answer the question, ''What will be my monthly payment on a $75,000, 30-year fixed loan with a 10% interest rate?''

Operational rules. The PAYMENT returns the amount of the periodic payment assuming the interest rate and term are in periodic amounts. Because most fixed loans have monthly periods, the interest and term often must be adjusted. For instance, suppose if the payments are to be made monthly, but the interest rate and term are given in annual terms, such as a 10% annual rate for 30 years. In this case, divide the annual interest rate by 12 and multiply the yearly term times 12. dBASE uses the following formula to calculate the PAYMENT:

princ * (int/(1 – (1 + int)^ – n))

princ = principal
int = interest rate
n = term

As with all financial functions dealing with annuities (fixed payments), payments are assumed to be made at the end of each period. The formula to calculate the term if the payments are made at the beginning of each period is:

```
PAYMENT(princ,rate,term)/(1 + rate)
```

Example.

```
. Pmt = PAYMENT(75000,.1/12,30*12)
658.18
```

The function calculates the monthly payment on a 30-year fixed rate loan of $75,000 at a 10% interest rate.

The formula below calculates the total paid over the 30 years: pmt * term * 12. Running this calculation is not advised to those with weak stomachs or newly purchased homes:

```
? Pmt * 12 * 30
236944.32
```

See also: FV( ) *p. 206.*
PV( ) *p. 239.*

PCOL( )

Description. PCOL( ) returns the column number position where the printer head currently is.

Operational rules. The PCOL( ) function is used in conjunction with the @...SAY...GET command that places a display in a particular position on the screen or printed page. The @ command places the display on the screen using the following syntax:

```
@ <row>,<col> SAY <expression>
```

For instance, the command

```
@ 5,30 SAY "HI THERE"
```

would display the words HI THERE on the fifth row on the screen, in column 30. When the command SET DEVICE TO PRINT has been given, all @...SAY commands are sent to the printer.

After each @...SAY, the cursor is then positioned at the end of the expression. Therefore, the PCOL( ) function would return 38 after printing the expression in the example above. This allows you to use the PCOL( ) function to display an expression on the screen relative to another expression.

Examples.

```
SET DEVICE TO PRINT
@ 5,30 SAY Mstring
IF PCOL( ) >68
   @ 5, PCOL( ) SAY "Y)es or N)o"
ELSE
   @ 6, 30 SAY "Y)es or N)o"
ENDIF
```

The program prints a message after the expression Mstring (assuming it is of variable lengths). If Mstring places the cursor too far to the right, the program places the message on the next line, otherwise it is placed right next to Mstring.

This program prints a string continuously until it reaches the end of the screen:

```
DO WHILE PCOL( ) < 75
    @ 10, PCOL( ) SAY Mstring
ENDDO
```

The operator $ can also be used with the @ SAY...GET command interchangeably with POL( ). For instance the following commands are valid:

```
@ 5,30 SAY Mstring
@ 5. $ SAY "Y)es or N)o"
```

The difference between PCOL( ) and $ is that PCOL( ) can also be used in a conditional statement, as in the two examples above. Also, $ can be used to relatively address the screen or printer, while PCOL( ) can only be used with the printer, and COL( ) can only be used with the screen.

See also: COL( ) *p. 187.*
PROW( ) *p. 238.*
ROW( ) *p. 251.*

PI( )

Description. The PI function returns the number π (approximately 3.1415926). This value is used in engineering and drafting calculations, often in conjunction with trigonometric functions (COS, SIN, ACOS, etc.) The ratio between the circumference of a circle and its diameter is always pi.

Operational rules. Because it is a constant, there are no arguments to the PI function. The function is usually entered in formulas, such as:

PI( )*3^2	the area of the circle with radius of 3
COS(PI( ))	the cosine of the half circle

Examples.

```
. SET DECIMALS TO 5
. ? PI( )
      3.14159
```

The formula below calculates the area of a circle with a 5 inch radius:

```
. ? PI( ) * 5^2
      78.53982
```

See also: COS( ) *p. 189.*
SIN( ) *p. 256.*

POPUP( )

Description. POPUP returns the name of the most recent popup menu activated.

Operational Rules. The command that activates a popup menu is ACTIVATE POPUP. A popup menu is a menu that pops up on the screen with a specific message. The POPUP ( ) function returns the name of only the active popup menu. Once the menu is deactivated, it is erased from the screen, and the screen is restored to its previous contents.

To create a popup menu, you must use the commands DEFINE POPUP. This command assigns the coordinates and prompts of the menu. To create a popup menu where the user can make selections, use the DEFINE BAR command in conjunction with DEFINE POPUP.

The companion function, BAR( ) returns the number of the bar most recently chosen.

Examples.

```
. ? POPUP( )
MAIN
```

See also: ACTIVATE POPUP *p. 90.*
DEFINE POPUP *p. 110.*
DEFINE BAR *p. 108.*

PRINTSTATUS( )

Description. PRINTSTATUS returns logical true (.T.) is the printer is online.

Operational Rules. This function can be used to determine whether a command that sends output to the printer will print. Examples of these commands are SET PRINT ON, SET DEVICE TO PRINT, Ctrl – P, or any of the commands that accept the "TO PRINT" clause.

Four most common reasons that the printer is not on-line are:

- ☐ The printer is not turned on.
- ☐ The printer's on-line toggle is not on.
- ☐ The cable between the printer and the computer is disconnected.
- ☐ The computer is not set to send output to the correct printer port. Use the MODE command from DOS to change this setting.

When a print command is given and the printer is not on-line, dBASE will respond with the message Printer not Ready (125) or Printer is either not connected or turned off (126). The PRINTSTATUS( ) function is helpful in circumventing these errors.

Examples.

```
IF .NOT. PRINTSTATUS( )
    ? "The printer is not on or is not connected. Please turn it "
    ? "on-line, and try to run this option again. "
    WAIT
    RETURN
ENDIF
REPORT Form Maillist TO PRINT
```

The program checks the print status before running a report to the printer.

See also: SET PRINT ON *p. 169.*

PROGRAM( )

Description. PROGRAM returns the name of the program that was running when the last error occurred.

Operational Rules. This command can be used at the dot prompt, in a program, or in the Debugger. To use PROGRAM( ) from the dot prompt, the program must be suspended. This function is very useful when used in conjunction with the ON ERROR command.

The ON ERROR command is given at the beginning of a program, but waits until an error occurs before performing. When ON ERROR is triggered by an error, the command may call a program, a procedure, or a user-defined function. The syntax for the command is ON ERROR <command>.

The PROGRAM( ) function can be used in conjunction with the program that ON ERROR branches to. The program can display the different program that was being run when the error occurred. The MESSAGE( ) function can also be helpful in this routine, as it displays the error message that would appear if the ON ERROR( ) command was not present

This function can also be used in the Breakpoint or Display window of the the Debugger. If the error occurred while running a procedure, PROGRAM( ) returns the name of the procedure, not the procedure file.

Examples.

Mailprog.PRG

```
ON ERROR DO Errtrap
USE Maillist
SET PRINT ON
DO  WHILE .NOT. EOF( )
     ? Lname, Fname
     SKIP
ENDDO
```

The program calls an error routine command named ERRTRAP.

Errtrap.PRG

```
SET PRINT OFF
? "An error has occurred. "
? "The error is: ", MESSAGE( )
?
? "It occurred in the program: ",PROGRAM( )
? "on line :",LINENO( )
RETURN TO MASTER
```

See also: ON ERROR *p. 130.*
MESSAGE( ) *p. 225.*
LINENO( ) *p. 217.*

PROMPT( )

Description. PROMPT returns the name of prompt selected in the currently defined popup menu.

Operational Rules. The command that activates a popup menu is ACTIVATE POPUP. A popup menu is a menu that pops up on the screen with a specific message. To create a popup menu, you must use the commands DEFINE POPUP. This command assigns the coordinates and prompts of the menu. To create a popup menu where the user can make selections, use the DEFINE BAR command in conjunction with DEFINE POPUP.

The companion function, BAR( ) returns the number of the bar most recently chosen. The function POPUP( ) returns the name of the current popup menu. If there is no menu current, PROMPT( ) returns a null string.

Examples.

```
. ? PROMPT()
Run Report
```

See also: ACTIVATE POPUP *p. 90.*
DEFINE POPUP *p. 110.*
DEFINE BAR *p. 108.*

PROW( )

Description. PROW( ) returns the row number position where the printer head currently is.

Operational Rules. The PROW( ) function is used in conjunction with the @...SAY...GET command that places a display in a particular position on the screen or printed page. The @ command places the display on the screen using the following syntax:

```
@ <row>,<col> SAY <expression>
```

For instance, the command

```
@ 5,30 SAY "HI THERE"
```

would display the words HI THERE on the fifth row on the screen, in column 30. When the command SET DEVICE TO PRINT has been given, all @...SAY commands are sent to the printer.

After each @...SAY, the cursor is then positioned at the end of the expression. Therefore, the PROW( ) function would return 5 after printing the expression in the example above. This allows you to use the PROW( ) function to keep track of the rows printed, and place page breaks accordingly.

Examples.

```
USE Maillist
SET DEVICE TO PRINT
@ 1,1 SAY "Phone Listing "
DO WHILE .NOT. EOF()
    IF  PROW() >55
        EJECT
        @ 1,1 SAY "Phone Listing "
```

```
    ENDIF
    @ PROW( ) + 2,1 SAY Fname + Lname
    @ PROW( ) + 1,1 SAY Phone
    SKIP
ENDDO
```

The program prints a phone directory. Each name uses two lines: one for the name and one for the phone number. Each time the printer head reaches the 55th line, the program ejects a page, and reprints the title.

The operator $ can also be used with the @...SAY...GET command interchangeably with PROW( ). For instance, the following commands are valid:

```
DO WHILE .NOT. EOF( )
    @ $ + 2,1 SAY FNAME + LNAME
    @ $ + 1,1 SAY PHONE
    SKIP
ENDDO
```

The difference between PROW( ) and $ is that PROW( ) can also be used in a conditional statement, as in the two examples above. Also, $ can be used to relatively address the screen or printer, while PROW( ) can only be used with the printer, and ROW( ) can only be used with the screen.

See also: COL( ) *p. 187.*
PCOL( ) *p. 233.*
ROW( ) *p. 251.*

PV(<principal>,<rate>,<term>)

Description. The @PV function returns the present value on a loan with fixed payments at a rate of interest rate for term periods.

Operational Rules. The PV returns the amount of the present value assuming the interest rate and term are in periodic amounts. Because most fixed loans have monthly periods, the interest and term often must be adjusted. For instance, if the payments are monthly, but the interest rate and term are annual, divide the annual interest rate by 12 and multiply the yearly term times 2. dBASE uses the following formula to calculate the PV:

pmt * ((1 – (1 + int)^ – n))/int

pmt = periodic payment
int = interest rate
n = term

As with all financial functions dealing with annuities (fixed payments), payments are assumed to be made at the end of each period. The formula to calculate the term is the payments are made at the beginning of each period is:

PV(pmt,int,term)*(1 + int)

This function is the companion to PMT which returns the payment given principal, interest and term. The PV will answer the question, "How much can I borrow if my loan will be 30-year fixed, 10% interest rate, with a monthly payment of $500?".

Example.

```
. ? PV(500,.1/12,30*12)
      56975.41
```

The following example calculates the principal on a 30-year fixed rate loan with payments of $500 at a 10% interest rate. Because the interest and term are in annual figures, the arguments in the PV formula divide the annual interest by 12 and multiply the annual term times 12.

The next example calculates the principal left on the same loan after 2 years of payments:

```
. ? PV(500,.1/12,2*12)
      10835.43
```

See also: PAYMENT( ) *p. 232.*

RAND( )

Optional. The optional syntax is (RAND (<expN>)).

Description. RAND returns a number between 0 and 1 that changes each time you request the function.

Operational Rules. Because it is a constant, there are no arguments to the RAND function. The optional numeric argument is used as a seed to create a new random number sequence.

The default seed is 100001. Although this function is named after the "random" expression, the sequence of numbers returned from a series of RAND( )s will always be the same if started from the same seed. However, if you use a negative number as the argument, the seed is taken from the system clock.

Although the number returned by RAND is less than 1, you can get larger numbers. First choose the highest and lowest numbers you would like to generate. Create a formula that multiplies RAND by the highest minus lowest number, and then adds the lowest number:

RAND	a random number between 0 and 1
RAND*5+1	a number between 1 and 6

The RAND is used in some statistical modeling applications as well as computer games. (Random numbers are often used to ensure that the game does not start the same way every time.)

Example.

```
. ? RAND()
    0.47
. ? RAND()
    0.80
. ? RAND()
    0.88
```

The following sequence starts with a seed taken from the system clock:

```
. ? RAND(-5)
    0.55
. ? RAND()
    0.62
. ? RAND()
    0.53
```

READKEY( )

Description. READKEY( ) returns a number that represents the most recent key pressed on the keyboard to exit a full screen command.

Operational Rules. The full-screen command that READKEY can detect are: APPEND, BROWSE, CHANGE, CREATE, EDIT, INSERT, MODIFY, and READ. READKEY( ), like the INKEY( ) function, can detect the exact keystroke pressed (such as a Ctrl key combination or an arrow key), unlike other interactive commands such as READ and ACCEPT.

The READKEY function is different than INKEY( ), however, in that it only reads the key pressed in the last full-screen command (such as READ, or ACCEPT), while INKEY( ) pauses to receive the keystroke (or captures it during a noninteractive command). The value returned by READKEY will be different depending on whether any data was changed during the command. The LASTKEY( ) function, which also captures keystrokes, is different in that it is used with any type of interactive command (such as ACCEPT), and it returns the same value whether data was changed or not.

Table 4-2. The READKEY return values.

Non-Updated Code Number	Updated Code Number	Key	Description
0	256	Ctrl – S Ctrl – H ←	back 1 character
	256	backspace	back and erase
1	257	Ctrl – D Ctrl – L →	forward 1 character
4	260	Ctrl – E Ctrl – K ↑	back one field
5	261	Ctrl – J Ctrl – X ↓	forward one field
6	262	Ctrl – R PgUp	backward one screen
7	263	Ctrl – C PgDn	forward one screen
12		Ctrl – Q Esc	Abort
	270	Ctrl – W Ctrl – End	Save, Quit
15	271	Enter Ctrl – M	Enter to next field
16		Enter Ctrl – M	Enter at new record in APPEND mode
33	289	Ctrl – Home	turn on/off menu display
34	290	Ctrl – PgUp	zoom out
35	291	Ctrl – PgDn	zoom in
36	292	F1	Help

Table 4-2 lists all READKEY return values. Notice that there are only codes for those keystrokes that exit from a full screen command.

Examples.

```
*       Mailing List Program
DO WHILE .T.
   PRN = "P"
   ZSORT = "A"
```

```
    @ 1,1 SAY "Press ESC to Return to Main Menu, PgDn for Help"
    @ 3,1 SAY "Display on Printer or Screen? (P/S) " GET PRN
    @ 5,1 SAY "Sort by Zip or Alpha? (A/Z) " GET ZSORT
    READ
    IF READKEY( ) = 12                              && if ESC, return to menu
          CLEAR
          ? "Returning to Master Menu"
          RETURN
    ENDIF
    IF READKEY( ) = 7 .OR. READKEY = 263               && if PgDn, run Help
          CLEAR
          DO HELPER
          LOOP
    ENDIF
    DO MAILLIST
    EXIT
ENDDO
```

The program instructs the user to press escape to abort the program and return to the main menu. The READKEY function reads whether that key was pressed.

See also: ON KEY( ) *p. 130.*
INKEY( ) *p. 208.*
LASTKEY( ) *p. 213.*

RECCOUNT( )

Optional. The optional syntax is RECCOUNT(<alias>).

Description. RECCOUNT returns the number of records in a database file.

Operational Rules. This function returns the number of records in a file, as displayed on the LIST FILES directory. This is the same number received by running the COUNT command without any options. However, the COUNT command takes a much longer time to return the same answer.

RECCOUNT( ) will return the total number of records, regardless of whether the commands SET DELETED or SET FILTER have been turned on.

RECCOUNT( ) will return the number of records in the current file unless an argument is provided. The optional alias can be either the alias name or work area. Work areas are designated from 1 to 10 or A through J. If no file is open in the designated area, RECCOUNT( ) returns zero. If the designated alias name does not exist, RECCOUNT( ) returns an error message.

Examples.

```
. SELECT A
. USE Coa
. SELECT B
. USE Journal
. ? RECCOUNT( )
   20
. ? RECCOUNT("A")
     8
. ? RECCOUNT(1)
     8
```

The example assumes that there are 20 records in JOURNAL.DBF, and there are 8 records in COA.DBF.

See also: DBF( ) *p. 191.*
RECSIZE( ) *p. 245.*

RECNO( )

Optional. The optional syntax is RECNO(<alias>).

Description. RECNO returns the number of the record that dBASE is currently positioned at.

Operational Rules. This function returns the record number of the current record, except in the following occasions:

RECNO( ) =	when
0	no current file
1	no records in database
1	record pointer is at BOF( )
RECCOUNT( )+1	record pointer is at EOF( )

RECNO( ) will return the number of records in the current file unless an argument is provided. The optional alias can be either the alias name or work area. Work areas are designated from 1 to 10 or A through J. If the designated alias name does not exist, RECNO( ) returns an error message.

Examples.

```
  . USE Coa
  . GO 5
COA: Record No 5
  . ? RECNO( )
      5
```

```
. GO BOTTOM
COA: Record No 8
```

See also: DBF( ) *p. 191.*
RECSIZE( ) *p. 245.*

RECSIZE( )

Optional. The optional syntax is RECSIZE(<alias>).

Description. RECSIZE returns the size of a record in the database file.

Operational Rules. This function returns the length of a record, which is the total of the lengths of each field plus 1. This is the number displayed during the CREATE or MODIFY STRUCTURE commands. The following formula will return the number of bytes used by the data in the database:

```
RECCOUNT( ) * (RECSIZE)
```

All database files have a header record at the top of the file. The header record uses the following amount of space:

```
32 * <number or fields> + 35
```

RECSIZE( ) will return the length of the records in the current file unless an argument is provided. The optional alias can be either the alias name or work area. Work areas are designated from 1 to 10 or A through J. If no file is open in the designated area, RECSIZE( ) returns zero. If the designated alias name does not exist, RECSIZE( ) returns an error message.

Examples.

```
. USE Maillist
. LIST STRUCTURE
Structure for database: D:MAILLIST.DBF
Number of data records:      6
Field    Field Name     Type         Width
   1     LNAME          Character       10
   2     FNAME          Character       10
** Total **                             21
. ? RECSIZE( )
      21
. ? RECSIZE( ) * RECCOUNT( ) + (32 * 2 +35)
      225
```

See also: DBF( ) *p. 191.*
RECCOUNT( ) *p. 243.*

REPLICATE(<expC>,<expN>)

Description. REPLICATE( ) returns a character string <expC>, repeated <expN> number of times.

Operational Rules. This function is useful when creating lines for report headings, and section breaks. The character string can be more than one character, but the resulting character string cannot be more than 254 characters.

The SPACE( ) function is equivalent to using REPLICATE( ) with " " as the character argument.

Examples.

```
. ? REPLICATE("-",40)
----------------------------------------

. ? REPLICATE("yeah ",3
yeah yeah yeah

. ? REPLICATE("* ",10)
* * * * * * * * * *
```

See also: SPACE( ) *p. 257.*

RIGHT(<expC>,<expN>)

Description. The RIGHT( ) function returns the last <expN> letters of a string.

Operational Rules. The RIGHT( ) function returns a substring of <expC>. There is no difference between the RIGHT( ) function and the SUBSTR(*string, start-number,length*) function where the start-number is the <expN>, and the length is to the end of the string. If the number <expN> is larger than the length of the string, the result will be the string itself. If the number is 0, the function will return the null string.

dBASE IV, unlike previous versions, allows you to perform the RIGHT( ) function on a memo field.

Example.

```
? RIGHT("California",5)
ornia

? RIGHT("California",0)
                              (a null string)

MM = "11-Nov-89"
? RIGHT (MM,2)
```

```
89
? RIGHT ("Hello",9)
Hello
```

See also: LEFT( ) *p. 214.*
SUBSTR( ) *p. 259.*

RLOCK( )

Optional. The optional syntax is RLOCK(<list of records>,<alias>). The RLOCK function is identical to the LOCK( ) function.

Description. The RLOCK( ) function locks the record(s) in a database, so that other users cannot make any updates to them. Record locking (as with file locking) is only performed on mutli-user systems running on networks. The LOCK( ) function is completely interchangeable with the RLOCK( ) function.

When the SET LOCK command is on, many commands automatically lock the record without using RLOCK( ). Some commands lock the record regardless of whether the SET LOCK is on or off. These commands include: APPEND BLANK, REPLACE, @...GET/READ, and EDIT. See the SET LOCK section for a list of all commands that explicitly lock the file, and/or records.

The RLOCK( ) function is still useful, however, because it can be used to check whether the record is currently locked, and it can lock the record before issuing a command. RLOCK( ) returns a logical false (.F.) if the record is already locked.

Although a locked record cannot be updated by other users, it can be opened on a read-only basis.

RLOCK( ) will lock the current file, unless the second argument is provided. The optional alias can be either the alias name or work area. Work areas are designated from 1 to 10, or A through J.

Three ways to unlock records that have been locked with RLOCK( ) are:

- ☐ Use the UNLOCK command.
- ☐ Close the file with the USE or CLOSE command.
- ☐ Quit dBASE.

RLOCK( ) will return a logical true (.T.) and lock the file, if the specified record is not currently locked. On single-user systems, RLOCK( ) always returns true (.T.) The companion function FLOCK( ) is used to lock all records in a database.

If relationships have been set with other files, the associated records in the other files will also be locked. If any of those records cannot be locked, RLOCK( ) will return .F.

Examples.

```
USE Maillist
INPUT "Enter record number to Edit " GET MRec
GOTO Mrec
IF .NOT. RLOCK( )
     ? "This name cannot be edited now, because the record is locked."
     ? "Try again later."
     WAIT
     RETURN
ENDIF
EDIT
```

This program checks whether a record is locked before running a command that will automatically lock the file.

Following are examples of the RLOCK( ) function used to lock multiple records and files:

```
. SELE A
.USE Maillist
.GO 4
.? RLOCK"( )
.T.
.? RLOCK(6,7)
.T.
.SELE B
.? RLOCK(6,Maillist)
.T.
```

See also: SET LOCK *p. 178*
SET REPROCESS *p. 170.*
UNLOCK *p. 152.*
FLOCK( ) *p. 203.*

ROLLBACK( )

Description. The ROLLBACK( ) function returns .T. if the last ROLLBACK command was successful.

Operational rules. The ROLLBACK command is used to undo changes in a database (or databases). The command must be used in conjunction with the BEGIN TRANSACTION command. When BEGIN TRANSACTION is issued, dBASE creates a log file that tracks all further change in the file(s). The ROLLBACK command can undo changes in all files changed or just in selected files.

ROLLBACK( ) will return a logical true (.T.) if the last ROLLBACK (in the current session) was successful. Otherwise, the command returns logical false (.F.) True is the default value of ROLLBACK( ).

The companion function is COMPLETED( ), which tests whether the commands between BEGIN TRANSACTION and END TRANSACTION have all been performed completely.

The two most common reasons why a transaction is not completed are:

- ☐ The user pressed Esc while the command(s) were processing.
- ☐ An error occurred during the processing.

Examples.

```
. Use Maillist
. LIST Fname,Lname
 RECNO    FNAME     LNAME
     1    John      Smith
     2    Joe       Brown

. BEGIN TRANSACTION
. REPLACE ALL LNAME WITH UPPER(Lname)

.LIST Fname,Lname
 RECNO    FNAME     LNAME
     1    John      SMITH
     2    Joe       BROWN

. ROLLBACK
. LIST FNAME, NAME
 RECNO    FNAME     LNAME
     1    John      Smith
     2    Joe       Brown

? . ROLLBACK( )
.T.
```

Below is an example of a program that increases the prices in a file by 10%. The transaction can be aborted in the middle of the process if the user presses Esc (and then chooses Ignore at the prompt), or if an error occurs while the command is running. The program checks whether this has happened:

```
USE Prices
BEGIN TRANSACTION
REPLACE All Price WITH Price * 1.1
END TRANSACTION
```

```
IF .NOT. COMPLETED( )
   ROLLBACK
   IF .NOT. ROLLBACK( )
        ? "The prices have been corrupted. Please use the backup"
        ? "copies from your data disks. "
        WAIT
   ENDIF
ENDIF
RETURN
```

See also: BEGIN TRANSACTION *p. 93.*
ROLLBACK *p. 143.*
COMPLETED( ) *p. 188.*

ROUND(<expN>,<expN>)

Description. The ROUND function returns the first number x rounded to the second n number of decimal places.

Operational rules. The first argument is the number that you are rounding. The second argument is the number of decimal places to be rounded.

To truncate at the decimal (always rounding down), use the INT( ) function. Numbers will display with less decimal places (see SET DECIMAL TO), but they will calculate the decimals that do not show.

If the second argument is a negative number, the number will round to multiples of 10, 100, etc. For instance, rounding to –1 places will return a multiple of 10, and rounding to –2 places will return a multiple of 100.

Example.

```
. ? ROUND(5.22,0)
         5
. ? ROUND(5.29,1)
         5.3

. ? ROUND(-5.22,0)
        -5

. ? ROUND(8,-1)
        10

. ? ROUND(125,-2)
       100
```

See also: INT( ) *p. 209.*
SET DECIMAL TO *p. 160.*

ROW( )

Description. ROW( ) returns the row number position where the cursor is currently positioned.

Operational rules. The ROW( ) function is used in conjunction with the @SAY...GET command that places a display in a particular position on the screen or printed page. The @ command places the display on the screen using the following syntax:

```
@<row>,<col> SAY <expression>
```

For instance, the command

```
@ 5,30 SAY "HI THERE"
```

would display the words HI THERE on the fifth row on the screen, in column 30.

After each @...SAY, the cursor is then positioned at the end of the expression. Therefore, the ROW( ) function would return 5 after printing the expression in the example above. This allows you to use the ROW( ) function to keep track of the rows displayed on the screen.

Examples.

```
USE Maillist
@ 1,1 SAY "Mailing List  "
DO WHILE .NOT. EOF()
   IF ROW() > 22
      WAIT
      CLEAR
      @ 1,1 SAY "Mailing List  "
   ENDIF
   @ ROW()+2,1 SAY  Fname + Lname
   IF Phone <> "          "
      @ ROW()+1,1 SAY  Phone
   ENDIF
   SKIP
ENDDO
```

The program displays a list of information on the screen. Each name may use one or two lines: if they do not have a phone number, it does not print one. Each time the screen fills with names down to row 22, the program pauses, and waits for the user to press a key to continue.

The operator $ can also be used with the @SAY . . . GET command interchangeably with ROW( ). For instance, the following commands are valid:

```
DO WHILE .NOT. EOF( )
   @ $+2,1 SAY  FNAME + LNAME
   @ $+1,1 SAY  PHONE
   SKIP
ENDDO
```

The difference between ROW( ) and $ is that ROW( ) can also be used in a conditional statement, as in the two examples above. Also, $ can be used to relatively address the screen or printer, while PROW( ) can only be used with the printer, and ROW( ) can only be used with the screen.

See also: COL( ) *p. 187.*
PCOL( ) *p. 233.*
ROW( ) *p. 251.*

RTOD(<expN>)

Description. RTOD converts a number, representing an angle measured by radians, into degrees.

Operational rules. Fractions of a degree, usually represented by minutes and seconds, are by represented by decimals. For instance, 45 minutes is depicted as .75 degrees.

Figure 4-1 in the ACOS( ) section shows a circle with points marked in radians (0 to PI). This helps illustrate the conversion of degrees to radians.

Use the SET DECIMALS command to change the number of decimals which appear in the answer. The DTOR( ) function is used to conversely change degrees to radians.

Examples.

```
. ? RTOD (PI( )/2)
 90

. ? X1 = 45.75
45.75
. ? RTOD(X1)
2621.28
```

See also: ACOS( ) *p. 178.*
DTOR( ) *p. 195.*
SET DECIMALS *p. 160.*

RTRIM(<expC>)

Description. The RTRIM( ) function removes all trailing spaces from a string.

Operational rules. The RTRIM( ) function is often used to trim off the blanks at the end of a field, because the display commands do not do this automatically. It is also often used with the SEEK command, to make sure that there are no blanks at the end of the string being searched for.

The only command that automatically trims trailing spaces when displaying expressions is the LABEL command.

The companion function to RTRIM( ) is LTRIM( ), which removes all leading spaces from an expression.

Examples.

```
 . USE Maillist
. ? FNAME,LNAME
 John            Smith

. ? RTRIM(FNAME),LNAME
 John Smith

. ? RTRIM(FNAME) + LNAME
 JohnSmith
```

The example first shows how fields are displayed when the RTRIM( ) is not used. The second example shows how RTRIM( ), when used in conjunction with a comma, leaves one space between the two strings. The third example shows how RTRIM( ), when used in conjunction with a plus sign, leaves no spaces between the two strings.

See also: LTRIM( ) *p. 220.*

RUN(<expC>) (version 1.1 only)

Description. The RUN( ) function runs an operating system command and returns a number that tells whether the command was successfully run.

SEEK( )<exp>)

Optional. The optional syntax is SEEK(<exp>,<alias>).

Description. The SEEK( ) function looks up a record in an indexed database.

Operational rules. The SEEK( ) function returns logical true (.T.) if the expression is found in the index, otherwise it returns false (.F.) At this time, the record pointer is moved to the record that matches, otherwise it is moved to the end of the file (EOF( )).

The SEEK( ) function was introduced with dBASE IV can be used in place of the SEEK command, which moves the record pointer, followed by the FOUND( ) function, which states whether a match was found.

SEEK( ) will perform the lookup on the current file, unless the second argument is provided. The optional alias can be either the alias name or work area. Work areas are designated from 1 to 10, or A through J.

Examples.

```
USE Maillist INDEX Mailname
ACCEPT "Enter Last Name of Person to Edit  " TO MLNAME
IF SEEK(MLNAME)
  EDIT
ELSE
  ? "NO MATCHING RECORDS FOUND!"
  WAIT
ENDIF
```

The example is program that looks for a name in an indexed database, and edits the record that matches. If no records match, a message is displayed. Notice that the SEEK( ) function replaces the use of the SEEK command followed by the FOUND( ) function, as used in previous versions of dBASE.

See also: FOUND( ) *p. 205.*
SEEK *p. 146.*

SELECT( )

Description. The SELECT( ) function returns the highest work area number that is currently not selected.

Operational Rules. The use of this function can insure that the area being selected is not currently being used. SELECT( ) will return the highest unselected work area, with 1 being the lowest, and 10 the highest.

Examples.

```
. USE Coa IN 10
. USE Jnl IN 2
. ? SELECT()
9
. USE Batch IN SELECT()
```

The example opens two files, and then opens a third file named Batch in the next available work area.

See also: USE( ) *p. 153.*

SET(<expC>)

DESCRIPTION. The SET( ) function returns the current status of a particular SET command.

Operational rules. The argument for this function is the name of the SET command. Examples are: BELL, CARRY, MEMOWIDTH, STATUS, and other SET commands. The argument is not case sensitive.

The SET( ) function returns ON or OFF, depending on the current status of the command. Some SET commands, such as MEMOWIDTH return an integer. For some commands that can be set as an integer or on/off, the function will only return the on/off status. For commands that have a setting other than on/off or an integer, the function will return an error.

Examples.

```
   . ? SET ("memowidth")
       60
   . ? SET("STATUS")
ON
   . ? SET("Carry")
OFF
```

See also: SET *p. 155.*

SIGN(<expN>)

Description. The SIGN( ) function returns a number that represents whether the argument is a positive number, negative number, or zero.

Operational rules. SIGN( ) returns a 1 for positive numbers, a −1 for negative numbers, and a 0 for zero. This function, which was introduced with dBASE IV, replaces the following function:

```
IIF(X > 0,1,IIF(X > 0,-1,0))
```

Examples.

```
. ? SIGN(55)
   1
. ? SIGN(0)
   0
. ? SIGN(M55)
  -1
```

See also: IIF( ) *p. 207.*

SIN(<expN>)

Description. SIN( ) returns the sine of an angle.

Operational rules. The sine represents the y-axis value at any point of the circle with the radius pi/2. Therefore it will always be between −1 and 1.

It is often better to use memory variables as the argument, because the function will then use 20-place numeric accuracy. You can change the number of decimal points displayed in the answer with the SET DECIMALS command.

Examples.

```
? SIN(0)
    0
? SIN(PI( )/6)
    .5
```

See also: ASIN( ) *p. 180.*
ACOS( ) *p. 178.*
COS( ) *p. 189.*

SOUNDEX(<expC>)

Description. The SOUNDEX( ) function returns a code that can be used to determine how much the strings sound alike.

Operational rules. In brief, the SOUNDEX( ) code is a four-digit code, made up of the following:

- ☐ The first digit is the first character of the string.
- ☐ After the first digit of the string, all occurrences of the letters a,e,h,i,o,u,w,and y are ignored.
- ☐ It assigns a number to the remaining letters:

b,f,p,v	= 1
c,g,j,k,q,s,x,z	= 2
d,t	= 3
l	= 4
m,n	= 5
r	= 6

- ☐ If two letters next to each other have the same code, it only uses the code of the first letter.
- ☐ It stops at the first character that is not a letter. If the first character of the string is not a letter, it returns "0000".

The companion function, DIFFERENCE( ), calculates the difference between the SOUNDEX( ) codes of two strings.

Examples.

```
. ? SOUNDEX("HUMDINGER")
H535
```

You can index a file on the soundex code of a name to help look up names where you do not know the exact spelling:

```
. USE Clients
. INDEX ON SOUNDEX(Lname) TO Clisound
. SEEK SOUNDEX("BALISTERI")
. ? FNAME,LNAME
. JOHN            Ballestros
```

See also: DIFFERENCE( ) *p. 192.*

SPACE(<expN>)

Description. The SPACE( ) function returns a string of spaces, with length <expN>.

Operational rules. The SPACE( ) function is often used to pad a string on the left so that it displays at a certain position. The argument can be any number between 0 and 254.

Examples.

```
. Title = "Income Projection"
. Padding = (80/2) - LEN(Title)/2      && PAD = screen/2 - title/2
. ? SPACE(Padding) + Title
                              Income Projection
```

The example calculates displays the character string in the center of an 80-character screen:

See also: LEN( ) *p. 215.*

SQRT(<expN>)

Description. The SQRT function returns the square root of the argument.

Operational rules. The value x can be either a type F (floating point binary, as used in dBASE III) or type N (the more accurate binary coded) numbers. The answer is always a type F number.

A negative argument will return an error message, as it is impossible to take the square root of a negative number. Either the ABS or IF functions can be used to circumvent this problem:

```
SQRT(ABS(-100))
IIF(Amount<0,0,SQRT(Amount * -1))
```

Examples.

```
. ? SQRT(100)
    10
. ? SQRT(ABS(-100) )
    10
```

See also: ABS( ) *p. 177.*

STR(<expN>)

Optional. The optional syntax is STR(<expN,<length>,<decimals>).

Description. The STRING function returns the number x as a string representing the number.

Operational rules. This function is helpful when used to display a number with a specified width. The <length> argument represents the length of the string, including decimal points and places. If the number is longer than the requested length, the STR( ) function returns asterisks.

The <decimal> argument represents the number of digits left of the decimal point. If the number has more decimal places than requested, STR( ) rounds it.

The default length is 10. The default decimal places is 0.

The companion function is the VAL( ) function which converts a string to a numeric value.

Example.

```
. ? STR(5,6,2)
 5.00

. ? STR(5,6)
. ? 5
```

The following example uses the LTRIM( ) (trim off leading blank spaces) to left justify a number.

```
 . Owe = 500
 . ? "You have 10 days to pay the $", LTRIM(STR(Owe)), "that you owe."
You have 10 days to send the $ 500 that you owe.
```

See also: VAL( ) *p. 263.*

STUFF(<expC1>,<expN1>,<expN2>,<expC2>)

Description. The STUFF function replaces a portion of <expC1> with <expC2> in a specified position.

Operational rules. STUFF( ) removes the <expN2> number of characters from <expC1>, starting at position <expN1>. Then it takes <expC2>, and places it within <expC1> at the <expN1> position. If <expN1> is greater than the length of <expC1>, then STUFF appends <expC2> to the end of <expC1>. If <expN2> is zero, then no characters are eliminated from <expC1>, and <expC2> is simply inserted into the string.

The STUFF( ) function, which was introduced with dBASE IV, can be used in place of the following command:

```
. Oldstring = "I am happy"
New string = LEFT(Oldstring,5) + " very" + SUBSTR(Oldstring,5)
I am very happy
```

In this case, Oldstring is <expC1>, "very" is <expC2>, and 5 is <expN1>. <expN2> is zero because no characters are eliminated from <expC1>.

The STUFF( ) function is not supported in memo fields.

Example.

```
. mm = "I am happy"
. ? stuff(mm,6,0,"very )")
I am very happy
. ? stuff (mm,6,5,"hungry")
I am hungry
```

To replace all occurrences of the word Exxon with Arco in a character field named DESC:

```
. SET FILTER TO "Exxon" $ Desc
. REPLACE Desc WITH STUFF(Desc,AT("Exxon",DESC),5,"Arco")
```

See also: REPLACE *p. 140.*
LEFT( ) *p. 214.*
SUBSTR( ) *p. 259.*

SUBSTR(<expC>,<start position>)

Optional. The optional syntax is SUBSTR(<expC>,<start position>, <number of characters>).

Description. The SUBSTR function returns the rest of the string <expC>, starting at the start number position.

Operational rules. If the third argument is given, the SUBSTR( ) function returns a substring of that length. When no third argument is entered, the answer ends at the last character of <expC>. If the third argument is larger than the number of characters left in the string, then the third argument is ignored. If the number is 0, the function will return the null string.

If the second argument is larger than the number of characters in <expC>, an error will occur. This is also true of negative numbers as the argument.

dBASE IV, unlike previous versions, allows you to perform the SUBSTR( ) function on a memo field.

Example.

```
. ? SUBSTR("California",5,3)
for

. ? SUBSTR("California",5)
fornia

. ? SUBSTR("California",0)
                                (a null string)

. MM = "11-Nov-89"
. ? SUBSTR(MM,4,3)
Nov
```

See also: LEFT( ) *p. 214.*
RIGHT( ) *p. 246.*

TAG(<expN>)

Optional. The optional syntax is TAG(<mdx filename>,<expN>,<alias>).

Description. TAG returns the name of the .mdx tag in the current work area, or a specified work area. The argument <expN> designates the index order number.

Operational rules. Each index file is given an order number, depending on the order that it was opened. The SET INDEX TO and USE INDEX commands open the indexes. The first file in the list is the master index, or 1. The SET ORDER TO command can be used to change the order of currently opened index files.

A multiple index file is created with the INDEX ON command, in conjunction with the TAG keyword. Multiple indexes end with the extension MDX and can maintain up to 47 different key expressions.

The optional alias can be either the alias name or work area. Work areas are designated from 1 to 10, or A through J. If no file is open in the designated area, NDX( ) returns a null string.

The companion function MDX ( ) returns the name of the multiple index file in the current work area, or specified work area.

See also: SET ORDER TO( ) *p. 168.*
USE( ) *p. 153.*
MDX( ) *p. 222.*

TAN(<expN>)

Description. TAN ( ) returns the tangent of an angle. The tangent is cos x divided by sin x.

Operational rules. A circle is marked with points in radians (0 to PI). The cosine represents the x-axis value at any point, and the sine represents the y-axis value at any point. The tangent, therefore, if SIN (x)/COS(x). This ratio can be any number other than PI( )/2 or 3PI( )/2 which have sine values of 0.

Examples.

```
. TAN(0)
      0
. TAN(30*PI/180)
      .5
```

See also: COS( ) *p. 189.*
SIN( ) *p. 256.*

TIME( )

Description. TIME returns the system time as a character string.

Operational rules. The system time is kept through DOS and can be set with the TIME command at the DOS prompt. Many computers come with battery clocks that keep the system time current.

The TIME( ) format is hh:mm:ss.

Examples.

```
. ? TIME( )
 16:35:36
```

See also: DATE( ) *p. 190.*

TRANSFORM(<exp>,<picture string>)

Description. The TRANSFORM function returns expression <exp> formatted with a PICTURE format.

Operational rules. The PICTURE formats are used to display numbers, strings, logicals, and dates in a set format. They are usually used in conjunction with the @...SAY command. Examples of a few picture formats:

Variable:	Format:	will print as:
5000	"###,###.##"	5,000.00
5000	"$ ####.#"	$ 5000.0
"hello"	"@!"	HELLO

The TRANSFORM function allows these picture formats to be used in commands other than @...SAY. This command is often used with any of the DISPLAY commands, and in the report generator.

Examples.

```
. MM = 66000
. ? TRANSFORM(MM,"###,###.##")
  66,000.00

. PIC = "$ #,###,###")
. ? TRANSFORM(MM,PIC)
  66,000
```

See also: @...SAY *p. 87.*

TYPE(<exp>)

Description. TYPE returns a code that signifies the type of variable of <exp>.

Operational rules. TYPE( ) will return one of the following codes:

Code	Type of Variable
C	Character
N	Numeric
D	Date
L	Logical
M	Memo
F	Floating Point Number
U	Undefined

This function is useful when checking whether a certain variable exists in a file.

Examples.

```
. USE Mail
. ? TYPE("ZIP")
  C
. MM = TYPE("ZIPCODE")
  U
```

See also: DATE( ) *p. 190.*

UPPER(<expC>)

Description. The UPPER( ) function converts all the letters in a string to uppercase letters.

Operational rules. The companion function is LOWER( ), which converts all letters in the expression to lowercase. Numbers and other non-alphabetical characters are not affected.

Examples.

```
? UPPER("Hello")
HELLO

? UPPER("hello")
```

See also: LOWER( ) *p. 219.*

USER( )

Description. The USER( ) function returns the name used to login to a protected system.

Operational Rules. Each user is named into the system with the PROTECT command. PROTECT is also the command you use to set the privilege schemes that define what each access level can do. There are two types of privileges: file and field.

The protection scheme only works with multi-user systems.

When writing programs on network systems, it is a good idea to check the access level of the current user in the beginning of the program. The ACCESS( ) function returns this level.

Examples.

```
Mname = USER( )
? "Hello, ", Mname, "We are about to start the main menu program."
WAIT
DO MENU
```

The program checks the name of the user and uses it in displays.

See also: ACCESS( ) *p. 177.*

VAL(<expC>)

Description. The VAL function returns the character <expC> as a number.

Operational rules. This function is helpful when used to read the numeric value of a character string. If the string has no numbers in it, the VAL( ) function returns zero. VAL( ) reads the numeric characters in the string until it reaches a non-numeric character.

The companion function is the STR( ) function which converts a numeric value to a string. The SET DECIMALS command can be used to change the number of decimal places displayed.

Examples.

```
. ? VAL("5")
        5.00

. ? VAL("500 West Street")
    500
```

See also: STR( ) *p. 258.*

VARREAD( )

Description. The VARREAD( ) function returns the name of the variable that the user was editing immediately before exiting.

Operational rules. This function is used in conjunction with the full-screen function @...GET and READ. When the user exits the screen with one of the following keys: Esc, PgDn, Ctrl–End, or On key, they can be placed in any variable on the screen. The VARREAD( ) function returns a character string of the name of the variable.

This function can be used to create context-sensitive help screens.

Examples.

```
USE Maillist
@ 1,1 SAY "Press ESC to get help for a particular field"
@ 3,1 GET Lname
@ 4,1 GET Fname
READ
IF READKEY( ) = 12
   DO Helpit
ENDIF
```

Helpit.Prg

```
DO CASE
     CASE VARREAD( ) = "Lname"
             ? "Help for Lname Field"
     CASE VARREAD( ) - "Fname"
             ? "Help for Fname Field"
ENDCASE
RETURN
```

The program displays context-sensitve help.

See also: ON KEY *p. 130.*
READ *p. 138.*
READKEY( ) *p. 241.*

VERSION( )

Description. The VERSION( ) function returns the version number of dBASE currently being used.

Operational rules. The version will always be the same as the number displayed at the dBASE sign-on message.

Examples.

```
. ? VERSION( )
dBASE IV 1.0
```

YEAR(<expD>)

Description. YEAR returns the number of the year when given a date expression.

Operational rules. You can enter a date as an argument three ways:

- ☐ Enclose the date in curly brackets: {12/5/89}.
- ☐ Use the CTOD function: CTOD("12/5/2010")
- ☐ Reference a field name or memory variable.

Examples.

```
. ? YEAR({9/6/89})
1989

. ? YEAR({12/25/89})
1989
```

See also: DAY( ) *p. 191.*
MONTH( ) *p. 229.*

5

System Memory Variables

THE SYSTEM MEMORY VARIABLES ARE SPECIAL FUNCTIONS THAT ALLOW YOU TO change certain characteristics of your dBASE program. Many of these variables pertain to printing characteristics, such as the page length used by the report generator.

System memory variables return the current settings, although they can also be used to change these settings. For instance, the page length variable is _plength. To display the current page length setting, use:

```
? _plength
```

To change the current setting, change the value of the system memory variable. The following command changes the page length from the 66 line default to the 84 lines needed for legal length paper:

```
_plength = 84
```

Following is a list of the system memory variables.

_alignment

Description. This variable determines the alignment of the output displayed through the ? command. The default is left alignment. The choices are LEFT, RIGHT, and CENTER. The right margin setting (_rmargin) will determine the placement of centered and right-aligned materials. This variable can only be changed when the wrap function (_wrap) is set to True (.T.).

Example.

```
. _wrap = .T.
. _alignment = "RIGHT"
. ? "Date: ",DATE( )
                                                        Date: 12/31/89
```

_box

Description. This variable determines whether or not boxes are displayed. Boxes are defined with the DEFINE BOX command. If _box is set to True (.T.), the boxes will display. Otherwise, they will not. This variable does not affect boxes displayed with the @...TO command. The default is True (.T.)

_indent

Description. This variable determines the number of spaces that the first line is indented for output displayed through the ? command. The default is 0 spaces. The choices are any number up to the right margin setting. The _indent can be less than the left margin. In fact, it can be up to the negative of the _lmargin setting. This variable can only be changed when the wrap function (_wrap) is set to True (.T.).

Example.

```
. _wrap = .T.
. _rmargin = 30
. _indent = 5
     This is a test of
the word wrap function
with indent.
```

_lmargin

Description. This variable determines the left margin for output displayed through the ? command. The default is 0 spaces. The choices are any number from 0 to 254. This variable can only be changed when the wrap function (_wrap) is set to True (.T.).

Example.

```
. _wrap = .T.
. _lmargin = 25
                         This is a test of the word wrap function
                         with a large left margin.
```

_padvance

Description. This variable determines the method used for advancing the paper with the EJECT command. The default is FORMFEED. The choices are FORMFEED and LINEFEED.

The FORMFEED setting causes the paper to advance the same number of lines as the form-feed button on the printer. This can cause a problem if the internal workings of the printer are not set for the correct page length. The LINEFEED setting assures that the paper will advance the correct number of lines according to the page length set with the _plength variable (default 66 lines).

This command only affects the EJECT command. Displaying function CHR(12) will send a form feed regardless of the _padvance setting.

_pageno

Description. This variable determines the page number to printed on a REPORT FORM or other printed output (except output created with the @ commands). The default _pageno is 1. For output other than report forms, dBASE tracks the current page number depending on the page length set through _plength, and the number of lines printed. This variable can be used to change the number printed on the first and preceding pages on a report.

_pbpage

Description. This variable determines the page to begin printing for a REPORT FORM or other printed output. The default _pbpage is 1. This variable can be used if a printout was aborted after a certain number of pages, and you do not want to print those pages again. A _pbpage number greater than _pageno skips the pages before _pbpage by not printing them to the screen or printer.

_pcolno

Description. This variable determines the column position of the output displayed through commands other than the @ commands. This variable can be used to change the column position of text to be displayed. Changing the _pcolno number will have different effects depending on whether the output is being sent to the printer.

If SET PRINT is ON, and _wrap is false (.F.), then lowering _pcolno will cause the last printed text to overstruck by the new text. If SET PRINT is OFF, or it is ON and _wrap is false (.T.), then lowering _pcolno will cause the last printed text to be replaced by the new text.

Example.

Strike.Prg

```
_wrap = .F.
SET PRINT ON
? "This function will strikeout"
_pcolno = _pcolno - 10
?? "---------"
?? "some text."
?
```

The program will cause the word "strikeout" to appear as the following:

This function will ~~strikeout~~ some text.

_pcopies

Description. This variable determines the number of copies of a PRINTJOB to be printed. The default _pcopies is 1. This command can only be used for printing with the PRINTJOB or REPORT FORM commands. You must set _pcopies for issuing the PRINTJOB command.

_pdriver

Description. This variable determines the current printer driver. The default is set through the CONFIG.DB file. Printer drivers determine such print characteristics as boldface, underlining, and italics. These characteristics can be set with the STYLE argument of the ? command or through the report generator.

Printer drivers are files with a .pr2 extension. The extension does not need to be included when changing the _pdriver.

Example.

```
. _pdriver = "LX80"
```

This command sets the printer driver for an Epson LX-80.

_pecode

Description. This variable determines the control codes sent at the end of a PRINTJOB. The default _pecode is a null string.

This command is often used in conjunction with the _pscode which sends out a certain control code before printing. After the PRINTJOB is finished, the printer can be set back to its default mode. Otherwise, all subsequent printing will be printed with the _pscode style.

This variable can only be used for printing with the PRINTJOB or REPORT FORM commands.

Example.

```
_pscode = "{15}"
_pecode = "{18}"
REPORT FORM Maillist TO PRINT
```

In this example, the report prints in condensed print, but then sets the printer back to normal pitch. The example is for an Epson printer where CHR(15) sends the printer into condensed mode, while CHR(18) sets it to 10 pitch.

_peject

Description. This variable determines when an eject is sent within a PRINTJOB. The default _peject is BEFORE. The choices are BEFORE, AFTER, BOTH, NONE. This command can only be used for printing with the PRINTJOB or REPORT FORM commands.

_pepage

Description. This variable determines the page to end printing for a REPORT FORM or other printed output. The default _pepage is 32,767 or the last page of the output, whichever comes first. This variable can be used to reprint an output without printing all the way to the end. A _pepage number less than the number of pages of the entire printout skips the last pages by not printing them to the screen or printer.

_pform

Description. This variable determines the print form file. Print form files set characteristics such as _pageno, _pcopies, _pscode, etc., for report and label forms. You can change all these settings with one command by placing them in a print form file, and then changing _pform before issuing the REPORT FORM or LABEL FORM command. Printer form files have a .prf extension. The extension does not need to be included when changing the _pform.

Example.

```
. _pform = "MONTH"
. REPORT FORM Journal
```

The command sets the print form file to the file Month.Prf.

_plength

Description. This variable determines the page length for printed output. The default is 66. If the page length is different than that set within the mechanism of the printer, this command will not always effect the page length advanced with the EJECT command. To ensure that the page ejects correctly, set _padvance to LINEFEED before issuing EJECT.

_plineno

Description. This variable determines the line position of the output displayed through commands other than the @ commands. The default _plineno is 0. dBASE keeps track of this number as it prints each line. Users of previous dBASE versions were forced to increment the line numbers with a repetition of ? commands because there was no _plineno variable.

_ploffset

Description. This variable determines the left side of the screen and print page. The default is 0 spaces. This is the same variable changed with the SET MARGIN TO command.

This variable is different than the _lmargin variable, because it determines the column to begin counting left for the _lmargin. In other words, you can change the _ploffset, and all _lmargin changes will change relatively. If _ploffset is 0, and the _lmargin is 5, the display will begin in column 5 of the screen. If _ploffset is 10, and the _lmargin is still 5, the display will begin in column 15 of the screen.

_ppitch

Description. This variable determines the current printer pitch. The default _ppitch is DEFAULT, which is equivalent to the setting in the printer mechanism. The choices are PICA, ELITE, CONDENSED, and DEFAULT. This command can only be used if the correct printer driver is set, otherwise the pitch must be changed by sending character strings to the printer using the ? command or _pscode variables.

_pquality

Description. This variable determines the current mode of the printer. The default _pquality is false (.F.), or draft mode. The choices are true (.T.), which is letter quality and false (.F.), which is draft mode. This command can only be used if the correct printer driver is set, otherwise the quality must be changed by sending character strings to the printer using the ? command or _pscode variables.

_pscode

Description. This variable determines the control codes sent at the beginning of a PRINTJOB. The default _pscode is a null string. This variable can only be used for printing with the PRINTJOB or REPORT FORM commands.

Example.

```
_pscode = "{15}"
REPORT FORM Maillist TO PRINT
```

In this example, the report prints in condensed print. The example is for an Epson printer where, CHR(15) sends the printer into condensed mode.

_pspacing

Description. This variable determines the line spacing. The default is single spacing, or 1. The choices are 1, 2, and 3. This variable effects all outputs except those created with the @ commands.

_pwait

Description. This variable determines whether dBASE pauses between pages so the user can put in a new piece of paper. This is needed for printing on separate sheets of paper when there is no sheet feeder of paper bin. The default value is false (.F.). The choices are false (.F.), which is no pausing, and true (.T.), which turns on the wait mode.

This variable can only be used with any command that send information to the printer. It pauses at each occurrence after the EJECT command, and at each point that the _plength is reached.

_rmargin

Description. This variable determines the right margin for output displayed through the ? command. The default is 80 spaces. The choices are any number from 1 to 254, although the right margin must be at least 1 space greater than the _lmargin setting. This variable can only be changed when the wrap function (_wrap) is set to true (.T.).

Example.

```
. _wrap = .T.
. _rmargin = 25
```

```
This is a test of the
word wrap function with
a small right margin.
```

_tabs

Description. This variable determines the tab settings for output displayed through the ? command. The tabs are only affected when the tab character, CHR(9) is displayed.

The default tab setting is every 8 spaces, or "8, 16, 24, commas. This vari able may be changed whether the wrap function (_wrap) is set to true (.T.) or false (.F.).

Changing this variable is equivalent to changing the tab changing the Tab settings in the Config.db file.

Example.

```
 . ? "Col 1",CHR(9),"Col 2", CHR(9),"Col 3"
Col 1   Col 2     Col 3
 . _tabs = "15,30,45"
Col 1             Col 2           Col 3
```

_wrap

Description. This variable determines the word wrap is on. When _wrap is true (.T.), text that is longer than the area between the left and right margins will automatically wrap to the second line, breaking between words.

The default is false (.F.). The choices are true (.T.), which turns word-wrap on, and false (.F.), which turns it off. The _lmargin, _rmargin, _indent, and _alignment variables are only effective when _wrap is true (.T.).

6

Performing Queries

DURING THE 1970S, IBM DEVELOPED TWO DIFFERENT DATABASE QUERYING APPLIcations, Structured Query Language (SQL) and Query By Example (QBE). Both of these are implemented in dBASE IV, and SQL is discussed extensively in Chapter 7. This chapter focuses on QBE, labeled as "Queries" in the Control Center.

QBE is one of the best improvements of dBASE IV over dBASE III+. It is often difficult for new users to get the information they need out of a database. Learning to use QBE is relatively easy, enabling first time users to quickly learn how to perform queries.

The queries are classified into two types, view queries and update queries. Views are created as *virtual* files, meaning that its data comes from one or more underlying tables, while the view does not exist as a file itself. After a view is defined, it can be saved and will reflect the contents of the underlying tables whenever it is used.

Update queries are used to manipulate records in one database, performing one of the four following operations: Append, for adding records; Replace, for altering values of many records at once; Mark, for marking records for deletion; and Unmark, for unmarking records for deletion.

The Query Design Screen

The query design screen appears in Fig. 6-1. The pull-down menu options are on the top row, and can be invoked by pressing the F10 key, or by holding

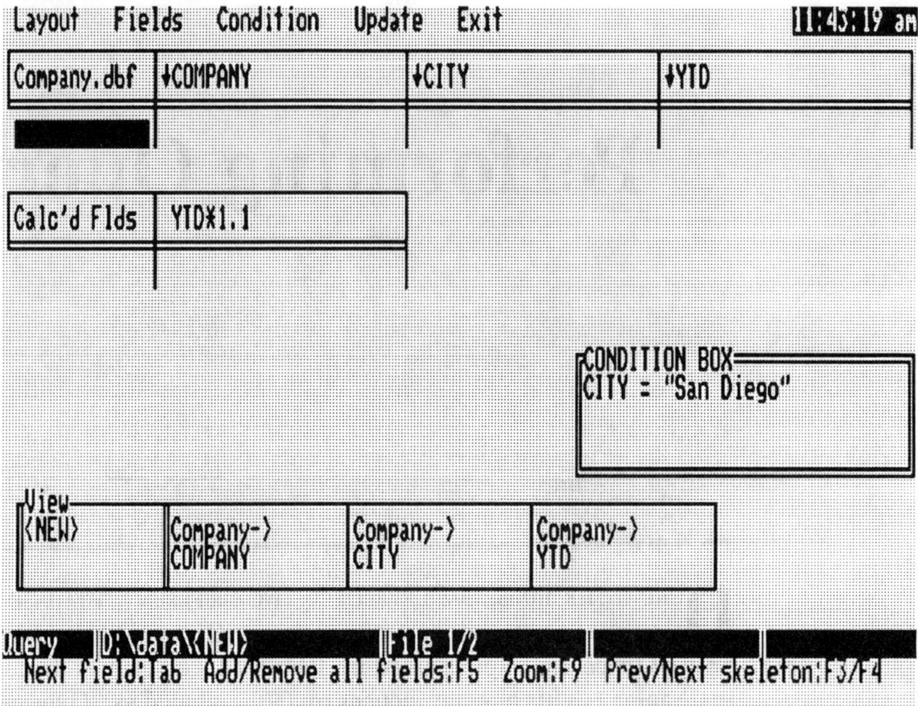

Fig. 6-1. The Query design screen.

down Alt and simultaneously pressing the first letter of the menu option desired.

Immediately below the menu options is a file skeleton. A file skeleton exists for each file used in a query, showing from where the data originates. Query criteria can be entered in the rows below the column headings.

At the bottom of the screen is the view skeleton, only one of which can exist. The view skeleton selects which columns are to be displayed in the resulting query, whether they are from a file skeleton or a calculated field skeleton.

Above the view skeleton on the left is the calculated skeleton. Its columns can contain expressions of columns in the file skeletons.

Above the view skeleton and to the right is the condition box. You can enter dBASE-like limiting criteria here, complete with .AND., .OR., and .NOT. logical operators. It is provided because sometimes conditional expressions are too complex to be accomplished easily using the file skeletons.

Basic Skeleton Movement

Some basic keys to use in skeletons are now introduced. Other keys and their functions are mentioned later as they pertain to a particular subject.

The F3 and F4 keys move the cursor to a different skeleton or box. F3 advances the cursor to the next query design structure, and F4 moves the cursor back to the previous structure. When trying to go beyond either the beginning or the end, the cursor "loops around."

The Tab key moves to the right one column, and Shift – Tab moves to the left one column. If more columns exist than are displayed, the fields will scroll while keeping the database file name's column on the left locked.

Ctrl – right arrow moves the cursor to the right-most position within the field. If already in the right-most position, Ctrl – right arrow advances you to the next field. Ctrl – left arrow works similarly.

Pressing End moves to the far right column, and Home moves to the far left column.

File Skeletons

The file skeletons are used to show where data originated, to enter criteria for queries, and to help define the resulting view by selecting columns to appear in the view.

To add a file skeleton, select the Layout option from the queries menu. Next choose the first option, Add file to query. All the files in the current catalog will be displayed. If no catalog is active, database files in the current directory will be displayed. Position the light bar over the desired file and press Return. You can have up to eight file skeletons in use at a time. It is possible to select the same file more than once, allowing you to relate files to themselves.

The name of the database file being used is in the left-most column of the file skeleton, with only the first letter capitalized, and .dbf shown as the extension. The other columns are the fields that appear in the file.

When in file skeletons, the up and down arrow keys move the cursor from row to row. PgUp and PgDn are used to move to the next screen of file skeletons if many exist. Ctrl – PgUp and Ctrl – PgDn move to the first and last row, respectively, of a file skeleton.

The F5 key behaves differently, depending on what column the cursor is in currently. If under the left-most column (below the <file>.dbf header), pressing F5 toggles between adding all columns of the skeleton to the view and removing all columns of the file skeleton from the view. Otherwise, pressing F5 while the cursor is under the field columns only adds or removes that particular field named.

View Skeleton

The view skeleton determines the fields (or functions of fields) from various files to display in the query result. While there can be many file skeletons, there is only one view skeleton. Update queries do not use views.

When in the left-most column of a file skeleton, pressing F5 results in adding all of its fields into the view. Pressing F5 again removes all fields from the view. If under a field's column instead, pressing F5 adds or removes just that particular column. The same ends can be accomplished by the Add field to view option and the Remove field from view option in the Fields submenu.

When inside the calculated field skeleton, F5 is also used to add and remove the calculated fields to and from the view. However, when adding a calculated field you are prompted to include name for the field if it does not yet exist.

When working within the view structure, you can type column names in the highlighted column. It will not affect the column definition, for that appears in the box below. The column names will appear as headings after performing the query and the browse/edit mode is entered.

The order in which the columns in the view appear can be changed, and you can even move several adjacent columns at once. First, move to one of the columns to be moved by using Tab and Shift–Tab. Next, press F6 (Extend Select). The field should now be surrounded by a large box. Use Tab and Shift –Tab to expand the adjacent columns to be moved. After all the desired columns are boxed, press Return. Now press F7 (Move), and use the right and left arrow keys to move the columns to their new location. When finished, press Return.

If you are using version 1.1, the skeleton column widths will be the same as their respective fields.

Calculated Field Skeleton

When you wish for some column in a view to be the function of one or more fields in a file, the calculated field skeleton must be used.

To invoke the skeleton, select the Create calculated field option from the Fields submenu. You can now enter dBASE expressions in the skeleton, with a total of up to 20 calculated fields. To include the calculated fields in the view, go to the desired field and press F5.

Condition Box

Sometimes when working with complex queries it might be easier to type the query criteria in the condition box. The criteria resembles what would follow "FOR" in dBASE statements, allowing the logical operators .AND., .OR., and .NOT.. In addition, the query criteria can be a combination of both the condition box and example variables.

To use the condition box, select the Add condition box from the Condition submenu. The Delete condition box option will remove the box. Show condition box will hide the condition box by removing it from the screen, although it will still be in effect.

When entering a particularly long criteria, press the F9 (Zoom) key. It will pop up a large editing window to enter the criteria.

Performing Queries

We have thus far covered from where data is obtained (file skeletons), what fields of data is to be displayed (view skeleton), how to compute expressions of fields (calculated fields skeleton), and how to use additional criteria (condition box). Now we perform actual queries, with emphasis on entering criteria within file skeletons.

Query criteria is entered in the rows beneath the column headings, in the appropriate columns. For example, to obtain a view of all those companies in the company database that are in Houston, "Houston" is entered in the city column, as shown below:

Company.dbf	Company	City	YTD
		"Houston"	

Because City is of type character, Houston is enclosed with quotes. Otherwise, Houston will be considered a memory variable.

F2 is pressed to perform the query. When completed, the resulting view switches to browse mode. The F2 key now toggles between browse and edit mode for added flexibility. You can edit the contents of the view fields, and the underlying tables will automatically be updated. This does not apply to view fields that came from the calculated file skeleton. Furthermore, no fields in the view may be modified if a view is defined using any of the aggregate operators AVG, CNT, MAX, MIN, or SUM. The same is true if more than one file skeleton is used in the definition of the view, or a sorting order is specified on a field that lacks an index file for the same field.

Use the Exit option to return to query design screen. Pressing Escape instead returns you to where the query design screen was invoked, such as the Control Center.

A field's condition is not restricted to the width of the column on the design screen. The entry will scroll within the column if more space is needed. You might instead prefer to press F9 (Zoom) to expand the entry space, and press F9 again when finished.

Query Operators

You could have entered = "Houston" instead of just "Houston" in the earlier example. Equals is taken as the default operator. This leads us to the fact that many different operators are available. If > "Houston" was entered, for example, the resulting view would include all those companies in cities that alphabetically follow Houston. The allowable operators are summarized in the table below.

Operator	Description
=	Equals
>	Greater than
<	Less than
<>, #	Not equal to
>=	Greater than or equal to
<=	Less than or equal to
$	contains substring
Like	Pattern matches
Sounds like	Soundex match

The first operators are straightforward, but the last three are worthy of more discussion.

The $ operator is used to see if a certain string is found within (as a substring of) a field's character string. For example, "son" is a substring of "Personal Computer". The $ operator is used the same way throughout dBASE, except in QBE the string following $ is used as the substring to look for. In the rest of dBASE, the substring appears on the left of $, and on the string to search in appears on the right.

The Like operator employs wildcard characters to find matching patterns. These are the asterisk (*) and the question mark (?), both of which behave the same way here they do in DOS. The asterisk replaces zero or more characters. For example, entering Like "*tech" in the Company column would return companies like Megatech, Gentech, and Computech. The question mark replaces exactly one character. For example, entering Like "Anders?n & Associates" in the company column would return Anderson & Associates and Andersen & Associates if they exist.

The Sounds like operator is similar to the dBASE SOUNDEX( ) function. If the field's character string is pronounced similarly to the specified string, the record will be included in the view. For example, if you are not sure of a company name's spelling, and Sounds like "megatech" is entered in the Company column, some of the possible spellings include Megatech, MegaTech, Megatec, and MegaTek.

The criteria is not restricted to being compared solely to constants; the myriad of dBASE functions are at your disposal as well. Pressing Shift–F1 (Pick) pops up a listing of operators, functions, and field names you can select for use in your queries.

Multi-Conditional Operations

In some queries, you might want more than one condition to be met for a record to be included in the resulting view. This is effectively known as an AND operation. To implement an AND operation in QBE, the conditions are simply put on the same row.

For example, to query those companies that have done at least $1000 worth of business with your company (Year-To-Date) AND are in Chicago, the following conditions should be entered:

Company.dbf	Company	City	YTD
		"Chicago"	**> = 1000**

You can also enter more than one condition in the same column by separating them by a comma. This way you can AND together two expressions of the same column to check a range of values.

For example, to obtain all the companies that have done between $1000 and $2000 worth of business with your company this year, use the query as displayed:

Company.dbf	Company	City	YTD
		"Chicago"	
			> = 1000

If you want records to be included in the view if one condition is true or another condition is true, this is effectively an OR operation. To perform ORs, the conditions are put on different rows of the file skeleton.

If the two conditions in the earlier example with the city of Chicago and Sales exceeding 1000 dollars were put on different rows, the query would have a very different meaning.

As displayed above, the query returns all the companies that are either in Chicago *or* have done at least $1000 worth of business with your company so far this year.

Using Aggregate Operators

Within QBE, you can easily obtain basic statistical information that provides insight to database data. The operators are AVG (or AVERAGE), CNT (or COUNT), MIN, MAX, and SUM.

For example, to determine the average sales to clients in New York City this year, enter the query below:

Company.dbf	Company	City	YTD
		"New York"	**Avg**

After performing the query, note that there will only be one row in the resulting view, the average sales for New York. You cannot edit this result or any others derived from aggregate operators. For these type of queries, dBASE will display only the minimum amount of information needed to interpret the result. In the example above, only the YTD column has a value.

These aggregate operators cannot be used in conjunction with the comparison operators like =, >, < =, etc. This is because an entry like > = AVG does not know the average value at the onset of the query, so it cannot perform the query by stepping through the database only once.

Using the Find Operator

The Find operator allows you to begin browsing at the first occurrence that the criteria is fulfilled, where the criteria is entered in the normal matter in the file skeleton. When Find is used the records are not filtered by the criteria, so all records will be displayed. The criteria instead instructs where to begin browsing. To use Find, the keyword Find is entered in the left-most column of the skeleton, below the file skeleton's name.

Using the Unique Operator

Sometimes duplicate records appear in the database, that is two or more records that have identical entries in every field. The query's resulting view will contain these redundant and often undesirable entries. To prevent the duplicate entries from appearing in the view, enter the keyword Unique in the leftmost column of the skeleton, below the file skeleton's name.

Grouping

It is often useful to group information by some category when analyzing data. The Group By operator performs this task, used in conjunction with the aggregate operators.

For example, to obtain the average sales per company grouped by city, the following could be entered.

Company.dbf	Company	City	YTD
		Group By	**Avg**

The resulting view contains an entry for each city. The view is somewhat different from that in which AVG was used without the Group By operator. Although the Company field is not relevant to this particular query, a company appears for each city. This seems like a peculiar result, because you are only interested in the YTD and City fields, which are computed here for several different companies. Simply ignore the values in the Company field, they are just the last company appearing in each group (in this case, each city). When grouping with any of AVG, CNT, or SUM, ignore these values. However, when using MIN and MAX, the other fields become very important, giving information about the record that satisfies the minimum or maximum criteria.

Sorting

There are four ways of sorting rows in the resulting view:

Asc	Ascending ASCII (A..Za..z,0..9)
Desc	Descending ASCII (z..aZ..A,9..0)
AscDict	Ascending Dictionary (Aa..Zz,0..9)
DescDict	Descending Dictionary (zZ..aA,9..0)

There are two ways to select on which field to sort. Move to the desired field and invoke the Fields menu. Then select the Sort on this field option, and choose one of the four options above on the right.

Instead, you can just type in the words that appear in the first column. A number follows the sort keyword to determine the priority of the sort so that nested sorts can be done.

For example, to obtain all the records in the database sorted by City, and then sorted by Company within each city, enter the following:

Company.dbf	Company	City	YTD
	Asc2	**Asc1**	

If just one field is sorted, it is unnecessary to include a 1 following the sort operator. If there are more than one sort operators without a priority operator, the default is sort in the order that they appear in the file skeleton, from left to right.

You can combine sort operators with Group By operators. When you have several operators, generally Group Bys are computed first, in the order of the priority of the operators that follow them.

For example, if the field Co_type categorizes companies, the following would have the total YTD sorted by each type of company, and for each type within each city:

Company.dbf	City	YTD	Co_type
	Group By, Asc2	Sum	Group By, Asc1

Linking Databases

Sometimes you might want to relate databases together on a common field and extract data from both. This is called *linking*, easily facilitated by QBE.

To select additional file skeletons to appear on the query design screen, recall that the Layout submenu option Add file to query is used. Also note that you can have the same file appear more than once, allowing you to relate a file to itself.

Files are linked together by example variables. These are given arbitrary names by the user and are placed in both file skeletons in the field that they are to be related by.

For example, to relate the Company database to a database named Invoices on the Comp_code field, the following is entered.

Company.dbf	Comp_code	Company	City
	Comp		
Invoices.dbf	Inv_num	Comp_code	Total
		Comp	

The fields in both files do not have to necessarily be of the same name, just as long as the two can be related. Linking is usually done when at least one of the files contain unique records, otherwise every combination of records that can be linked on the linking field will be appear in the view.

The variable Comp was chosen arbitrarily. The menu can also be used to link files together, by selecting the Create link by pointing option from the Layout submenu. The menu is invoked while in one of the desired fields to link. Then move to the field in the next file that it is to be linked to, and press Return. The name it chooses for the variable is not very descriptive. The menu method is not advantageous to use, so you might just want to link files manually.

Self-Joins

As mentioned earlier, you can have two file skeletons on the query design screen that are the same file. This way you can relate a file to itself by treating it as two identical but separate files.

For example, to obtain all the companies that are in the same city as Computronix, the following is entered.

Company.dbf	Comp_code	Company	City
		"Computronix"	**X**

Company.dbf	Comp_code	Company	City
			X

The variable X creates the relation on the City field. Computronix is included on one of the lines in one of skeletons, producing an AND operation, that one company must be Computronix, the other in the same city as Computronix.

Using Every in Links

In the earlier Company-Invoices example, records appeared in the view only when a Comp_code appeared in both files. Sometimes you might want to see all the records in a file, even for those that lack a record in another file to link it with. QBE uses the Every operator to accomplish this, with Every preceding the linking variable in one of the files. Every can only be used once for the link.

Using the Company-Invoices example again, Comp is replaced with Every Comp below:

Company.dbf	Comp_code	Company	City
	Every Comp		

Invoices.dbf	Inv_num	Comp_code	Total
		Comp	

Upon query execution, all the companies in the Company database will be displayed, even if their company codes do not appear in the Invoices database.

Using First in Links

Another linking related operator is First. Preceding the linking variable with First will result in only the First occurrence of a link between the two files to display. First is put in the database file skeleton that has several entries to one entry in the other file:

Company.dbf	Comp_code	Company	City
	Comp		

Invoices.dbf	Inv_num	Comp_code	Total
		First Comp	

Only the first invoice in the Invoices file for each company will be in the resulting view.

Update Queries

Update queries allow you to efficiently operate on several records of a database at the same time. Only one database is used in update queries, denoted by the word Target that appears above the file skeleton name when an update is being performed. Unlike view queries, no view skeleton exists because no view results.

Four operators are categorized as Update operators: Replace, Append, Mark, and Unmark. These can be selected from the Update submenu's Specify update operation option or you can simply type one of the four update operators in the left-most column of the skeleton below the file skeleton name.

Updating with the Replace Operator

The Replace operator functions much the same as the dBASE command REPLACE. It allows you to change the values of a field in several records at the same time. The criteria for which records to change is entered as criteria normally is. The operator Replace is entered in the left-most column below the file skeleton name. Enter the new values to assign below the desired fields, by writing the keyword With followed by an expression.

For example, to increase the price of all items in inventory purchased from Pacificomp by 5%, the following is entered:

Inventor.dbf	Partnum	Vendor	Price
Replace		**"Pacificomp"**	**With Price*1.05**

Updating with the Append Operator

The Append operator allows you to insert records into a database by explicitly entering values, or by using variables to copy several records from another file.

The first method is demonstrated in the example below. Append is entered in the left-most column below the file skeleton name, and field values are then assigned.

Inventor.dbf	Partnum	Vendor	Price
Append"	**1040-SX"**	**"Iris Corp."**	**853.00**

For the second method, two file skeletons are needed, one for the source and one for the destination. The Append operator will appear in the destination file, becoming the Target file. Variables are entered in the source file as shown below. These variables then appear in the Target file skeleton to show from what fields to take values. The criteria is entered in the source file skeleton to specify which records form the source to append from.

In the example following, all entries in the Items database are copied into the Inventor database:

Items.dbf	Part	Sell	Dist
	Partno	**Sell_price**	**Who**
Inventor.dbf	Partnum	Vendor	Price
Append	**Partno**	**Who**	**Sell_price**

Updating with the Mark Operator

The Mark operator functions as the dBASE DELETE command. Records are marked for deletion, meaning they still physically exist in the database, but will not appear if SET DELETED is ON. To remove records marked for deletion in the database, the PACK command can be performed in dBASE interactive mode. Alternatively, when inside the database design screen, the Organize submenu option Erase marked records can be selected.

To reinstate records that have been marked for deletion but not yet packed, the Unmark operator can be used.

The criteria is entered in the skeleton to specify which records to mark for deletion. You might want to take some care here. Even though records are only marked for deletion, proceeding to perform a pack without making sure that no other records were accidentally marked could have some unfortunate results. Entering Mark with no criteria will cause all records to be marked for deletion.

In the example below, an entire line of items have been discontinued, those whose part numbers begin with ABX:

Inventor.dbf	Partnum	Vendor	Price
Mark	**Like "ABX*"**		

Updating with the Unmark Operator

The Unmark operator performs the opposite task of the Mark operator, reinstating records marked for deletion. The criteria is entered in the file skeleton, and Unmark is entered under the file skeleton name. It does not hurt anything to unmark records that are already unmark. Entering Unmark with no criteria will unmark all records.

In the example below, the ABX line of items is reinstated.

Inventor.dbf	Partnum	Vendor	Price
Unmark	**Like "ABX*"**		

Saving Queries

Queries can be saved so that you may use them again in the future. To do so, select the Save this query option from the Layout submenu. Provide a name, and press Return. If the query is a view query, it will be given a .qbe file extension, and if it is an update query, it will be given a .upd file extension.

You can also save the query when exiting with the Exit menu. Select the Save changes and exit option.

The queries will now appear in the Control Center in the Queries column. To use one of them, just position the light bar on your choice and press Return.

Queries can also be called from the dot prompt or in programs. Use the MODIFY QUERY or MODIFY VIEW command. To create a query from the dot prompt or in programs, use the CREATE QUERY or CREATE VIEW command.

7

dBASE IV Structured Query Language

IN THIS PART OF THE BOOK, WE TURN OUR ATTENTION TO dBASE IV'S STRUCTURED Query Language, or SQL. An overview of the language is presented in this chapter to show SQL basics to get users unfamiliar with SQL up and running quickly. The majority deals with creation of objects and manipulation of data. Then some other aspects of SQL are introduced. The next section contains a detailed SQL command reference and goes into much greater depth for each command. Because SQL can be used interactively or as a language, a section on embedding SQL into your dBASE programs is also included in the latter part of the text. Finally, information regarding the system databases SQL uses and the Appendices are given.

SQL Description

The Structured Query Language came about as a result of research performed in the mid-1970s at IBM. It was accepted enthusiastically by many companies after it was released, and rapidly became popular. In recent times, SQL has been gaining ground in the personal computer community as well, exemplified by Ashton-Tate's decision to implement it into its tremendously successful dBASE software.

The reason for SQL's popularity is because it is easy to use, but still very powerful and able to perform complex database functions. A difficult task in database environments is to relate one database to one or more other separate databases to share information and store data more efficiently. (This is known as *relating files* or working with *relational databases.*) Those who have set up relations when programming in dBASE before know that this can be a difficult task at times. On the other hand, SQL is a much easier vehicle to use in accomplishing this.

When using databases, a primary concern of the user is the ability to extract information easily. This is where the "Q" for Query in SQL comes from, and the major focus of the SQL designers at IBM. Obtaining data from files with the smaller, simpler command set of SQL makes queries less difficult.

Starting SQL

SQL has two modes—interactive, and embedded SQL for programming. To begin SQL in interactive mode, you must first be at the dBASE dot prompt (.). If you are in the dBASE control center, press Escape and select the Yes option when asked to confirm exiting.

At the dot prompt, type:

```
SET SQL ON
```

The dot prompt should now be replaced with the SQL prompt (SQL.). When you decide to exit from SQL mode, type

```
SET SQL OFF
```

Then the dBASE dot prompt will reappear.

It is possible to begin in interactive SQL mode when dBASE IV is first run by modifying the CONFIG.DB file in the dBASE directory. Simply add the line

```
SQL = ON
```

to the file. If you are unfamiliar with modifying a configuration file, consult a DOS manual.

Keep in mind that while in SQL mode, many, but not all, dBASE IV commands and functions will work. However, dBASE IV version 1.1 allows you to run many more commands (such as APPEND, BROWSE, and LABEL) while in SQL mode. They handle files a little differently, and have commands with the same name that perform different duties, depending on whether SQL or dBASE is activated. A prime example is the SELECT command. In dBASE, SELECT chooses a work area; in SQL, SELECT chooses which data is to be pulled out of tables.

In dBASE, simply pressing Return at the end of an entry will enter commands. However, when using SQL, a semicolon (;) is used at the end of the end of the command to terminate the entry (plus a Return to enter it). It is very easy to forget the semicolon, but failure to do so produces an annoying error message, Incomplete SQL Statement.

The reason why a semicolon is required is because often it is helpful to enter a command on more than one line. Then at the end of the final line, a semicolon can be placed. To issue a command in this manner, the "Zoom" editing mode can be invoked by Ctrl – Home (holding down the control key and pressing Home). After completing the entry, Ctrl – End is pressed, and the command is executed. Throughout the book, commands are typed this way to make them easier to decipher, and we recommended that you enter complex commands this way, too.

Databases, Tables, and Views

The normal dBASE jargon speaks of database files as being described by fields and containing records that hold the data. In SQL, we refer to those databases as *tables*. The columns of the table can be thought of as the fields, where each row contains a record. To use proper SQL terminology, databases are called *tables*, fields are called *columns*, and records are called *rows*.

Before tables are created, a database has to be made. No other information about this special database needs to be provided except for the name. Once the database is in use, all tables, indexes, views, and other information can be managed by SQL. Therefore, for each different application, a different database is used.

Figure 7-1 demonstrates the relationship between databases, tables, and views. The foundation for each application is the database, as previously described. Several tables of data can then be created, each table holding different kinds of information, but usually related. For example, one table can be for invoices and another for inventory.

Views are essentially *virtual* tables that contain information from one or more tables. They are virtual in the sense that no new database is made when creating a view, its contents come directly from other tables. Once defined, views can be treated just like a table, and if declared properly, updating a view will update the corresponding data in the table(s) from which the view was based.

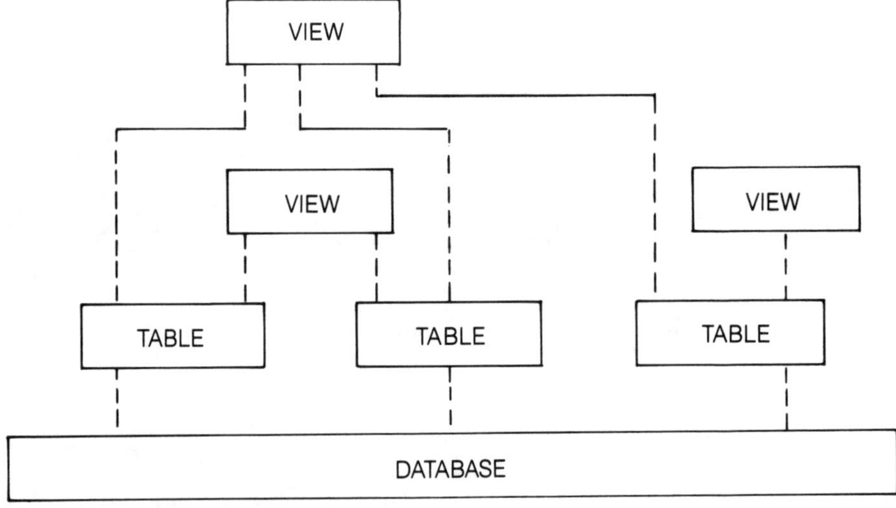

Fig. 7-1. Databases, tables and views.

Creating Databases

To create a database, the CREATE DATABASE command is used. The format is:

```
CREATE DATABASE [<path>] <database name>;
```

Path is optional. It determines where a new subdirectory is to be made. If no path is included, a subdirectory is created from the current directory.

The subdirectory takes on the name given by <database name>. Here, all the catalog tables (described later) and information concerning a certain application are to be kept. It's a nice, clean way of organizing the application.

For example, issuing the command

```
CREATE DATABASE Sales;
```

at the SQL prompt will result in a subdirectory named Sales being created, and a set of system catalog tables to manage Sales is copied to the Sales directory. (Don't forget the semicolon!)

Whenever a database is created, it is immediately activated, allowing the user to work with the application. If no database is active (i.e., you turn on the computer and run dBASE IV), you can activate an existing database with the command:

```
START DATABASE [<database name>];
```

The name must be a previously created database. Without starting a database, none of the associated tables can be used. You cannot have more than one database activated at a time. Not to worry though, you can have several TABLE in use at a time. That is where the actual data is stored. Remember, the database is a sort of shopkeeper for the entire application.

If you attempt to START another database while one is in use, the new one is activated, and the previous one is automatically closed.

The opposite of the START DATABASE command is the STOP DATABASE command, which quite simply, closes the specified database.

Creating Tables

Once the database has been made, tables can now be manufactured. Unlike dBASE IV, the column definitions and information is entered via the CREATE TABLE command instead of a database editor. The command's structure is:

```
CREATE TABLE <table name>
  (<column name> <datatype>
  [,<column name> <datatype>...]);
```

The table name cannot have the same name as an existing table for the currently active database.

Between the parentheses, the columns are defined and separated by commas. For each column name, a datatype must be given (a table of datatypes appears in the reference section for the CREATE TABLE command on p. *306*). These include types such as character, integer, and date.

When you enter the command, it is much better to visualize and compose by using the editing screen accessed by pressing Ctrl–Home. This way, several lines can be used to make up the command. When finished, Ctrl–End is pressed, and SQL tries to execute the command.

As an example, create a sample table for an enterprise called Eardrum Sound Systems which you will use later. Enter the following command (remember, an active database, such as "Sales," must be created earlier):

```
CREATE TABLE Inventor
L   (Partnum      CHAR(15),
     Descript     CHAR(30),
     Quantity     INTEGER,
     Minimum      INTEGER,
     Cost         NUMERIC(8,2),
     Sell         NUMERIC(8,2));
```

This will create a table named Inventor with the columns Partnum through Sell. "Inventor" is used here instead of "Inventory" because table names are limited to eight characters.

Altering Table Structure

What if you forgot a column in the table definition? The ALTER TABLE command can be used:

```
ALTER TABLE <table name>
L   ADD   (<column name> <datatype>
          [,<column name> <datatype>]);
```

As you can see, the format is similar to the CREATE TABLE command.

Using the same table as before, if it were decided to also keep track of the last time an item was sold, issue the command:

```
ALTER TABLE Inventor
  ADD (Lastsell DATE));
```

Now the column Lastsell is added as the last column in the database. Although you can add columns to the table, you cannot delete or alter them. However, the same ends can be accomplished in a roundabout method by creating a new table with the desired structure and inserting rows from the old one.

Entering Data into Tables

Data can be entered primarily in three ways:

1. Entering "manually," line by line by using the INSERT INTO command.
2. Inserting multiple lines from existing tables using the INSERT INTO command.
3. Importing data from other applications, such as dBASE, Lotus 1-2-3, and Framework II using the LOAD DATA command.

In this section, we present only the first method. The second and third schemes are discussed in the command reference section following.

The syntax of the INSERT INTO command is:

```
INSERT INTO <table name>
  [(<column list>)]
  VALUES (<value list>);
```

If the optional column list is provided, the VALUES must correspond to the column list. Otherwise, the values list must contain a value for each column in the table, in order of which they appear.

Using the Inventor table as an example,

```
INSERT INTO Inventory
  VALUES ("HR-5000", "Haiku Stereo Receiver", 5, 1, 293.00,
    389.00, {01/02/89});
```

will add a new row in the table. Note that the Lastsell column entry is included, because you previously ALTERed the table.

Updating data. When one or more rows of the data in the a table needs to be changed, the UPDATE command is used. It is analogous to the REPLACE command found in dBASE IV, with UPDATE's SET similar to REPLACE's WITH, and UPDATE's WHERE similar to REPLACE's FOR.The format of the command is:

```
UPDATE <table name>
  SET <column name> = <expression> [,<column name> =
      <expression>...]
      [<WHERE clause>];
```

The Inventory example is employed once more. Suppose you want to decrease the selling price of the items in inventory that haven't sold after a certain date by 10%. This can be achieved by entering:

```
UPDATE Inventory
  SET Sellprice = Sellprice * .90
  WHERE Lastsell < CTOD("06/01/88");
```

SET determines the values to be assigned, and the WHERE clause is the criteria for which rows to change. Be careful when specifying the WHERE clause, for it is easy to accidentally change the wrong rows.

Deleting rows. The DELETE command is straightforward and uses the same WHERE clause as the UPDATE command to determine which records to delete. The syntax is:

```
DELETE FROM <table name>
  [WHERE <clause>];
```

Suppose that an item in inventory was discontinued due to lack of sales. The item could be deleted from the table by entering the following command:

```
DELETE FROM Inventory
  WHERE Partnum = "AB-1000";
```

This will cause the row entry containing part number AB-1000 to be removed from the table. Once again it is very important here that care is taken with the WHERE clause. If it is omitted, SQL will interpret this to mean you wish to delete the entire table. However, it does give a ''last chance'' prompt to abort the command if you don't have a WHERE clause.

Retrieving Data with the Select Command

The next command introduced is of particular significance and discussed at great length in the reference section. It is the workhorse of SQL, with the ability to extract data from several tables at once based on a specified criteria. In addition, it is used as a subclause for other SQL commands. The command is SELECT, and its format is:

```
SELECT <clause>
  [INTO <clause>]
  FROM <clause>
  [WHERE <clause>]
  [GROUP BY <clause>]
  [HAVING <clause>]
  [UNION subselect]...
```

```
[ORDER BY <clause> /FOR UPDATE OF <clause>]
[SAVE TO TEMP <clause>];
```

SELECT appears overwhelming at first, but simple queries can be performed quite easily. Also, much of the time a lot of the clauses are not going to be used at once.

The SELECT clause determines which columns to display, and in what order. Or, by following SELECT with an asterisk (*), all the columns will display. To see all the data in all the columns of Eardrum Sound Systems' Inventory table, type:

```
SELECT *
  FROM Inventory;
```

The WHERE clause works exactly the same as it does in other commands. While SELECT determines what COLUMNS to display, WHERE determines which ROWS to display. Observe the following entry:

```
SELECT Partnum,Description,Quantity,Minimum
  FROM Inventory
  WHERE Quantity < = Minimum;
```

Upon execution, assuming that data exists, something like the following would display:

PARTNUM	DESCRIPT	QUANTITY	MINIMUM
HR-5000	Haiku Stereo Receiver	3	3
XP-92122	Oishi CD Player	2	4
:	:	:	:
SA-200-X	Anderson 3-Way Speakers	1	2

The resulting output is a list of the part numbers, descriptions, quantity on hand, and reorder minimum from the Inventor tables, as specified by the SELECT clause. The rows SELECTed are those items whose quantity on hand is less than or equal to the reorder minimum, so clerks will know when it is time to order more stereo equipment.

Indexes

Like in dBASE mode, in SQL mode index files can be created for tables. However, it is much different than dBASE. In dBASE, indexes are used to determine in what order the data is retrieved. In SQL, indexes are used to speed up the retrieval of information, but not to determine the order. This might sound silly to dBASE users at first. It does make sense because when a SELECT statement is issued, the ORDER BY and GROUP BY clauses determine the sequence of rows retrieved.

Even though indexes speed retrieval time, other considerations must be made. Updates are slowed down because the index files must be updated as well. As a general rule, try to limit the number of index files you create, and generate the index on the column you would ORDER BY in SELECT statements.

All of these indexes remain active when you use a table. The index actually used when the data is retrieved is the most efficient one determined by SQL.

The CREATE INDEX command's syntax is:

```
CREATE [UNIQUE] INDEX <index name>
  ON <table name>
  (<column name> [ASC/DESC]
  [,<column name> [ASC/DESC]);
```

The index is made solely from a list of column names, not expressions of column names. Using UNIQUE results in an index that does not allow duplicate rows. ASC/DESC determines if the index will be in increasing order (ASC) or decreasing order. (DESC) If neither is specified, it will default to ASCending order. To index on part number in the Inventor table, enter:

```
CREATE UNIQUE INDEX Part
  ON Inventor (Partnum);
```

UNIQUE is used to insure the same part number isn't in the table twice.

Views

After becoming familiar with tables, users can increase their SQL effectiveness by using views. A *view* is comprised of parts of one or more tables. It becomes a "virtual" table, meaning it functions like a table but isn't a true table. This is because it is the child of other tables with its data coming from its parents, and not an actual table in its own right. If a *view* is created as an "Updatable View", altering the contents of the *view* will alter the contents of tables that the view was created from, a very helpful data manipulation device.

The format of the command is:

```
CREATE VIEW <view name>
  [(<column name>, <column name> ...)]
  AS <SELECT statement>
  [WITH CHECK OPTION];
```

The view name is first provided, followed by a list of column names to define the view. The AS part is a bit more tricky—a SELECT statement must be included to define the view. The view can be thought of as a SELECT statement whose selected rows and specified columns get output to the view. The WITH CHECK OPTION involves updatable views and can be used to make sure that no changes are made to the table that violate the view definition.

The SELECT statement issued earlier can be created into a view, a view that contains products to reorder.

```
CREATE VIEW Reorder
  AS SELECT Partnum,Descript,Quantity,Minimum
  FROM Inventor
  WHERE Quantity < = Minimum;
```

To give an example using more than one table, assume a table called Invoices also exists. It contains the columns:

```
Invnum    CHAR(12),
Partnum   CHAR(15),
Qty_Ord   INTEGER,
```

Also assume that two of the lines are:

```
INVNUM   PARTNUM      QTY_ORD
12763    HR-5000            1
12763    SA-200-X           1
```

You desire information from the Inventory table—the price and description to complete the invoice. If you want to create a view to from both tables, you could type the following:

```
CREATE VIEW Inview
  AS SELECT Inventor.Partnum, Descript, Quantity, Sell
  FROM Invoices, Inventor
  WHERE Invnum = "12763" AND Invoices.Partnum = Inventor.Partnum
```

The SELECTed columns might have the names of columns from both tables. However, if a column name is the same, then the table name is followed by a period (.) and the column name. Here, Partnum is in both Inventor and Invoices. The resulting output is:

```
PARTNUM    DESCRIPT                    QTY_ORD    SELL
HR-5000    Haiku Stereo Receiver             1  389.00
SA-200-X   Anderson 3-Way Speakers           1  310.00
```

The DROP Command

We have covered the basics of views, tables, indexes, and databases. One more command is discussed, the DROP command. DROP is just a synonym for delete, to remove one of these structures from the system. Be careful when using this command, because DROPping a database will DROP all associated tables, views, and indexes. Similarly, DROPping tables will remove the views and index files associated with it. The syntax is:

```
DROP VIEW <view name>;
DROP INDEX <index name>;
DROP TABLE <table name>;
DROP DATABASE <database name>;
```

Use one of the above, depending on what you wish to drop.

More SQL Commands

The preceding was aimed at getting first time users up and running in dBASE IV SQL. Some other commands are now introduced as they pertain to other SQL concerns. The commands can be referred to in the reference section.

Database security. dBASE IV makes it fairly simple to implement a password protected system. You might want to be familiar with the dBASE IV command PROTECT that controls user IDs and passwords, information used in both dBASE IV mode and SQL mode.

A special user called the *SQL database administrator* (SQLDBA) has access to all tables, and other objects created in SQL. The SQLDBA and users can create tables and then give access to these tables to other users. The commands used for security are GRANT and REVOKE. As their names imply, GRANT allows access to tables, REVOKE takes back some or all of the GRANTed privileges. The SQLDBA has the power to GRANT to and REVOKE from anyone. See these commands in the reference section for more details.

Embedded SQL. Embedded SQL refers to the ability to "embed" SQL commands within another programming language, such as dBASE. In addition to the commands that can be used in both interactive and embedded SQL mode, there are special commands that are used exclusively in embedded SQL. In particular, the commands DECLARE CURSOR, FETCH, OPEN, and CLOSE use a powerful programming tool called *cursors*.

An entire section is devoted to embedded SQL following the command reference section.

Data importing and exporting. SQL provides two commands for importing and exporting data, LOAD and UNLOAD respectively. They have the ability to transfer to and from many of the most popular IBM PC-based applications' formats as well as Standard Data Format.

SQL catalog tables. SQL uses several catalog tables to keep track of tables, indexes, views and synonyms. A set of these tables exist for every database in the database's directory. They vary in amount of use and their function, but they contain vital information required by SQL. In addition, a master catalog table Sysdbs in the SQL home directory contains information on each database. The tables and the information they hold is summarized here:

Table	Information
SYSAUTH	Contains user privileges on tables and views. One row exists for each table a user has some privilege(s) on.
SYSCOLAU	Contains user privileges to UPDATE columns in tables and views. One row exists for each column in a table the user can UPDATE.
SYSCOLS	Contains column definitions for every table and view, including the catalog tables themselves. One row exists for each column in every table and view.
SYSIDXS	Contains all the table's indexes in the database. One row exists for each index.
SYSKEYS	Contains the description for every column used as an index key in each index. One row exists for each column for every index.
SYSSYNS	Contains the definitions for table and view synonyms. One row exists for each synonym.
SYSTABLS	Contains description of every table and view. One row exists for each table and view.
SYSTIMES	Contains time information to verify that users have up-to-date copies of SQL catalog tables in a multi-user environment. One row exists for each catalog table.
SYSVDEPS	Contains the tables each view is dependent on. One row exists for each table in every view definition.
SYSVIEWS	Contains view definitions and characteristics. One or more rows is used for each view.

Information in these tables can be accessed by using the SELECT command just like they were any other table. However, you cannot DELETE, UPDATE or ALTER the tables. (The SQLDBA can perform UPDATEs.)

To see all the basic table and view information for example, you can enter:

```
SELECT *
FROM Systabls;
```

The three catalog table maintenance commands are RUNSTATS (*p. 322*), DBCHECK (*p. 310*), and DBDEFINE (*p. 310*). RUNSTATS is used to optimize performance, and should be run periodically. DBCHECK verifies table and index structure. It should be run after altering table definitions. DBDEFINE creates catalog entries for dBASE files, allowing them to be used in SQL. DBDEFINE is also used to redefine tables if errors occur. See the following reference section for more details.

Alphabetical Listing of SQL Commands

The following section is a listing of SQL commands. This alphabetical list explains what each command does and gives the syntax of the command.

ALTER TABLE

The ALTER TABLE command is used to add columns to existing tables. Don't be misled by the word ALTER. You can add columns to tables but cannot delete or modify the definition of any existing columns. The syntax is:

```
ALTER TABLE <table name>
  ADD (<column name> <data type>
  [,<column name> <data type>...]);
```

Note the similarity of the ALTER TABLE command to the CREATE TABLE command. The <table name> must be an existing table in the current database. The <column names> must be unique within the table, and are 1 to 10 characters in length. The total number of columns cannot be more than 255, with the total width less than or equal to 4,000 bytes. Please refer to the table in the description of the CREATE TABLE command for the allowable data types on p. _.

If the new column is of type character, all rows are set to the empty string. If it is one of the numeric types, all rows are set to 0. If it is of type logical, all rows are set to .F..

Although views are often treated as tables in SQL, the ALTER TABLE command cannot be used on views, because they themselves are based on other tables.

While ALTER TABLE does not allow modification or deletion of existing columns, there is a roundabout method to do so. First, create a new table with the new structure. Then use the INSERT INTO command to extract data from the old table and place it into the new. For example:

```
ALTER TABLE Donors
  ADD  (Last_date DATE,
        Total NUMERIC(9,2));
```

Two columns are added to the Donors table, Last_date of type DATE for the last amount donated, and Total of type NUMERIC for the total amount given.

CLOSE

To deactivate a cursor that has been open, the CLOSE command is used. Its syntax is:

```
CLOSE <cursor name>;
```

The <cursor name> must be the name of the open cursor to close. This command is used only in embedded SQL.

A cursor can be reopened repeatedly, but it must be CLOSEd before each new OPEN. This is useful because the result table of the cursor as defined in the DECLARE CURSOR's SELECT clause can change in between OPENs. A cursor is closed automatically at the end of the program module if it was open, but it is better programming style to include the CLOSE.

You might want to be aware that the compiler is (unfortunately) very strict on the sequence that OPEN and CLOSE appears in a program. The compiler will generate an error if it does not see an OPEN in between two CLOSEs, even though the two CLOSEs might not ever both be executed because of IF-THEN or CASE conditional statements.

Refer to *p. 341* in the section on embedded SQL to see how CLOSE functions with other cursor-related commands.

CREATE DATABASE

The databases (as they are called) that SQL uses are not structures that contain user data in the traditional view. Instead, they contain information regarding a particular application. The actual user data is contained in structures called *tables*. The database organizes the various tables, views and indexes associated with a particular application, and creates a work area just for the application. The syntax of the command is:

```
CREATE DATABASE [<path>] <database name>;
```

If the optional path is included, the database will create and use the directory specified in the path. If it is not specified, a new subdirectory will be created from the current directory. The name assigned to the new directory will be the same as the database name. However, if the directory already exists, it will be redefined as a new database directory.

Within the new directory, special SQL catalog tables are created to keep track of all the tables, views, and other information concerning the application. In addition, the database is entered into the SQL master table Sysdbs.

After creating a database it automatically becomes active, allowing for tables to be created, and work to be done within the application. In future SQL sessions, use the START DATABASE command to activate the database. For example:

```
CREATE DATABASE People;
```

A new database named People is created, as well as a subdirectory named People. People is entered into the master catalog table, and the set of SQL catalog tables are defined in the People directory. Finally, the database is active.

CREATE INDEX

Indexes are a useful mechanism in increasing the speed of data retrieval. The syntax of the command is:

```
CREATE [UNIQUE] INDEX <index name>
  ON <table name>
  (<column name> [ASC,DESC]
  [,<column name> [ASC/DESC] ...] );
```

Including the optional keyword UNIQUE allows only nonduplicate values for the columns indexed on. The <index name> is the name you wish to call the new index, and the table that the index is based on is given by <table name>.

More than one <column name> may be used as an index key, each being separated by a comma. If more than one is specified, the index is first calculated by the first column named. Then, if there are entries with the same value in the first column, the index is figured on the second column within each value of the first column. If more columns are used, the process repeats.

Specifying ASC or DESC is optional, for ASC is taken as the default. ASC creates an index in increasing order, while DESC creates an index in decreasing order, both by the ASCII standard. If multiple columns are used, you cannot use both ASC and DESC; all columns must be one or the other. Columns that are of type logical cannot be indexed on. An important thing to keep in mind is that creating an index will not cause data to be retrieved in a particular order, for that is the function of the ORDER BY clause in the SELECT command. However with indexes, the speed of retrieval will increase. Ideally, indexes will be created based on columns that will be used in the SELECT statement's ORDER BY clause. When a SELECT is issued, dBASE IV SQL automatically chooses the most efficient index to use.

Because the index is essentially a list of row numbers for a certain table, updating the contents of table will cause the indexes to be updated as well. This might slow down updates somewhat, especially if the index is UNIQUE, and several indexes exist.

If the index is UNIQUE, tables are can be read but not written to when in dBASE mode.

As far as views are concerned, because views are based on underlying tables, data is retrieved based on the tables' indexes. If a view is updatable, the indexes based on the underlying tables are updated when data in the view is updated. For example:

```
CREATE UNIQUE INDEX Partnum
ON Inventor (Partnum);
```

An index named Partnum is created for the Inventor (Inventory) table, in ASCending order on the column Partnum. UNIQUE is used to insure that repetitions of the same part number does not exist in the table.

CREATE SYNONYM

The CREATE SYNONYM command, quite simply, allows the user to refer to tables by a different name other than the table name. The syntax is:

```
CREATE SYNONYM <synonym name>
  FOR <table name>;
```

The <synonym name> is the synonym to be created, and cannot be an existing name for a synonym, table, or view in the current database. The <table name> is the table that is to be given a synonym.

Synonyms can be useful if you want to refer to a table by a more descriptive name. Also, if a table name is long you can instead refer to it by a shorter name. For example:

```
CREATE SYNONYM In
  FOR Inventor;
```

Here, the synonym In is created for table Inventor.

CREATE TABLE

CREATE TABLE is utilized to construct the tables used to contain data in the currently active database. The syntax is:

```
CREATE TABLE <table name>
  (<column name> <data type>
  [,<column name> <data type>...] );
```

The <table name> given cannot be an existing table, view or synonym for the current database, and is 1 to 8 characters in length.

The columns can be thought of as the fields that are to hold data, so they must be descriptively defined. Each column name must be unique within a table, and 1 to 10 characters in length. There is a maximum of 255 columns in a table with a total width 4,000 bytes. The allowable data types in SQL for the columns are given below:

Data Type	**Description**
SMALLINT	Allows for "small" integer values, with up to 6 digits in length. A '+' or '−' is considered one digit, allowing values from −99,999 to 999,999, because no '+' is required for positive values.
INTEGER	Allows integer values, with up to 11 digits in length. A '+' or '−' is considered one digit, allowing values from −9,999,999 to 99,999,999, because no '+' is required for positive values.
DECIMAL(x,y)	Allows fixed decimal values with a total length of up to x, where x is from 1 to 20, and '+' and '−' are counted towards the total length. Parameter y specifies how many digits right of the decimal point to use, where y ranges from 1 to 18. Therefore, the length format of the decimal is (x − y).y.
NUMERIC(x,y)	Is similar to DECIMAL, only the decimal point '.' is also counted towards the total length. Fixed decimal values with a total length up to x is allowed, where x is from 1 to 20. Parameter y specifies how many digits to the right of the decimal point to use, where y ranges from 1 to 18. Therefore, the length format of the decimal is (x − y − 1).y.
FLOAT(x,y)	Allows floating point numbers with a total length up to x, where x is from 1 to 20 and the decimal point '.' and unary signs '+' and '−' contribute to the total length. Parameter y specifies how many digits to the right of the decimal point to use, where y ranges from 1 to 18. Numbers may be given in scientific notation, i.e. −1.23E+45. The floating point numbers may range from 10^−308 to 9.0*10^+307.
CHAR(n)	Allows up to an n character string to be entered, where n is from 1 to 254.
DATE	Allows a date in the special date format to be entered. The default format is mm/dd/yy, but can be altered using the SET DATE and SET CENTURY commands. In addition to accepting values from other date formatted columns and date variables, dates explicitly given can be specified within the dBASE function CTOD( ) (i.e., CTOD("01/01/89")) or brackets { } (i.e., {01/01/89}).

LOGICAL — Allows logical true or false values to be entered. The value "true" can be entered as either .T., .t., .Y., or .y.. The value "false" can be entered as either .F., .f., .N., or .n..

These types encompass, in one form or another, the types found in dBASE mode. The only one not covered by SQL are memo fields.

When a table is created, a new .dbf file is made, and the SQL catalog tables are updated. There might be an existing .dbf file in the database directory. If this occurs, it is overwritten by the new table.

If the dBASE command PROTECT has previously been executed, the new table will be encrypted. Only the SQL database administer or the creator can GRANT access to the table, using the GRANT command. The table will not be accessible outside of SQL mode. See PROTECT on p. # for more details.

An example of the command is:

```
CREATE TABLE Donors
(Lname    CHAR(15),
Fname     CHAR(12),
Address   CHAR(25),
City      CHAR(15),
State     CHAR(2),
Phone     CHAR(13),
Birthday  DATE,
Potntial     NUMERIC(9,2));
```

A table named Donors is created, using CHAR type for name and address information, DATE for birthday, and NUMERIC for giving potential.

CREATE VIEW

Within a database for an application, several tables can exist. SELECT statements can be executed to relate different tables together in various ways, but sometimes it is nice to be able to treat the resulting table from the SELECT as a table itself. Although the SAVE TO TEMP clause in SELECT could be used, it only exists for the current session, or it can be made into a permanent table with the addition of KEEP.

Many times it is more useful to use the CREATE VIEW command. The syntax is:

```
CREATE VIEW <view name> [(<column name>, <column name>...)]
  AS <subselect>
  [WITH CHECK OPTION];
```

As the name implies, it provides the ability to "view" portions of one or more tables. It saves space by being only the offspring of other tables. Furthermore, the resulting view can then be treated like a table, allowing more queries to be made on it. This can help as being an intermediate step in a very complex query. Also if defined properly, the contents can be updated, which will alter the tables from which it is based.

The <view name> is the name to be given to the view. AS <subselect> defines the view, where the subselect is just a SELECT statement. The tables used in the subselect are called *base* tables, being the underlying tables of the view. In the same vein, the view is then thought of as a *virtual* table. It is virtual because it is treated as being real, but is only derived from others and does not physically exist.

The column list is made up of column names (or expressions thereof). If the column list is not specified, the column names are given the same name of those from the SELECT's result table. If different column names are desired, or the SELECT contains derived columns (i.e., expressions), or duplicate columns, the column names must explicitly be given.

The WITH CHECK OPTION is used with updatable views. If it is included, the view definition is checked each time a row is updated to make sure it is not violated. A violation will cause the underlying tables to not be updated.

It is important to point out that a view cannot be created for all SELECT statements. FOR UPDATE OF, INTO, ORDER BY, SAVE TO TEMP, and UNION cannot be used within the SELECT statement. Also, a view created with GROUP BY cannot be joined later with another table or view.

More restrictions are applied for views that are updatable. The SELECT cannot contain DISTINCT, GROUP BY, or an SQL aggregate function. Nor can FROM reference a nonupdatable view, or FROM in a nested subquery, use the same underlying table.

One very beneficial use of views is for security. Because views can be made from parts of tables, you can allow users to have access to a view, but not the sensitive columns in the underlying tables. See GRANT on *p. 315* for determining user access to tables and views.

As in most things in life, with good things often come the bad. With all the benefits of views is one major disadvantage, speed. Because a view doesn't really exist as a physical table, performing operations like SELECT can slow down performance because of translation that must be done to use the base tables.

For example, assuming the company Iris Corporation's customer code is 2485, the following will create a view of all their invoices.

```
CREATE VIEW Iris_Inv
  AS SELECT *
  FROM Invoices
  WHERE Custcode = 2485;
```

Say a personnel database exists that you would like some employees to be able to manipulate, without having access to certain personal information like salary and medical information. After it is created, access can be GRANTed to the view and restricted from the table. The following view can be created, where the columns named are only nonsensitive columns:

```
              CREATE VIEW Emp
AS SELECT     Lname,Fname,Address,City,Zip,Phone,
              HireDate,Departm,Superv
              FROM Employee;
```

DBCHECK

DBCHECK is part of the trio of maintenance commands, DBDEFINE and RUNSTATS being the others. When an SQL table is manipulated in dBASE mode or the table's structure is altered, DBCHECK should be run to make sure the table will function properly. Its syntax is:

```
DBCHECK [<table name>];
```

If a table is specified, only that table and its index files in the current database are checked. Otherwise, all tables and their associated index files are checked.

This "checking" process entails verifying that catalog table entries are consistent with the .dbf and .mdx files. An error message will display for every inconsistency. To remedy the situation, follow the steps outlined under the DBDEFINE command.

DBDEFINE

DBDEFINE is used to bring dBASE files and their indexes into the current SQL database. In addition, it is used to correct inconsistencies with the SQL catalog files. The format is:

```
DBDEFINE <.dbf file>];
```

If a .dbf file is specified, catalog table entries are created for only the file and its .mdx file if it exists. Otherwise, all files and their indexes are given catalog entries and made available in SQL mode.

DBDEFINE cannot be issued for an index created in dBASE mode that used the UNIQUE option.

If operating in a multi-user environment, execute this command when the table is not being manipulated.

After successful completion, a documentation file named dbdefine.txt is created that contains table and index definitions which might be helpful later.

If DBCHECK or RUNSTATS produce errors, or it is desired to redefine the SQL tables and indices, the following four steps should be performed:

1. Exit SQL and backup the troublesome .dbf and .mdx files by copying them to another directory or diskette.
2. Go back into SQL, and DROP the tables that had errors, the ones that were backed up in step 1. The tables and its associated entities will be removed from the catalog tables.
3. Exit SQL once more, and recopy the .dbf and .mdx files back into the database directory.
4. Reenter SQL, and execute DBDEFINE for each table to be redefined. The indexes for each table will be redefined as well.

DECLARE CURSOR

To define a cursor in embedded SQL, the DECLARE CURSOR command is used. The syntax is:

```
DECLARE <cursor name> CURSOR
  FOR <SELECT statement>
  [FOR UPDATE OF <column list>/<ORDER BY clause>];
```

The cursor acts similar to a file pointer that advances from record to record. Instead of pointing to records in files, the cursor points to rows in a result table. The result table is determined by the SELECT statement following FOR.

The cursor definition is retained during the entire SQL session. To activate the cursor, the OPEN <cursor name> command (*p. 319*) is used, and the result table is then computed. (It is computed at the OPEN because what appears in the result table can change at different times, and it can be reopened after it is closed.) The FETCH command (*p. 314*) is then used to obtain values out of the current row and advance the cursor to the next row. See all of these commands for further details, as well as the section on embedded SQL to show how all these work together.

The FOR UPDATE OF clause in the SELECT statement must be included if you wish to update column values of the currently FETCHed row. This is accomplished using the UPDATE command. If FOR UPDATE OF is used, the

SELECT statement cannot contain ORDER BY, UNION, DISTINCT, GROUP BY, or HAVING clauses. In addition, SQL aggregate functions are not allowed, and the FROM clause may only contain one table or an updatable view, where the table might not reappear in a subquery. For example:

```
DECLARE Item CURSOR
  FOR SELECT Partnum, Descript, Qty, Minimum
  FROM Inventor
  WHERE Qty < Minimum;
```

A cursor named Item is created from the Inventor table for items that have a quantity on hand less than the minimum desired amount.

DELETE

The DELETE command allows rows to be removed from table. There are two forms of the command, their syntaxes being:

```
DELETE
  FROM <table name>
  [<WHERE clause>]
```

and

```
DELETE
  FROM <table name>
  [WHERE CURRENT OF <cursor name>];
```

There are two WHERE possibilities, as shown above. The first is used in command mode or embedded SQL mode, with the WHERE clause containing the criteria of which rows in the table to DELETE.

WARNING! Be very careful when specifying the condition for which rows to delete, for they cannot be restored, unlike in dBASE mode. It might be wise to first do a SELECT with the same WHERE clause to see which entries will be removed. Also, there is the danger of not including a WHERE clause. If it is omitted, SQL assumes that you wish to delete all the rows. Luckily, SQL detects this and gives you a last-chance prompt to abort. Nonetheless, be forewarned: mistakes with DELETE can have disastrous results. Therefore, it might be a good idea to not allow users to have the delete privilege, and allow only the database system operator to DELETE. See the GRANT command on p. 315 regarding this.

The second means of deletion is only in embedded SQL mode. It deletes the row that the cursor is currently pointing at, the cursor being specified following WHERE CURRENT OF. Usually, rows will be FETCHed one at a time, and possibly some action may be taken on it. Then an IF-THEN statement is often used to see if a condition is met, and if satisfied, the row will be deleted. See the section on embedded SQL for an example of using DELETE WHERE CURRENT OF on *p. 312*.

If BEGIN TRANSACTION is used, the deletions won't take effect until an END TRANSACTION is encountered. If it is used in embedded SQL, the deletions won't take effect until an END TRANSACTION is encountered and the cursor is CLOSEd. For example:

```
DELETE FROM Inventor
  WHERE Partnum = "XY-9000";
```

If an item was discontinued, it could be deleted form the inventory table Inventor be entering the above.

DROP DATABASE

When an application is no longer needed, it can be deleted by the DROP DATABASE command. The syntax is:

```
DROP DATABASE <database name>;
```

The database being dropped cannot be active. You can deactivate a database with the STOP DATABASE command. In addition, if working in a protected environment, only the database creator or the SQL database administrator can DROP the database.

Dropping a database will delete the .dbf and .mdx files in the database's directory. All tables, indexes, views, and the the like will cease to exist. The system catalog table Sysdbs is updated to reflect the deletion.

A last-chance prompt appears to verify the DROP, allowing the user to abort the operation.

DROP INDEX

The DROP INDEX command allows indexes that are no longer needed to be deleted. The syntax is:

```
DROP INDEX <index name>;
```

If a database or table is DROPped, its associated indexes are automatically DROPped as well. In addition, if working in a protected environment, only the creator of the index or the SQL database administrator can DROP the index.

DROP SYNONYM

The DROP SYNONYM command deletes table and view synonyms. Its syntax is:

```
DROP SYNONYM <synonym name>;
```

If a database, table, or view is DROPped, its associated synonyms are automatically DROPped as well. In addition, if working in a protected environment, only the creator of the synonym or the SQL database administrator can DROP the synonym.

DROP TABLE

If a table is no longer needed, it can be deleted with the DROP TABLE command. Its syntax is:

```
DROP TABLE <table name>;
```

If a table is DROPped, its associated views, indexes and synonyms are automatically DROPped as well. In addition, if working in a protected environment, only the creator of the table or the SQL database administrator can DROP the table.

DROP VIEW

If a view is no longer needed, it can be deleted with the DROP VIEW command. Its syntax is:

```
DROP VIEW <view name>;
```

If a database or table is DROPped, its associated views are automatically DROPped as well. In addition, if working in a protected environment, only the creator of the view or the SQL database administrator can DROP the view.

FETCH

After DECLARing and OPENing a cursor, the values in the result table can now be retrieved by using the FETCH command. The syntax is:

```
FETCH <cursor name>
  INTO <variable list>;
```

The first time FETCH is executed after an OPEN, the cursor is positioned at the first row in the result table, and the row's values are retrieved. Subsequent FETCHes advance the cursor one position and then retrieve the new row's values. When the end of the result table is encountered, no values are retrieved.

These values are assigned to the memory variables in the variable list in the INTO clause, in the same order that the columns were specified in the DECLARE CURSOR's SELECT statement. Make sure you have the same amount of memory variables as the SELECT statement's columns. The memory variables need not be previously defined.

After the OPEN command, the SQL system variable Sqlcnt will contain the number of rows in the result table. The other system variable Sqlcode is used to check the status of commands. If a FETCH is successful, Sqlcode will contain 0. If the cursor points beyond the last row of the table, Sqlcode will contain +100, a very useful fact. If an error occurred, Sqlcode will contain −1.

Refer to the section on embedded SQL for examples on how FETCH is used along with other cursor-related commands on *p. 341*.

GRANT

The GRANT command is used for determining which users can access what tables and their associated entities in a PROTECTed environment. The dBASE command PROTECT must have already been used to define users and their passwords. Please refer to PROTECT for more information. After they log in and enter SQL mode, GRANT will determine what privileges users will have. The syntax is:

```
GRANT ALL [PRIVILEGES]/<privilege list>
  ON [TABLE] <table list>
  TO PUBLIC/<user list>
  [WITH GRANT OPTION];
```

Users can CREATE tables which they can use, independent of GRANT. Afterwards only the SQL database administer or the creator can GRANT access to the table, or DROP it.

Several different privileges can be given on a table, the privileges being defined ALTER, DELETE, INDEX, INSERT, SELECT, and UPDATE[(column list)]. UPDATE can be followed by a column list enclosed in parentheses to allow only the values in certain columns to be modified, otherwise all columns will be assumed. These can be included in any combination in the privilege list, or ALL could be used instead to GRANT ALL privileges. However, ALL cannot be used when GRANTing access to views, for ALTER and INDEX are not allowable privileges on views. Having the keyword PRIVILEGES following ALL is optional and does not change the statement's meaning, but can be included as a matter of preference.

The table list allows similar privileges to be GRANTed to many tables at once to save time. TABLE is just an optional keyword in the same way PRIVILEGES is.

After specifying what privileges to allow on what tables, who is being GRANTED these privileges needs to be determined. Specifying PUBLIC allows everyone to have the same privileges in one easy command. Otherwise, users must be named explicitly in the user list. The users are specified by his or her ID name assigned in PROTECT.

Inclusion of the WITH GRANT OPTION allows those users GRANTed access to the tables to then GRANT the same privileges they have been bestowed to other users. If access was GRANTed TO PUBLIC, the WITH GRANT OPTION should not be included; everyone has access to the tables anyway.

To allow only partial access to nonsensitive columns in tables, you can create a view of the nonsensitive columns as described in the CREATE VIEW section, or use UPDATE to note those columns as described earlier.

Privileges on tables can be taken away from users by using the REVOKE command.

Some examples are:

```
GRANT ALL
  ON Contacts
  TO PUBLIC;
```

This code allows everyone to perform any operation on the Contacts table. In the following code,

```
GRANT SELECT, UPDATE(Address,City,State,Zip)
  ON Clients
  TO Remy, Molina
```

users Remy and Molina are granted the ability to perform SELECT queries and update address information on the Clients table.

INSERT

The INSERT command allows new rows of data to be entered into the table. The two forms of the command can be used in either the SQL command mode or embedded SQL. The syntaxes are:

```
INSERT INTO <table name>
  [(<column list>)]
  VALUES (<value list>);
```

and

```
INSERT INTO <table name>
  [(<column list>)]
  <subselect>;
```

The table name is the table into which to insert. The column list specifies into which columns to insert values. If it is omitted, it is assumed that values are being inserted into all the columns, in the order that the table is defined.

If VALUES is being used, the value list must correspond to the column list. That is, the values specified must be in the same order as the columns that they are being inserted into in the column list. Items in both lists are separated by commas. The command succeeds just as long as the values are of compatible data types as the columns in which they are being inserted. Therefore, it is possible to accidentally insert values into the wrong column that are of the same type.

When specifying values, constant character values are surrounded by quotes, and dates use either { } or CTOD( ). Values can be given explicitly by constants, by memory variables, or functions.

If the subselect technique is being employed, the values still must correspond to the column list. The subselect then must return column values in an order that is compatible with the data types of the INSERT's column list. For example:

```
INSERT INTO Donors
  Lname,Fname,Address,City,State,Zip,Ent_Date,Total
  VALUES("Alcas","Jaime","6559 Condor Dr","San Diego",
          "CA","92122",{06/01/89},150.00);
```

This would create a new entry in the Donors table for a first time donor. The following inserts basic name and address information for all entries in the Contacts table into the People table:

```
INSERT INTO People
  Last, First, Address, City, State, Zip
  SELECT Lname, Fname, Address, City, State, Zip
    FROM Contacts;
```

LOAD DATA

The LOAD DATA command has the ability to import data into tables from files that are not in SQL format. The syntax is:

```
LOAD DATA FROM [path] <filename>
  INTO TABLE <table name>
```

```
[[TYPE] SDF/DIF/WKS/SYLK/FW2/RPD/DBASEII/
DELIMITED [WITH BLANK/WITH <delimiter>];
```

The path specifies where to bring the data in from, be it from a floppy in the A drive, or another directory on a hard disk. The filename is the name of the file found at the location of the path.

The table name is the name of the table to load the data into. It must contain the as many columns as there are fields in the data being imported. The table's column definitions should also correspond in type, length, and order of the fields in the file being imported. If these differ, data might be truncated.

What if no table exists for the exact format being imported? A trick around this is to create a temporary table with exact definitions to fit the data. After LOADing, use the INSERT INTO command to place the data into the proper table(s). When finished, DROP the temporary table.

Including TYPE denotes what the format of the data is, including some from the more popular applications. They are:

Type	**Description**
SDF	Standard Data Format. Most applications, even those not well known, allow importing and exporting using to this standard ASCII format.
DIF	Visicalc format.
WKS	Lotus 1-2-3 format.
FW2	Framework II format.
RPD	Rapidfile format.
DBASEII	dBASEII format, for the unfortunate few!
DELIMITED	Fields are separated by a comma, records by a carriage return and linefeed, and character fields are surrounded by quotes. If WITH BLANK is used, spaces are field separators, and character fields have no delimiters. Using DELIMITED WITH <delimiter> will assume fields separated by commas, and character fields surrounded by the delimiter specified.

If no TYPE is given, dBASE .dbf format is taken as the default. When using .dbf files, the memo fields are not imported.

If a table named Phone exists, and Lotus 1-2-3 is on the C drive with a worksheet used as a phone list in its files subdirectory,

```
LOAD DATA FROM C:\lotus\files\phone.wks
  INTO TABLE Phone
  TYPE WKS;
```

means that the phone data will be read into table Phone.

OPEN

After a cursor has been defined with the DECLARE CURSOR command, it is opened with the OPEN command. The syntax is:

```
OPEN <cursor name>;
```

The <cursor name> is a cursor that has previously been DECLAREd.

Upon execution, the defining SELECT statement in the DECLARE statement is computed for the result table. The FETCH command can now be used to advance the pointer and retrieve values from the result table.

A cursor can be reOPENed over and over, but it must have been previously CLOSEd before each new OPEN. ReOPENing is useful because if the table is updated, the next OPEN will produce a different result table. In addition, the SELECT statement can contain memory variables in the WHERE clause that might change the result table's definition.

Two important SQL system variables are updated after an OPEN. The first, Sqlcnt, contains the number of rows in the result table, 0 if it is empty. It is useful in programming loops to FETCH the number of rows in the cursor's result table. The second, Sqlcode, is set to 100 if there are no more rows left to FETCH (then it is set to 100 if there are no rows in the result table). Otherwise, Sqlcode is 0 on successful execution of a command, or −1 if there was an error.

See the section on embedded SQL to see how OPEN (*p. 342*) is used in relation to other SQL commands.

REVOKE

The REVOKE command is used in conjunction with the GRANT command, which permits users to have access to tables. REVOKE performs the opposite task, withdrawing privileges previously given by the GRANT command. Its syntax is:

```
REVOKE ALL [PRIVILEGES]/<privileges list>
  ON [TABLE] <table list>
  FROM PUBLIC/<user list>;
```

In an environment where security exists, the PROTECT command must have been previously run, which configures user IDs and passwords. After users log in, they can CREATE tables and then GRANT access to them to other users. Similarly, they can REVOKE some or all of the GRANTEd access. Just as the SQL database administrator can GRANT access to anyone on any table, he or she can also REVOKE access from anyone, even if the SQL database administer didn't GRANT the access.

The privileges that are REVOKEd on a table can be those previously GRANTed. The privileges are listed explicitly in the privilege list or ALL can be used to REVOKE all privileges. Having the optional keyword PRIVILEGES following ALL does not alter the command's effects, but can be included as a matter of preference.

The <table list> allows privileges to REVOKEd on more than one table at the same time. TABLE is just an optional keyword in the same manner PRIVILEGES is.

The <user list> provides the ability to REVOKE privileges from more than one user at the same time. Using PUBLIC instead is a bit more tricky. It does not REVOKE privileges from everybody; it REVOKEs from those GRANTed privileges PUBLICly, but not from those GRANTed individually. In other words, think of each user as having two identities, their own and a PUBLIC one. That user can manipulate tables based on the combination of both.

When the WITH GRANT OPTION is used with the GRANT, it gives users GRANTed access to GRANT to others. If a user is REVOKEd privileges and he or she GRANTed privileges to others, their privileges are also automatically REVOKEd. This is because their privileges are based on another user's privileges. If a user has been given the WITH GRANT OPTION, the only way to effectively REVOKE the WITH GRANT OPTION is to REVOKE ALL privileges, and reGRANT privileges without the WITH GRANT OPTION.

A user (called A) can be GRANTed privileges to the same table by more than one user. Therefore, having one user REVOKE user A's privileges is not enough, A can still access the table. If A's privileges are to be REVOKEd, all must REVOKE his privileges, or have the SQL database administer REVOKE ALL A's privileges.

In the example:

```
REVOKE DELETE
  ON Clients
  FROM PUBLIC;
```

Assume ALL privileges were GRANTED previously to PUBLIC on the table Clients. The above command will disallow all users to DELETE entries from the Clients table. Note that if an individual user was explicitly (not PUBLICly) given the DELETE privilege previously, he or she will still have that ability.

ROLLBACK

Transaction processing is allowed in SQL mode as it is dBASE mode. If a transaction is unable to complete, the ROLLBACK command can be used as part of error recovery. The syntax is:

```
ROLLBACK [WORK];
```

WORK is just an optional keyword, included for compatibility with other SQL systems.

Transactions are defined to be the set of commands appearing between BEGIN TRANSACTION and END TRANSACTION. Usually the ON ERROR command is used such that if an error occurs during a transaction, the program can transfer control to an error recovery routine. Here, performing a ROLLBACK will bring the table or view back to its state before the BEGIN TRANSACTION command was executed.

The commands DBCHECK, DBDEFINE, ALTER, CREATE, DROP, GRANT, and REVOKE cannot be included within a transaction.

Some functions related to error recovery are:

COMPLETED( ); returns .T. if the transaction was successfully completed, .F. otherwise.

MESSAGE( ); returns the error message for the last error.

ROLLBACK( ); returns .T. if ROLLBACK successfully completed.

Also, the RETRY command can be used to return to the program where the error occurred and try to execute the troublesome command again. For example, within the program:

```
ON ERROR DO Err
BEGIN TRANSACTION
* Manipulate table, view here
END TRANSACTION
ON ERROR
* ON ERROR alone cancels "DO Err"
```

Within Err.prs:

```
@ 20,1 SAY MESSAGE( )
try = " "
@ 22,1 SAY "Try again? (Y/N)" GET try
READ
IF try $ "Yy"
  RETRY
ELSE
  ROLLBACK;
ENDIF
RETURN
```

RUNSTATS

To perform at an optimum level, SQL catalog tables keep statistical information that need to be updated using the RUNSTATS command. The syntax is:

```
RUNSTATS [<table name>];
```

If a table is specified, statistics on only that table is updated. Omission of a table name will result in the updating of all tables in the current database.

RUNSTATS should be run if a new table is created, DBDEFINE was just run, or a table's definition is altered. The same is true for indexes. In addition, RUNSTATS should be run periodically, when "normal" database operations are happening, to increase performance.

When executing this type of command that demands full use of a table in a multi-user environment, you should stop all other manipulations of the table.

SELECT

The SELECT command queries one or more tables, and produces a result table. The result is displayed, or it can be saved to a temporary table. SELECT is the cornerstone of SQL, and is found as a subclause to other commands. The syntax is:

```
SELECT <clause>
  [INTO <clause>]
  FROM <clause>
  [WHERE <clause>]
  [GROUP BY <clause>]
  [HAVING <clause>]
  [UNION <subselect>]...
  [ORDER BY <clause> / FOR UPDATE OF <clause>]
  [SAVE TO TEMP <clause>];
```

The clauses are broken down and described in the following sections.

The SELECT clause. The SELECT clause chooses which columns of the table to display (or expressions of), and whether or not each row is unique:

```
SELECT [ALL/DISTINCT] <expression list>
```

Uniqueness is determined by [ALL/DISTINCT], which are optional reserved words. Inclusion of ALL results in nondistinct rows being displayed. In other words, two or more rows with the same data contents will both be in the result table. This does not mean each row in a table will be output, for the WHERE clause chooses which rows to display; it just means duplicate rows are allowed. It is not necessary to include ALL in the statement, ALL is taken as the default.

On the other hand, using DISTINCT in the clause will not display duplicate rows, and will instead produce only one of the repeated row entries. The advantage of DISTINCT is to make the output more concise, and eliminate redundancies. When using DISTINCT, keep in mind the combined length of the columns listed may not be greater than 100 bytes.

The <expression list> contains the listing of columns to display and expressions of columns to display. Expressions can be functions of columns, and SQL aggregate functions can be used.

The asterisk (*) is used to denote to list all the columns in the SELECT clause, as opposed to having to list each column name explicitly. For example:

```
SELECT DISTINCT *
  FROM Clients;
```

Upon execution, this command will list all the DISTINCT entries for all the columns in the table named Clients. In this example,

```
SELECT Partnum,Quantity,Cost,Quantity*Cost
  FROM Inventor;
```

the columns Partnum, Quantity, and Cost are displayed, along with a fourth column labeled Exp1 that contains the Quantity multiplied by Cost for each item. The output would look something like:

PARTNUM	QUANTITY	COST	EXP1
AX-257	1	238.00	238
T-400-Q	2	175.00	350
:	:	:	:
WZ-9999	1	345.00	345

EXP1 is labeled as such because it is the first column that contains an expression in the column list.

When making SELECTs that have have many rows in the result table, the screen display can be stopped from scrolling by pressing Ctrl – S. Pressing Ctrl – S again will cause the screen to continue scrolling. It might be more convenient to issued SET PAUSE ON before performing the SELECT so the display will pause at each screen full of data.

Aggregate functions. In SQL mode, there are some special aggregate functions that can be used. They are:

Function	**Description**
AVG( )	Returns the average value of a column for the rows selected.
COUNT( )	Counts the number of rows selected.
MIN( )	Finds the minimum value of a column for the rows selected.

MAX( ) Finds the maximum value of a column for the rows selected.
SUM( ) Sums a numeric column for the rows selected.

All functions can be used with columns that are of numeric type. MAX( ), MIN( ) and COUNT( ) can be used with date and character types as well. When using MAX( ) and MIN( ), the returned value is based on the ASCII standard. (A is lower than Z, a is lower than z, and A is lower than a. A < Z < a < z.)

Enclosed in the parenthesis of the aggregate functions are the optional keywords ALL or DISTINCT followed by a column name or an expression. The expression cannot contain another aggregate function, and must include a column name.

This will return the total number of entries in the People table, the first name alphabetically, and the last name alphabetically:

```
SELECT COUNT(*),MIN(Lname),MAX(Lname)
  FROM People;
```

From the inventor table, each row (item) has its quantity multiplied by cost, then is summed up with the other items:

```
SELECT SUM(Quantity*Cost)
  FROM Inventor;

RESULT:
            SUM1
         82532.73
```

The final total will be the total value of the inventory on hand.

Here, information about the sales staff is displayed:

```
SELECT AVG(Sales),MAX(Sales),MIN(Sales)
  FROM Staff;

       OUTPUT:
          AVG1      MAX1      MIN1
       9324.54  22484.35   3476.75
```

They are the average, maximum and minimum amount of sales for the salespersons.

What if you wanted to find out how many people are in each zip code in a table named Donors, and the following was typed? (NOTE: This is incorrect.)

```
SELECT Zip, COUNT(*)
  FROM Donors;
```

The error message GROUP BY expected is displayed. This is because specifying a column name implies *one or more* values are to be returned, and specifying an aggregate function implies *only one* value is to be returned. The SQL interpreter is confused. However, if GROUP BY was specified, a count could be given for each unique value grouped on. When GROUP BY is discussed on p. 328, the proper way to accomplish this goal is demonstrated.

The INTO clause. The INTO clause is used in embedded SQL mode to transfer the values of the result table into memory variables:

```
INTO <memvar> [,<memvar>,...<memvar>]
```

If more than one row results, only the first row is used. The memory variables are assigned in the order that the columns specified in the SELECT clause. If no rows result, the memory variables are not created, and the special SQL system variable SQLCODE is set to +100. If INTO is included in the statement, the GROUP BY, HAVING, UNION, ORDER BY, FOR UPDATE OF, and SAVE TO TEMP clauses cannot be specified.

An example of the INTO clause follows:

```
SELECT Lname,Fname,Address,City
  FROM People
  INTO Mlast,Mfirst,Madd,Mcity
  WHERE Lname = "Jones";
```

This statement uses the table named People, and copies the last name, first name, address, and city into memory variables for the first occurence of the last name of Jones.

The FROM clause. The FROM clause specifies FROM which tables to base the query on. The syntax is:

```
FROM <table>/<view> [alias] [, <table>/<view> [alias]]...]
```

A view can be specified instead of a table, and several tables and views can be listed, separated by commas.

The alias is a special construct that allows a table to be given another name, provided they are not the single-letter names of A through J. Aliases are particularly useful in correlated subqueries and self-joins, which is discussed towards the end of the SELECT section. For example:

```
SELECT *
  FROM People Who;
```

this returns all row entries for all columns in the table People, and assigns the alias Who to the table People.

The WHERE clause. The WHERE clause determines the criteria for which rows to return. The format is:

```
WHERE [NOT] <search condition>
  [AND/OR [NOT] <search condition>...]
```

In addition, the WHERE clause can contain sub-selects, dBASE functions, predicates, and SQL aggregate functions. First, the search condition operators are covered:

Logical Operator	Description
NOT	Returns the rows which do not satisfy the search condition following NOT.
AND	Returns rows which meet the condition on both the right-hand side and left-hand side of the AND.
OR	Returns rows that meet either the condition on the right-hand side or the condition on the left-hand side.

The precedence determines the order in which the expressions are to be evaluated. NOT has highest precedence, followed by AND, followed by OR. Nevertheless, it is very wise to group expressions with parentheses for clarity when several operators appear in an expression.

The following are the comparison operators.

Comparison Operator	Description
<	Less than
>	Greater than
=	Equals
<=	Less than or equal to
>=	Greater than or equal to
< >, != or #	Not equal to
!<	Not less than
!>	Not greater than

Now some examples are presented to demonstrate these operators:

```
SELECT *
  FROM People
  WHERE City = "San Diego";
```

The result table will return all those persons in the People table living in San Diego.

If on a capital campaign for a charitable organization, entering the following would return all those donors who have a giving potential greater than or equal to $1000.

```
SELECT Lname, Fname, Phone
  FROM Donors
  WHERE Potential > = 1000;
```

Suppose you want to send birthday cards to individuals in the table named People. Then the following could be typed:

```
SELECT *
  FROM People
  WHERE (MONTH(Birthday) = 6 AND DAY(Birthday) > = 1 AND
    DAY(Birthday) < = 7) OR Lname = "Rumplestilskin";
```

The result table will contain those people who have a birthday in June (the 6th month) and the day of the month between the 1st and 7th, or for Mr. Rumplestilskin, who likes to get a birthday card every week.

In the above example, note the use of the dBASE functions MONTH( ) and DAY( ). These and the entire arsenal of dBASE functions help make SELECT statements very powerful.

The Between predicate. Other devices called *predicates* aid in constructing selects. Two are presented here, with others being discussed in relation to subqueries later. The first is BETWEEN, and like all predicates, is used in the WHERE clause.

Basically, BETWEEN...AND... replaces two search conditions ANDed together that are interested in a range of values. Using the Donors table, the following statement

```
SELECT *
  FROM Donors
  WHERE Potential > = 1000 AND Potential < = 2000;
```

could be replaced more concisely by:

```
SELECT *
  FROM Donors
  WHERE Potential BETWEEN 1000 AND 2000;
```

The LIKE predicate. LIKE has the ability to do string comparisons using wildcard characters, analogous to the ones found in DOS. '%' effectively same functions as '*' in DOS, meaning it replaces any string of zero or more characters. '_' (the underscore) effectively functions as '?' in DOS, meaning it replaces exactly one character. For example,

```
SELECT *
  FROM Clients
  WHERE Lname LIKE "M%cNeil";
```

will detect the names of both McNeil or MacNeil in the Clients table. Although it is unlikely to exist, it would even detect the name MZimbabwecNeil, because '%' replaces zero or several characters. The other wildcard character in the statement

```
SELECT *
  FROM Clients
  WHERE Lname LIKE "Anders_n"
```

will return names like Anderson and Andersen, i.e., those that begin with ''Anders'', followed by exactly one character, followed by and ended by ''n''.

The GROUP BY clause. The GROUP BY clause provides the means for a convenient way of grouping data together. The syntax is:

```
GROUP BY <column> [,<column>...]
```

The rows that result from a SELECT statement are grouped according to the columns specified. For each unique value in the column, the rows will be grouped. Adding more columns to the column list causes subgroupings within the group. The columns contained in the column list must also be contained in the column list following SELECT.

Only one GROUP BY clause can be in the entire SELECT statement, be it a subquery or not. Also, if GROUP BY is included in the SELECT statement, the INTO clause cannot be included. Furthermore, if a view is defined with the GROUP BY or HAVING clause, it cannot be used in a SELECT's FROM clause.

Aggregate functions can be used in the column list. This way information like COUNTs can be compared based on groups.

In this example, a listing of all persons in the Donars table results, grouped by Zip code:

```
SELECT Lname,Fname,Address,City,State,Zip
  FROM Donors
  GROUP BY Zip;
```

For the same table, if a count of how many donors are in each zip code were desired, the following would be typed:

```
SELECT Zip,COUNT(DISTINCT *)
  FROM Donors
  GROUP BY Zip;
```

The output would appear something like:

```
G_ZIP    COUNT1
02786        24
22834        10
  :           :
92806        35
```

The G_ (G underscore) before ZIP as a column heading in the result table implies that the results are grouped by zip code. The column heading COUNT1 is labeled as such because it is the result of the COUNT( ) function, and the first occurrence of one.

The HAVING clause. The syntax of the HAVING clause is:

```
HAVING [NOT] <condition>
  [AND/OR [NOT] <condition> ...]
```

The HAVING clause is similar to the WHERE clause in that it determines which results to display. However, WHERE affects all rows of the table individually, and HAVING affects the results of the GROUP BY clause. The group as a single unit must meet the criteria specified by having.

HAVING is usually used in conjunction with GROUP BY, but omitting GROUP BY will cause HAVING to operate on the entire table as one group. Only one GROUP BY clause can appear in a SELECT statement, and GROUP BY cannot be used if an INTO clause is used.

The condition specified in the GROUP BY clause must contain an SQL aggregate function.

Using the Donors table again to find out those cities which have a total giving potential greater than or equal to $10,000, the following could be entered:

```
SELECT City,SUM(Potential)
  FROM Donors
  GROUP BY City
  HAVING SUM(Potential) > 10000;
```

The output would appear as:

```
    CITY        SUM1
LOS ANGELES    42720
          :        :
PORTLAND       11200
```

The UNION clause. The UNION clause allows the results from two or more tables to be combined in one result table by having each of the SELECTs be separated by UNION. If more than two tables are being combined, parentheses must be used for each subUNION. UNION conveniently eliminates duplicate rows as well.

The usage of UNION is stringent. The columns specified in the column list of each SELECT statement must "match up." That is, the same number of columns must be specified, and each column in the list must correspond to another in the same position of the other column lists. The corresponding columns do not have to have the same name, but they do have to have the same datatype, and be of the same width. For example,

```
SELECT Last,First,Phone
  FROM Clients
  UNION
  SELECT Lname,Fname,Phone
    FROM Contacts;
```

In the above example, the last name, first name, and phone number of those individuals in the table Clients and the table Contacts are combined into the result table. Lname and Last are both of type character, and of the same width. Even though 2 of the column names correspond to a different column names in the other column list, it is legal because they are both of the same type and of the same width.

The ORDER BY clause. The ORDER BY clause specifies in what order the rows of the result table are to appear. The syntax is:

```
ORDER BY <column>/<integer> [ASC/DESC]
            [,<column>/<integer> [ASC/DESC] ];
```

The column or integer choice allows you to refer to columns explicitly by their name, or by the number that it appears in the column list in the SELECT clause. (The first column is 1, etc.) The columns used in the ORDER BY clause must be in the SELECT clause's column list as well. An advantage of using the numbering scheme is that you can refer to expressions of columns by using the number that it appears in the column list.

ASC and DESC determines if the order should be sorted in increasing order or decreasing order respectively, with ASC being the default.

If more than one column is used in the ORDER BY clause, the first one specified takes precedence, followed by the second and so on. So, suborders result within orders.

ORDER BY must be the last clause in the command, unless the SAVE TO TEMP clause is also used.

For example,

```
SELECT Name, Address, Zip
FROM Clients
ORDER BY Zip, Name
```

the resulting output would contain the client information, ordered by the zip code, then with all names within each zip code would be ordered alphabetically.

The FOR UPDATE OF clause. The FOR UPDATE OF clause is used in embedded SQL mode when a cursor definition is being given. The syntax is:

```
FOR UPDATE OF <column>
              [,<column>...];
```

The columns listed denote those columns whose values are allowed to change. See the UPDATE command for more details. If FOR UPDATE OF is employed, the INTO, ORDER BY and SAVE TO TEMP clauses are forbidden.

The SAVE TO TEMP clause. The SAVE TO TEMP clause allows the results from a SELECT statement to be saved to a temporary table. The syntax is:

```
SAVE TO TEMP <table> [(<column>
                     [,<column>] )]
                     [KEEP]
```

The table determines what to name the temporary table. Stating columns is not always necessary. They will have the same name as the columns listed in the SELECT clause unless otherwise specified. However, if the SELECT clause contains expressions of columns, column names must explicitly be given.

Including KEEP in the statement will save the table as a permanent .dbf database file, so that in subsequent sessions the table will still exist. If KEEP is not included, the table will exist only during the current session while the current database is in use.

Joins. The true power of SQL stems from its ability to relate tables together. Obtaining a result table by combining two or more related tables or even relating a table to itself is called a *join*.

Because two related tables often have the same column names, it is useful to include table names when specifying column names. This is done by using the format Tablename.Columnname. A simple example is first presented, although unnecessary. If there is a table Chars with column Comic, we could obtain a listing of all comic strips in Chars by typing:

```
SELECT DISTINCT Comic
  FROM Chars;
```

we could have also entered:

```
SELECT DISTINCT Chars.Comic
FROM Chars;
```

Expanding on this idea, assume there is a table that exists named Chars that includes columns Comic and Char, the comic strip and the character respectively. Also, assume a table Artists exists that includes the columns Comic and Artist. If we wish to see all the characters of the comic strips and the artist that draws them, the following join could be used:

```
SELECT Chars.Char, Chars.Comic, Artists.Comic, Artists.Artist
  FROM Chars, Artists
  HERE Chars.Comic = Artist.Comic;
```

The output would be something like:

```
Chars->Char   Chars->Comic        Artists->Comic      Artists->Artist
Calvin        Calvin and Hobbes   Calvin and Hobbes   Bill Waterson
Hobbes        Calvin and Hobbes   Calvin and Hobbes   Bill Waterson
      :                :                   :                    :
Snoopy        Peanuts             Peanuts             Charles Shultz
```

In the columns following SELECT, the expanded column notation is used. Note that Chars->Comic and Artist->Comic are duplicate columns. Both are displayed to show that the criteriain the WHERE clause is satisfied. Because it is not useful to have duplicate columns like this, one or the other should only be included, but not both.

In the above example, you might think it superfluous to even have two different tables in the first place. The reasoning for having multiple tables is to store data efficiently. If the Artist table also contained the address of the Artist, birthdate and other information, it wouldn't make sense to repeat this information over and over for each character if a single table was used.

It is very important that a WHERE clause is included in joins, it tells HOW the table are to be joined. If no WHERE clause is included, there is no limiting criteria, and SQL combines every row of the first table with every row of the second table.

For example, assume that there is a table named Letters with one column named Letter, having 26 entries A-Z. Also assume there is a table Numbers with 10 entries, 1-10 in column Number. What would happen if the following were entered?

```
SELECT Letter,Number
  FROM Letters,Numbers;
```

The ouput would look something like:

LETTER	NUMBER
A	1
A	2
:	:
A	10
B	1
:	:
Z	10

No WHERE clause is present, so SQL concatenates every row of LETTERS with every row of NUMBERS, producing a result table of 26*10 = 260 rows. When working with information from different tables and trying to establish a relationship, a result like this is usually not useful. Nonetheless, it is presented here to demonstrate how a join is actually accomplished.

Sometimes beneficial information is gained when a table is related to itself. Before presenting an example, alias names are discussed.

Aliases allow the user to refer to a table by another name. The earlier comic strip example (but this time without the duplicate column) could have also been entered as:

```
SELECT C.Char,C.Comic,A.Artist
FROM Chars C, Artist A
WHERE C.Comic = A.Comic;
```

The C following Chars defines C as an alias for Chars that can be used throughout the SELECT statement. Similarly, A is an alias for Artist. Here aliases save a little typing, but they also can be used to clarify table meanings.

The most interesting case of using aliases is when a table is related to itself. Employing the Chars comic strip table, if you wanted to match up each character in a strip with every other person in the same strip, the following could be entered:

```
SELECT X.Comic, X.Char, Y.Char
FROM Chars X, Chars Y
WHERE X.Comic = Y.Comic;
```

The output would appear something like:

X->Comic	X->Chars	Y->Chars
Calvin and Hobbs	Calvin	Calvin
Calvin and Hobbes	Calvin	Hobbes
Calvin and Hobbes	Hobbes	Calvin
:	:	:

The statement accomplished the task, but each character is matched up with each character twice, once as the first, once as the second. To remedy the situation and obtain only unique pairs, enter:

```
SELECT X.Comic, X.Chars, Y.Chars
FROM Chars X, Chars Y
WHERE X.Comic = Y.Comic AND X.Char > Y.Char;
```

Subqueries. With subqueries, it is possible to nest SELECT statements within one another via the WHERE clause. This allows the outer SELECT to query based on what the inner (nested) SELECT returns. The best way to see this is by example:

```
SELECT Name
FROM Clients
WHERE Custcode =
  (SELECT Custcode
  FROM Invoices
  WHERE Invnum = 2786);
```

In this example, you want to know what customer appears on invoice number 2786. Assume that the Clients table contains information about clients, including a customer code (Custcode). Also assume Invoices contains invoice information including the customer who purchased items by Custcode. Custcode appears in both tables and is the column by which the two tables are related.

The '=' operator is used in the WHERE clause, comparing Custcode on the left-hand side to some value on the right hand side to be returned by the subselect. Therefore, only one unique value should be returned from the subselect or an error will occur.

The value returned will be the customer code from invoice number 2786. Because "Custcode = " appears after the word WHERE, a Custcode of some sort is expected to be returned from the subselect. Thus Custcode is the column SELECTed to be returned in the inner select.

Predicates. A helpful instrument in doing subqueries are SQL's predicates. Two of them, BETWEEN and LIKE were introduced earlier. Not all are exclusively used in subqueries, but they are discussed here because of their particular relevance.

The IN predicate. What if the subquery returns many different values, unlike the last example? The IN predicate can then be used. First it is noted that IN can be used without a subquery as in:

```
SELECT Name,Address,City,State,Zip
FROM Clients
WHERE Zip IN ("92122","92806","90028");
```

The zip codes in parentheses following IN are a list of possible Zip values that will satisfy the SELECT criteria.

With subqueries, the values following IN can be replaced by an "inner" subquery, whose list of values returned will be used by the "outer" subquery. Another example is presented:

```
SELECT Name,Address,City,State,Zip
FROM Clients
WHERE Custcode IN
  (SELECT Custcode
  FROM Invoices
  WHERE Invdate > = {01/01/89});
```

Custcode appears in both the Clients and Invoices tables. The inner query returns a list of customer codes for those clients who have purchased something since January 1, 1989. The outer query then obtains a result table containing the name and address information of those clients.

NOT can be used in conjunction with IN to produce the opposite result. In the above example, if the line "WHERE Custcode IN" were replaced with "WHERE Custcode NOT IN", the result table would contain those clients who have NOT purchased anything since January 1, 1989.

The ALL predicate. The ALL predicate is used in conjunction with the comparison operators >, > =, <, < =, =, and < >. The operator precedes ALL, inferring that the condition must be true on the operator for ALL values returned by the subquery. An example best shows how ALL is used:

```
SELECT Partnum
FROM Inventor
WHERE Price > ALL
  (SELECT Price
  FROM Invoices
WHERE Invoice = 2387);
```

The items in inventory that have a price greater than the highest priced item on invoice # 2387 is returned. Here's how it works.

The inner query returns a list of values, the prices of all the items on invoice number 2387. The outer query then steps through the entire inventory, checking to see if any item's price is greater than ALL of the items on invoice 2387. (In other words, greater than the highest priced item on the invoice.)

Using < ALL would produce the opposite result. It would return items in inventory that are priced less than the least priced item.

Even = ALL is a valid combination. The inner query would be evaluated true if the outer query's column value equals ALL of the inner query's returned list. This is only possible if the inner query returns ALL of the same value (only one unique value), equivalent to the outer query's column value.

Specifying < ∧ ALL has the same effect as NOT IN. The column being queried on cannot equal any of the values returned by the inner query.

The ANY predicate. The ANY predicate is also used in conjunction with operators. The operator followed by ANY infers that the condition must be met by ANY of those items returned by the subquery. In the example presented below, you can see that nested subqueries are allowed:

```
SELECT Custcode
FROM Invoices
WHERE Total > ANY
  (SELECT Total
  FROM Invoices
  WHERE Custcode =
    (SELECT Custnum
    FROM Clients
    WHERE Name = "Iris Corp."));
```

We will analyze this in a bottom-up fashion. The bottom (innermost) subquery returns a single value, the customer code for the Iris Corporation. The query immediately above then finds all the invoice totals for Iris Corporation.

Finally, the query above that then asks to find the customer codes for those customers who have had an invoice total greater than any of Iris Corporation's. (In other words, greater than the lowest of Iris Corporation's invoice totals.)

The < ANY condition is met when the outer query's value is less than any of the inner query's returned values. = ANY has the same effect of IN. The condition is fulfilled if the outer query's value is equivalent to any of the inner query's returned values. Following the same logic, < ∧ ANY produces the same result as NOT IN.

The EXISTS predicate. Yet another predicate, EXISTS, has the capability to determine the "existence" of any values returned by the subquery. Thus, the subquery will return true if the subquery condition was met, or false if it was not. Here you are not really interested in what the particular values of the subquery are, just the fact that some exist. This leads to two noteworthy observations: First, it does not matter which columns are returned by the subquery, so a "*" or any column can be specified as the column list. Secondly, by the nature of EXISTS, a column from the outer query should be present in the inner query.

Often, there are many ways to accomplish the same task. The following example shows another way to display those clients who have purchased something after January 1, 1989.

```
SELECT Name, Address, City, State, Zip
FROM Clients
WHERE EXISTS
  (SELECT *
  FROM Invoices
  WHERE Clients.Custnum = Invoices.Custcode
    AND Invdate > = {01/01/89});
```

Both Clients and Invoices contain a column named Custcode, so the "table.column" format is used in the inner query to avoid ambiguity.

For each row in the Clients table, its Custcode is compared with the Custcode in the Invoices table. If a match occurs the invoice date (Invdate) is checked if it is on or follows January, 1989, by virtue of the AND connector. If both conditions are met, the Name is output in the result table.

Correlated subqueries. Thus far, the queries executed in the above examples (except for those in EXISTS) have worked in the following manner: the inner query is computed, then returns its resulting value(s) to the outer query. The outer query is then steps through each row in its table, making some comparison based on what the inner query returned, one unchanging result.

A correlated subquery works a little differently. A column from the outer query is compared to one in the inner query. This way a row's values from the outer query's table are given to the inner query, whose result is then given back to the outer query to be evaluated. This process is repeated for each row in the outer query's table. For example,

```
SELECT A.City, A.Lname, A.Fname
  FROM Donors A
  WHERE Total > =
    (SELECT AVG(B.Total)
    FROM Donors B
    WHERE A.City = B.City)
  ORDER BY A.City;
```

The above will return all those persons in each city who have donated an amount greater than or equal to the average donation amount for that city. Note that aliases were employed because the same table is used in both the outer and the inner query. The inner query obtains a city for a donor from the outer query, then calculates an average for the city (WHERE A.City = B.City). If the donor has contributed at least the average, he/she will appear in the result table.

SHOW DATABASE

The SHOW DATABASE command provides a listing of the SQL databases, as entered in the master catalog table Sysdbs. The syntax is:

```
SHOW DATABASE;
```

The master catalog Sysdbs contains the information listed, which includes the database name, the date created, who created it, and the DOS path where the database directory exists.

This command can be useful when you would like to access a known table, but forgot under which database it is found.

START DATABASE

To activate a database to access its tables and views, the START DATABASE command is used. Its syntax is:

```
START DATABASE <database name>;
```

You can specify a default database to start automatically in the config.db file by adding SQLDATABASE = <database name>. Otherwise, START DATABASE will usually be one of the first commands executed in SQL, in order to access tables.

Only one database can be active at a time. If you wish to use another database, you can START the next one without STOPping the current one. The current database will automatically be deactivated.

There is no need to START a database after CREATing one, it is automatically activated.

STOP DATABASE

The STOP DATABASE command deactivates the current database. The syntax is:

```
STOP DATABASE;
```

When START DATABASE is used, the previous database is automatically closed, so it is not necessary to use this command in this case. However, to DROP a database, it must not be active. STOP DATABASE will close the DATABASE so that it may be DROPped.

UNLOAD DATA

The UNLOAD DATA command has the ability to export data into files that are not in SQL format so that other applications may use it. The syntax is:

```
UNLOAD DATA TO [path] <filename>
  FROM TABLE <table name>
```

```
[[TYPE] SDF/DIF/WKS/SYLK/FW2/RPD/DBASEII/
DELIMITED [WITH BLANK/WITH <delimiter>]];
```

The path specifies where to export the data in to, be it to a floppy in the A: drive, or another directory on a hard disk. The default is taken as the current user directory.

The <filename> is the name of the file to create at the location specified by the path. The <table name> is the name of the table to unload the data from. The field definitions, size and name are directly obtained from the table's column definitions. The column name will appear as a column heading in spreadsheets.

Including TYPE denotes what the format of the data is to be, including some from the more popular applications. They are:

Type	**Description**
SDF	Standard Data Format. Most applications, even those not well known, allow importing and exporting using this standard ASCII format.
DIF	Visicalc format.
WKS	Lotus 1-2-3 format.
FW2	Framework II format.
RPD	Rapidfile format.
DBASEII	dBASEII format.
DELIMITED	Fields are separated by a comma, records by a carriage return and linefeed, and character fields are surrounded by quotes. If WITH BLANK is used, spaces are field separators, and character fields have no delimiters. Using DELIMITED WITH <delimiter> will assume fields separated by commas, and character fields surrounded by the delimiter specified.

If no TYPE is given, dBASE .dbf format is taken as the default. When using .dbf files, the memo fields are not imported.

If a table named Phone exists, and Lotus 1-2-3 is on the C drive with a subdirectory named files

```
UNLOAD DATA TO C:\lotus\files\phone.wks
FROM TABLE Phone
TYPE WKS;
```

will read the Phone table's data into a file named phone.wks.

UPDATE

The UPDATE command provides the ability to change column values in rows of tables or updatable views. There are two forms of the command, their syntaxes being:

```
UPDATE <table name>/<view name>
  SET <column name> = <expression>
  [,<column name> = <expression>...]
  [WHERE <search condition>];
```

and

```
UPDATE <table name>
  SET <column name> = <expression>
  [,<column name> = <expression,...]
  WHERE CURRENT OF <cursor name>;
```

The table name is the table to update. Following the keyword SET is a listing of column assignments, each separated by a comma. The expressions can be constants, memory variables, or functions.

The two forms of the command differ in their WHERE clause. The first can be employed in either embedded or interactive SQL. Following WHERE is search condition that determines the criteria for which rows in the table or updatable view to UPDATE. Take care here, for you don't want to accidentally UPDATE the contents of the wrong row. It is a good idea to do a SELECT statement using the same WHERE clause to make sure that those are the rows you do indeed wish to UPDATE.

The second form of the command can be used only in embedded SQL. It has WHERE CURRENT OF followed by a cursor name. The UPDATE is made only on one row, the row that the cursor is currently pointing to. The cursor must have been DECLAREd, OPENed, and a row FETCHed. This is useful when stepping through a cursor's result table row by row, making some kind of IF-THEN comparison, and UPDATing single rows appropriately. See the section on embedded SQL for an example on using UPDATE-WHERE CURRENT OF.

In the example,

```
UPDATE Inventor
  SET Sell_price = Cost * 1.1
  WHERE Sell_price/Cost < 1.1;
```

Sell_price is the selling price of an item, and Cost is the purchase cost. The above would increase the selling price of those items in inventory to a 10% markup over the cost for those items whose selling price has less than 10% of a markup from its cost.

Embedded SQL

Embedded SQL refers to embedding SQL commands within another language. In this case, embedding SQL commands within dBASE can take advantage of the power of SQL and the programming constructs of dBASE IV. Familiarity with dBASE programming and SQL commands will help in understanding dBASE embedded SQL.

This chapter will emphasize SQL techniques in programs, and as a result, the examples presented try to keep the dBASE commands fairly simple to highlight the SQL commands. The SQL commands within the program are in boldface to further accentuate them.

Switching between dBASE and SQL Modes

The compiler must know when to switch from dBASE mode into SQL mode and vice versa. This can be done by the file extension given to program source code files. The .prg files are used to denote that dBASE mode is to be used. The .prs files, ''s'' for SQL, are used to denote that SQL mode is to be used. This way dBASE files can call an embedded SQL file with the DO command. Similarly, SQL .prs files can call dBASE .prg files via the DO command. The context of the calling program, and what mode it is in is automatically restored when the called program returns. This allows the programmer the flexibility to accomplish various tasks using either of the two methods.

Recall that in dBASE .prg files, the semicolon is used as a continuation character, indicating that a program statement continues on the following line. The semicolon has the same effect for dBASE commands in .prs files as .prg files, but it also acts to mark the end of SQL commands, as it does in SQL interactive mode. Keep this in mind to avoid errors at compile time.

The MODIFY COMMAND editor is used to edit .prs files as well as .prg files. However, since MODI COMM assumes a .prg file extension as the default, make sure you explicitly include .prs in the filename. When compiling and no file extension is given, the compiler will first look for a .prg and then a .prs file.

Many dBASE commands can be used in embedded SQL mode, but files must be accessed using SQL commands, not dBASE file commands. In addition, dBASE file-related functions cannot be used.

Sqlcode and Sqlcnt. SQL has two built-in system variables you can use to aid in your programs. The first, Sqlcode is a status variable that can have three different values, depending on the effect of last SQL command executed. A value of -1 indicates an error. A value of 0 indicates that the last SQL command was successfully executed. A value of $+100$ warns that either of the following happened, depending on the command: an attempt was made to FECTH beyond the last row of the result table, a SELECT statement has no rows in its result table, or UPDATE, DELETE, or INSERT did not affect any rows.

Sqlcnt contains the number of rows affected by the last SQL command. For example, after OPENing a cursor, Sqlcnt will contain the number of rows in the cursor's result table. Or, performing a DELETE with a criteria in the WHERE clause that removes 4 rows from a table will cause Sqlcnt to contain 4.

Some considerations. A maximum of ten "work areas" can be used, whether operating in dBASE mode or SQL mode. To calculate how many work areas are being used, use the following as a guideline:

- ☐ When switching from dBASE to SQL mode, any work areas left open in dBASE are still active. Therefore, it is best to try and close these.
- ☐ 1 work area is used for each table reference (even one repeated) in a SELECT statement.
- ☐ 1 work area for each GROUP BY or ORDER BY clause.
- ☐ 1 work area if SAVE TO TEMP is used.
- ☐ 1 work area for each open cursor.
- ☐ 1 or more for a transaction, depending on what is done. (A transaction is defined as the block between BEGIN TRANSACTION

It is beneficial to use indexes in applications for faster data retrieval. However, the more indexes, the slower the time it takes to perform updates. Weigh these factors in choosing how many indexes to have.

The folks who created dBASE SQL recommend that an application be recompiled later after much data has been entered and the index scheme changed. This way the compiler can optimize performance by making better decisions with the current information.

A Simple Inventory Example

The examples' main goal is to show how SQL can be used without complexity, but they also tie together in a simple inventory application. The inventory application can insert, update, and delete items in inventory. Then, purchase orders can be made, and the quantity of items can be updated in the inventory automatically when the items ordered in the purchase order are received.

A quick note on the modules that are presented. The LASTKEY( ) function returns the ASCII value of the key that caused the exiting of a READ command, like Return, Esc, PgDn, etc. The ASCII value of Escape is 27. The Escape key is detected to allow the user to exit from modules The modules will have DO WHILE .T. loops to continuously repeat until it is encounters EXIT.

Inserting. The first example of embedded SQL is now introduced. It does not use cursors, but examples that do will appear later. The object is to insert new items into an inventory table. Its definition is given by the command:

```
  CREATE TABLE Inventor
(Partnum    CHAR(15),
Descript    CHAR(30),
Quantity    INTEGER,
Minimum     INTEGER,
Cost        NUMERIC(8,2),
Sell        NUMERIC(8,2));
```

Memory variables are used to obtain the new values through @...SAY...GET statements. After the input is received, a SELECT statement is used to verify no other entries exist for that item, as specified in the WHERE clause. Finally, the INSERT command is used. The program follows. It is easy to create a different table and change the columns and memory variables for developing your own applications:

INV_INS.PRS:

```
                DO WHILE .T.
                STORE SPACE(15) TO mpartnum
                STORE SPACE(30) TO mdescript
                STORE 0 TO mquantity,mminimum,mcost,msell
                STORE 0 TO mcount
                CLEAR
                @  3,10 SAY "INSERT"
@  5,10 SAY     "      Part Number:" GET mpartnum
@  6,10 SAY     "      Description:" GET mdescript
@  7,10 SAY     "         Quantity:" GET mquantity
@  8,10 SAY     "Reorder Minimum:" GET mminimum
@  9,10 SAY     "   Purchase Cost:" GET mcost PICTURE "99999.99"
@ 10,10 SAY     "   Selling Price:" GET msell PICTURE "99999.99"
@ 12,10 SAY     "Press ESC To Exit"
READ
```

```
* See if ESC was pressed
IF LASTKEY() = 27
 RETURN
ENDIF
* See if part already exists
SELECT COUNT(*)
    INTO mcount
    FROM Inventor
    WHERE Partnum = mpartnum;
  * mcount now contains the number of entries for the part.
  * If mcount > 0, it already exists, so loop back
  IF mcount > 0
    @ 15,0 SAY "Cannot Insert, Part Already Exists!"
    WAIT
    LOOP
  ENDIF
  * OK, enter into table.
INSERT INTO Inventor
        VALUES (mpartnum,mdescript,mquantity,mminimum,
                mcost,msell);
ENDDO
RETURN
```

Updating. After items have been entered in inventory, you might wish to edit the entries by using the UPDATE command. In the program below, a part number is asked for. SELECT is used to read the values of the part entry INTO memory variables. Note that Sqlcnt contains the number of rows returned by the SELECT statement. Thus, if Sqlcnt is 0, no rows are returned, so the program goes back to the top of the loop. Next, the entries are edited, and the UPDATE command is used.

INV_ED.PRS:

```
DO WHILE .T.
  STORE SPACE(15) TO mpartnum
  STORE SPACE(30) TO mdescript
  STORE 0 TO mquantity,mminimum,mcost,msell
```

```
CLEAR
@ 0,5 SAY "EDIT"
@ 2,5 SAY "Part Number:" GET mpartnum
@ 4,5 SAY "Press ESC To Exit"
READ
* See if ESC was pressed
IF LASTKEY( ) = 27
  RETURN
ENDIF
SELECT *
   INTO mpartnum,mdescript,mquantity,mminimum,mcost,msell
   FROM Inventor
   WHERE Partnum = mpartnum;
* See if part exists.
IF Sqlcnt = 0
  @ 6,0 SAY "No Such Part Exists!"
  WAIT
  LOOP
ENDIF
* OK, edit.
CLEAR
    @  5,10 SAY "        Part Number:" GET mpartnum
    @  6,10 SAY "        Description:" GET mdescript
    @  7,10 SAY "           Quantity:" GET mquantity
    @  8,10 SAY "    Reorder Minimum:" GET mminimum
    @  9,10 SAY "      Purchase Cost:" GET mcost PICTURE "99999.99"
    @ 10,10 SAY "      Selling Price:" GET msell PICTURE "99999.99"
READ
* Update table entry.
UPDATE Inventor
    SET    Partnum = mpartnum,
           Descript = mdescript,
           Quantity = mquantity,
           Minimum = mminimum,
           Cost = mcost,
           Sell = msell
   WHERE Partnum = mpartnum;
ENDDO
RETURN
```

Deleting. The module to delete items is similar to the others. The INTO clause is used in the SELECT so that the item can be displayed in the same format it was entered, and then verified. The program follows:

INV_DEL.PRS:

```
DO WHILE .T.
  STORE SPACE(15) TO mpartnum
  STORE SPACE(30) TO mdescript
  STORE 0 TO mquantity,mminimum,mcost,msell
  STORE "Y" to yn
  CLEAR
  @ 0,5 SAY "DELETE"
  @ 2,5 SAY "Part Number:" GET mpartnum
  @ 4,5 SAY "Press ESC To Exit"
  READ
  * See if ESC was pressed.
  IF LASTKEY() = 27
    RETURN
  ENDIF
  SELECT *
    INTO mpartnum,mdescript,mqty,mminimum,mcost,msell
    FROM Inventor
    WHERE Partnum = mpartnum;
  * See if part exists.
  IF Sqlcnt = 0
    @ 6,0 SAY "No Such Part Exists!"
    WAIT
    LOOP
  ENDIF
  * OK, display & double check.
  CLEAR
  @  5,10 SAY " Part Number: " + mpartnum
  @  6,10 SAY " Description: " + mdescript
  @  7,10 SAY " Quantity: " + STR(mquantity)
  @  8,10 SAY " Reorder Minimum: " + STR(mminimum)
  @  9,10 SAY " Purchase Cost: " + STR(mcost,8,2)
  @ 10,10 SAY " Selling Price: " + STR(msell,8,2)
  @ 13,10 SAY "Are You Sure? (Y/N)" GET yn PICTURE "!"
  READ
  IF yn = "Y"
    * Remove from table
```

```
    DELETE
      FROM Inventor
      WHERE Partnum = mpartnum;
  ENDIF
ENDDO
RETURN
```

Cursors. Cursors allow an additional flexibility in programming. It provides a convenient means of doing row-by-row processing for certain rows of a table. The UPDATE (*p. 340*) and DELETE (*p. 312*) commands have special forms that are specific for cursors to use. The other cursor commands are DECLARE CURSOR (*p. 311*) to define the cursor; OPEN (*p. 319*) to obtain the cursor's result table and open the cursor; FETCH (*p. 314*) to advance the cursor pointer to the next row and read in its values into memory variables; and CLOSE (*p. 304*) close the cursor, allowing it to be reopened later. These commands are all detailed in the reference section in Chapter 2.

A typical segment of a program using cursors might appear something like:

```
DECLARE <cursor name> CURSOR
FOR <SELECT statement>;
:
OPEN <cursor name>
:
DO WHILE .T.
  FETCH <cursor name>
  INTO <variable list>;
  * See if done FETCHing, then EXIT loop
  IF SQLCODE = 100
    EXIT
  ENDIF
  :
  <do something like UPDATE, DELETE>
ENDDO
CLOSE <curser name>;
```

Updating with cursors. For the first example, the previous inventory editing module is rewritten, this time using cursors. Even though a cursor's real power comes in multi-row processing, it can be used here when the cursor's result table returns only one row. It basically follows the format of the above outline, but there is no DO-WHILE loop for the FETCHes because only one row is FETCHed. When UPDATE is used, the WHERE CURRENT OF clause is included, that way the only row that will be updated is the currently FETCHed row:

INV_EDC.PRS:

```
DECLARE Item CURSOR
  FOR SELECT *
  FROM Inventor
  WHERE Partnum = mpartnum
  FOR UPDATE OF Partnum,Descript,Quantity,Minimum,Cost,Sell;
DO WHILE .T.
  STORE SPACE(15) TO mpartnum
  STORE SPACE(30) TO mdescript
  STORE 0 TO mquantity,mminimum,mcost,msell
  STORE "Y" to yn
  CLEAR
  @ 0,5 SAY "EDIT"
  @ 2,5 SAY "Part Number:" GET mpartnum
  @ 4,5 SAY "Press ESC To Exit"
  READ
  * See if ESC was pressed
  IF LASTKEY( ) = 27
    RETURN
  ENDIF
  OPEN Item;
  * See if part exists.
  IF Sqlcnt = 0
    @ 6,0 SAY "No Such Part Exists!"
    WAIT
  ELSE
  FETCH Item
    INTO mpartnum,mdescript,mquantity,mminimum,mcost,msell;
  * OK, edit.
  CLEAR
@  5,10 SAY    " Part Number: " GET mpartnum
@  6,10 SAY    " Description: " GET mdescript
@  7,10 SAY    " Quantity: " GET mquantity
@  8,10 SAY    " Reorder Minimum: " GET mmini-
               mum
@  9,10 SAY    " Purchase Cost: " GET mcost PIC-
               TURE "99999.99"
```

```
@ 10,10 SAY                    " Selling Price: " GET msell PICTURE
                               "99999.99"
    READ
    * OK, enter into table.
    UPDATE Inventor
      SET Partnum = mpartnum,
          Descript = mdescript,
          Quantity = mquantity,
          Minimum = mminimum,
          Cost = mcost,
          Sell = msell
        WHERE CURRENT OF Item;
  ENDIF
  CLOSE Item;
ENDDO
RETURN
```

Deleting with cursors. This is similar to the previous example, only the entry is verified, and the WHERE CURRENT OF clause is included in the DELETE command.

INV_DELC.PRS:

```
DECLARE Item CURSOR
  FOR SELECT *
  FROM Inventor
  WHERE Partnum = mpartnum
  FOR UPDATE OF Partnum,Descript,Quantity,Minimum,Cost,Sell;
DO WHILE .T.
  STORE SPACE(15) TO mpartnum
  STORE SPACE(30) TO mdescript
  STORE 0 TO mquantity,mminimum,mcost,msell
  STORE "Y" to yn
  CLEAR
  @ 0,5 SAY "DELETE"
  @ 2,5 SAY "Part Number:" GET mpartnum
  @ 4,5 SAY "Press ESC To Exit"
  READ
  * See if ESC was pressed
  IF LASTKEY() = 27
    RETURN
  ENDIF
```

```
OPEN Item;
* See if part exists.
IF Sqlcnt = 0
  @ 6,0 SAY "No Such Part Exists!"
  WAIT
ELSE
  FETCH Item
    INTO mpartnum,mdescript,mquantity,mminimum,mcost,msell;
  * OK, verify.
  CLEAR
@  5,10 SAY  " Part Number:       " + mpartnum
@  6,10 SAY  " Description:       " + mdescript
@  7,10 SAY  " Quantity:          " + STR(mquantity)
@  8,10 SAY  " Reorder Minimum:   " + STR(mminimum)
@  9,10 SAY  " Purchase Cost:     " + STR(mcost,8,2) PICTURE "99999.99"
@ 10,10 SAY  " Selling Price:     " + STR(msell,8,2) PICTURE "99999.99"
@ 13,10 SAY "Are You Sure? (Y/N)" GET yn PICTURE "!"
READ
IF yn = "y"
    DELETE
      FROM Inventor
      WHERE CURRENT OF Item;
  ENDIF
ENDIF
CLOSE Item;
ENDDO
RETURN
```

Purchase Order Example

The Purchase Order modules are now presented, with more interesting cursor examples. The definition for the PO table is:

```
CREATE TABLE PO
(Ponum   INTEGER
Part     CHAR(30)
Qty      INTEGER);
```

The entries would be used on the lines that appear on a Purchase Order, with Ponum (the PO number), designating what PO the entries belong on.

PO line inserting. The INSERT module for the PO's to insert new lines essentially mimicks the insert routine in the inventory:

PO_INS.PRS:

```
* Assign outside of loop, so the same PO number will be taken
* as the default if additional entries are made.
STORE 0 TO mponum
* Continually loop to make many entries.
DO WHILE .T.
  STORE SPACE(15) TO mpart
  STORE 0 TO mqty,mcount
  STORE "Y" to yn
  CLEAR
  @  6,10 SAY "Purchase Order Number: " GET mponum
  @  7,10 SAY " Part Number: " GET mpart
  @  8,10 SAY " Quantity: " GET mqty
  @ 10,10 SAY "Press ESC To Exit"
  READ
  * See if ESC was pressed.
  IF LASTKEY() = 27
    RETURN
  ENDIF
  * Check if part already in PO
  SELECT COUNT(*)
  INTO mcount
  FROM PO
  WHERE Ponum = mponum AND Part = mpart;
  * mcount now contains the number of entries for the part.
  * If mcount > 0, it already exists, so loop back
  IF mcount > 0
    @ 13,0 SAY "Cannot Insert, Already Have Entry For Part!"
    WAIT
    LOOP
  ENDIF
  * OK, enter into table.
  INSERT INTO PO
    VALUES (mponum,mpart,mqty);
ENDDO
RETURN
```

PO updating and deleting. To edit a purchase order after inserting lines, cursors are utilized. The lines are stepped through one by one and displayed, and then the user is given the opportunity to UPDATE the line, DELETE the line, or go on to the next line. It combines the UPDATE and DELETE commands seen earlier, but this time more than one row will be in the cursor's result table. Although it is not an elegant way to edit Purchase Orders, they typically will not be too long. The main purpose is to see SQL in use.

PO_ED.PRS:

```
DECLARE Line CURSOR
  FOR SELECT Part,Qty
  FROM PO
  WHERE Ponum = mponum
  FOR UPDATE OF Part,Qty;
DO WHILE .T.
  STORE SPACE(15) TO mpart
  STORE 0 TO mponum,mqty
  STORE "Y" to yn
  CLEAR
  @ 0,5 SAY "EDIT"
  @ 2,5 SAY "Purchase Order Number:" GET mponum
  @ 4,5 SAY "Press ESC To Exit"
  READ
  * See if ESC was pressed.
  IF LASTKEY() = 27
    RETURN
  ENDIF
  OPEN Line;
  * See if PO exists.
  IF Sqlcnt = 0
    @ 6,0 SAY "No Such PO Exists!"
    WAIT
  ELSE
    DO WHILE .T.
      * Get next row
      FETCH Line
        INTO mpart,mqty;
      * See if any rows left to process
        IF Sqlcode = 100
          EXIT
        ENDIF
```

```
            STORE "N" TO udn
            CLEAR
            @  6,10 SAY " Purchase Order #: " + STR(mponum)
            @  7,10 SAY " Part Number: " + mpart
            @  8,10 SAY " Quantity: " + STR(mqty)
            @ 11,10 SAY "(U)pdate, (D)elete, or (N)ext?" GET udn PICTURE;
               "U,D,N"
            READ
            DO CASE
              CASE udn = "U"
                @ 7,10 SAY " Part Number: " GET mpart
                @ 8,10 SAY " Quantity: " GET mqty
                READ
                  UPDATE PO
                    SET Part = mpart,
                         Qty = mqty
                    WHERE CURRENT OF Line;
              CASE udn = "D"
                @ 13,10 SAY "Delete, Are You Sure? (Y/N)" GET yn PICTURE "!"
                READ
                IF yn = "Y"
                  DELETE FROM PO
                    WHERE CURRENT OF Line;
                ENDIF
              CASE udn = "N"
                LOOP
            ENDCASE
          ENDDO
        ENDIF
        CLOSE Line;
      ENDDO
    RETURN
```

Updating inventory with a Purchase Order. After receiving the items from a Purchase Order, the inventory can be updated quickly and easily by the following program module.

The Purchase Order to receive is first entered by the user. If it exists, each line in the Purchase Order is FETCHed row by row by the cursor. The Inventor table is UPDATED by adding the quantity of items received of a particular part to the existing quantity on hand. No cursor is used for the Inventor table, just for the PO table, so a noncursor UPDATE is used. Next, the row is DELETEd from the PO table, using the WHERE CURRENT OF clause on the cursor Line.

PO_INV.PRS:

```
DECLARE Line CURSOR
  FOR SELECT Part,Qty
  FROM PO
  WHERE Ponum = mponum
  FOR UPDATE OF Part,Qty;
DO WHILE .T.
  STORE SPACE(15) TO mpart
  STORE 0 TO mponum,mqty
  CLEAR
  @ 0,5 SAY "RECEIVE PO"
  @ 2,5 SAY "Purchase Order Number:" GET mponum
  @ 4,5 SAY "Press ESC To Exit"
  READ
  * See if ESC was pressed.
  IF LASTKEY() = 27
    RETURN
  ENDIF
  OPEN Line;
  * See if part exists.
  IF Sqlcnt = 0
    @ 6,0 SAY "No Such Purchase Order Exists!"
    WAIT
  ELSE
    DO WHILE .T.
      * Get next row.
      FETCH Line
         INTO mpartnum,mquantity;
      * See if any more lines
      IF Sqlcode = 100
        EXIT
      ENDIF
      * Update Inventor
      UPDATE Inventor
         SET Quantity = Quantity + mqty
         WHERE Part = mpart;
      * Delete the PO Line
```

```
        DELETE FROM PO
            WHERE CURRENT OF Line;
      ENDDO
    ENDIF
    CLOSE Line;
  ENDDO
  RETURN
```

Tying It Together

A simple main menu appears below to tie the modules together:

INV.PRS:

```
SET TALK OFF
choice = " "
DO WHILE .T.
  CLEAR
  @  4,20 SAY "A-> Insert Items Into Inventory"
  @  5,20 SAY "B-> Edit Items In Inventory"
  @  6,20 SAY "C-> Delete Items From Inventory"
  @  8,20 SAY "D-> Insert Lines Into Purchase Orders"
  @  9,20 SAY "E-> Edit Lines In Purchase Orders"
  @ 10,20 SAY "F-> Receive Items From Purchase Orders"
  @ 12,20 SAY "Your Choice?" GET choice PICTURE "!"
  READ
  IF LASTKEY() = 27
    RETURN
  ENDIF
  DO CASE
    CASE choice = "A"
      DO INV_INS
    CASE choice = "B"
      DO INV_ED
    CASE choice = "C"
      DO INV_DEL
    CASE choice = "D"
      DO PO_INS
    CASE choice = "E"
      DO PO_ED
    CASE choice = "F"
      DO PO_INV
  ENDCASE
ENDDO
```

Error recovery. If errors occur while trying to UPDATE or DELETE rows, the ROLLBACK command can be used to restore any tables to their previous state. The BEGIN TRANSACTION and END TRANSACTION commands are used to define a block of commands in a program as a transaction. Many rows of a table can be processed within the transaction, and ROLLBACK will make the tables appear as they did before the transaction.

You want ROLLBACK to be executed only if an error occurs. Errors can be detected using the ON ERROR command. ON ERROR is followed by a command to execute if an error occurs, usually DO an error recovery program, such as the following:

ERR.PRS:

```
@ 20,1 SAY MESSAGE( )
try = " "
@ 22,1 SAY "Try again (Y/N) " GET try
READ
IF try $ "Yy"
  RETRY
ELSE
  ROLLBACK;
ENDIF
RETURN
```

The MESSAGE( ) function contains the error message for the error. RETRY will go back to the command that caused the error, and try again.

The program PO_ED.PRS is modified below such that it processes all lines in a purchase order as one transaction:

```
DECLARE Line CURSOR
  FOR SELECT Part,Qty
  FROM PO
  WHERE Ponum = mponum
  FOR UPDATE OF Part,Qty;
DO WHILE .T.
  STORE SPACE(15) TO mpart
  STORE 0 TO mponum,mqty
  STORE "Y" to yn
  CLEAR
  @ 0,5 SAY "EDIT"
  @ 2,5 SAY "Purchase Order Number:" GET mponum
  @ 4,5 SAY "Press ESC To Exit"
```

```
READ
* See if ESC was pressed.
IF LASTKEY( ) = 27
  RETURN
ENDIF
* If an error occurs, execute ERR.PRS
ON ERROR DO ERR
* Define the beginning of the transaction
BEGIN TRANSACTION
OPEN Line;
* See if PO exists.
IF Sqlcnt = 0
  @ 6,0 SAY "No Such PO Exists!"
  WAIT
ELSE
  DO WHILE .T.
    * Get next row
    FETCH Line
      INTO mpart,mqty;
    * See if any rows left to process
    IF Sqlcode = 100
      EXIT
    ENDIF
    STORE "N" TO udn
    CLEAR
    @  6,10 SAY " Purchase Order #:     " + STR(mponum)
    @  7,10 SAY " Part Number:          " + mpart
    @  8,10 SAY " Quantity:             " + STR(mqty)
    @ 11,10 SAY "(U)pdate, (D)elete, or (N)ext?" GET udn PICTURE;
       "@MU,D,N"
    READ
    DO CASE
      CASE udn = "U"
        @ 7,10 SAY "       Part Number: " GET mpart
        @ 8,10 SAY "       Quantity: " GET mqty
        READ
        UPDATE PO
         SET Part = mpart,
             Qty = mqty
```

```
            WHERE CURRENT OF Line;
         CASE udn = "D"
         @ 13,10 SAY "Delete, Are You Sure? (Y/N)" GET yn PICTURE "!"
         READ
         IF yn = "Y"
            DELETE FROM PO
               WHERE CURRENT OF Line;
         ENDIF
      CASE udn = "N"
         LOOP
   ENDCASE
  ENDDO
ENDIF
END TRANSACTION
* Cancel the ON ERROR command.
ON ERROR
CLOSE Line;
```

8

dBASE IV Programming

IN THIS CHAPTER THE SUBJECT OF PROGRAMMING IS ADDRESSED. THE PRIMARY intent of this book is to provide information in a reference-based manner. All commands and functions are presented in other sections, many of which are used here. For a more in-depth survey of dBASE IV programming, you might wish to acquire an additional publication, although the material here might be adequate for your needs. First, the editor is discussed. Our attention then turns toward programming, where a few basics are mentioned. Finally, an example program for managing a mailing list database is presented and analyzed in detail.

Since the early days of dBASE II, programming in a dBASE language has rapidly evolved from being somewhat awkward to being sophisticated and powerful. The main idea was to allow a sequence of dBASE commands (normally executed at the dot prompt) to be executed in succession, while providing some programming constructs for decision making and control. This is still true, but the tools at the programmer's disposal have much improved.

One major flaw of the dBASE III + editor has been corrected. Previously, command files could not be more than 5,000 bytes. Now they can be much larger, limited only by storage space or up to 32,000 lines of code.

Using the Editor

dBASE has its own built-in editor for editing program files. The editor can be invoked in two ways: MODIFY COMMAND followed by a file name can be entered at the dot prompt, or a file can be selected or created from the Applications panel in the Control Center. To save a little bit of typing when at the dot prompt, MODI COMM can be entered instead of MODIFY COMMAND.

If you wish to use another program such as WordStar or WordPerfect to edit your files, you can modify the config.db file in the dBASE home directory. Add an additional line TEDIT = <editor>, where <editor> is the name of the program you wish to use to edit files (i.e., WS, WP).

Editing Keys

Basic cursor keys function as you would expect when editing files. Table 8-1 shows all editing keys.

Indentation

The editor automatically indents when you edit files. After pressing Return on a line, the cursor appears immediately below the first non-space character in the previous line. If the left arrow key is now pressed, the cursor jumps back to the end of the previous line, and does not move to the empty space to the left. Just remember this—pressing Shift – Tab will allow you to move to left, specifically to the previous tab setting. Forgetting this fact might result in experiencing some annoyance. The Enable automatic indent option from the Words menu can be used to turn indentation ON or OFF.

Copying and Moving Text

The pull-down menus don't show that the editor has the ability to copy and move text. For both operations, first go to the beginning of the desired block of code. Press F6 (Select) and then expand the highlighted area using the cursor arrow keys. After all lines are highlighted, press Return.

Now position the cursor where the block is to be copied or moved. Finally, press F7 to move the block, or press F8 to Copy the block.

Other Features

A few other features are mentioned.

The Go To menu allows you to jump to the specified line number of the program and continue editing. This is useful when compiling programs and dBase notifies you on what line number the error occurred.

Speaking of line numbers, in the Print menu you can print out your programs with line numbers as well as have greater control over your printer.

Table 8-1. All editing keys and their actions.

Key	Description
Arrow keys	Move left, right, up, down
Ctrl →	Move one word to the right
Ctrl ←	Move one word to the left
Home	Go to the beginning of the line
End	Go to the end of the line
Tab	Go to the next tab
Shift – Tab	Go to the previous tab
PgUp	Move up one screen
PgDn	Move down one screen
Ctrl – PgUp	Go to the beginning of the file
Ctrl – PgDn	Go to the end of the file
Ctrl – Y	Delete line
Ctrl – T	Delete to the end of the word
Ctrl – N or Return	Insert blank line
Backspace	Delete previous character
Ctrl – Backspace	Delete previous word
Ins	Toggle insert/typeover modes
F10	Use the pull down menus
F6 (Select)	Select a block of text
F7 (Move)	Move block of text
F8 (Copy)	Copy block of text
Del	Delete character or block
Shift – F5	Search for specified string
Shift – F3	Search for previous occurrence of string
Shift – F4	Search for next occurrence of string
Shift – F6	Find and replace string
Esc	Exit editor without saving work
Ctrl – Return	Save work and remain in editor
Ctrl – End or Ctrl – W	Save work and leave editor
Ctrl – K R	Insert file into text
Ctrl – K W	Write text to file

The last option of the Exit menu, Debug program, should not be overlooked. It allows you to run your programs one line at a time to pinpoint problems quickly.

Modular Design Programming

In programming, it is often easier to complete a large task by breaking it down into smaller, more manageable tasks. This is known as *modular program-*

ming. Each module of a program is dedicated to performing one operation, making designing and debugging a much easier process.

To execute a program from the dot prompt, enter the DO command followed by the desired filename is entered. If the file has been modified, it will be compiled first. Within your programs, you can also include DO commands, having programs call other subprograms, while all public variables are still retained in memory for use of the subprograms.

A more structured approach is to use *procedures*. A procedure is found in a program file that does not necessarily bear its name, as in the above method. A procedure begins with the keyword PROCEDURE followed by the procedure name. The lines of code to execute are next, and the procedure is terminated by a RETURN statement. For example, a procedure to print "Hello, world" appears below:

```
PROCEDURE Hello
  ? "Hello World"
RETURN
```

To execute this within a program, the line DO Hello is included.

There is another species of animals called procedure files. We won't go into detail here, but basically it is a file of procedures that your programs can call with the DO command, after first setting SET PROCEDURE TO followed by the name of the file that contains all the procedures.

Procedures can also have parameter passing, but that is not discussed here.

Setting Up the dBASE Environment

When the highest level program is executed, usually the first lines of programming code set the environment. These will include CLEAR ALL to release existing variables in memory and close any open files, and many SET commands. There are several SET commands available that can be found in the Command reference Chapter 3. They allow you to do things like suppress system responses to commands in order to keep the screens neat (SET TALK OFF).

Memory Variables

After setting up the environment, variables should be initialized. You can have statements like x=y appear for the the first time x is used, but it is better style to assign x to a constant when it is declared, rather than another variable. In addition, in @...SAY...GETs, the memory variable following the GET must to already exist. In the memory variable's declaration, the variable can be set to some default constant like 0 (for type numeric), today's date or null dates (for type date), or a string of spaces of a specified length (for type character).

The two ways of initializing memory variables are by using an assignment statement (x = 0), or by using the STORE command (STORE 0 to x). The STORE method might seem more verbose, but it offers the advantage of having the ability to assign the same value to more than one variable at a time.

To assign x, y, and z to 0 using assignment statements, you would enter:

```
x = 0
y = 0
z = 0
```

Using the STORE command instead, the following is entered:

```
STORE 0 TO x,y,z
```

Memory variable arrays are a new feature of dBASE IV. They can be either one- or two-dimensional arrays. The number of elements in the array must be included in the declaration. For example, to declare an array name for 20 entries and 2 elements (last name and first name) for those 20 entries, enter:

```
DECLARE names[20,2]
```

Assignments to the names array can now be made:

```
name[1,1] = "Lambert"
name [1,2] = "Julie"
```

The elements of an array can have different types. You can copy the contents of a record to an array using the COPY TO ARRAY command. Similarly, new records can be added by inserting values into an array and using the APPEND FROM ARRAY command. These two commands allow you to shorten up the length of your programs a bit performing several actions in just one statement.

Memory Variables and Fields

One concern that can be frustrating for first-time programmers (speaking from experience!) is using fields of records in files and memory variables together in programs. A memory variable can have the same name as field in a file. The important thing to remember is that STORE and assignment statements change the value of memory variables only. To change the value in a field, the REPLACE command must be used. The format of the REPLACE command is

```
REPLACE <field> WITH <value>
```

where <value> is a constant or expression of variables or fields. Observe the following program excerpt:

```
USE Names
STORE "Fred" to name
REPLACE name WITH name
name = "Barney"
```

Assume the field name exists in the database Names. The file is open and is at the first record. "Fred" is initialized to the memory variable name. The field name in the current record is replaced with the contents of the memory variable name, "Fred". The memory variable name is then assigned the value "Barney".

To avoid confusion, good dBASE programming style will precede with an "m" memory variables that are to be used as tempory variables for fields. The above code could then be easier understood:

```
Use Names
Store "Fred" to mname
REPLACE name WITH mname
mname = "Barney"
```

Decision Making

Three tools are available to facilitate decision making: IF statements, CASE statements, and IIF statements. See these commands in Chapter 2 if not familiar with them.

Loops

Just one looping mechanism exists, the DO WHILE loop. Again, refer to the command reference section.

The People Sample Application

We present a sample application to introduce some typical programming techniques. A database named People is used that contains mailing list information, phone number, the date it was entered, and a numeric field for a dollar amount of potential business to be obtained from this person. The structure is:

Field	Field Name	Type	Width	Dec	Index
1	LNAME	Character	20		Y
2	FNAME	Character	15		N

3	ADDRESS	Character	30		N
4	CITY	Character	20		N
5	STATE	Character	2		N
6	ZIP	Character	10		N
7	PHONE	Character	14		N
8	ENT_DATE	Date	8		N
9	POTEN	Numeric	8	2	N

To improve readability in the program listings provided, the conventions used for capitalization are: all dBASE keywords are in uppercase; memory variables and field names are in lowercase; procedures and files begin with a capital letter followed by lowercase letters.

The Main Program

In the highest-level program (the one that executed first and calls other subprograms), the environment for the entire application is set up, and the main menu is put into action.The program is first listed, and then discussed:

Main.prg:

```
* Set-up environment
SET TALK OFF
SET HEADING OFF
SET STATUS OFF
SET SCOREBOARD OFF
SET BELL OFF
CLEAR ALL
* Open People database
USE PEOPLE ORDER LNAME
* Do menu definition
DO Def_Main
* Repeat Until "Exit" is selected from menu
DO WHILE BAR( ) # 10
  CLEAR
  ACTIVATE POPUP main
ENDDO
RETURN

PROCEDURE Def_Main
  DEFINE POPUP main FROM 1,30 to 12,50
  DEFINE BAR 1 OF main PROMPT " PEOPLE DATABASE" SKIP
  DEFINE BAR 3 OF main PROMPT " Insert Entries"
```

```
    DEFINE BAR 4 OF main PROMPT " Edit Entries"
    DEFINE BAR 5 OF main PROMPT " Delete Entries"
    DEFINE BAR 6 OF main PROMPT " Report"
    DEFINE BAR 7 OF main PROMPT " Labels"
    DEFINE BAR 8 OF main PROMPT " Pack"
    DEFINE BAR 10 OF main PROMPT " Exit"
    ON SELECTION POPUP main DO Main_opt
RETURN

PROCEDURE Main_opt
    DO CASE
        CASE BAR( ) = 3
            DO Insert
        CASE BAR( ) = 4
            DO Edit
        CASE BAR( ) = 5
            DO Delete
        CASE BAR( ) = 6
            DO Report
        CASE BAR( ) = 7
            DO Labels
        CASE BAR( ) = 8
            DO Packem
        CASE BAR( ) = 10
            RETURN TO MASTER
    ENDCASE
RETURN
```

The first executed command, CLEAR ALL, releases memory variables (if they exist) from memory, closes all files, and sets the work area to 1. In other words, any leftover garbage from previous work is cleaned up.

The SET commands used are the typical ones that many applications use. They insure that dBASE messages are not printed on the display to mess up the screen, column headings don't appear when using the LIST command, and the somewhat annoying BELL is turned off.

Next, the USE command opens the database for adding, editing, or listing records. ORDER specifies which index tag to use for the indexing order. Recall in the structure above that the field lname had a ''Y'' in the Index column. You will want to use the People database ordered on the field lname. For those dBASE III + users, this is a new indexing scheme used in dBASE IV. See the INDEX command on p. *121* for more details.

Now we discuss a new ("really neat") feature of dBASE IV, pop-up menus. There are three components to working with the menus, the definition, the activation, and the actions to take based on the menu's result.

The *definition* is put in procedure Def_Main. The DEFINE POP-UP command names the pop-up menu and gives the placement and dimensions of the menu. DEFINE BAR is used to describe the lines in the menu. For BAR 1, the keyword SKIP is included at the end so that "PEOPLE DATABASE" will appear as a heading and not as an option that can be selected. There is no BAR 2 definition so that a line will be skipped between the heading and the options. ON SELECTION POPUP determines what procedure to execute after an option has been selected. If no DO <procedure> follows, the course of action is to take is to do nothing, and execution of the program continues following the line in which the menu was ACTIVATEd.

After being defined, a menu can be activated with the ACTIVATE POPUP command. After execution of subprograms, control automatically returns to the pop-up menu.

The actions to take appear in procedure Main_opt. The function BAR( ) contains the value of the bar last selected. Typically, a CASE statement appears to select the course of action next.

The menu normally can be deactivated by pressing Escape or by using the DEACTIVATE POPUP command. In this case however, after pressing Escape, the menu is deactivated and then reactivated because of the DO WHILE BAR( ) # 10 loop.

Don't be misled by the DO WHILE BAR # 10 (# means "does not equal") loop. As stated above, when returning from each subprogram such as Insert, the menu will remain in control. However, if in a subprogram (or its subprograms) and RETURN TO MASTER is encountered, the flow of control shifts to the line following the ACTIVATE POPUP command in the main program, as opposed to returning to the menu as it normally would. RETURN TO MASTER can be used anywhere, and it basically shifts control to the highest level calling program without having to retrace level by level. Therefore, the DO WHILE loop will then reactivate the menu after a subprogram uses RETURN TO MASTER.

Use this as a model for your pop-up menus, and the DO WHILE part for your main menu. Compactly,

```
DO Def_Main ACTIVATE POPUP main
PROCEDURE Def_Main
   DEFINE POPUP main FROM .. TO ..
   DEFINE BAR 1 OF main PROMPT ......
   :
   ON SELECTION POPUP main DO Main_opt
```

```
RETURN
PROCEDURE Main_opt
  DO CASE
    :
RETURN
```

Insert

The Insert program allows new records to be inserted into the database. The program follows:

Insert.prg:

```
DEFINE WINDOW again FROM 10,26 TO 14,54
DEFINE WINDOW insert FROM 6,10 TO 19,60
ACTIVATE WINDOW insert
* Repeat forever
DO WHILE .T.
  * Initialize variables
  STORE SPACE(20) TO mlname,mcity
  STORE SPACE(15) TO mfname
  STORE SPACE(30) TO maddress
  STORE "  " TO mstate
  STORE SPACE(10) TO mzip
  STORE SPACE(14) TO mphone
  STORE { / / } TO ment_date
  STORE 0 TO recnum,mpoten
  STORE "Y" TO yn
  * Obtain values
  @  1,1 SAY " Last Name:     " GET mlname
  @  2,1 SAY " First Name:    " GET mfname
  @  3,1 SAY " Address:       " GET maddress
  @  4,1 SAY " City:          " GET mcity
  @  5,1 SAY " State:         " GET mstate PICTURE "!!"
  @  6,1 SAY " Zip:           " GET mzip PICTURE "99999-9999"
  @  7,1 SAY " Phone:         " GET mphone PICTURE "(999) 999-9999"
  @  8,1 SAY " Entry Date:    " GET ment_date
  @  9,1 SAY " Potential:     " GET mpoten PICTURE "99999.99"
  @ 11,1 SAY "Press ESC To Abort"
  READ
  * See if Escape was pressed
```

```
IF LASTKEY() = 27
   DEACTIVATE WINDOW insert
   RETURN
ENDIF
   * Add new record
APPEND BLANK
   * Replace field values
REPLACE lname WITH mlname, fname WITH mfname, ;
     address WITH maddress, city WITH mcity, ;
     state WITH mstate, zip WITH mzip, ;
     phone WITH mphone, ent_date WITH ment_date ;
     poten WITH mpoten
   * See if user wants to continue insertions
   ACTIVATE WINDOW again
   @ 1,1 SAY "Insert Another? (Y/N):" GET yn PICTURE "!"
   READ
   DEACTIVATE WINDOW again
   IF yn <> "Y"
     DEACTIVATE WINDOW insert
     RETURN
   ENDIF
ENDDO
```

Windows are used here for a clean-looking entry screen that can be laid over the menu. The first two lines define two windows, again and insert, and give their coordinates. Each time this program is executed from the main menu the windows will be redefined. This won't hurt anything, but you could have had the definitions appear in the main program so they are only executed once.

Next the insert window is activated. Now when printing is done to the screen, it will be bounded by the window, and coordinates are now relative within the window, not the entire screen. In other words, @ 0,0 will appear at 0,0 within the window, but will be at 7,11 on the screen.

A DO WHILE .T. loop appears next. The .T. denotes the Boolean value true as the loop condition, so the loop is instructed to repeat indefinitely. However, the loop can left by two methods: by an EXIT command, in which case the next command to execute is the command following ENDDO; or by the RETURN command, to RETURN to the calling program.

The program is structured to allow many insertions to be made without having to go back to the main menu. Thus, the variables are initialized within the loop, otherwise on subsequent insertions the previous values will appear. The memory variables are initialized to reflect the definitions of the fields that appear in the database that they will replace.

@...SAY...GETs are used to obtain the new record's values. The PICTURE clauses are used to format variables into their desired appearances.

It is nice to allow users the opportunity to abort an operation if they changes their mind or pressed the wrong key. The LASTKEY( ) function returns the ASCII value of the last key that was pressed in exiting a READ. You can check if Escape was pressed here, and if so deactivate the insert window, and return to the main menu. Escape's ASCII value is 27.

Pressing Escape does not always halt program execution. It depends where in the program you currently are. Pressing Escape in a READ will exit the READ. Pressing Escape when selecting a pop-up menu option will deactivate the menu. If executing other statements that do not involve a built-in dBASE procedure, then the current program will be interrupted.

After obtaining user input, we can now create a new record to hold the data. The APPEND BLANK command creates an empty record at the end of the database and becomes the current record. The REPLACE command is employed to transfer the values in the memory variables into the proper fields in the record. Several fields in a record can be replaced at once, separated by commas. In the program note that semicolons appear at the end of the line. The semicolons tell dBASE that the command continues on the next line.

Finally, the user is given the opportunity to insert another record. The again window is activated and the user is prompted. Whether the user answered yes or no, the window is no longer needed, so it is immediately deactivated. If the answer was not "Y" for yes, the insert window is deactivated, and we return to the main menu. Otherwise, the end of the loop will be encountered, and the program will loop back to the top and obtain the next record.

Insert Using Arrays

An alternative Insert program is presented to demonstrate using arrays and how they can shorten the length of your programs somewhat. APPEND FROM ARRAY creates a new record with the contents of the specified array. The code follows:

```
* Declare the array named stuff, 9 elements
DECLARE stuff[9]
DEFINE WINDOW again FROM 10,26 TO 14,54
DEFINE WINDOW insert FROM 6,10 TO 19,60
ACTIVATE WINDOW insert
* Repeat forever
DO WHILE .T.
```

```
  STORE SPACE(20) TO stuff[1],stuff[4]
  STORE SPACE(15) TO stuff[2]
  STORE SPACE(30) TO stuff[3]
  STORE " " TO stuff[5]
  STORE SPACE(10) TO stuff[6]
  STORE SPACE(14) TO stuff[7]
  STORE { / / } TO stuff[8]
  STORE 0 TO recnum,stuff[9]
  STORE " " TO yn
  @  1,1 SAY " Last Name:      " GET stuff[1]
  @  2,1 SAY " First Name:     " GET stuff[2]
  @  3,1 SAY " Address:        " GET stuff[3]
  @  4,1 SAY " City:           " GET stuff[4]
  @  5,1 SAY " State:          " GET stuff[5] PICTURE "!!"
  @  6,1 SAY " Zip:            " GET stuff[6] PICTURE "99999-9999"
  @  7,1 SAY " Phone:          " GET stuff[7] PICTURE "(999) 999-9999"
  @  8,1 SAY " Entry Date:     " GET stuff[8]
  @  9,1 SAY " Potential:      " GET stuff[9] PICTURE "99999.99"
  @ 11,1 SAY "Press ESC To Abort"
  READ
  * See if Escape was pressed
  IF LASTKEY( ) = 27
    DEACTIVATE WINDOW insert
    RETURN
  ENDIF
  * Add new record
  APPEND FROM ARRAY stuff
  * See if user wants to continue insertions
     ACTIVATE WINDOW again
  @ 1,1 SAY "Insert Another? (Y/N):" GET yn PICTURE "!"
  READ
  DEACTIVATE WINDOW again
  IF yn <> "Y"
    DEACTIVATE WINDOW insert
    RETURN
  ENDIF
ENDDO
RETURN
```

Edit

With the Edit program, existing records can retrieved and modified. The program follows:

Edit.prg:

```
* Initialize memory variables STORE SPACE(20) TO mcity
STORE SPACE(15) TO mfname
STORE SPACE(30) TO maddress
STORE " " TO mstate
STORE SPACE(10) TO mzip
STORE SPACE(14) TO mphone
STORE { / / } TO ment_date
STORE 0 TO reccnt,mpoten
DEFINE WINDOW err FROM 10,20 to 14,60
DEFINE WINDOW edit FROM 6,10 to 19,60
DEFINE WINDOW key FROM 4,35 TO 21,75
ACTIVATE WINDOW key
* Repeat forever
DO WHILE .T.
   * Clear part of window
   @ 2,0 CLEAR TO 15,36
   STORE 0 TO recnum
   STORE SPACE(20) TO mlname
   * Get desired name
   @ 0,1 SAY "Enter Last Name:" GET mlname
   @ 15,1 SAY "Press ESC To Abort"
   READ
   * See if Escape was pressed.
   IF LASTKEY( ) = 27
      DEACTIVATE WINDOW key
      RETURN
   ENDIF
   mlname = TRIM(mlname)
   SEEK mlname
   * Error if not found
   IF .NOT. FOUND( )
      ACTIVATE WINDOW err
      @ 1,1 SAY "Not Found! Press Any Key To Continue."
      WAIT " "
```

```
  DEACTIVATE WINDOW err
  LOOP
ENDIF
* List all matches
DO WHILE lname = mlname
  @ 2,0 CLEAR TO 15,36
  @ 1,0
  reccnt = 0
  SCAN WHILE lname = mlname .AND. reccnt < 10
    LIST NEXT 1 TRIM(lname) + ", " + TRIM(fname)
    reccnt = reccnt + 1
  ENDSCAN
  IF lname = mlname
    ?
    WAIT
  ENDIF
ENDDO
@ 13,0 SAY " Enter Record # To Edit:" GET recnum RANGE 1,RECCOUNT( )
@ 15,0 SAY " Press ESC To Abort"
READ
* See if Escape was pressed.
IF LASTKEY( ) = 27
  DEACTIVATE WINDOW key
  RETURN
ENDIF
* Goto the record, assign fields to memory variables.
GOTO recnum
mlname = lname
mfname = fname
maddress = address
mcity = city
mstate = state
mzip = zip
mphone = phone
ment_date = ent_date
mpoten = poten
ACTIVATE WINDOW edit
@  1,1 SAY " Last Name:    " GET mlname
@  2,1 SAY " First Name:   " GET mfname
@  3,1 SAY " Address:      " GET maddress
```

```
    @  4,1 SAY " City:          " GET mcity
    @  5,1 SAY " State:         " GET mstate PICTURE "!!"
    @  6,1 SAY " Zip:           " GET mzip PICTURE "99999-9999"
    @  7,1 SAY " Phone:         " GET mphone PICTURE "(999) 999-9999"
    @  8,1 SAY " Entry Date:    " GET ment_date
    @  9,1 SAY " Potential:     " GET mpoten PICTURE "99999.99"
    @ 11,1 SAY "Press ESC To Abort"
    READ
    * See if Escape was pressed
    IF LASTKEY( ) = 27
      DEACTIVATE WINDOW edit
      LOOP
    ENDIF
    REPLACE lname WITH mlname,fname WITH mfname ;
            address WITH maddress, city WITH mcity ;
            state WITH mstate, zip WITH mzip ;
            phone WITH mphone, ent_date WITH ment_date ;
            poten WITH mpoten
    DEACTIVATE WINDOW edit
  ENDDO
```

First, the variables are initialized. They don't need to be part of a loop here as they were in Insert.

Three windows are defined. One is for a record not found error, one for editing, and one for selecting which record to edit.

After the window is activated, a DO WHILE .T. loop appears so that users can edit records for as long as they so desire. The window is cleared of its previous contents, and the user is prompted to enter the last name of the person to look up. Here again as in Insert, the Escape key is checked after a READ.

Next mlname is trimmed to remove trailing spaces, very important for string comparisons. The default dBASE uses in string comparisons is to compare the two strings only up to the length of the string on the right. For example, if the following is typed at the dot prompt,

```
. ? "program" = "pro"
.T.
```

a value of true is returned, it considers these two strings equivalent. However the following will return false:

```
. ? "program" = "pro "
.F.
```

The spaces are not ignored.

The SEEK command also functions this way. If mlname = "D", SEEK goes through the database indexed on lname and stops at the first occurrence of a last name beginning with "D". This is useful if the user is unsure of the spelling or doesn't want to type in a long name. Just the first few letters can be entered.

After executing a SEEK, the function FOUND( ) is true if SEEK found a match, otherwise it is false. If no names match the mlname pattern, the err window is activated, and an error message is displayed. WAIT " " causes the program to wait until a key is pressed by the user. Normally WAIT has its own error message, but you can instruct it to print your own; in this case " " infers not to print anything. After a key is pressed, the window is deactivated. LOOP causes the flow of the program to jump to the instruction immediately following DO WHILE .T.. The next part is a bit tricky. If SEEK was successful, the DO WHILE lname = mlname loop is executed. The idea here is to list all the records that match mlname. Because the database is indexed on the last name, all the records that meet the lname = mlname condition will appear one after another.

First, part of the window is cleared, the cursor is position @ 1,0 in the window, and a counter, recent, is set to 0.

A SCAN WHILE loop then appears within the DO WHILE loop. The SCAN WHILE loop is a new dBASE construct, and used here in the following

```
SCAN WHILE <condition>
  :
ENDSCAN
```

has the same meaning as:

```
DO WHILE <condition> .AND. .NOT. EOF()
  :
  SKIP
ENDDO
```

The SCAN's condition in the Edit program is to loop as long as the lname field in the current record equals mlname, up to ten times by keeping track of reccnt.

Within the SCAN WHILE loop, one record's lname and fname fields are displayed, and the record counter (reccnt) is incremented.

If reccnt is equal to 10, the loop exits. A check is made to see if lname equals the new current record. If so, more records are going to have to be displayed, so a line is skipped and a WAIT is issued to allow the user to see the existing records so far.

Although you're now outside the SCAN WHILE loop, we're still inside the DO WHILE loop. Because lname = mlname, the process repeats; the window is cleared, and the next 10 records are scanned, and so on.

After listing all matching records, the user can select which person to edit by their record number. The @...SAY...GET statement uses the RANGE clause to make sure nonexistent record numbers are not entered. RECCOUNT( ) is equal to the number of records in the database.

If the Escape key wasn't pressed, you GOTO the record number chosen by the user. Next, memory variables are assigned the values in these fields.

The rest should look familiar—it is similar to Insert. The edit window is activated, and the values are edited and replaced. Encountering ENDDO will cause program flow to jump back to the top of the loop, where another entry can be retrieved.

Edit Using Arrays

Just as two different Insert programs were shown, two Edit programs are demonstrated as well. Once again the second version uses an array. The COPY TO ARRAY command copies the contents of of the current record into the specified array. The program follows:

```
* Declare an array named stuff, 9 elements
DECLARE stuff[9]
STORE SPACE(20) TO mlname
DEFINE WINDOW err FROM 10,20 to 14,60
DEFINE WINDOW edit FROM 6,10 to 19,60
DEFINE WINDOW key FROM 4,35 TO 21,75
ACTIVATE WINDOW key
DO WHILE .T.
  @ 2,0 CLEAR TO 15,36
  STORE 0 TO recnum
  STORE SPACE(20) TO mlname
  * Get desired name
  @ 0,1 SAY "Enter Last Name:" GET mlname
  @ 15,1 SAY "Press ESC To Abort"
  READ
  * See if Escape was pressed.
  IF LASTKEY( ) = 27
    DEACTIVATE WINDOW key
    RETURN
  ENDIF
  mlname = TRIM(mlname)
  SEEK mlname
  * Error if not found
  IF .NOT. FOUND( )
```

```
    ACTIVATE WINDOW err
    @ 1,1 SAY "Not Found! Press Any Key To Continue."
    WAIT " "
    DEACTIVATE WINDOW err
    LOOP
  ENDIF
  * Display all matches
  DO WHILE lname = mlname
    @ 2,0 CLEAR TO 15,36
    @ 1,0
    reccnt = 0
    SCAN WHILE lname = mlname .AND. reccnt < 10
      LIST NEXT 1 TRIM(lname) + ", " + TRIM(fname)
      reccnt = reccnt + 1
    ENDSCAN
    IF lname = mlname
      ?
      WAIT
    ENDIF
  ENDDO
  @ 13,0 SAY " Enter Record # To Edit:" GET recnum RANGE 1,RECCOUNT( )
  @ 15,0 SAY " Press ESC To Abort"
  READ
  * See if Escape was pressed.
  IF LASTKEY( ) = 27
    DEACTIVATE WINDOW key
    RETURN
  ENDIF
  * Goto the record, assign fields to memory variables.
GOTO recnum
COPY NEXT 1 TO ARRAY stuff
ACTIVATE WINDOW edit
@  1,1 SAY " Last Name:    " GET stuff[1]
@  2,1 SAY " First Name:   " GET stuff[2]
@  3,1 SAY " Address:      " GET stuff[3]
@  4,1 SAY " City:         " GET stuff[4]
@  5,1 SAY " State:        " GET stuff[5]
@  6,1 SAY " Zip:          " GET stuff[6]
@  7,1 SAY " Phone:        " GET stuff[7]
@  8,1 SAY " Entry Date:   " GET stuff[8]
@  9,1 SAY " Potential:    " GET stuff[9]
```

```
@ 11,1 SAY "Press ESC To Abort"
READ
* See if Escape was pressed
```

Delete

The Delete program is very similar to edit. The program follows:

Delete.prg:

```
* Initialize
STORE SPACE(15) TO mfname
STORE 0 TO reccnt
DEFINE WINDOW err FROM 10,20 to 14,60
DEFINE WINDOW delete FROM 6,15 to 10,60
DEFINE WINDOW key FROM 4,35 TO 21,75
ACTIVATE WINDOW key
DO WHILE .T.
  @ 2,0 CLEAR TO 15,36
  * Initialize variables
  STORE SPACE(20) TO mlname
  STORE "N" to yn
  STORE 0 TO recnum
  @ 0,1 SAY "Enter Last Name:" GET mlname
  @ 15,1 SAY "Press ESC To Abort"
  READ
  * See if Escape key was pressed.
  IF LASTKEY() = 27
    DEACTIVATE WINDOW key
    RETURN
  ENDIF
  mlname = TRIM(mlname)
  SEEK mlname
  * Error if not found
  IF .NOT. FOUND()
    ACTIVATE WINDOW err
    @ 1,1 SAY "Not Found! Press Any Key To Continue."
    WAIT " "
    DEACTIVATE WINDOW err
    LOOP
  ENDIF
  * List all matches
  DO WHILE lname = mlname
```

```
      @ 2,0 CLEAR TO 15,36
      @ 1,0
      reccnt = 0
      SCAN WHILE lname = mlname .AND. reccnt < 10
        LIST NEXT 1 TRIM(lname) + ", " + TRIM(fname)
        reccnt = reccnt + 1
      ENDSCAN
      IF lname = mlname
        ?
        WAIT
      ENDIF
    ENDDO
    @ 13,0 SAY " Enter Record # To Delete:" GET recnum RANGE 1,RECCOUNT( )
    @ 15,0 SAY " Press ESC To Abort"
    READ
    * See if Escape was pressed
    IF LASTKEY( ) = 27
      DEACTIVATE WINDOW key
      RETURN
    ENDIF
    * Goto the record, assign fields to memory variables.
    GOTO recnum
    mlname = lname
    mfname = fname
    * Last chance prompt
    ACTIVATE WINDOW delete
    @ 0,1 SAY TRIM(lname) + ", " + TRIM(fname)
    @ 2,1 SAY "Delete: Are You Sure? (Y/N):" GET yn PICTURE "!"
    READ
    IF yn = "Y"
      DELETE
    ENDIF
    DEACTIVATE WINDOW delete
  ENDDO
```

Again, it is similar to Edit, only the record selected is to be deleted not edited. An Are You Sure? prompt appears with the record in the delete window to verify the user's selection.

Keep in mind that when records are "deleted" they are marked for deletion only. They are physically removed from the database only when a PACK is performed.

Report

Both the Report and Labels program try to emphasize how to use previously created reports in programs, the scopes of variables, and how to obtain the criteria with which to filter those reports. The program follows:

Report.prg:

```
* Initialize variables
STORE SPACE(20) TO mlname, mcity
STORE SPACE(15) TO mfname
STORE SPACE(30) TO maddress
STORE " " TO mstate
STORE SPACE(10) TO mzip
STORE SPACE(14) TO mphone
STORE { / / } TO ment_date
STORE 0 TO mpoten1
STORE 99999.99 TO mpoten2
STORE " " TO criteria
* Get criteria DO Crit
SET FILTER TO &criteria
* Get destination
DO Dest
REPORT FORM Peorep
SET PRINT OFF
SET FILTER TO
WAIT
CLEAR
RETURN
```

When memory variables are declared in dBASE, they can be accessed by the program in which they were declared, or by the subprograms that the current program calls. If a memory variable is declared in a subprogram that was called, the program that called it cannot access the variable.

This point is brought up because in Report two subprograms are called, Crit, to obtain criteria, and Dest, to select the print destination. We desire Crit to return a criteria that we may use in this program. Because we aren't using procedures with parameter passing, the memory variables must be declared here. The Crit program is discussed later.

After Crit is executed, the memory variable criteria will now contain the criteria for the report. To use this information, the SET FILTER TO &criteria command is used. Note that criteria is preceded with an ampersand (&), making criteria a macro. This means ''substitute '&criteria' with the contents of criteria, and execute this statement.'' For example, if mac = "DO MAIN", typing &mac at the dot prompt will execute main.

Next Dest is executed to select where to output the report, to the screen or printer.

We assume an existing reporting exists called Peorep, created in the Reports section of the Control Center. See the Reports section in Chapter 1 for creating Reports. The report Peorep is run.

Afterwards, if the printer was selected, SET PRINT OFF will deselect it. No harm is done in saying SET PRINT OFF if it wasn't previously set on.

The filter condition is removed with SET FILTER TO command followed by nothing. WAIT pauses execution, CLEAR clears the screen, and finally the program returns.

Crit. Crit allows users to set a filter condition that is entered into the memory variable criteria. The program follows:

Crit.prg:

```
DEFINE WINDOW crit FROM 6,10 TO 21,60
ACTIVATE WINDOW crit
@  0,1 SAY " ENTER CRITERIA:"

@  2,1 SAY "   Last Name:" GET mlname
@  3,1 SAY "   First Name:" GET mfname
@  4,1 SAY "      Address:" GET maddress
@  5,1 SAY "         City:" GET mcity
@  6,1 SAY "        State:" GET mstate PICTURE "!!"
@  7,1 SAY "          Zip:" GET mzip PICTURE "99999-9999"
@  8,1 SAY "        Phone:" GET mphone PICTURE "(999) 999-9999"
@  9,1 SAY "   Entry Date:" GET ment_date
@ 10,1 SAY "  Potent > = :" GET mpoten1 PICTURE "99999.99"
@ 11,1 SAY "  Potent < = :" GET mpoten2 PICTURE "99999.99"
@ 13,1 SAY "Press ESC To Abort"
READ
* See if Escape was pressed
IF LASTKEY() = 27
  DEACTIVATE WINDOW crit
  RETURN TO MASTER
ENDIF
* Trim all variables
mlname = TRIM(mlname)
mfname = TRIM(mfname)
maddress = TRIM(maddress)
```

```
mcity = TRIM(mcity)
mstate = TRIM(mstate)
mzip = TRIM(mzip)
mphone = TRIM(mphone)
* For each variable, check and see if it was used, * and if so, add it to criteria
DO CASE
  CASE LEN(mlname) > 0
    criteria = criteria + "lname = mlname .AND."
  CASE LEN(mfname) > 0
    criteria = criteria + "fname = mfname .AND."
  CASE LEN(mcity) > 0
    criteria = criteria + "city = mcity .AND."
  CASE LEN(mstate) > 0
    criteria = criteria + "state = mstate .AND."
  CASE LEN(mzip) > 0
    criteria = criteria + "zip = mzip .AND."
  CASE LEN(mphone) > 0
    criteria = criteria + "phone = mphone .AND."
  CASE DAY(ent_date) > 0
    criteria = criteria + "ent_date = ment_date .AND."
  CASE mpoten1 > 0
    criteria = criteria + "poten > = mpoten1 .AND."
  CASE mpoten2 < 99999.99
    criteria = criteria + "poten < = mpoten2 .AND."
ENDCASE
* Get rid of last " .AND."
IF LEN(criteria) > 1
criteria = LEFT(criteria, LEN(criteria) - 6)
ENDIF
DEACTIVATE WINDOW crit
RETURN
```

The first part of the program isn't anything new. There are two ''poten'' fields, allowing a range of potential values to be entered.

Here's how it works. Only those memory variables where an entry has been made are counted toward the criteria. If more than one field is filtered on, they are ANDed together.

After input is read, all string variables are trimmed to remove trailing spaces. The CASE statement checks each variable to see if it has an entry. An entry will exist if the length of the variable is greater than 0. If an entry does exist, it is added to criteria. " .AND." appears at the end of all the strings to allow all the conditions to be ANDed together.

The last " .AND." is removed by the LEFT( ) function. LEFT( ) takes the substring of criteria starting at the left and continuing for length of criteria minus 6 characters, the length of " .AND.".

Dest. The Dest program selects the destination for report output. The program follows:

Dest.prg:

```
* Do menu definition Do Def_dest
ACTIVATE POPUP dest
RETURN

PROCEDURE Def_dest
  DEFINE POPUP dest FROM 10,55 TO 16,70
  DEFINE BAR 1 OF dest PROMPT " PRINT TO" SKIP
  DEFINE BAR 3 OF dest PROMPT " Screen"
  DEFINE BAR 4 OF dest PROMPT " Printer"
  DEFINE BAR 5 OF dest PROMPT " Abort"
  ON SELECTION POPUP dest DO Destpop
RETURN

PROCEDURE Destpop
  DO CASE
      CASE BAR() = 4
        SET PRINT ON
      CASE BAR() = 5
        RETURN TO MASTER
  ENDCASE
  DEACTIVATE POPUP
RETURN
```

The pop-up menu is similar to the Main program's main menu.

If Printer is selected, the printer is set on. Selecting screen does nothing, for the output will appear on the screen anyway. The last option allows the user to Abort the entire operation, and returns control to the main program via RETURN TO MASTER.

DEACTIVATE POPUP deactivates the most recently activated pop-up menu, in this case the menu dest.

Labels

The Labels program is exactly like the report program, except that the REPORT FORM command is replaced with a LABEL FORM command, assumed to have already exists. The program follows:

Labels.prg:

```
* Initialize variables
STORE SPACE(20) TO mlname, mcity
STORE SPACE(15) TO mfname
STORE SPACE(30) TO maddress
STORE " " TO mstate
STORE SPACE(10) TO mzip
STORE SPACE(14) TO mphone
STORE { / / } TO ment_date
STORE 0 TO mpoten1
STORE 99999.99 TO mpoten2
STORE " " TO criteria
* Get criteria
DO Crit
SET FILTER TO &criteria
* Get destination DO Dest
LABEL FORM Peolab
SET PRINT OFF
SET FILTER TO
WAIT
CLEAR
RETURN
```

Packem

The Packem program is a brief program that uses the PACK command to remove those records marked for deletion from the database. The code follows:

Packem.prg:

```
CLEAR
SET TALK ON
@ 1,1 SAY "One moment, please..."
PACK

SET TALK OFF
WAIT
CLEAR
RETURN
```

Recall that in Main.prg we SET TALK OFF. Packing can take quite a while for large databases. Not seeing anything change on the screen for a long time while only hearing the hard drive going can sometimes cause anxiety. SET TALK ON allows users to see the process take place. Afterwards the talk is set off again.

The dBASE IV Applications Generator

The previous section explained how to program a dBASE IV command file. Although simple programming is quite easy, it can take hundreds of hours of practice before a user becomes efficient at programming more sophisticated applications. Fortunately, dBASE IV has an Applications Generator that will create programs for you. Once you set the parameters and menu options, the Applications Generator creates the actual command (.PRG) file.

In this chapter, we create a menu system that allows the user to add, edit, and print reports on the PEOPLE.DBF database described in the previous chapter. The main menu will be a horizontal bar of options, with each option displaying a vertical popup of suboptions. Figure 8-1 shows an example of the menu.

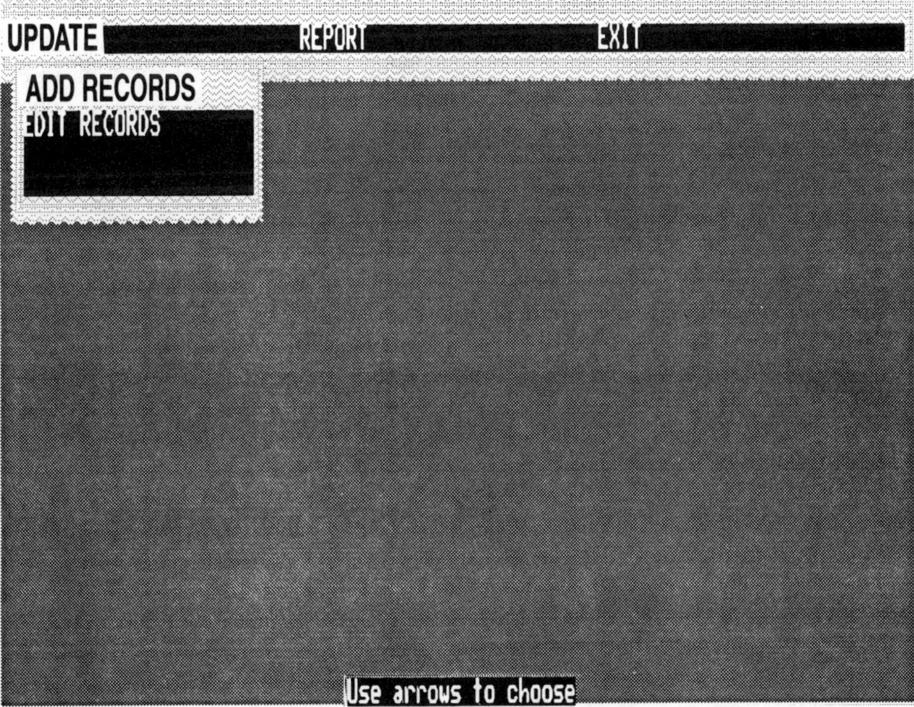

Fig. 8-1. The bar menu created by the Applications Generator.

To run this example, the following files must already be created.

PEOPLE.DBF	(database from previous chapter)
PEOPLE.FMT	(screen format for PEOPLE.DBF)
PEOPLE.FRM	(report form for PEOPLE.DBF)

Creating the Application

To create the menu system, go through the following steps:

1. Start the Applications Generator and name the application.
2. Design the horizontal bar main menu.
3. Design the vertical popup menus.
4. Attach popup menus to bar options (assign actions).
5. Assign actions to popup menu options.
6. Generate program.

Starting the Applications Generator. To enter the Applications Generator from the dot prompt, type CREATE APPLICATION. From the Control Panel, choose Applications, <create> and Applicaitons Generator. It will automatically add an .APP extension to the application file name.

At the Application Definition screen, enter the following information:

Application name	: **PEOPLE**	(file PEOPLE.APP)
Description	: **Add, Edit and Report**	(comment in PEOPLE.PRG)
Main menu type	: **BAR**	(press spacebar for other options)
Main menu name	: **PMENU**	(name of bar menu (.BAR) file)
Database/view	: **PEOPLE**	(name of data (.DBF) file)
Set INDEX to	:	(name of index (.NDX or .MDX) file)
ORDER	:	

Press Ctrl – End when done.

The next screen shows the application object. This screen always displays when you go in to modify the application. You can also make this screen come up as the first screen of the application. Change the banner by erasing the default greeting (use Ctrl – Y to delete each line) and typing in your own. Change the banner as follows:

```
JOE'S COMPUTER CONSULTING
        SAN DIEGO, CA
         (619)555-1566
```

Designing the Menus

The Applications Generator menu. To design the rest of the application, use the Applications Generator menu at the top of the screens. Press F10 to access the menu. The options are:

Design Application Generate Preset Exit

You can choose an option at any time by holding down Alt and pressing the first letter of the option. You can also choose an option by highlighting it and pressing Enter. In the following sections, we refer to choosing an option as pressing the ALT – letter combination.

Designing the horizontal bar main menu. The steps for designing a horizontal bar menu are:

1. Press Alt – D, and choose Horizontal bar menu.
2. Choose <create>. Enter the following:

Name	: **PMENU**	(file PMENU.BAR)
Description	: **Add, Edit and Report**	(shows when modifying application)
Message Line	: (leave blank)	(shows when running application)

3. Press Ctrl – End when done.
4. Now, to type the options in the menu, you must press F5 before and after each option. Press F5, type UPDATE, and then press F5 again. Use the spacebar to move out to the middle of the screen for the next option. Follow these steps for the following menu:

   UPDATE
   REPORT
   EXIT

5. You can highlight each option by pressing Ctrl – Right arrow.
6. You must designate that the bar menu will have pull-down menus for the options. Press Alt – M for the Menu option. Choose Attach pull-down menus. Answer Yes at the question Pull down associated menus ....
7. Press Alt – M, Put away menu, Save changes . . ..

Designing the vertical popup menus. To design the vertical popup menus:

1. Press Alt – D, and choose Popup menu.
2. Choose <create>. Enter the following:

Name	: **UPDATE**	(file UPDATE.POP)
Description	: **Add and Edit Records**	(shows when modifying application)
Message Line	: **Choose desired option**	(shows when running application)

3. Press Ctrl – End when done.
4. Now, to enter the options, simply type them in the designated box. For the UPDATE menu, type:

   ADD RECORDS
   EDIT RECORDS

5. The popup menu will look better if it is moved up on the screen directly below the bar option. To move it, press F7, and choose Entire Frame. Use

the arrows to move under the UPDATE option in the horizontal bar and press Enter. You can also change the size of the popup menu by pressing Shift – F7 and adjusting the dimensions of the box.

6. Press Alt – M, Put away menu, Save changes ... .

Follow steps 1 through 6 for the other two popups. For the next popup, use these lines for the second step:

Name : **REPORT**
Description: **Prints a Report**

and this line for the fourth step:

PRINT MAILING LIST

For the last popup menu, use these lines for the second and fourth steps:

Name : **EXIT**
Description: **EXIT TO DOS**

Attaching popup menus to bar options. To attach the popup menus to a bar menu:

1. Press Alt – D, and choose Horizontal bar menu.
2. Choose PMENU. Highlight the first option, UPDATE.
3. Press Alt – I, choose Change action and choose Open a menu. Enter the following:

Menu type : **POPUP** (press the spacebar to change type)
Menu name : **UPDATE** (file UPDATE.POP)

4. Press Ctrl – End when done.
5. To attach a popup to the next option, press PgDn. Notice that the status line displays REPORT.

Repeat steps 3 through 5 using the popup menus REPORT and EXIT.

Assign Actions to Popup Menu Options

With the menus designed, the next stpes are to make the menus functional:

1. Press Alt – D, and choose Popup menu.
2. Choose UPDATE. Highlight the first option, ADD RECORDS.
3. Press Alt – 1, choose Change action and choose Edit Form. Change the following defaults:

Format File : **PEOPLE** (uses PEOPLE.FMT screen file)
Mode : **APPEND**

4. Press Ctrl – End when done.

5. Press PgDn to get to the next option in the pop-up menu, EDIT RECORDS (notice the change in the Status line). Repeat steps 3 through 4 for this option, following the default changes listed in the following table.
6. Repeat steps 1 through 4 for the other menu options listed in the table.

The default changes for each menu item are:

Menu	Item	Change action (from Item menu)
UPDATE	EDIT RECORDS	Edit form Format: **PEOPLE** Mode: **EDIT**
REPORT	PRINT MAILING LIST	Display or Print Report Form Name: **PEOPLE**
EXIT	EXIT TO DOS	Quit Quit to DOS

Generating the Program

Now that all menus have been defined, we can generate the code. This is the process where dBASE actually writes the .PRG file based on the parameters you have specified:

1. Press Alt – G, and choose Display during generation. Choose Yes to see the program as it is created.
2. Choose Begin generating. You should see the program scroll down the screen as it is generated.
3. To exit the Applications Generator, press Alt – E, and choose Save all changes.

Running the program. Because the Applications Generator creates a program file, you can run it as you would any other program, by typing DO <app. filename> at the dot prompt. From the Control Panel, choose Applications, then choose the application that you want, and Run application.

Additional Hints

This book does not cover all aspects of the Applications Generator. The previous exercise simply shows the basics of creating a program. However, several additional features that can be very useful. Descriptions of each follow.

Generating a quick application. This option automatically creates a single menu program that allows the user to add/edit records, browse, and pack a database. The menu options and actions are already set in the program, although you may change the wording with the Preset option. If you select a screen format, report, label, and/or index file, the program will also include these features. To create a quick application, simply choose Generate Quick Application from the Application menu.

Assigning a batch process. In the example application, we assigned menu options that edited the database, ran a report form, and quit. If you want a menu option to run a group of commands, you must use a batch process. To do this, you must first define it from the Design menu by choosing Batch Process, giving it a name, and entering the commands you wish processed. To assign the batch to a menu option, highlight the option, and choose the following from the Item menu:

Change action
Run program
Execute BATCH process

Then enter the name of the desired batch process.

Sign-on banner. When the application is run, you can make it first display a screen with information such as the programmer's name and a copyright notice. To design this initial screen, go to the Preset menu, and choose Sign-on defaults. To use the application object as the initial screen at run-time, choose Display sign-on banner from the Application menu.

Index

B

E

F

N

O

P

S

Y

Z